3/11

W9-AHE-231

THE ILLINOIS GOVERNORS

Most

Ta

C

University of Illinois at Springfield, Springfield, Illinois

T

ISBN-13: 978-0-938943-26-6
ISBN-10: 0-938943-26-X

This book is a revised and updated edition of *Mostly Good and Competent Men: Illinois Governors 1818 to 1988*, published in 1988 by *Illinois Issues* and the Illinois State Historical Society, Springfield, Illinois. A second edition of *Mostly Good and Competent Men: The Illinois Governors* was published by the University of Illinois at Springfield in 1999.

Executive Editor: Peggy Boyer Long
Projects Editor: Beverley Scobell
Assistant Editors: Amy Karhliker, Dan Egler, and Joanna Tweedy
Art Director: Diana L. C. Nelson
Cover Illustration: Mike Cramer
Printer: United Graphics

Unless otherwise indicated, all photographs courtesy of the Abraham Lincoln Presidential Library

ABRAHAM LINCOLN
PRESIDENTIAL LIBRARY & MUSEUM

Printed in the United States of America

10 9 8 7 6 5 4 3 2 1

CENTER FOR STATE POLICY AND LEADERSHIP
Center Publications/*Illinois Issues*
One University Plaza, MS HRB 10
University of Illinois at Springfield
Springfield, IL 62703-5407

Phone: 217-206-6502 • Fax: 217-206-7257
Web site: http://cspl.uis.edu/centerpublications

Contents

Preface to the Second Edition v
Acknowledgments vii
Introduction ix
    1st Governor: Shadrach Bond 2
    2nd Governor: Edward Coles .8
    3rd Governor: Ninian Edwards 18
    4th Governor: John Reynolds 30
    5th Governor: William Lee Davidson Ewing 38
    6th Governor: Joseph Duncan 42
    7th Governor: Thomas Carlin 52
    8th Governor: Thomas Ford 58
    9th Governor: Augustus Chaplin French 68
    10th Governor: Joel Aldrich Matteson 74
    11th Governor: William Henry Bissell 82
    12th Governor: John Wood 88
    13th Governor: Richard Yates 92
    14th Governor: Richard James Oglesby 102
    15th Governor: John McAuley Palmer 112
    16th Governor: John Lourie Beveridge 122
    17th Governor: Shelby Moore Cullom 128
    18th Governor: John Marshall Hamilton 138
    19th Governor: Joseph Wilson Fifer 142
    20th Governor: John Peter Altgeld 148
    21st Governor: John Riley Tanner 158
    22nd Governor: Richard Yates 164
    23rd Governor: Charles Samuel Deneen 170
    24th Governor: Edward Fitzsimmons Dunne 178
    25th Governor: Frank Orren Lowden 184
    26th Governor: Lennington Small 192
    27th Governor: Louis Lincoln Emmerson 200
    28th Governor: Henry Horner 206

29th Governor: John H. Stelle 214

30th Governor: Dwight Herbert Green 220

31st Governor: Adlai Ewing Stevenson 228

32nd Governor: William Grant Stratton 236

33rd Governor: Otto Kerner 244

34th Governor: Samuel Harvey Shapiro 252

35th Governor: Richard Buell Ogilvie 258

36th Governor: Daniel Walker .266

37th Governor: James Robert Thompson
                updated by Peggy Boyer Long 274

38th Governor: Jim Edgar by Peggy Boyer Long 288

39th Governor: George Ryan by Taylor Pensoneau 304

40th Governor: Rod Blagojevich by Taylor Pensoneau . .314

Appendix A: Roster of Governors 326

Appendix B: The Constitutions of Illinois and the Power
             of the Governor .328

Appendix C: Gubernatorial Vote Totals 336

Bibliographical Essay 342

Bibliography 344

Index 363

About the Center for State Policy and Leadership 387

About the Authors 388

Preface to the Third Edition

Illinois politics is in constant motion. Not much more than a decade transpired between publication of the first and second editions of Robert Howard's biographical history of the Illinois governors. Now, eight years and two administrations later, we've decided to update his classic collection again.

We began by recasting the title. In 1988, Howard chose to call his history *Mostly Good and Competent Men*, a title that lent itself to interpretation. But while we wanted to retain his suggestiveness, we also wanted to reflect shifts in the state's social and political culture as we head into this new century, including the possibility that Illinoisans will one day elect a woman chief executive. We hope Howard would approve of our simple solution. We titled this most recent collection *The Illinois Governors: Mostly Good and Competent.*

Much has changed since the second edition of *Mostly Good*. Illinoisans elected, then reelected, the first Democratic governor in a quarter century. The locus of administrative power moved from Springfield to Chicago. A former governor was convicted of public corruption. And the state's fiscal fortunes declined.

All of these changes are reflected in the two new chapters about Governors George Ryan and Rod Blagojevich written by Taylor Pensoneau, a political historian who was once an Illinois Statehouse reporter for the *St. Louis Post-Dispatch*. Pensoneau is a good choice to follow in Howard's footsteps; he covered five of this state's governors, including Richard Ogilvie and Dan Walker. His experience reporting on those last two governors inspired a couple of Pensoneau's own must-read biographies. He is a co-author of *Dan Walker: The Glory and the Tragedy* and author of *Governor Richard Ogilvie: In the Interest of the State*, which the *Chicago Sun-Times* called one of the 10 most notable political books of 1997.

Howard designed his book to explain who the governors were and how they responded to the challenges of leadership. Our aim in this collection is to sketch, as well, some of the larger context and highlight a few of the people and events that fill out the portrait of each governor's era.

Editorial assistants Beverley Scobell and Amy Karhliker, with the help of the staff at the Abraham Lincoln Presidential Library, tracked down additional images for this book that help to tell the story of Illinois as it has evolved through 40 administrations. Among the photographic narratives are those of John Hossack II, an Ottawa businessman and abolitionist who was arrested in 1859 under the Fugitive Slave Act for rescuing a slave and helping him to freedom in Canada. We've included others from the Chicago Fire of 1871, a tragedy that changed the face and politics of that city, from the dedication of the 1893 World's Columbian Exposition, and from the 1931 rededication of Lincoln's Tomb in Springfield with President Herbert Hoover in attendance.

In a sense, the making of this book has taken nearly two decades. Howard began his biographies in 1933 when he came to Springfield as a correspondent for The Associated Press. He wondered, he wrote in the preface to the first edition, "about the personalities and problems of the former governors — there were then 27 — whose portraits in double tier lined the walls of Henry Horner's reception room and private office." Yet biographical information was sparse.

Through his half-century as a Statehouse reporter, including a stint with the *Chicago Tribune*, Howard came to know 10 Illinois governors personally. Then, sometime after 1950, he began collecting information on the governors and preparing to write the history of the state's executive leaders himself. By the time he died in 1989, Howard had finished a one-volume *Illinois: A History of the Prairie State* and *Mostly Good*.

Illinois Issues is honored to have published all three editions of Howard's book about the governors. The first edition, envisioned by former *Illinois Issues* Publisher J. Michael Lennon, was produced jointly with the Illinois State Historical Society. The second edition, published in 1999 under the direction of former *Illinois Issues* Publisher Ed Wojcicki, updated Governor James R. Thompson's biography and added Governor Jim Edgar. Rodd Whelpley deftly edited that edition. This third edition was published in partnership with the Abraham Lincoln Presidential Library.

Illinois Issues Projects Editor Beverley Scobell has made an essential contribution to all three editions. Her editorial and research skills, and her grounding in the history of this state and its governors, has helped further Robert Howard's legacy.

Peggy Boyer Long
Executive Editor, *Illinois Issues*
Director, Center Publications
Center for State Policy
& Leadership
University of Illinois at Springfield

Acknowledgments

Although Robert P. Howard died shortly after the publication of *Mostly Good and Competent Men*, his scholarship provided the foundation for the second and third editions of the book.

Special thanks go to Beverley Scobell, too, who played a critical role from the beginning. She ably edited and fact-checked the text, beginning with the original, and selected the photographs for all three editions. Mary Michals supplied the photographs for each, initially through the Illinois State Historical Library and now, with the help of Roberta Fairburn, through the Abraham Lincoln Presidential Library and Museum, which partnered with *Illinois Issues* magazine for this edition.

We owe a debt of gratitude, as well, to two former publishers of *Illinois Issues*. J. Michael Lennon teamed up with State Historian Michael Devine of the Illinois State Historical Society to publish the first edition. Ed Wojcicki directed publication of the second edition.

Charles N. Wheeler III read portions of the second and third editions and checked many of the facts about the modern governors. Rodd Whelpley, who served as editor-in-chief of the second edition, built a solid base for this one by streamlining the text and deftly correcting errors. Diana Nelson provided the design of the second and third editions, including the covers. Peggy Boyer Long updated Howard's chapter on Governor Thompson and wrote the chapter on Governor Edgar for the second edition. Taylor Pensoneau wrote the chapters on Governors Ryan and Blagojevich for this edition.

We had a lot of additional help on the third edition. Dan Egler served as chief copy editor. Joanna Tweedy proofed the entire book. Amy S. Karhliker helped copy edit the chapters on the early governors and helped round up photographs.

Of course, Howard did not work alone on the first edition, either. So it is appropriate here to acknowledge those who contributed to the original text. Their work informs this edition.

Howard said the book would not have been written in the first place had it not been for his father, J. R. Howard, a lifetime observer of the political process; C. F. Littell, professor of political science at Cornell College; and Paul M. Angle, who first encouraged him to read Illinois history. And Howard never forgot Milburn P. Akers, an Associated Press colleague who presided over his introduction to Springfield.

The entire first edition manuscript was read by Fred H. Bird, Jr., Cullom Davis, William L. Day, Samuel K. Gove, and James D. Nowlan.

Some chapters were read by John R. Chapin, Irving Dilliard, Dan Egler, Harold E. Gibson, Raymond H. Hammes, David Kenney, Thomas B. Littlewood, and Mark Plummer. Others who helped with information and advice included Carl R. Baldwin, John D. Buenker, Janet Cornelius, Rodney O. Davis, William W. Downey, Paul M. Green, John Hoffmann, Daniel D. Holt, Robert W. Johannsen, Donald F. Lewis, Michael Maher, Archie Motley, Taylor Pensoneau, John Y. Simon, and Robert Sutton, along with Michael Devine, state historian and Illinois Historic Preservation Agency director, and staff members of the State Historical, Lincoln, and Sangamon State University (now the University of Illinois at Springfield) libraries.

Finally, the first edition might not have been finished had not Robert's wife Beth believed that at age 78 he needed a word processor.

Special help with the second edition included Kevin Flanagan, assistant librarian at the American Legion, who helped verify some facts about Governor Stelle. Greg Koos of the McLean County Historical Society verified some facts about Governors Hamilton, Fifer, and Stevenson. Phil Germann of the Historical Society of Quincy and Adams County supplied facts about Governor Wood. Bill Harris at McKendree College supplied information on Governor French, and Catherine "Kay" Schlichting at Ohio Wesleyan helped track down facts about Governor Hamilton. Bill Barnhart, co-author of *Kerner: The Conflict of Intangible Rights*, shared information to make the second edition's biography of that governor more accurate. Governor Jim Edgar granted Long an interview during the last hectic days of his administration and provided invaluable insight. Edgar Press Secretary Eric Robinson provided copies of valuable documentation. Dave Joens read through the entire text and made helpful suggestions and corrections.

It can be fairly said that through three editions, *Mostly Good* has been a labor of love for many. And for good reason. Illinois has a compelling and colorful political past, and no characters have a more commanding role in this history than its chief executives.

Introduction

The unwritten job specifications for governor of Illinois call for a melding of the best qualities of a statesman, an administrator, and a politician. The governor should understand what the people want and what they can afford. He or she should act evenhandedly and promptly in establishing priorities and managing the dozens of agencies in an expanding bureaucracy, and he or she should be a leader who can win the legislature's cooperation and the public's support. The ideal person rarely exists.

From 1818 to 2007, 40 men have occupied the office of the governor, with Rod Blagojevich becoming the 40th in 2002. No one pretends that the chief executives represent a cross section of Illinois citizenry. All have been white males. In the state's first 180 years, only two women, Dawn Clark Netsch and Judy Baar Topinka, ran as a major-party candidate for governor, and only one black man, Roland Burris, entered his name in a major party's primary race for the state's highest office. All trace their ancestry to Europe. William H. Bissell and Edward F. Dunne were Roman Catholics, Rod Blagojevich is Eastern Orthodox, and Samuel H. Shapiro and Henry H. Horner were Jews. Otherwise, active or nominal Protestants have had a monopoly on the office.

Yet within this seemingly narrow demographic, the governors have been men of diverse backgrounds, talents, and philosophies. Three governors — Edward Coles, Ninian Edwards, and Adlai Stevenson — came from elitist families with a tradition of public service. They are far outnumbered, however, by those who rose from obscurity and made their way upward, in the Abraham Lincoln tradition, by hard work, brains, and personality, with good luck always an additional factor. In that category are such prominent figures as William H. Bissell, Richard J. Oglesby, John M. Palmer, John P. Altgeld, and Frank O. Lowden. Some governors were reared in political atmospheres. When they ran for the top office, Stevenson, William G. Stratton, and Otto Kerner were emulating fathers who had been state officials. Shelby M. Cullom was the son of a state legislator. And the state's twenty-second governor, Richard Yates, followed directly in his father's footsteps. (Richard Yates, Sr. was governor during the Civil War.) Edward F. Dunne's and Richard B. Ogilvie's fathers were business executives. Charles S. Deneen was the son of a Latin professor. Len Small and James R. Thompson grew up in the homes of doctors. At the other extreme, Thomas Ford and Jim Edgar were reared by widowed mothers who had to scrimp to make ends meet. Some governors acquired considerable wealth, with Governor Lowden apparently not the only millionaire. As time passed, the governors tended to be better educated. The recent ones are all college graduates. As to intelligence, some were obviously quite bright, and some were slower in their capacity to understand and evaluate difficult situations.

Politically, Illinois has had 22 Republican governors, 15 Democrats, and one Whig. (The first three preceded the arrival of political parties in Illinois.) The net result, through 2007, is that Republicans have served as chief executive for 114 years, and Democrats for 59 years. The Republican advantage in number and in years served was built up between the Civil War and the Depression, and there was a Republican mini-boom after the mid-1970s.

The Constitution of 1970 requires only that governors be United States citizens who are at least 25 years old and have been residents of the state for three years. Along with some detail about the mechanics of the office, the Constitution without qualification or elaboration states that "the governor shall have the supreme executive power, and shall be responsible for the faithful execution of the laws." In real life, however, there are limitations on the executive. Naturally, a governor with a legislative agenda must work with members of the General Assembly to frame the laws that put the administration's policies into practice. But executive decisions are not the sole preserve of the governor. In Illinois, the governor must share the responsibility and prestige of the executive branch with other officials — the attorney general, secretary of state, comptroller, and treasurer — who are accountable only to the people and may be affiliated with a party different from the governor's. These other executive branch officers may be more concerned with personal ambition than with the harmonious operation of state government.

Even so, Illinois has never lacked applicants for the underpaid office in which there is no assurance that good work will be rewarded with a four-year extension in tenure. Indeed, the rise of the multiple-term governor is a relatively modern phenomenon. Under the 1818 and 1848 Constitutions, governors were prohibited from immediate reelection. Since the direct reelection of governors was permitted by the 1870 Constitution, only Lowden, who had presidential ambitions, and Louis L. Emmerson, who was 69 years old, retired voluntarily after one term. For governors who want more than one term, the easy way is to concentrate on reelection and leave the hard decisions for the future — or for the last term. A more difficult road is to follow Governor Horner's example of imposing a necessary retail sales tax in 1933 and then — somehow — winning a second term in 1936. Like Horner, Governor Ogilvie used determination, time, party loyalty, the logic of necessity, and official favors to break down resistance to putting in place a state income tax. His foresight, however, was not so handsomely rewarded, and he yielded his office to Dan Walker.

Former Illinois governors have a limited political future. The office has not turned out to be a warm-up for the White House, and only Stevenson was nominated for president by a united major political party. (Governor Lowden's name was placed in nomination, but he didn't win the nod and Governor John Palmer was the nominee of an anti-Bryan Gold Democratic faction in 1896.) Charles S. Deneen in 1924 was the last governor to reach the U.S. Senate. None has been appointed to a president's cabinet, although Stevenson, as ambassador to the United Nations, had cabinet rank. In addition to Stevenson, only Cullom and Lowden became nationally prominent. Former governors who went on federal payrolls were Kerner, a judge of the U.S. Court of Appeals, and Joseph W. Fifer, an Interstate Commerce commissioner a century ago. In terms of longevity in office, as a rule U.S. senators and congressmen have more durable careers than governors. Being less visible, holders of the lower state offices also can hope for repeated reelection.

Thus, so far, the governorship of this state has represented the pinnacle of the public service careers of the 40 men who have held the job. But many Illinoisans would be hard-pressed to name more than a handful of them. While there is no Abraham Lincoln or Stephen A. Douglas on the roster, the life stories of these men are worth knowing. Through them, we can draw inferences about the evolving nature of political power and leadership and understand the personalities of the men who shaped our state.

The fundamental question is whether Illinois' governors were good men who effected good public policy. A large majority — possibly three-quarters — have been men of good will, character, and competence who deserve the respect of the generations that did not know them. Nearly a dozen would qualify as statesmen whose wisdom, vision, and leadership provided showpieces of good government, often in difficult times. Most Illinois governors left behind reputations for probity and honesty. Their stories are lessons on the proper measure of courage and ability in service to the public.

But it would be unrealistic to expect any state, especially one with a short attention span for reform movements, to routinely elect super-statesmen. If we remember that large-scale land title frauds involved prominent territorial figures and that Illinois qualified for statehood with a dishonest census, we must assume that some of our early governors would not be exempt from the scandals that too often have given state and local government a bad name. So the best men are not always elected, which is a characteristic of democracies, and the state's top office occasionally has been filled by chairwarmers and crooks. Since the middle of the 20th century, Governors Otto Kerner, Dan Walker, and George Ryan, some other executive branch officials, and a number of legislators have been convicted for various financial crimes that, with one exception, involved official business. (Walker's troubles grew out of private investments after he left office. William Stratton, too, was indicted after he left office but was acquitted on tax evasion charges.) Most convictions were obtained by federal prosecutors, which might be a reflection on state law enforcement. Two earlier governors, Joel A. Matteson and Len Small, had narrow escapes when they came under intrastate investigation. To be blunt about it, the inaugural oath has been administered to three governors who went to prison, two others who might have, two or more incompetents, and an oddball. Another was constitutionally unqualified for the office. The stories of these men are lessons of power gone awry.

This book will acquaint you with the faces and names of the men — good and bad — who have brought Illinois into the new millennium. Today, perhaps more than ever, we face questions about the abilities and the moralities of our elected officials. With every election, we judge how candidates will handle the precarious demands of gathering power, governing efficiently, and retaining personal integrity. And soon, perhaps, the demographics of our pool of chief executives will expand to include women and minorities. But we have no crystal balls to guide us. Instead, our state offers us the lessons of a rich and colorful history punctuated by the life stories of the mostly good and competent men who have been the governors of Illinois.

1st Governor

Shadrach Bond
1773-1832

1773 — Born November 14 near Baltimore, Maryland
1809 — Illinois becomes a territory separate from the Indiana Territory.
1810 — Marries Achsah Bond, a distant cousin
1812 — Becomes Illinois Territory representative to Congress
1814 — Settles near Kaskaskia; works as receiver of public money
1818 — Illinois Constitutional Convention adopts a state constitution and selects
    Kaskaskia as the state capital August 6; Bond becomes first governor of Illinois
    October 6; President Monroe signs resolution making Illinois the 21st state.
1820 — General Assembly declares Vandalia the state capital for 20 years.
1822 — Term as governor ends; becomes record keeper at Kaskaskia land office
1826 — Makes a failed bid for Congress
1830 — Makes a failed bid for Senate
1832 — Dies at his farm April 12

Held office
October 6, 1818 to December 5, 1822

The first governor of the state of Illinois was a big, gregarious farmer with limited education and average ability. He owned land, slaves, and foxhounds, and he held desirable public offices most of his adult life. Shadrach Bond was Illinois' first representative to Congress as a nonvoting territorial delegate. He became governor in 1818. He was elected to both offices without opposition.

For his time, Bond was an adequate governor who accepted his only opportunity to play a statesman's role. As a member of the state Council of Revision, he joined Supreme Court justices in vetoing a bill to establish an uncapitalized and unregulated state bank. The veto was overridden, and the bank turned out to be one of the worst mistakes ever made by an Illinois legislature. When the new state found itself in debt, it wasn't the governor's fault. Statehood had arrived prematurely, and the Bond Administration marked time waiting for a flood of settlers to come down the Ohio River and across from Kentucky. Bond was busier before and after his term when, by presidential appointment, he was receiver and then registrar of the federal land office at Kaskaskia.

The Bonds of the Indiana Territory

Shadrach Bond was born November 14, 1773, somewhere in Maryland. According to his tombstone, a family-inspired biography, and some historians, the birthplace was Frederick, Fredericktown, or

Frederick County, which are synonymous. Local historians there have never heard of him, however, and a Maryland genealogist who is a Bond family specialist believes he probably was born in the Back River Upper Hundred, which is part of Baltimore County. His father paid taxes there in 1773; most of the Bonds lived in the Baltimore vicinity; and there is no evidence that Nicodemus and Rachel Stevenson Bond, Shadrach's parents, lived or visited in Frederick that year. Originally from England, by way of Virginia, the Bonds were prolific, minor members of the plantation and slave-owning class. Opportunities were limited, and Shadrach, the sixth of ten children, headed for the frontier in 1794.

Two Shadrach Bonds, uncle and nephew, were an early first family of Illinois, when Illinois was still part of the Indiana Territory. The elder, known as Shadrach Senior or Judge Bond, had been a civilian scout with George Rogers Clark's "Illinois Regiment" in the Revolutionary War and was one of the first English-speaking frontiersmen to make a home on the American Bottom, the area from Alton to the Kaskaskia River.

The future governor was the nephew, Shadrach Junior. Under his uncle's tutelage, Bond became a landowner and farmer at the New Design community. In 1810, at Nashville, Tennessee, Shadrach was married to a distant cousin, Achsah Bond, a native of the Baltimore vicinity. They had five daughters and two sons.

The two Bonds steadily advanced in political prominence, sitting in both houses of the Indiana territorial legislature and in local courts as appointed judges. When the court system was reorganized, the younger Bond was a justice of the peace. When Illinois was part of the Indiana Territory, the Bonds generally were factional allies of Governor William Henry Harrison. Their opponents included Kaskaskia's richest men, John Edgar and Robert Morrison, who were not pleased that Harrison supported investigations of land grant frauds. (Neither Bond was ever accused of obtaining land fraudulently.)

Bond's Public Service to the Illinois Territory

When Illinois became a separate territory in 1809, Bond showed little interest in asserting leadership. He usually sided with Jesse B. Thomas, who had been instrumental in achieving separation from Indiana, and against Ninian Edwards, Illinois' territorial governor, who would later become the state's third governor. That was especially true after Edwards did not appoint Bond commander of the St. Clair County militia.

Contrary to two published biographies, the first governor was neither an Indian fighter nor a hero of the War of 1812. He declined an opportunity to run for colonel against William B. Whiteside, a member of a prominent family of Indian fighters. In 1812, Edwards made him one of four aides-de-camp. But late that year, when Edwards personally led an expedition against Indian villages at Peoria, Bond was on his way to Washington by horseback and stage to serve as the Illinois Territory's first nonvoting delegate to Congress. Also contrary to legend, Bond did not participate in the defense of Washington when it was burned by the British on August 14, 1814. By that time he was back in Illinois with a political plum, a presidential appointment as receiver of public money for the Kaskaskia land office.

The only record of the 1812 vote that sent Bond to Congress is a petition "complaining of the undue election of Bond." He served in Washington for 15 months. He worked for a bill to raise 10 companies of mounted rangers and also proposed that a road connect Shawneetown and Kaskaskia.

In 1814, after he became a land office official, Bond moved to a farm west of Kaskaskia, the territorial capital, and built a two-story brick house that was considered palatial. Men of his position needed slaves for field and house work, and the 1820 census showed that the governor owned "14 Negroes." When he died in 1832, he bequeathed nine slaves valued at $1,210 to his wife and daughters.

Bond as State Governor

At the approach of statehood, in a factional truce, prominent Democrats Ninian Edwards and Jesse B. Thomas took for themselves the state's two U.S. senatorships. Bond announced his candidacy for the single congressional seat against John McLean, a Thomas partisan, and Daniel Pope Cook, an Edwards kinsman. For unstated reasons, Bond announced a month before the election that he would rather be governor of the new state. The official returns have been lost, but the *Illinois Intelligencer* said Bond received 3,628 votes, with only a handful being cast for some other man. When the legislature met, his majority was officially given as 3,427. Legislative journals contain no details.

A justice of the peace swore in Bond and Lieutenant Governor Pierre Menard, the only elected state officials, on October 6, 1818. In his inaugural message, Bond declared that the treasury was empty and the state's credit impaired. As a temporary solution, he recommended borrowing rather than increasing taxes. As one source of income, he proposed that the state lease its salt works outside Shawneetown and the two sections of land that had been donated by Congress for a seminary.

Because the best transportation was by water, Bond was justified in asking for internal improvements, especially the digging of a canal between Lake Michigan and the Illinois River. He also asked for a revision of the territorial code and more humane criminal laws. He wanted to abolish whipping and confinement in stocks and pillory for minor offenses and death sentences for arson, horse stealing, murder, and rape. He proposed that counties be required to build strong and substantial jails, and that the state, when it could afford it, should build a prison where convict labor could pay part of the operating costs.

More than most other early governors, Bond had some success in dealing with the legislature. Because of a funding shortage, it authorized borrowing $50,000. But the legislature also approved private lottery schemes to finance river and drainage improvements. (These failed because of the shortage of money.)

Midway through his term, when the Second General Assembly met in the new capital at Vandalia, Bond announced that the treasury was solvent. He recommended that a "seminary of learning" be built near Vandalia. He chose not to veto a "black code" patterned after the laws of slave states.

Taking the unpopular side of the chief pocketbook issue — the shortage of money in the western country — the governor objected to proposals to manufacture prosperity by creating state banks with the authority to issue paper money and make unsecured loans. He warned that the result could be "a state of things still more embarrassing," but the legislature ignored him. The General Assembly overrode his vetoes of the bank bill and a "stay" law that gave settlers a legal excuse not to pay their debts. As he predicted, the state soon faced a monetary crisis, a heavy debt, and echoes of scandal.

Back to the Land Office

Two months after Bond's term ended, President James Monroe appointed him to the Kaskaskia land office as registrar, or record keeper. President John Quincy Adams reappointed him to the prestigious position four years later. Always a politician, the former governor took his turn in 1826 at trying to defeat Congressman Daniel P. Cook, who had beaten John McLean twice and Elias Kent Kane once. Running as a supporter of William H. Crawford for the presidency, he polled approximately a third of the vote. In 1830, when a Senate vacancy was filled, only nine legislators voted for him. (The state legislature elected senators at that time.)

The elder statesman was the first grand master of the first Masonic Lodge in Illinois. Appointed by the legislature, he served on the commission that built the first state penitentiary at Alton. When a second state bank was created, he was made a director of its Edwardsville branch. He served on the governing boards of private companies chartered to dig a canal from the Illinois River to Chicago and to improve the Kaskaskia River. Both ventures failed.

Still holding the land office job, Bond died of pneumonia in his farm home on April 12, 1832. The inventory of his estate included "several farms," nine slaves, livestock, and a barrel of "very old" whiskey valued at $14.

In 1879, his remains were moved from the family cemetery on the farm to Evergreen Cemetery atop a hill in Chester, the new county seat. Two years later, Kaskaskia and the farm were swept downstream when the flooded Mississippi River changed its course.

Courtesy of the Abraham Lincoln Presidential Library

Inauguration of Shadrach Bond, as depicted by Robert A. Thom; sitting, left, Ninian Edwards; standing, next right, Elias Kent Kane; standing, in front of the window, Pierre Menard; standing to the right of Bond, Jesse B. Thomas, Nathaniel Pope, and Daniel Pope Cook

2nd Governor

Edward Coles
1786-1868

1786 — Born December 15 in Albemarle County, Virginia

1814 — Writes letter to Thomas Jefferson urging him to head an emancipation movement

1815 — Travels west; buys land near Edwardsville

1818 — Attends the Illinois constitutional convention

1822 — Elected governor with only 33 percent of the vote because pro-slavery candidates split the majority vote; inaugurated December 5

1824 — Voters refuse to call a convention aimed at amending the 1818 Constitution to allow slavery. Coles leads this victorious anti-slavery movement.

1830 — Makes a failed bid for Congress

1832 — Moves to Philadelphia, Pennsylvania; continues his anti-slavery work

1835 — Appointed head of Illinois' Board of Canal Commissioners

1862 — President Lincoln signs the Emancipation Proclamation September 22; Coles' son Robert, a slave-holder in Virginia and a Confederate captain, is killed in battle.

1868 — Dies July 7

Held office
December 5, 1822 to December 6, 1826

Edward Coles became governor by a minority vote only three years after he migrated to Illinois. He lacked rapport with the public and never attracted a personal following during the 11 years he lived in Illinois. But during his term in office, Coles played the leading role in preventing Illinois from becoming a slave state. Only Thomas Ford, who became governor two decades later, did as much to influence the course of Illinois history.

In 1824, Governor Coles responded to the legislature's pro-slavery order of a referendum for a constitutional convention to legalize the *de facto* human bondage existing in early Illinois. Lacking power to veto the resolution, he assumed leadership in defining the issue, raised money for publicizing his views, and mobilized public sentiment against the pro-slavery movement. In what seemed to be a hopeless campaign, the cause of freedom triumphed — 6,640 votes to 4,972.

The Young Abolitionist

Enniscorthy plantation in Albemarle County, Virginia, was an unusual spawning ground for an abolitionist. Edward's parent's — John Coles, who had been a Revolutionary War colonel, and Rebecca Elizabeth Tucker Coles — moved in a social circle that included presidents and governors. Patrick Henry and Dolley Madison were their cousins.

They had extensive property holdings, obtained in part through grants from the British crown. The Coles' sons and sons-in-law were influential, and Isaac, one of Edward's brothers, had been called "the most perfect gentleman in America" when he was Thomas Jefferson's private secretary.

Edward Coles was born December 15, 1786, the eighth of 12 children. His education — at Hampden Sidney College and then at the College of William and Mary — was impeccable. Bishops and professors taught that slavery might be wrong in principle but that it must be tolerated because of the difficulty of getting rid of it. Because of the "peltings and upbraidings of conscience," young Coles could not accept that reasoning. In a brief autobiography, he wrote decades later that "at William and Mary I imbibed the belief that man could not of right hold property in his fellow man and under this conviction determined to remove the chain of slavery and to emigrate to and reside with my colored people in one of the new states or territories." Shortly before graduation he was called home to help supervise the plantation during his father's final months. Soon he inherited 782 acres and 20 slaves. Had his father known that he planned to free them, they would have been bequeathed to someone else.

Upon hearing of his plans to free the slaves, Coles' shocked family begged him not to be impetuous. Virginia law required freed slaves to leave the state within a year, and the plantation could not be sold in the economic situation before the War of 1812. So Coles accepted President James Madison's invitation to become his private secretary, in part because it provided an opportunity to collect information about the free country beyond the Alleghenies. A major item in anti-slavery literature is an 1814 letter in which Coles urged Thomas Jefferson to head a movement for emancipation of Virginia slaves and to "put into practice the hallowed principles contained in the renowned Declaration of Independence of which you are the immortal author." Jefferson declined because of advanced years but encouraged Coles to follow his own conscience. Three years earlier, Coles had been the go-between who arranged the reconciliation of Jefferson and John Adams.

During his White House years, Coles never wavered in his determination to leave Virginia, as his autobiography reveals:

> The existence of war, and the difficulty of selling, and when sold, of collecting the money made me remain in this situation for six years. On peace being made, I resigned the secretaryship and set out for the western country to seek a permanent home in Ohio, Indiana or Illinois.

Coles Moves West

Accompanied by a slave, he traveled westward in 1815. That year he bought 6,000 acres near Edwardsville. "Were I a married man, I think I could set myself down and be very happy in the Illinois Territory," Coles wrote. "I do not think I am extravagant in my calculation when I say that $10,000 in the hands of a tolerably judicious man will in five or six years be worth $100,000 by the gradual and certain increase in the value of property."

A trip to Russia, made at Madison's request, delayed his settlement in Illinois. Traveling in the first American warship to enter the Baltic Sea, Coles straightened out a misunderstanding with Czar Alexander I and then leisurely toured the continent and the British Isles.

On a second journey to Illinois in 1818, Coles carried a letter of introduction from President James Monroe to Ninian Edwards, the territorial governor, and attended the constitutional convention at Kaskaskia. He knew that some delegates wanted Illinois to be a slave state, but he didn't think it would happen.

National politics also was involved. In early maneuvering for the 1824 presidential election, Coles supported Treasury Secretary William H. Crawford as the most able (if least popular) man in a crowded field. Thomas Ford wrote that Coles was sent to Illinois to counteract the influence of Edwards, who favored John C. Calhoun.

Returning to Virginia, Coles finally collected the debt for the plantation sale. In a dramatic scene on two Ohio River flatboats lashed together, Coles announced to his slaves (two aged women had been left behind, with provision for their care) that they were free, immediately and unconditionally. He gave each family a quarter section of land. He hired some to work on his Edwardsville farm, while the others found jobs nearby or in St. Louis.

In Illinois, Coles was both a farmer and a federal official, for Monroe had appointed him receiver, or money collector, of the land office at Edwardsville. Courteous and helpful to land buyers, always well-dressed in a rough environment, he was soon known by reputation in much of the state. As the Bond Administration drew to a close, slavery became a political issue, and in 1822 the aristocrat became a candidate for governor.

A Rocky, but Principled Governorship

Without public announcement, slavery advocates planned to call a constitutional convention after the 1822 election. Joseph Phillips was the choice of the dominant faction led by Jesse B. Thomas, one of the

Illinois Territory's early representatives to Congress. Phillips was so confident he would be elected the second governor of Illinois, he resigned from the Illinois Supreme Court in 1822. In a two-man race he would have defeated Coles easily, but political parties did not exist in the Old Northwest. The two chief factions, both of which favored slavery, divided their vote between Phillips and another Supreme Court justice, Thomas C. Browne, backed by Ninian Edwards' supporters. A fourth candidate, James B. Moore, did little campaigning. The proponents of slavery were shocked by the outcome. With only 33 percent of the vote, Coles was elected by a plurality of 167 over Phillips. Together the two pro-slavery candidates polled 59 percent. In his disappointment, Phillips left Illinois.

The new governor was a polished gentleman, tall and handsome. But he was also stiff, slightly awkward, and he lacked personal magnetism. He did not consult legislators and opposition leaders about his plans for the state, and he never hesitated to be blunt when he criticized them in public messages. His inaugural speech was a diplomatic failure, especially in its outspoken treatment of the racial issue. Demanding justice and humanity for all, he asked that the indenture system and a black code be abolished, that the kidnapping of free blacks be stopped, and that freedom be granted to the descendants of slaves who had been brought to Illinois during the French period. Hooper Warren, the crusading editor of the *Edwardsville Spectator*, accused the governor of precipitating a crisis. And this was not altogether untrue: A week later, a legislative committee recommended that a constitutional convention consider the governor's requests. The report did not specifically ask for legalized slavery, but the inference was clear.

By high-handedly reversing a contested election, the pro-slavery forces obtained the necessary two-thirds vote in the House of Representatives. Several hours after the final vote to reverse the representative's election, a raucous and alcoholic celebration erupted outside the governor's rooming house. John Reynolds, himself a leader in the anti-Coles forces, wrote in later years that the legislature's action "looked revolutionary, and was condemned by all honest and reflecting men."

Approval of the referendum calling for a pro-slavery constitutional convention seemed inevitable at the start of the unusually bitter 18-month campaign. Coles quickly met friendly legislators and issued a call to arms. In the campaign, he worked long hours, wrote extensively, and contributed more than the $4,000 that was his four-year salary. Coles bought the *Illinois Intelligencer* and contributed almost weekly articles. Morris Birkbeck, who with George Flower had established English colonies on the prairie near the Wabash River, expressed regret that he could not pay for the printing of pamphlets he wrote under the name of Jonathan Freeman. Financial help and other pamphlets came from Nicholas Biddle, president of the Bank of United States, and Roberts Vaux of Philadelphia, whom Coles had known since his White House days. They emphasized that slavery was unprofitable and cruel, and quoted the opinions of men who had lived in the South.

In heavy balloting August 2, 1824, Coles' supporters cast 57 percent of the vote and won — 6,640 to 4,972. Had the result been reversed, Illinois would have been in turmoil for years: The pro-slavery faction undoubtedly would have written a Southern-style constitution and made every effort to put it into effect. With multiplying controversies, their attempt to override the Ordinance of 1787, which prohibited slavery in the Northwest Territory, then including Illinois, would have been challenged in federal courts and Congress. And the character of immigration would have changed, with easterners hesitating to come to Illinois. As it was, pseudoslavery existed almost until the Civil War, and the black code was not repealed until after the war. Had Illinois been a slave state, Abraham Lincoln might have launched his political career elsewhere.

Coles Faces the Fallout for Sticking to His Convictions

Thereafter, Coles encountered petty persecution. When he gave his slaves certificates stating that he was restoring their inalienable right to liberty, he had not known of a month-old law requiring a $1,000 bond for each free black to prevent him from becoming a public charge. Vindictive Madison County officials obtained a $2,000 judgment against the governor, but the legislature, which after 1824 had an anti-slavery majority, canceled the penalty. Supreme Court Justice John Reynolds, who presided at the trial level during the court hearing, had refused to admit Coles' evidence, ruling against him on all points. In other litigation, a libel suit was dropped, probably because the governor was anxious to go to court on the issue. The Senate meanwhile refused to confirm the appointment of Morris Birkbeck as secretary of state after he had served three months. The chamber had previously rejected Coles' nomination of William H. Hamilton for secretary.

Without success, Coles advocated tax-supported schools. During the 1825 legislative session, Senator Joseph Duncan, who would become governor in nine years, sponsored a bill enabling counties to levy taxes to support free schools for whites between the ages of 5 and 21. On paper, the law placed Illinois ahead of other states, but the bill contained an out clause: No person could be taxed for schools without his consent. Because no one would consent to be taxed voluntarily, Duncan's law was soon repealed. Schools continued on a subscription basis for 30 years.

Coles criticized the legislature for having created an uncapitalized and unregulated state bank and for allowing borrowers to postpone debt payments. The people would be better off, he said, if forced to rely on their own industry and economy.

Coles and his lieutenant governor, Adolphus Frederick Hubbard, an uneducated lawyer from Shawneetown, were opposites. When Ninian Edwards resigned from the U.S. Senate, Coles scornfully rejected two Hubbard schemes: that the governorship be turned over to Hubbard, who would appoint Coles to the Senate; or that Coles appoint Hubbard senator. Coles, who refused to "sneak into the senate," wrote that "the more I see and know of the politicians in this state, the less respect and confidence I have in them."

Hubbard sought revenge the next summer by claiming that the governor had forfeited his office by taking a trip east. Contending that he was the legal chief executive during the rest of the term, Hubbard announced the appointment of William Lee D. Ewing, a future governor, as militia paymaster general. Both the legislature and the Supreme Court rejected Hubbard's pretensions. Coles might have been unpopular, but his opponents were not ready to put an obviously unqualified man in his place.

When left alone to do his job, Coles was a detail-oriented administrator. He wrote his own state papers, including the copies that went into the archives, in a small precise hand. He gave close attention to management of saline lands, settlement of French claims at Peoria, the location of seminary townships, and revenues from school sections.

An Active Retirement Away from Illinois

After his term ended, the electorate snubbed Coles and his anti-slavery followers, but the losers in the 1824 referendum were rewarded with senatorships and other high offices. Almost to a man, the new leaders of the old Jesse B. Thomas faction lined up behind Andrew Jackson and benefited from his frontier popularity. Many of those who backed Coles on the slavery issue also were receptive converts to Jackson's Democratic Party.

The governor had lost friends in 1824 by supporting Crawford for the presidency. When the legislature elected a senator to succeed Edwards, Coles, who never wavered in his criticism of Jackson, received only four votes on the first ballot and one on the tenth. In his final candidacy, he ran for Congress in 1830 and finished third.

With no prospect for again attaining influential office, Coles left Illinois. In the autumn of 1832, he moved to Philadelphia, a city of culture where he had a widening acquaintance. A year later, he married Sally Logan Roberts, 24, a member of a prominent Quaker family. They had two sons and a daughter.

When Governor Duncan visited Philadelphia in 1838, he went with Coles "to a literary club where I met many of the first citizens and spent a delightful evening." Three years earlier, Duncan appointed Coles to the presidency of the state Board of Canal Commissioners, hoping that he could borrow $500,000 to complete the waterway. Because the state was unwilling to pledge its faith in repayment of a loan, eastern investors were not interested in the canal.

As a private citizen, Coles maintained an interest in politics and corresponded extensively with public men, including historians and former presidents. One of his letters urged Madison to free his slaves. In 1854, he started a flap with Stephen A. Douglas, who was arguing that extension of slavery into the territories should be left to popular sovereignty. In an open letter, Coles insisted that the Ordinance of 1787 made slavery illegal in the Old Northwest. Douglas published a vehement reply citing Indiana and Illinois indenture laws and saying that, where it existed, slavery was local in character and not attributable to Congress.

Two years later, in a paper read before the Historical Society of Pennsylvania, Coles replied:

> Of course, the continuance of the remnant of the French slaves for so long a time in Illinois rose from the fact of its being quietly acquiesced in, and not brought to the decision of the courts of justice. If the question had even been brought before me as governor of the state, I would not have hesitated for a moment to decide, and if necessary to have enforced that decision, that slavery did not legally exist in Illinois, and of course held all in service, as such, were entitled to their freedom. This opinion I expressed in my inaugural address, and in messages to the legislature.

The former governor was wealthy, with a major part of his income coming from valuable blocks in downtown St. Louis. At one time he had title to 23 sections of bounty land in the Military Tract, a favorite area for speculation by some governors. He was paying taxes on part of it in his final years. Prairieland Farm in Madison County covered 474 acres. Coles also owned 4,890 acres in Missouri, a house and four lots in Edwardsville, and three houses in Philadelphia. At the start of the Civil War, he held leases on holdings of nearly 1,000 acres in Virginia. His philanthropic efforts included longtime support of the American Colonization Society, which sought resettlement of blacks in Africa.

In 1861, he closed his autobiographical letter by writing:

> The longer I live, the more I see and hear of the disgraceful proceedings of the present day, the more pleasing the consolation I feel in reflecting on the efforts and agency I had in our succeeding efforts in the cause of freedom and against the curse of slavery and its expansion over the lovely state of Illinois. But I must stop, or my nervous headache, always made worse by writing, will drive me mad.

During his final years, Coles wrote that he never expected to be happy again. His younger son, Roberts Coles, had bought a plantation in Albemarle County and had become a slaveowner. When the Civil War broke out, Coles wanted his son to return to Philadelphia or go abroad as a neutral. Instead, Roberts, as a Confederate captain, was killed in 1862 while defending Roanoke Island in unimportant fighting. Governor Coles lingered past his 81st birthday. He died July 7, 1868, but he lived long enough to know that all slaves had been freed.

Courtesy of the Abraham Lincoln Presidential Library

Artist's depiction of Edward Coles freeing his slaves on the Ohio River on the way to Illinois

Edward Coles

Sally Logan Roberts Coles

At the request of Governor William G. Stratton, Sidney Williams, executive secretary for the National Urban League, laid a wreath on the grave of Edward Coles in Philadelphia. The ceremony was a special feature of the league's annual conference in 1953 to mark Coles' efforts when governor to prevent Illinois from becoming a slave state. Others not identified

3rd Governor

Ninian Edwards
1775-1833

1775 — Born March 17 in Mount Pleasant, Maryland

1790 - 1791 — Attends Dickinson College

1794 — Sent to Kentucky to look after his grandfather's holdings; quickly becomes politically active and is twice elected a state representative

1803 — Marries Elvira Lane, a cousin; becomes a circuit judge

1806 — Withdraws from congressional contest; becomes a member of the Kentucky Court of Appeals

1808 — Becomes Chief Justice of the Kentucky Court of Appeals

1809 — President James Madison appoints Edwards governor of the newly created Illinois Territory on April 24.

1812 — Calls for a referendum to make Illinois a territory of the second grade; voting rights are granted to all white males over 21 who pay taxes and who have lived in the territory for a year.

1812 - 1814 — Serves disastrously in the War of 1812, leading an unimpressive campaign against friendly American Indians; he is forced to allow officers from other territories to command troops in the Illinois territory.

1818 — Ends his term as territory governor; begins term as a U.S. senator

1824 — Resigns from the Senate in the wake of the "A.B. Plot," a smear campaign in which Edwards ("A.B.") charged Treasury Secretary William Crawford with gross negligence

1826 — Becomes governor of the state of Illinois

1830 — Retires from the office of governor

1832 — Makes a failed bid for Congress

1833 — Dies July 20 in a cholera epidemic

Held office
December 6, 1826 to December 6, 1830
(Territorial Governor April 24, 1809 to October 6, 1818)

The imposing Ninian Edwards was governor of Illinois for 13 years. He served nine as the presidentially appointed governor of the territory of Illinois, from 1809 to 1818, and, beginning in 1826, four more years as the popularly elected chief executive of the state. In the interval, he was a U.S. senator. Regarded by contemporaries as one of the great men of the western country, Edwards was the leader of one of two early political factions in Illinois. A fluent orator and writer, he was an authority on frontier government and a businessman whose enterprises included farming, merchandising, banking, and land speculation. In addition, he was a man of compassion to whom the moneyless went for free medical consultation.

His term as the state's third governor came at the end of a controversial career. His popularity had peaked at the end of the territorial period, when he willingly surrendered his office and helped his constituents get the greater political privileges that went with statehood. Thereafter, he was less effective.

Though Edwards was a man of commanding appearance and superior intellect, he lost major battles with political rivals. He was pompous, vain — some thought him arrogant and overbearing — and he was guilty of errors in judgment. Part of his biography is a recital of failure to meet expectations. Nevertheless, John Francis Snyder, a 19th century physician and author, believed Edwards was the most able man in Illinois.

Edwards as Kentucky Politician and Lawyer

In his native Maryland, the future governor was reared in an elite, intellectual household. He was born March 17, 1775, the oldest son of Benjamin and Margaret Beall Edwards, at Mount Pleasant, their farm home in Montgomery County. The father, a native of Virginia, was a merchant and farmer who served in the Maryland House of Delegates, represented his district in the state convention that ratified the federal Constitution, and was elected to a two-month vacancy in the Third Congress. His brother, John Edwards, was elected from Kentucky to both houses of Congress. His mother's family, the Bealls, also were an important Maryland family.

Young Ninian was educated by private tutors, one of whom was William Wirt, a future attorney general of the United States, and he attended Dickinson College for the 1790-1791 school year. Edwards was a member of the Dickinson class of 1792, though he did not graduate. Ninian Wirt Edwards, the governor's son, wrote that "it was required of the law class that they should read, for one-half of the time, history, but young Edwards having, under the instruction of his father, become a good historian, devoted that portion of the time required for that study to the reading of medicine."

Like many other seaboard planters, the Edwards family moved to better land in the newly opened West. When he was 19, the family sent Ninian to Kentucky to take charge of his grandfather's holdings and find land for other family members. In Nelson County, he opened and improved land, built distilleries and tanyards, and generally displayed a capacity for business. Beginning a political career, he was elected state representative before he was 21 and was reelected almost unanimously. In his early Kentucky period, young Edwards drank too much and became an unsuccessful gambler. He reformed and thereafter was opposed to gambling, profane swearing, and Sabbath breaking.

In 1799, Edwards moved to Russellville in Logan County, where he developed a law practice serving Kentucky and western Tennessee. He acquired more than 2,000 acres and became militia major and presiding judge of the General Court. In 1803, he became a circuit judge and married Elvira Lane, a cousin from Maryland. In 1804, as a presidential elector, he voted for Thomas Jefferson. Two years later, facing certain defeat, he withdrew from a congressional contest. In 1806, he was a member of the Court of Appeals, the highest in the state, and two years later advanced, at the age of 33, to the chief justiceship. His prospects were for a long career of judicial eminence and increasing wealth in Kentucky, but his tenure as chief justice lasted only one year.

The Territorial Governor's First Step Toward Statehood

When the Illinois Territory became separate from the Indiana Territory in 1809, John Boyle, one of Edwards' associates, was appointed governor and collected a $138.88 salary for 21 days. Then they traded jobs: Boyle resigned and became chief justice of the Kentucky Court of Appeals, and President James Madison appointed Edwards to replace him, on the recommendation of Henry Clay, William Wirt, and Senator John Pope, an uncle.

Edwards, one month past his 34th birthday, was younger than any of the chief executives elected after statehood. Appointed for a three-year term, he was commander-in-chief of the militia, superintendent of Indian affairs, and superintendent of the government-owned salines that were the frontier's chief source of salt. A cousin, Nathaniel Pope, as secretary of the territory, was the new governor's right-hand man. Completing the official hierarchy were three federal judges with whom the governor shared legislative power. One was Jesse B. Thomas, an experienced Indiana-Illinois political infighter who, for two decades, would be Edwards' associate and rival. Each territorial governor received a 1,000-acre land grant, and Edwards, who arrived with his slaves and livestock herds three months after appointment, settled on the American Bottom between Kaskaskia and Prairie du Rocher. He named his farm Elvirade, in honor of his wife.

Included in the welcoming speeches when Edwards arrived at the capital were pleas for patronage. These were followed by conflicting private advice as to who deserved preference. The governor, who hoped he would not have to become a partisan, retained civil employees who had received emergency appointments from Pope. For the militia, he canceled all appointments and proclaimed that company officers would be elected by the men and the regimental staff by the captains, with the understanding that he would commission the winners. It was a means of involving the public in the democratic process and of avoiding tough decisions. His uncle, a Kentucky senator, told Edwards he should accept full legal responsibility. Thereafter, Edwards made his own appointments and became the head of one of the two major factions in Illinois politics. In the new alignment, Jesse B. Thomas took over leadership of the anti-Edwards group.

The governor and the judges proclaimed that Indiana statutes not otherwise inconsistent would be effective in Illinois. To meet western conditions, they followed the example of Indiana and did not hesitate to borrow from the codes of newer states, especially Kentucky, even though it was contrary to the guidelines of the Northwest Ordinance of 1787.

The governor solved the dilemma over the extension of suffrage to the Illinois frontier, a major factor in the march toward statehood. The law gave him responsibility for determining if and when a majority of the populace wished to advance to second grade government, which would permit election of a legislature and a delegate to Congress. The Ordinance of 1787 permitted voting only by freeholders who owned 50 acres and had lived two years in the territory. That would have been obnoxious in Illinois, where the complexities of fraudulent land grant titles had delayed the sale of the public domain. As a result, settlement was largely by squatters, and only an estimated 10 percent of the adult men could qualify as freeholders. In early 1812, Edwards called for an April referendum on the question of advancing to second grade government. It carried overwhelmingly. Then he waited five months before setting an October date for the election of the legislature and delegate. Meanwhile, at his request, Congress extended the right of suffrage in Illinois to all white males of 21 years who paid a county or territorial tax and had lived in the territory one year. As a result, Illinois was the most democratic of the territories, and Edwards had kept the richest men at Kaskaskia, John Edgar and Robert Morrison, from getting control of the legislature. Shadrach Bond won the position as delegate to Congress. Bond was not an Edwards ally, but he worked with Edwards.

Edwards' Farcical War of 1812

During the War of 1812, it was important for Illinois to have a man in Washington. However, for Edwards the war was a personal disaster. He was both an alarmist, afraid that white settlements would be overrun by Indian hordes, and a patriot who spent his private funds to buy presents for Indian chiefs, help build blockhouses, and equip mounted ranger companies. The governors of Indiana and Missouri also expected trouble, but Edwards overstated his case. In complex sentences and almost endless paragraphs, he sent letter after letter to Washington warning of attacks that never came. Secretary of War William Eustis trusted his own sources of information. Edwards believed that the Madison Administration did not appreciate the situation, especially after a massacre at Fort Dearborn in which nearly 75 men, women, and children lost their lives. Meanwhile, the delay of his reappointment increased the governor's insecurity.

Edwards, who never forgot that he commanded the Illinois militia, was offended when William Henry Harrison, the hero of Tippecanoe, was made a brigadier general and given command of operations from Indiana westward. Accepting at face value rumors that at Lake Peoria, four days away, the natives were massing a large force, Edwards took the offensive. At Fort Russell, which guarded Edwardsville, he collected 350 rangers and mounted volunteers whom he personally led northward. Near Peoria, they burned several villages, killed two dozen Indians, captured four others and 80 horses, and returned in 18 days with one man wounded. Constituents were impressed, but not officials in Washington; the burned villages belonged to Jack Partridge, who had befriended the whites at Fort Dearborn, and Gomo, who had been an intermediary in diplomatic efforts to confine the Indians to a neutral role.

The governor came into even greater disrepute after he sent an expedition by boat to the small French settlement at Peoria. Captain Thomas Craig, an Indian-hater from Shawneetown, was ransacking the nearly deserted town when Thomas Forsyth, a highly regarded government agent, returned and assured Craig that the few Indians there were powerless and at least potentially friendly. A few days later, when a shot was fired at one of Craig's boats, the white force raided the settlement, destroyed considerable property, and took captive Forsyth and some 40 Frenchmen. In midwinter, they were released below Alton without food.

The administration soon showed its displeasure. Benjamin Howard resigned as governor of Missouri and, as a brigadier general, led a federal force into Edwards' territory. At Peoria he built the 100-foot-square Fort Clark. Having forfeited his last chance for an army command, Edwards left Illinois to visit his family, which he had sent to Kentucky a year earlier for safety. He complained to Secretary of State James Monroe that during the war Madison had given him neither instructions on what to do, nor thanks for arduous work. "I have not till the present time been one day absent from my post since the indians [sic] first commenced their depredations — and with a constitution very delicate indeed I do believe that I have since August last undergone as much fatigue and hardship as any soldier in the army," he wrote.

As hostilities ended and immigration speeded up, Edwards was appointed one of three commissioners to negotiate treaties on the Indiana, Illinois, and Missouri frontiers. With Governor William Clark of Missouri and Auguste Choteau of St. Louis as co-negotiators, he prevailed upon tribesmen to give up title to more than 8 million acres, for which the American Indians received $18,400. Fort Edwards, which had an eight-year existence on the Mississippi River at present day Warsaw, was named for the governor who never became a military hero.

On to Statehood

Friction between the federally appointed judges and other officials was common. In 1812, the governor suspected that his character was being besmirched, and he and Jesse B. Thomas were on the verge of a duel. There were complaints that the judges, holding court infrequently, were not earning their salaries. The judges retorted that frontier travel was a hardship. The legislature went to the extreme of passing laws to govern the jurisdiction and procedures of federal courts. Congress settled the controversy with a law that backed up the legislature.

To avoid charges that he was a tyrant, Edwards went out of the way to avoid vetoes. Nevertheless, as a matter of principle, the legislature in 1814 petitioned for abolition of the absolute veto. His only veto, which prevented the abolition of de facto slavery, was amazing for its inconsistencies. Edwards said he personally opposed slavery, but he refused to let the legislature abolish the indenture system under which it existed in Illinois. In practice, Edwards not only bought and sold indentured servants, but also rented out some people for their forced labor. Later, in the U.S. Senate, he voted for the Missouri Compromise of 1820, which let Maine enter the union as a free state and Missouri enter as a slave state. He held that extending slavery into Missouri would dilute its evil.

In 1818, the territorial congressional delegate Nathaniel Pope guided a measure to grant Illinois statehood through both houses. Once the enabling act passed, a constitutional convention convened on August 3, and finished its work 23 days later.

The Controversial Senator Edwards

Edwards' career as a U.S. senator was a disappointment. With the arrival of statehood, he and Jesse B. Thomas, old-time enemies, took for themselves, in what was a political deal, the two Senate seats. When the new legislature met, he was elected senator on the first ballot. Not until the fourth ballot did Thomas get the necessary majority vote of the two houses. Then Edwards' luck turned bad. When the two senators drew straws, Thomas won the six-year term, and Edwards had to stand for reelection in four months. By that time, their political deal had expired, and Edwards barely defeated Michael Jones, an early land office official.

On patronage matters, President James Monroe favored Thomas, who also got a prized assignment to the public lands committee. As slaveholders, both senators voted for the Missouri Compromise, which was sponsored by Thomas. The July 4, 1820, *Edwardsville Spectator* accused Edwards of a conflict of interest, saying he owned 22 blacks whom he had hired out in Missouri.

The senator, a land speculator, placed his private interests over those of his constituents when he opposed an 1820 law that reduced government land prices to $1.25 from $2 an acre and allowed purchases of 80 acres, half the previous figure. Because it abolished credit sales, Edwards insisted that settlers were being unfairly treated. He ignored the point that speculators did not want price-cutting by the government. Henceforth, that vote was used as a political issue against Edwards.

A controversy known as the "A.B. Plot," which for two years occupied the attention of federal officials and partisan newspapers, forced Edwards to return to Illinois as a private citizen. He caused trouble for himself by writing several *Washington Republican* articles that he signed "A.B." in which he accused Treasury Secretary William H. Crawford of malfeasance in his official dealings with unstable western banks. Edwards, in 1818, had helped organize the Bank of Edwardsville and had used his influence to have it made a land office depository. Finding the bank in trouble, he resigned as a director in 1821 before the bank's failure cost the government $46,800. At the heart of the A.B. controversy was whether Crawford had been notified that Edwards believed government money should be withdrawn from the bank.

Politics at the national level was involved. In advance of the 1824 campaign, many regarded Crawford as the strongest candidate for president. As was customary, the two Illinois senators split, with Thomas backing Crawford and Edwards supporting John C. Calhoun, who was, not coincidentally, backed by the *Washington Republican*.

Edwards told the governor-historian Thomas Ford that he made the original charges against Crawford under a promise of support from President Monroe, Calhoun, Andrew Jackson, and John Quincy Adams. But when he was unable to get supporting evidence in the A.B. dispute, Edwards became unhappy in the Senate. He wanted to become minister to Mexico but Monroe nixed the idea. Adams later made the appointment. While Edwards was on his way to his new post, William H. Crawford told the House that he had never been advised of the Edwardsville bank's condition. Called back to testify before a House committee, Edwards proffered formal charges but could not substantiate them. When the committee exonerated Crawford, Edwards had no option but to resign his diplomatic post.

Edwards the State Governor

That Edwards could be elected governor in 1826, a watershed year, was a political miracle. Newer settlers had little interest in retaining the Edwards family in office. His record in the Senate was tainted. And after his ministerial position fell through, the state legislature — now dominated by his factional enemies — refused to send him back to the Senate. He had lost favor with President John Quincy Adams and could not expect another federal post. He could not run for Illinois' one seat in Congress because it was held by Daniel Pope Cook, his son-in-law and ally. The new western hero was Andrew Jackson, whose followers were incensed because Cook had cast Illinois' vote for Adams when the House of Representatives elected the president in 1825. Edwards refrained from criticizing Jackson, but was not accepted by the Jacksonians.

Like Edward Coles four years earlier, Edwards would have been defeated had the opposition centered on one candidate. Adolphus Frederick Hubbard, the unqualified lieutenant governor, insisted on running for governor, even though Thomas Sloo Jr., a state senator of good reputation but small acquaintance, was backed by a majority of the disorganized Jacksonian Democrats. Edwards won a single-handed, one-issue campaign by boldly telling the frontiersmen that his enemies were responsible for the state's financial dilemma. He blamed them for creating a worthless bank, for the law requiring that depreciated bank notes be received at par for payment of taxes and other bills, for auditors' warrants worth one-third of face value, for an enormous state debt, and for a real estate tax system that would continue annual deficits. He won with slightly less than half of the vote, with Sloo finishing only 447 votes behind.

In office, Governor Edwards had a four-year running fight with the legislature, chiefly over the management of the Bank of Illinois, which it had established in 1821. His main opposition came from the 1826-1827 legislature, which a history published in 1874 called "one of the worst that has ever been inflicted on the state." (The unofficial "worst legislature" citation has been frequently awarded in most states, but not in Illinois in recent decades.) In his inaugural address he berated officers of the branch bank at Edwardsville, accusing them of fraud and perjury and recommending impeachment and trial. Specific charges followed in special messages that named some of the state's most powerful politicians, all enemies of the governor. Heading the list was Theophilus T. Smith, who was both a Supreme Court justice and cashier of the Edwardsville bank. Others named included Shadrach Bond, who had been governor eight years earlier, and Thomas Carlin, who would be in 12 more years.

The legislature exonerated the men involved. Today, it seems probable that Edwards had right on his side — Thomas Ford believed that the investigating committee was stacked — but the governor's belligerence and self-righteous air helped spoil his case. John Reynolds noted that Edwards was not gifted with prudence and tact. Ford criticized Edwards for the scatter-gun charges that weakened his case by naming some men of good reputation.

Edwards retracted some of his critical statements, so that his administration made some progress in straightening out the financial situation. The legislature passed a law that would tighten bank regulation. It also abolished five circuit judgeships and assigned the Supreme Court justices to do their work, an economy measure the governor advocated. Another law granted some relief to debtors; however, like Bond and Coles, Edwards protested.

His midterm message introduced a new States' Rights Doctrine. The verbose governor asserted that all public lands within its borders belonged to the state and that the federal government could only own land needed for forts, naval facilities, and necessary public buildings. Both Congress and the electorate ignored him, but the legislature, just to be on the safe side, petitioned Congress to accept the governor's assertion.

Edwards the Man

During his busy political career, Edwards also carried on several business ventures. Historian John Moses called Edwards the foremost merchant in the state. He was said by his son to have established eight or 10 stores at such places as Kaskaskia, Belleville, Carlyle, Alton, and Springfield in Illinois, and at St. Louis, Franklin, and Chariton in Missouri. Edwards also established saw and grist mills. To some extent, his business affairs suffered because he had to leave hired managers in charge for long periods. The agriculture of Illinois benefited from the improved breeds of horses, cattle, and sheep he brought to the state and from choice fruit trees, grapes, and shrubbery he imported.

Edwards moved from his Elvirade farm outside Kaskaskia to Edwardsville in 1818 and to Belleville in 1825. Belleville, which had been made the county seat in 1814 when it was only a cornfield, was one of his many speculations. The governor bought the townsite a few years later and offered to sell lots for $60, soon to be increased to $100, with special concessions to blacksmiths and other craftsmen. In addition to townsite speculations, some with his son-in-law Daniel Cook as a partner, he had heavy holdings in agricultural land that usually was offered for resale with hope of a quick, if not large, profit.

Edwards, who never was good at organizing campaigns and who never condescended to the common low arts of electioneering, made one more effort to reenter public life. In 1832, he belatedly became a candidate for Congress and finished second in a three-man field.

Thomas Ford described Edwards as a large, well-made man, with a noble, princely appearance. He was credited with major virtues, among them humor, compassion, truth, and charity. He was an amateur doctor with a sizable charitable practice. When General Winfield Scott came to northern Illinois to fight the Black Hawk War, he brought along with his troops a cholera epidemic that spread down the Mississippi River and reached Belleville. Caring for stricken neighbors, Edwards refused to flee from his home. On July 20, 1833, the epidemic numbered the former governor as one of its victims.

The governor's first grave was at Belleville. He was twice reburied at Springfield, at Hutchinson's Cemetery in 1855 and at Oak Ridge Cemetery in 1866.

Painting of Fort Dearborn Massacre, 1812, which occurred before Illinois became a state

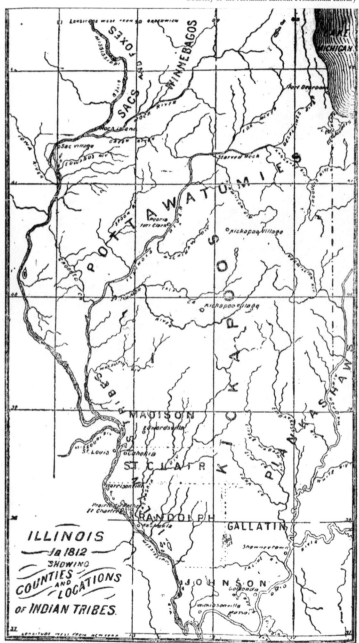

1812 map showing the early counties and the location of American Indian tribes

4th Governor

John Reynolds
1788-1865

1788 — Born February 26 in Montgomery County, Pennsylvania

1800 — Comes to the Illinois Territory with his family

1812 — Serves as advance guard for Governor Edward's quixotic Lake Peoria Indian campaign

1816 — Becomes judge advocate of the militia's second regiment

1818 — Defeated in a bid to become a constitutional convention delegate

1818 - 1825 — Serves as a justice of the Illinois Supreme Court

1823 — Makes unsuccessful bid for Senate

1827 - 1830 — Serves in the 5th and 6th General Assemblies

1830 — Defeats Lieutenant Governor William Kinney; becomes governor

1831 — Treaty of Chicago, the last Indian treaty pertaining to Illinois land, is signed.

1832 — The Black Hawk War, precipitated when Chief Black Hawk refuses to stay west of the Mississippi; after the war, all American Indian tribes are ordered out of Illinois.

1834 — Resigns governorship before his term expires to serve in the U.S. House

1836 — Loses his bid for reelection to the U.S. House

1839, 1840 — Wins election to the U.S. House

1853 - 1855 — Wins election to Illinois House and serves as speaker

1858 — Loses election for superintendent of public instruction

1865 — Dies May 18 at his home in Belleville

Democrat
December 6, 1830 to November 16, 1834

John Reynolds, the "Great Oddball" of Illinois officialdom, realized that he lacked the intellectual stature to serve as governor, Supreme Court justice, congressman, and speaker of the state House of Representatives. Still, he didn't let that stop him from running for — and winning election to — all those offices. A compulsive campaigner, the state's fourth governor also many times found himself on the short side of the vote tally.

Reynolds called himself the "Old Ranger," to remind people that he had served in the War of 1812. Highly prejudiced and a man of many idiosyncrasies, he avoided extreme positions in important political contests. Thomas Ford, a contemporary, described how Reynolds, a collector of friendships, adopted the protective coloration of frontier society:

> No one would suppose from hearing his conversation and public addresses that he ever learned more than to read and write and cypher to the rule of three....

He had been a farmer, a lawyer, and a soldier, a judge, and a member of the legislature. He had passed his life on the frontiers among a frontier people; he had learned all the bye-words, catch-words and figures of speech invented by the vulgar ingenuity and common among a back woods people; to these he had added a copious supply of his own, and had diligently compounded them into a language peculiar to himself, which he used on all occasions, both public and private. He was a man of remarkably good sense and shrewdness for the sphere in which he chose to move, and he possessed a fertile imagination, a ready eloquence, and a continual mirthfulness while mingling with the people.

Undereducated, eccentric, and opinionated, he normally espoused only policies that were popular among the frontiersmen upon whose votes he depended. However, on major controversies such as banking and finance, he cannily avoided future embarrassment by eavesdropping or cautious questioning when in the presence of his intellectual superiors. Hints thus acquired were translated into official policy with the result, all things considered, that he had a respectable administration. He wasn't an executive, but the state's shaky fiscal condition improved somewhat during his four years in office. It could have been worse.

The Rise of the Old Ranger

The future governor was born February 26, 1788, in Montgomery County, Pennsylvania, six months after his Protestant Irish parents, Robert and Margaret Moore Reynolds, landed at Philadelphia. He was soon taken to Tennessee and reached Illinois when he was 12, driving one of his father's two teams of horses. The family was headed for upper Louisiana but settled outside Kaskaskia at the urging of a land speculator involved in the wholesale frauds. He spent part of his boyhood in the Goshen neighborhood east of Edwardsville, and a one-year stint at a seminary in Knoxville, Tennessee, got him a pseudoclassical education. Back in Illinois, under the informal procedures of the pre-statehood period, he was accepted into the ranks of the attorneys, proving that not all self-schooled lawyers were of Lincoln's caliber.

His law practice was unimportant, but he became well-to-do early in life as an associate of a cousin, Joseph A. Beaird. Like many prominent men of his time, Reynolds speculated in land, apparently successfully, although he left no details. He did reveal that he bought and sold two stores worth $10,000 each. Once he offered a $50 reward for an escaped slave, which could have indicated that he had been in the business of buying and selling slaves. He believed that slavery was morally and legally right.

His military career was long enough for him to have a service record and safe enough to ensure that he would one day live to be an *Old* Ranger. He was a member of a spy (advance guard) company on Ninian Edwards' unimpressive Lake Peoria expedition in late 1812. "I never fired a gun, as I saw no occasion for it," he recalled. He did confiscate a sack of corn, soon abandoned because it became rain-soaked, and he saw Governor Edwards unhorsed in a deep mudhole. Later he was a member of a Missouri-Illinois force that built Fort Clark at Peoria. He saw no action, but he wrangled a sergeancy for himself. Three years later, he was judge advocate of the militia's Second Regiment, which was a political appointment. Thereafter, he was continually running for office, almost any office.

A Lifetime of Campaigning Begins

Reynolds hated many people, especially Jesse B. Thomas, who defeated him for election as a delegate to the 1818 constitutional convention. Reynolds went to the opening session of the General Assembly when officials were being elected. He probably would have taken a job as door keeper, but he was elected an associate justice of the Illinois Supreme Court, a $1,000-a-year job he claimed not to have asked for.

During his term as a Supreme Court justice (1818-1825), Reynolds took the unpopular side on one important issue. He joined the 3-to-2 majority in attempting to veto the 1822 bill that created a state bank that left the new state heavily in debt. Normally, he would have voted to please the great mass of uninformed voters who believed that the uncapitalized bank would ensure prosperity. On other court business, the few opinions he wrote were undistinguished. Sitting at the trial level, he ruled against Governor Coles on all counts in the Madison County case involving bonding of freed slaves. On appeal, the other Supreme Court justices ruled for Coles.

Reynolds was denied reelection at the end of his Supreme Court term. When the legislature created five new circuit judgeships, his name was absent. Seeking both opportunity and revenge, he ran for the U.S. Senate in 1823 while he was still on the bench, but lost to Jesse B. Thomas, 16 to 26.

With nothing better being available, he then ran for state representative, losing once and winning twice. In the legislature, his major interest was establishment of a state penitentiary and abolition of flogging and the pillory as punishment for crime.

The Fourth Governor

Considering the alternative, Illinois was fortunate that Reynolds, a "milk and cider" or moderate Jacksonian Democrat, was its fourth chief executive. In 1830, no more men of the caliber of Ninian Edwards, the retiring governor, were available. The "whole hog" Jacksonians wanted his successor to be Lieutenant Governor William Kinney, a convivial Baptist preacher whose administrative incompetence would be demonstrated when the legislature put him in charge of construction of state-owned railroads. Sued for funds he hadn't accounted for, Kinney left a bankrupt estate. By contrast, Reynolds' public and private lives were scandal-free and his home life exemplary. He did not use alcohol, although he freely bought it to treat voters. For many of his virtues, credit goes to the bad example of his father, who once created a drunken disturbance in his son's courtroom and who, in the investigation of territorial land frauds, was indicted on 17 counts of perjury and forgery.

The choice was difficult. Kinney, who was said to have campaigned with a Bible in one hand and a bottle in the other, undiplomatically criticized church people who weren't Baptists. Reynolds never went to church and in his conversation was habitually profane, perhaps more so than any other Illinois governor. Because they expected Kinney to carry the state handily, the remnants of the Edwards faction and the Henry Clay Whigs did not enter a candidate. Reynolds won easily by virtue of the anti-Kinney vote.

In the 1830 campaign, Reynolds said he had always been against the disastrous state bank and, echoing Edwards, blamed Kinney and other bank officials for the heavy tax burden. In reply, the Jacksonians pointed out that he had borrowed from the bank. Reynolds allowed Edwards, a former enemy, to write his inaugural speech and thus passed up an opportunity to lead a movement for debt repudiation. He called for winding up the bank's affairs as rapidly as possible and set a precedent for Governor Thomas Ford's stand for fiscal responsibility 10 years later. In his book *My Own Times*, Reynolds said little in justification of his stands on this and other issues. If public sentiment was divided, he usually kept still.

In his messages to the legislature, like other governors, he was for education and public improvements. He did not stir up trouble by engaging in crusades, however. In 1830, he supported the proposition to build a canal from the Illinois River to Chicago over Kinney's protest that it would bring more Yankees to Illinois.

In the Black Hawk War, he waited to determine that expulsion of Indians was a popular cause before he called out the militia and asked for the help of federal troops. Accompanied by a staff of colonels, he used the commander in chief's prerogative to go along on two military expeditions into northwest Illinois. His personal bravery became suspect when a combined federal-state force of 2,500 men reached Vandruff's Island on which Indians might be concealed. Suddenly ill, the governor went below decks.

Reynolds did sign two Indian treaties. In the summer of 1831, he and General Edmund P. Gaines met with 30 Sac chiefs who confirmed an 1804 land cession and agreed to stay west of the Mississippi River. The next year, he and General Winfield Scott signed the Treaty of Fort Armstrong that for all practical purposes ended the Indian occupation of Illinois.

An Early Departure to Greener Pastures

Reynolds left the governor's seat just days before the end of his term to begin an intermittent career in Congress. In his diary, John Quincy Adams called Reynolds untruthful, vulgar, and knavish. Reynolds switched positions on a tariff issue in his first term, ultimately opposing it. In 1836, he lost to Adam W. Snyder, a perennial rival. Reynolds was later elected again and served from 1839 to 1843.

During one of his out-of-office intervals, Reynolds lost $17,000 as the principal investor in the first Illinois railroad, a six-mile, wooden-railed line from the American Bottom bluffs, where he owned coal land, to the Mississippi River opposite St. Louis. It used horse-power and crossed a lake on a rickety bridge.

If Reynolds ever had been a statesman, he forfeited that rating in 1839. The legislature authorized Governor Thomas Carlin to borrow $4 million to finance the Illinois and Michigan Canal. Reynolds was totally unqualified for the assignment, but he talked Carlin into sending him to Europe as a special commissioner. With three associates, he made ill-advised and bungling deals that caused heavy losses to the state.

The European junket was a honeymoon tour at state expense for Reynolds and his second wife, Sarah Wilson, whom he met while a congressman and married in 1836. She was tall, stately, and 20 years younger. He bought an expensive home for her in Belleville, where he moved in 1831. His first wife, Catherine Manegle, daughter of Julien Dubuque, the Canadian Indian trader, died in 1834 after 17 years of marriage. Reynolds, who had no children by either marriage, acted as a father to his first wife's three children.

Reynolds was elected for the last time when he ran for state representative in 1853 and was rewarded with the speakership.

The Old Ranger Passes On

In his later years, he became a prolific author whose chief talent was a remarkable if disorganized memory for names, faces, dates, and places. Two of his books have merit. *The Pioneer History of Illinois* (1852) ends with statehood in 1818. Reynolds got help for this volume from John Mason Peck and John Russell. *My Own Times* (1855) is an auto-biographical sequel. Together they contain details not found elsewhere about settlement and people. The author's prejudicial thoughts about morals, religion, politics, history, and science fill a plotless novel, *The Life and Adventures of John Kelly* (1853). A trip to a New York exposition resulted in *Sketches of the Country* (1856). And he wrote *Friendship's Offering* in 1858 as a tribute to his friend Peck. Reynolds wrote rapidly and never corrected or interlined the words he scrawled on a pad held on his knee. Unemployed printers set books and occasional newspapers on a secondhand press in the law office in the back of his Belleville home. But Reynolds himself learned to set type and could quickly issue broadsides that gave his views on current events. His final book, *The Balm of Gilead*, was a 48-page defense of slavery.

With the approach of the Civil War, Reynolds hated Stephen A. Douglas even more than he hated Abraham Lincoln. He openly sympathized with the South and blamed abolitionists and "black Republicans" for sectional strife. He ran for office the last time in 1858 on the Buchanan ticket as a candidate for superintendent of public instruction, finishing third and last. In 1860, he was a John C. Breckenridge delegate to the Democratic National Convention at Charleston but was denied a seat. During the war, his outspoken support of secession attracted considerable attention, but old age and past prominence saved him from military arrest. He outlived Lincoln by a month.

Reynolds, an agnostic to his final hour, died of pneumonia May 18, 1865, at his Belleville home. When a minister called to tell the Old Ranger of his last chance for repentance, he contemptuously gasped, "The hell you say."

Drawing of Wolf's Point in Chicago, 1833, where the branches of the Chicago River meet; the new town's first trustees were elected and town meetings were held in the Sauganash Hotel.

The Merchandise Mart sits east of Wolf's Point, which, in 1860, was the site of the Wigwam, built for the Republican National Convention that nominated Abraham Lincoln for president.

5th Governor

William Lee Davidson Ewing
1796-1846

1796 — Born March 1 in Logan County, Kentucky

1818 — Reaches Shawneetown, Illinois

1830 — Elected state representative; becomes speaker of House in the 7th General Assembly

1832 — Elected state senator; is chosen leader of the Ilinois Senate and serves until 1837

1833 — Becomes acting lieutenant governor on March 1 when Lieutenant Governor Zodok Casey leaves his post to become a member of Congress

1834 — Becomes governor on November 17 when Reynolds leaves to serve in the U.S. House before his term expires; leaves office on December 3 when Governor-elect Duncan is sworn into office; returns to his Illinois Senate seat

1835 - 1837 — Serves as U.S. senator from Illinois while also serving in the Illinois Senate (He is appointed to fill the seat vacated upon the death of Senator Elias Kent Kane on December 12.)

1839 - 1843 — After defeating Lincoln for the speakership of the Illinois House in 1838, serves as speaker for the 11th and 12th General Assemblies

1843 - 1846 — Is the auditor of public accounts (an office dissolved by the 1970 Illinois Constitution and resurrected in 1973 as comptroller); dies in office March 25

Democrat

November 17, 1834 to December 3, 1834

William Lee Davidson Ewing, governor for 16 days, completed the unexpired term of John Reynolds, who resigned as chief executive to go to Washington as a newly elected congressman. Later, Ewing was a U.S. senator for two years, again filling a vacancy.

A friendly Scotch-Irishman who held an unusual sequence of public offices, mostly minor, Ewing was an attorney who lived in Vandalia and seldom practiced law. He had little to do during his half-month as governor. At the start of Governor Joseph Duncan's administration, he sent a message to the legislature that loyally followed Jacksonian doctrine by criticizing the Bank of the United States. Already reelected to the state Senate, he advocated another effort to establish a state bank, but didn't say how it should differ from the disastrous Bank of Illinois created by the 1821 legislature. Loyalty to the Jackson political creed helped in his pursuit of patronage jobs and public office.

Ewing's Early Years

His signature read Wm. Lee D. Ewing, and he was named for his maternal grandfather, a general who was killed in the Revolutionary

War. He was born March 1, 1796, in Logan County, Kentucky, the son of Finis and Margaret Davidson Ewing. His father, a Presbyterian minister, was one of four men who organized the Cumberland Presbyterian Church in 1810.

Details of his early life are vague, but the future governor seems to have become a lawyer before he reached Shawneetown sometime in 1818. Early in 1821, he was appointed one of eight trustees of Vandalia, the new capital. When the government opened a land office at Vandalia in 1820, Ewing was appointed receiver, a job he lost as the result of a robbery of the Bank of Illinois three years later. He kept two sacks of specie [coins] in his house because it was safer there than in any other house in town. Government regulations called for land office receipts, minus expenses, to be deposited in the Bank of Illinois at Shawneetown, which was a long way off. He then asked Ninian Edwards to help him get a government job as a surveyor in Iroquois County. Early in his Vandalia career Ewing married Caroline Berry, daughter of Elijah Berry, the first state auditor. They had six children, of whom two daughters reached adulthood.

The poverty of his early Vandalia years was not permanent. Ewing became a land speculator. There is a record that he bought 54 quarter-sections and sold 101 in the Military Tract before 1833. Incomplete land office records about purchases would account for the discrepancy. In 1830, the census showed that he owned two slaves.

One of the few militia officers who performed creditably during the Black Hawk War of 1832, he was major of a spy battalion that did advance patrol work in pursuing Indians out of Illinois and across Wisconsin to the Mississippi River at Bad Axe.

The Career Path of a Seat Warmer

In a unique political career, he was elected speaker for three of the terms he served in the Illinois House of Representatives. The path upward started in 1826 with two terms as clerk of the House. He then was elected state representative in 1830 and senator in 1832.

Ewing backed into the governorship. He was not elected lieutenant governor, but as Senate leader he was next in line when Lieutenant Governor Zodok Casey resigned after his election to Congress. Then, when Governor Reynolds resigned for the same reason, Ewing became governor for half a month, after which he automatically resumed his seat in the Senate.

He was appointed to fill Illinois' U.S. Senate seat upon the death of Elias Kent Kane on December 12, 1835. Late in 1836, when more influential Democrats wanted to assure a future vacancy in the Senate, Republican Abraham Lincoln and a group of anti-Jackson men perversely maneuvered Ewing's reelection. True to form, he lost that Senate seat in two years, but almost at once returned to the Illinois House to serve two terms as speaker. Again without interruption, he was back in his starting job as clerk of the House in 1842. He soon prevailed upon his colleagues in the legislature to elect him state auditor, a position he held until his death on March 25, 1846.

Perhaps Ewing's greatest political triumph is that he twice defeated Lincoln for the speakership of the Illinois House. The first time, in 1838, the Whigs had a nominal majority, but three were absent. Party discipline was not important, so several legislators from neighboring districts found reason to vote for the Vandalia resident.

A few months later, when he was trying to prevent the removal of the state capital to Springfield, Ewing called Lincoln a "coarse and vulgar fellow" and a "low and obscure colleague." Today, of course, Governor Ewing is not so easily remembered, while the vulgar Mr. Lincoln is somewhat less obscure.

Governor Samuel Shapiro accepted this portrait of Governor Ewing, who served the shortest term in Illinois history and, until 1968, did not have an official portrait in the Hall of Governors. Allen Stults, president of American National Bank and Trust Company of Chicago, right of painting, commissioned it to commemorate the state's sesquicentennial.

6th
Governor

Joseph Duncan
1794 - 1844

1794 — Born February 22 in Paris, Kentucky
1812 - 1814 — Served in the War of 1812
1824 — Elected to the first of two terms in the Illinois Senate
1826 — Elected to the first of four terms in Congress
1831 — Begins service as a major general in the Black Hawk War
1834 — Elected governor while in Washington
1837 — The legislature votes to move the state capital from Vandalia to Springfield
March 3; a mob in Alton kills Elijah P. Lovejoy, editor of the abolitionist paper, the
Alton Observer.; financial panic of 1837 hits the state, severely hampering the internal
improvements initiative to build railroads and the Illinois and Michigan Canal.
1838 — Ends his term as governor
1841 — Federal government sues Duncan, the signer of a surety bond for his brother-in-law,
for losses resulting from his brother-in-law's defaults
1842 — Runs as the Whig nominee for governor; gets 45 percent of the vote
1844 — Dies January 15

Whig
December 3, 1834 to December 7, 1838

Joseph Duncan, the only Whig governor of Illinois, was elected in absentia by voters who assumed he was still a Democrat. The four-term congressman stayed in Washington until after the 1834 election, made no campaign speeches, and still won with 54 percent of the vote in a four-man field. Meanwhile, he changed from an admirer to a critic of President Andrew Jackson, a move that caused Duncan to suffer politically and financially.

Like Jackson, Duncan was a western man with a military background. He might have had a long career as a Jacksonian Democrat, but he refused to be stampeded by the great western mass movement that swept Jackson into the White House in 1828. Instead, in Washington, the Democrat found himself more comfortable as a follower of John Quincy Adams and Henry Clay.

Duncan did not publicly announce he was changing parties. The political leaders got the message when Duncan voted to override vetoes of bills to improve the Wabash River and the Chicago harbor and when he defied Jacksonian policy by introducing an amendment to recharter the Bank of the United States. But, the informality of election procedures and the slowness of frontier communication permitted Duncan's surprise election. Congress did not adjourn until July 1, and his wife's illness delayed their return to Illinois until after the election one month later. Not until inauguration day on December 3 did the rank-and-file realize the new governor was a Whig — not the reliable Jackson man they thought they sent to Washington. At the time, a formal Whig Party organization did not exist in Illinois.

After Duncan's election, Jackson supporters — the lineal descendants of Thomas Jefferson's Democratic Republicans — organized their Democratic Party at the state level. Thereafter, they made certain election-day support centered on a single slate of candidates. With Jackson's name as their inspiration and Stephen A. Douglas as their tactician, Democrats controlled Illinois politics for two decades, until party alignments were fractured by the uproar over slavery that brought on the Civil War.

The new governor denied that he was an apostate, saying he held steadfastly to the principles on which Jackson was first elected in 1828. Duncan still believed in one-term presidencies, in economy and reform, and in keeping the spoils system out of government. But the legislature, dominated by Jacksonian Democrats, was even more unfriendly than it had been toward Coles, Edwards, and Reynolds.

Among the governors of Illinois, Duncan deserves honorable mention for his opposition to ill-timed and expensive programs for the construction of state-owned railroads and the chartering of another state bank that brought on Illinois' severest financial crisis. Time soon demonstrated that he was the best of the four men in the campaign for governor. Had the voters realized that Duncan was not a true Jacksonian, William Kinney, the "whole hog" extremist whom John Reynolds defeated for governor four years earlier, would likely have been elected. Thomas Ford, who defeated Duncan for the governorship in 1842, held a high opinion of the man. Ford said the Whig governor "had a sound judgment, a firm confidence in his own convictions of right, and a moral courage in adhering to his convictions which is rarely met with."

Military Service and Early Political Career

Born in Paris, Kentucky, on February 22, 1794, the future governor was the third son of Joseph and Anna Maria McLaughlin Duncan, Virginians of Scotch and Scotch-Irish lineage. His father, an army major who built a 20-room stone inn among the log cabins at Paris, died when Joseph was 12. Three years later, his mother married an army captain who died within two years. His older brothers had been educated at Yale and at Transylvania University in Kentucky, but instead of going to college, young Joseph assumed responsibility for his mother's finances. At 21, he was appointed guardian of his sister and two younger brothers.

He migrated to Illinois because an uncle and a brother had ties to Territorial Governor Ninian Edwards. His uncle, Robert K. McLaughlin, had been appointed territorial treasurer. At Edwards' request, Joseph's brother Mathew, a Kentucky newspaperman, printed the Illinois territorial laws. Mathew Duncan then moved to Kaskaskia, edited *The Herald*, and published the first book printed in Illinois. At Brownsville in Jackson County, Joseph Duncan farmed and operated a mill. Before statehood, he was appointed a justice of the peace. Governor Bond commissioned him a major general of the militia, an honor both military and political. His formal education was limited, but Duncan radiated intelligence and leadership qualities.

Midway through the Coles Administration, he was elected state senator, where he introduced the first bill for free common school education for all children. Duncan was a director and later president of the 1821 state bank's branch at Brownsville. A report during the Edwards Administration showed that Duncan borrowed $2,000 from the bank and repaid $275. Other officers and directors had similar records.

In 1826, as a comparative newcomer, he challenged Edwards' son-in-law, the popular Daniel Pope Cook, by running for the state's only seat in Congress. He won easily and, as a Jackson man, had no difficulty winning three more terms. In Congress, he served on the public lands committee and gave his attention to western causes such as preemption, early completion of surveys, sale of the public domain at low prices, and the prohibition of tollgates on the National Road.

During his first term at a dinner given by President John Quincy Adams, the Illinois congressman met socialite Elizabeth Caldwell Smith, a semi-invalid, who was four feet, five inches tall. In her diary, she wrote that Henry Clay told her that Duncan "was not only a good looking fellow but was a good son and brother, having taken care of his mother and educated his sister and two brothers." The next year they honeymooned in Illinois and established their residence at Jacksonville, where Duncan ordered construction of the first frame house.

In 1831, as a major general in the first year of the Black Hawk War, Duncan commanded a mounted militia force of 1,500.

The Split with Jackson

Early in the Jackson Administration, Duncan began to have doubts about the man for whom he had campaigned in 1824 and 1828. He was disappointed in Jackson's Cabinet, and he objected to the president's appointment of a Tennessee man as superintent of the Galena lead mines. Duncan, who had rigid views about keeping politics out of civil service, refused to endorse his brother's application for a federal job as an Indian agent. The congressman continued to believe in single terms, economy and retrenchment, and governmental reforms. He was disappointed when the president abandoned his original causes in the process of mobilizing public opinion behind new programs. Duncan thought that rechartering the Bank of the United States, which Jackson vetoed, was essential to the nation's economy. He returned to Illinois and, more than a year in advance, announced that he was a candidate for governor in 1834.

In the election, Jackson supporters split their strength between two "whole hog" candidates. A Belleville caucus backed William Kinney, while a group at Vandalia entered Robert K. McLaughlin, Duncan's uncle and a lawyer who had been territorial and state treasurer, served in both houses of the legislature, and married a niece of Shadrach Bond. An unimportant fourth candidate was anti-Jackson. Backed by Whigs and "milk and cider" Democrats, the absent Duncan won easily.

Building Infrastructure in a Faltering Economy

At his inauguration the governor criticized Jacksonian doctrine, advocated tax-supported education, and said that "to keep the government poor, and the people rich, is a political maxim which ought never to be forgotten." Much of the speech expressed concern about a grassroots demand that the state enter the transportation and banking businesses. When the legislature disregarded his advice, financial disaster followed. The period of prosperity marked by optimism and inflated real estate prices at the start of the Duncan Administration was followed by the Panic of 1837, caused when President Martin Van Buren restructured the over-inflated easy-credit banking system.

Of the three expensive projects undertaken during his administration, Duncan favored only the Illinois and Michigan Canal, connecting Chicago with the Illinois River, which had been advocated by all governors since Shadrach Bond. In his inaugural address, Duncan asked for a waterway wide enough for steamboats to pass, with the federal government to provide financing through a larger land grant or a direct appropriation. Congress never helped, but before the economic crash, the legislature put up enough money for digging to start at Bridgeport on July 4, 1836. Later, Duncan paid his own way to New York in a partially successful effort to raise funds.

Duncan opposed the 1837 internal improvements legislation under which Illinois constructed an extensive network of state-owned railroads. The Supreme Court justices joined him in a veto that was promptly over-ridden. Duncan believed in railroads as well as the canal, but he insisted that the work be done by private corporations and that the state's partici-pation be limited to the purchase of part of the capital stock. With the onset of the 1837 panic, Duncan urged a special legislative session to repeal the internal improvements law. The lawmakers ignored his advice, which Duncan repeated at the end of his term.

Had the other members of the Council of Revision supported him, he would have followed Shadrach Bond's example and vetoed an 1837 bill that, repeating the 1821 mistake, chartered another State Bank of Illinois. Because President Andrew Jackson put the Second Bank of the United States out of business, Stephen A. Douglas and other Democrats in Illinois supposed that Duncan would approve state banks. The governor, accept-ing the Whig doctrine that the United States needed a well-regulated national banking system, announced in his inaugural message that he would look with disfavor upon another state bank. With the help of some Democrats, the state bank bill was barely passed by inconsistent Whigs, chiefly from the Alton area, who hoped to become rich by diverting Mississippi River trade from St. Louis. Bank stock soon sold at a premium, and the belief spread that dividends could pay for the projected canal and railroads. Duncan approved an investment of not more than $100,000, but shortly before the crash, the legislature raised the state's share of bank capital to $2 million.

The panic forced the closing of state banks, and Duncan placed the blame on former President Jackson. His final I-told-you-so message to the legislature reminded the state that it would not be in financial trouble if his recommendations had been followed. When he took office, the state debt was $217,276. Four years later it was $6,688,784, and the retiring governor couldn't be blamed.

Duncan as a Temperate, Anti-Abolitionist

Duncan was consistent in a conservative stand on slavery. He denounced as outrageous the murder of Elijah Lovejoy, an abolitionist editor, but simultaneously blamed the violence and discord on anti-slavery agitators. He was ready to resign as a trustee of Illinois College under the impression that the president and most professors were abolitionists, but he was told it was not true. He held that "it is wrong, morally and politically, for any citizen or public institution to teach or advocate doctrines or principles in this country which cannot be carried into practice peaceably without violating the constitution of the United States, or forcibly without civil war." The 1820 census listed Duncan as owning two slaves in Jackson County.

The abolition issue was involved in a dispute that led to efforts by Duncan and others to organize a second Presbyterian church at Jacksonville. When it failed, he transferred his membership. For years he was a trustee of Illinois College. He was the first president of the board of trustees of the Illinois Institution for the Education of Deaf Mutes. A prohibitionist, Duncan regretted the "dreadful ravages and baneful effects of intemperance." During his four years as governor, he donated half his $1,000 salary to support an Illinois temperance paper.

Another Attempt for the Governor's Office

In the 1838 election, the Whigs ran Cyrus Edwards who narrowly lost to Thomas Carlin. But in 1842, the Whigs nominated Duncan again for governor, largely in a play for the Mormon vote, which two years prior had gone to Whigs. Missouri Democrats drove Joseph Smith from that state, and the Mormons founded Nauvoo on the Illinois side of the Mississippi in 1839. As the city grew — by 1845 it would be the state's largest city — it obtained incredible political power. Its city charter, granted by the legislature in 1840, gave the city unique rights, such as the power to make laws contrary to the state and federal constitution, the ability to raise its own militia, and annexation authority. Even so, Governor Carlin honored requests from the Missouri governor to have Smith arrested. But Democrats in the judiciary saved Smith from extradition. The Mormon leader urged Mormons to vote Democrat in 1842. The Whigs countered by nominating Duncan, perhaps as an appeal to tradition. But when Democratic candidate Adam W. Snyder died just prior to the election, the Democrats ran Thomas Ford, a Supreme Court justice who had no connection with recent Mormon controversies. Thus, Ford won the Mormon vote.

A Riches to Rags Retirement

Before and during his term as governor, Duncan was wealthy as a result of years of land speculations. No record of his total holdings has been preserved, but Duncan's daughter said he had personal investments "in Chicago, Sandusky, Michigan City, Jacksonville and lands through out central Illinois." He also was involved in the promotion of villages that never became cities. He paid $450,000 for a quarter interest in Oquawka, which was platted after the Black Hawk War. He also invested in Illiopolis, Marshall, and Warsaw. As the geographic center of the state, Illiopolis was promoted as a possible successor to Vandalia as the state capital in 1837, but there has been no intimation that the governor used his official position in an effort to gain financially.

Ongoing federal litigation clouded the 1842 gubernatorial campaign. His only sister, Polly Ann, had married William Linn, a personable scoundrel who, while Duncan was in Congress, was appointed receiver at the Vandalia land office. Duncan also appointed his brother-in-law as a canal commissioner. (Democrats criticized him for that inconsistency in his views on patronage.) Because he signed Linn's bond as one of nine sureties, the governor was liable when Linn defaulted on land office collections. That gave the Jackson Administration the opportunity to punish Duncan for turning Whig, and in 1841 three federal court judgments totaling $76,714 were issued. During litigation that dragged on for several years, Duncan claimed that Linn had been appointed to a second term after discovery of the defalcation (which, in an 1839 speech, Abraham Lincoln said totaled $55,000). Duncan, unaware of the shortage, had signed a second bond. Apparently the result of official connivance, the other sureties turned out to be insolvent, and Duncan was sued for the entire amount.

Claiming he was being persecuted, Duncan in 1841 said he had been put to the expense of defending four suits in federal courts, two of which were appealed to the Supreme Court, and asked "that I may be allowed to pay the debt without ruinous sacrifice of our property in times like the present." But the government insisted on forced sales that, at depression prices, wiped out Duncan's fortune. Court records no longer exist, but a daughter wrote that the government realized only $35,000 when:

> thousands of acres of the best and most carefully selected lands in Illinois were sold at 10¢ an acre. Some of the handsomest residential property in Jacksonville was sold at $3 or $4 a lot, and nearly forty acres comprising Duncan's Addition to Chicago, now in the heart of the city, were sold at from $5 to $7 a lot.

Survived by his widow and seven children, Duncan died January 15, 1844, in his Jacksonville home after a short illness. Except for a trust fund, he left his widow penniless. Two decades later the Duncan family was resisting efforts in court to break the trust. Mrs. Duncan, who was remembered as "a delicate, kindly little lady, always dressed in black silk and lace, and always expecting to be waited on," once sold a cow so that a daughter could attend a St. Louis concert by the "Swedish Nightingale," Jenny Lind. The former first lady lived until 1876.

Woodcut of Elijah Lovejoy, a Presbyterian minister and the editor of the **Alton Observer,** *which he used to preach against slavery; he was killed defending his press and buried on his 35th birthday.*

Drawing of the Alton riot of November 7, 1837, made from an 1838 woodcut; a pro-slavery mob stormed the warehouse holding the newest press of Elijah Lovejoy, killing him and dumping his press in the Mississippi River, the fourth one to be destroyed. Governor Duncan, who had owned slaves, condemned the murder but blamed both sides for the lawlessness.

Elizabeth Caldwell Smith Duncan

Lithograph of Alton, circa 1836, made by Nathaniel Currier before he joined Ives (original artist unknown); note the wall on the far left center showing part of the state's first penitentiary.

7th
Governor

Thomas Carlin
1786-1852

1786 — Born July 18 near Fankfort, Kentucky
1821 — Becomes first sheriff of Greene County
1825 - 1833 — Served in the Senate in the 4th through 7th General Assemblies
1831 - 1832 — Captain of Greene County militia companies in Black Hawk War
1838 — The first Democrat nominated at a state convention, Carlin wins gubernatorial election.
1844 — Loses congressional election to Stephen A. Douglas
1849 — Serves an unexpired term in the state legislature
1852 — Dies February 14

Democrat
December 7, 1838 to December 8, 1842

Two years after Andrew Jackson left the White House, Illinois Democrats, accepting the advice of young Stephen A. Douglas, began holding nominating conventions and finally elected a governor who was a "whole hog" Jacksonian. Thomas Carlin, a farmer who barely won the 1838 election, was an uncompromising partisan. Because he wasn't a party leader and hadn't recently been involved with state government, he couldn't be held responsible for the mistakes of the previous few years. He was the first guinea pig testing a briefly held Democratic theory that nonleaders make preferred candidates. The theory was valid with the election in 1842 of Thomas Ford, who was one of Illinois' great governors, and in 1846 of Augustus C. French, who was adequate. Carlin, however, rates at or near the bottom of the roster of chief executives.

The first convention-nominated governor, Carlin has been characterized as honest but ignorant by two historians, Theodore C. Pease and R. Carlyle Buley. John F. Snyder, a contemporary, said Carlin was "not brilliant." Other writers made a point of crediting him with nonintellectual virtues, but no one dissented from the basic premise that he lacked the background and capacity to govern a major state, especially one in financial difficulty. His personal integrity and his complete loyalty to Jackson were never questioned. Baffled by the complexities he faced, Carlin accepted conflicting advice that led to shifting policies. Both content and literary style indicate that his state papers were written by a changing cast of advisers.

Carlin, a muscular man with sandy hair, a thin face, and fair complexion, was the last of the Indian-fighter governors. In the War of

1812, he was a member of a spy company on Ninian Edwards' Peoria expedition. In both years of the Black Hawk War, he was the captain of Greene County militia companies that didn't see action.

Joseph Gillespie, an Edwardsville judge with a long memory, recalled that Carlin had great physical prowess and personal courage, that he was always ready for a rough-and-tumble fight, and that as a fine horseman, woodsman, and marksman he was an invaluable member of frontier society. "He was always intensely proslavery, or at least Negro-hating," Gillespie concluded. "He hated banks and he was suspicious of Yankees, unless they were Democrats."

The Road to the Governorship

Of Irish ancestry, the future governor was born July 18, 1786, near Frankfort, Kentucky, the son of Thomas and Elizabeth Evans Carlin. The family moved to Missouri in 1803. Carlin's father died seven years later, leaving his widow and seven children, of whom Tom was the oldest. Educational opportunities were limited, and he did not learn to read during his boyhood. He came to Illinois in time to serve as a mounted ranger in the War of 1812, married Rebecca Huitt in 1814, built a log cabin opposite the mouth of the Missouri River, and operated a ferry for four years. He was the first sheriff when Greene County was organized in 1821. Carrollton, the county seat, was located on his property, and he donated land for public buildings. He served two terms as state senator and in 1834 was appointed receiver for the land office at Quincy, where he lived during his term as governor.

Carlin was the Democrats' second choice for governor in 1838. The first Democratic convention nominated James W. Stephenson of Galena, a land office official who withdrew when it was discovered that his accounts were delinquent. As a good Jacksonian, Carlin promised in the campaign that rigid compliance with bank charter requirements would be profitable for the state. He was against monopolies and wanted the state to own and operate all railroads. The Whig candidate, Cyrus Edwards, a businessman at upper Alton who was the youngest brother of the former governor, ran as a friend of internal improvements and lost by 926 votes, the closest a Whig candidate came to carrying the state.

Inconsistent Treatment of the Mormons

Carlin, who had joined in a bipartisan welcome to Mormon refugees from Missouri, routinely signed the charter that gave almost unlimited local governmental powers to Joseph Smith and his associates at Nauvoo. Later, he approved Missouri warrants for the extradition of

Smith as a fugitive from justice. Smith, who did not suspect trouble was ahead, was arrested a few hours after he had been treated with respect when he called at the governor's home. The political and legal situation surrounding the Mormon controversy was increasing in complexity when the time came to transfer responsibility to Governor Ford.

Infrastructure Financing Pulls State into the Red

The departing Governor Duncan recommended scrapping the 1837 internal improvements program that provided public funding for waterway improvements and the Illinois Central Railroad system. But Carlin optimistically opened his administration by ignoring the financial panic that had closed banks and stifled commerce. He had vague reservations about a large-scale railroad program on which the state spent $2 million, but he was confident about the future. The public wanted railroads, the legislature agreed, and projects totaling $1 million were added to the transportation program. Within a year, all hands, including the governor, realized that it was impossible for the young state to finance and construct that many railroads. Reversing his position, Carlin called a special session of the legislature, which abandoned the internal improvements pipe dream but left a stupendous debt.

The Illinois and Michigan Canal to Chicago required bond financing, and the 1839 legislature authorized the governor to borrow $1 million. Duncan ignored a Whig suggestion that he negotiate with financial houses. Not knowing how to get the capital, Carlin appointed former Governor John Reynolds to be his official agent in Europe. But Reynolds used a European junket more as a vacation than as a mission to find financial backers. At Philadelphia and in Europe, the incompetent Reynolds borrowed money on unfavorable terms, with the state losing more than $150,000 on two transactions. One contract was with the London banking house of Wright and Company, which went bankrupt while Carlin debated whether he should approve it. Illinois' financial condition sunk even lower when the state sold bonds with a face value of $804,000 for only $261,500, their market value at the time. The selling of these bonds remained a political controversy for nearly 20 years. Because of money woes, canal construction was suspended in 1842.

The Jacksonian governor blamed the state bank and the Bank of Illinois at Shawneetown for his financial headaches. In his inaugural message he warned that banks become enmeshed in politics, resist regulation, encourage speculation, and add to the hardships of frontier farming. The state bank came under the control of Whigs, who lost money by investing in Alton interests. When there was bipartisan support for state purchase of an additional $3 million of stock in expectation that dividends would pay the entire bill for canal and internal improvements, Carlin warned against it and was supported by the Senate committee on banks. As a partial solution, the General Assembly levied an inadequate one-mill property tax to be applied to bond interest.

An Undistinguished End

Four years as governor made Carlin a pessimist. His final despondent message to the legislature again blamed the banks for economic ills that Duncan had traced to Jackson's veto of the Bank of the United States and his order that settlers must pay for their farms with gold or silver. Because it wasn't Democratic Party policy, Carlin recommended that Illinois not accept a share of the proceeds from federal land sales. However, he wanted Congress to donate more land for the canal. He didn't know how the interest on the debt could be paid because taxes were unpopular and therefore couldn't be increased. The message, a jumble of inconsistencies, recommended that the legislature repeal the charters of the state and Shawneetown banks. Carlin promised Thomas Ford, the incoming governor, that he would not ask for the repeal. Ford wrote that his predecessor "had not the genius to see how money might be raised to complete [the canal] except by petitioning Congress for an increased donation of land, then certain never to be granted."

Out of office, Carlin returned to Greene County and spent the rest of his life as a farmer, yet he was still ambitious politically. Well in advance of the 1844 election, he announced he was a candidate for Congress, but he lost to Stephen A. Douglas, who had been a late entry. Victory that fall sent Douglas into national politics. Carlin threatened to run against him in 1846 but thought better of it. His final political appearance came in 1849 when he served an unexpired term as state representative.

Survived by his widow and seven of 13 children, Carlin died at home February 14, 1852.

Courtesy of the Abraham Lincoln Presidential Library

A drawing of one mile of Chicago, circa 1840, with the view from the prairie; the sales pitch accompanying the picture lists the population as 4,470, with nearly $4,000,000 in imports.

The Newberry and Dole warehouse, located on the north side of the Chicago River just east of the present-day Rush Street Bridge, served as Chicago's first elevator. In 1839, 3,678 bushels of Illinois wheat were loaded onto ships through a chute lowered from the upper floor.

Governor Carlin's house in Carrollton, where he died in 1852

8th Governor

Thomas Ford
1800 - 1850

1800 — Born December 5 in Uniontown, Pennsylvania

1823 — Admitted to the bar

1841 - 1842 — Serves on the Illinois Supreme Court

1842 — When Democratic gubernatorial nominee Adam W. Snyder dies, Ford becomes the substitute nominee because he is thought to be the candidate least offensive to the large Mormon voting bloc; he wins the election with 54 percent of the vote; Ford realizes that debt must be retired and the economy must grow; work on the Illinois and Michigan Canal resumes after a hiatus.

1844 — Mormon leader Joseph Smith is held in a Carthage jail and is shot by a mob. This is the climax of increasing unrest between the Mormons and their neighbors, who charge the Mormons with abusing annexation powers, counterfeiting, and polygamy.

1846 — Gathers six Illinois regiments for the Mexican War; the Nauvoo Mormons leave the state in the spring.

1848 — Illinois adopts a new state constitution.

1850 — Dies November 11

1854 — Ford's history, *Illinois from Its Commencement as a State in 1818 to 1847*, is published.

Democrat
December 8, 1842 to December 9, 1846

Governor Thomas Ford, a man of unusually sound judgment and integrity, solved frontier Illinois' biggest problem. He saw how the massive internal improvement debt could be paid, and, despite considerable opposition from within his own party, he dominated the legislature and made possible the state's future solvency. Debt management was his great accomplishment, and for that he ranks alongside Edward Coles, the other great governor of the pre-Civil War period.

He was neither an administrator nor a leader of the Democratic Party, and on his scrawny shoulders rests part of the blame for the assassination of Joseph Smith, the Mormon prophet. Like Coles, he was not a politician, and he had no talent for negotiation and compromise. At times he was indecisive, vacillating, diffident, stubborn, and opinionated. Nevertheless, his critics conceded that he had been right about three major issues: that a compromise be reached with the unpopular banks; that provision be made for completion of the canal to Chicago; and that, to show its good faith, the state should dedicate a special property tax to the eventual payment of the massive debt incurred during preceding administrations. He was an able jurist, one of the best in Illinois. He reasoned clearly and might have had a long, eminent career on the Supreme Court if he had not transferred to the executive branch.

Scarcely five-and-a-half feet tall, he was by no means charismatic. Homely features included a sharp nose bent slightly to one side. His voice was squeaky. Charles Ballance, a Whig lawyer who became mayor of Peoria, wrote that at his inauguration, Ford had begun to read his speech "when his voice failed and he sank down upon the seat or table upon which he was standing" while another man picked up and read the message clearly.

Ford's second great contribution was authorship of an Illinois history that, based on his personal observation, covers the first three decades of statehood and survives as a remarkable treatise on governmental philosophy.

From Pennsylvania to the Illinois Supreme Court

Ford was born December 5, 1800, near Uniontown, Pennsylvania, and reared by his twice-widowed Irish mother who seems to have had unusual native intelligence, energy, and ambition for her large family. The former Elizabeth Delaney's first husband was killed in a coal mine accident. Little is known about the second husband, Robert Ford, who disappeared, presumably killed by highwaymen, in 1803. Desperately poor, she took her seven children to St. Louis the next year to find that the Louisiana Purchase had spoiled her hope of obtaining free land west of the Mississippi; she made a home at New Design in Monroe County. There, the future governor, a bright lad, walked three miles to his first school. However, to the impoverished family, the boy's education was less essential than his wages as a farm laborer and a servant in a country tavern.

Ford's half brother George Forquer, who was six years older, acted as Ford's foster father and political sponsor. A successful lawyer and eloquent speaker, Forquer served in both houses of the legislature, held such appointive positions as secretary of state and attorney general, and was defeated by Joseph Duncan when he ran for Congress. In that campaign, Ford entered politics by writing anti-Duncan newspaper articles.

For one term, Ford studied law at Transylvania University in Kentucky, until Forquer's business failed. The future governor walked back to Illinois, did farm work, taught school, and studied law under Daniel Pope Cook, a pioneer lawyer who became the state's first attorney general, a member of Congress, and the namesake of Cook County. After admission to the bar in 1823, Ford worked briefly for a pro-Jackson paper at St. Louis. Thereafter, he practiced law at Waterloo and at Edwardsville, where in 1828 he married Frances Hambaugh, a 15-year-old. They moved to Galena where he failed to establish a law practice and failed again when he was a candidate for justice of the peace. He held a minor position as a member of a commission to establish the state's northern boundary. Much of his time was spent at Vandalia, especially when the legislature was in session and, over the years, such jobs as committee clerkships had given him a thorough knowledge of the details and background of Illinois government and politics.

Forquer rescued him from Galena in 1830 by getting him appointed and reappointed state's attorney for the Military Tract district. Ford, who had moved to his father-in-law's farm near Versailles in Brown County, was recognized as a top-grade lawyer when he served as one of three defense counsels in the 1833 impeachment trial of Supreme Court Justice Theophilus W. Smith, who was acquitted. When Forquer became a state senator, Ford was promoted and served two terms as circuit judge and one on the Chicago Municipal Court. In 1841, when the Democratic legislature increased the membership of the Supreme Court from four to nine, one of the openings went to Ford. Assigned to the northern district, he moved to Oregon in Ogle County, where he lived for two years. All his public positions had been in northern or western Illinois. He had never been a candidate for county office, the legislature, or Congress.

The Unruly Puppet

Ford, who had never been involved with litigation or legislation concerning the controversial Mormons, became the Democrats' substitute nominee for governor in 1842. The Mormons had been Whig supporters two years earlier, but Joseph Smith decreed that they should vote for the Democrats, whose nominee for governor was State Senator Adam W. Snyder. A member of the Democratic inner circle, Snyder died in May 1842, three months before the election. Public sentiment had begun to turn against the Mormons, and the Whigs saw a chance for their candidate, former Governor Joseph Duncan. Ford was given the Snyder vacancy on the theory that any other Democrat probably would lose. His chief asset was that little in his record could be attacked by Duncan. Ford received 54 percent of the vote, and Democrats won big majorities in both houses of the legislature.

The new governor knew that he was an outsider in his own party. In his *History of Illinois*, he wrote that he was nominated:

because I was believed to have no more than a very ordinary share of ambition, because it was doubtful whether any of the leaders could be elected, and because it was thought that I would stand more in need of support from leaders than an actual leader would. To this cause, and perhaps there were others, I trace the fact that I was never able to command the support of the entire party which elected me. ... After my election I ascertained that quite a number of such leaders imagined that they, instead of myself, had been elected; and could only be convinced to the contrary on being referred to the returns of the election.

Fiscal Policies

Ford's *History* gives details of the enormity of the financial problems and the legislature's inability to solve them without the guidance of a strong executive. The governor began by rejecting the final recommendation of Thomas Carlin, his predecessor, that the legislature cancel the charters of the state bank and the Bank of Illinois at Shawneetown. Ford wanted to avoid any action that might alarm the far-off financiers from whom additional loans would be needed.

The state couldn't afford to buy postage stamps. Its credit had been exhausted in the accumulation of a debt — Ford itemized it at $15,187,348.81 — for the unfinished Illinois and Michigan Canal to Chicago, the disastrous project for state-owned railroads, and other expenditures. The new governor estimated that not more than $200,000 or $300,000 of good money was circulating in the state. The settlers and business firms were in debt. No one wanted to pay taxes, and few could. In that climate, the Democratic Party hadn't taken a stand on debt repudiation.

The new governor believed that if he had done nothing, repudiation would have been automatic, with the result that settlers would avoid Illinois and that the state's economic development would be delayed. He was convinced, as he stated in his inaugural message, that somehow principal and interest must be paid in full. He had confidence in the people and the future of Illinois, and he assured creditors that the money could be raised in due time by moderate taxation.

For the 1842-1843 legislative session, Ford drafted a compromise bill that allowed the two banks to surrender their charters after exchanging state bonds, the auditor's warrants, and scrip (worth 14 cents on the dollar) for depreciated bank stock. The trade, which extinguished $2,306,000 of the state's debt, was introduced as an administration measure and passed with Whig support. The governor and auditor were authorized to sell land and property acquired during the internal canal and railway-building improvements experiment. Reversing a Carlin policy, Illinois accepted from the federal government its share of the proceeds from land sales. Two boards that had been created by the 1837 legislature, and were in large part responsible for the debt, were abolished. The governor was empowered to borrow $1.6 million to complete the canal. Negotiations for the loan were started in New York and Europe, but first Ford had additional work for the legislature.

In a letter to an opponent of debt payment through taxation, Ford urged that the state preserve its honor by levying a permanent tax, part of which would be used to reduce and eventually pay off the debt. The plan, which according to Ford was authored by Justin Butterfield, a Chicago attorney, was widely printed in eastern and Illinois newspapers and commended by canal bondholders and the public. The new legislature approved a mortgage arrangement that had been reached. Eastern financiers loaned the money and controlled both construction and operation of the canal until toll collections retired the debt. Under the agreement, the bond holders named two members of a board of trustees, and the governor served as the third.

In a situation that would be repeated many times in Illinois, the reluctant legislature passed the tax bill only because the governor said the action could not be avoided under existing circumstances. Looking back, he could point to mammoth results. The new levy on property enabled the state to pay its bills and set aside revenues to pay interest on the debt. Construction of the canal resumed, and its 1848 opening helped speed the growth of northern Illinois. The property tax requirement was written into a new state constitution adopted in 1848. Collection of tolls provided a new revenue source. Other features of the Ford program enabled the state, so long as it operated frugally, to pay its bills. By the time the debt was paid off, a tradition of Spartan government was deeply ingrained in Illinois.

The Mormon Crisis

Ford received criticism for his handling of another major problem. It involved law enforcement, especially in Hancock County, where he left Joseph and Hyrum Smith to the mercy of unfriendly militia. The climax came on June 27, 1844. Fearing violence, the governor went to Carthage, the county seat, where he was asked to call out the militia to aid in the arrest of Mormon officials who had destroyed an opposition newspaper. Already on hand were 2,500 armed men, western Illinois Democrats and Whigs who were united in hatred of the bloc-voting

Mormons. Ford swore them into the militia, lectured them about the sanctity of the law, and asked for and accepted their pledge that the accused Mormons would not be molested.

Having received the governor's promise of protection, the Smiths and several other Mormon leaders surrendered at Carthage. Ford, who believed that the executive branch should not interfere in judicial matters, stood by while an anti-Mormon justice of the peace did not follow the letter of the law when new charges were filed against Joseph and his brother Hyrum. When Ford marched to Nauvoo to look for evidence of law violations, the Smiths begged to be taken along. Instead, they were left behind, supposedly guarded by militia companies that did not prevent their murder. Since then, all Mormon historians have held the governor responsible for the deaths of the men whose safety he had promised.

Until the Mormons left for Utah two years later, Illinois government could not maintain law and order in the territory around Nauvoo. To his credit, Ford tried, but at the end of his term, he reported to the legislature:

> No leading man of either party could be arrested without the aid of an army, as individuals of both parties were justly afraid of surrendering for fear of being murdered; and when arrested, each trial was likely to end in a civil war, and ... as a conviction was impossible, the administration of criminal justice was completely at an end, whilst the Mormons remained in the country.

Murder, arson, and lesser crimes were common where the Mormon and anti-Mormon factions were seemingly equal in armed strength and mutual hatred. The Ford Administration sent in militia that restored temporary quiet. Determined that the murderers of the Smiths would be brought to justice, the governor employed lawyers to collect evidence, obtain indictments, and prosecute the ringleaders. Outside and within the courthouse at Carthage, the anti-Mormon sentiment was so rabid that verdicts of acquittal ended trials for murder and press destruction. Because of factional rivalries, some Democratic leaders failed to cooperate in efforts to enforce the law. Ford sent General John J. Hardin, a Whig, into Hancock County twice with volunteers. The first expedition forced cancellation of a "wolf hunt," which obviously would have resulted in casualties among rural Mormons. The second briefly established a truce after a Mormon force was driven from the courthouse at Carthage.

After Hardin and other leaders left for the Mexican War and the evacuation of Nauvoo had begun, a "Mormon War" continued and a force assembled by Ford could not prevent cannon fire. Volunteer negotiators from Quincy managed to arrange a final cease-fire.

Governor Ford was continually under criticism by factions in the Nauvoo area as well as by Whig newspapers elsewhere in Illinois. In his *History*, he admitted that his power was inadequate but insisted that his efforts were correct and his critics unfair. In his defense, some Whigs volunteered statements that the governor was doing everything possible to keep the Mormon controversy under control. The Mormon custom of bloc voting, usually for Democratic candidates, added to the factionalism. Some militia officers who were Democrats declined to assume commands when Ford found it necessary to recruit volunteers for peace-keeping missions. The governor commended prominent Whigs, especially Hardin, for answering his calls for assistance.

Other Law-and-Order Problems

Lawlessness was not confined to the Mormon settlement. At the close of the frontier period, state government was too weak to enforce the criminal code in other border areas where elected officials could not cope with wide-scale crime. At times, after appeals for help, members of the law-abiding element took the law in their own hands, not always successfully. In far-off southeastern Illinois, horse thieves, counterfeiters, and robbers long terrorized the Massac and Pope counties region, where the militia refused to turn out when the governor ordered them to assist the presumably honest faction among local officials. General John T. Davis, who had been ordered to investigate a situation involving rival gangs, supposedly calmed the situation, but trouble broke out again. In 1846, Supreme Court Justice Walter B. Scates was threatened with lynching after several regulators were indicted. At the end of the Ford Administration, law enforcement in Massac County was unfinished business.

At the outbreak of the Mexican War in 1846, Ford called for enlistment of three regiments, the Illinois quota. The response was enthusiastic, and eventually three more regiments were formed with the War Department's permission. There were mix-ups, however, for which the governor received some blame. While he was away from Springfield, he accepted companies without notifying his office, with the result that some acceptance orders had to be canceled. In other counties, Ford was blamed because the sheriffs did not enforce the militia law, which was falling into disuse. He vacillated and left the decision to an arbitration board when Hardin and Edward D. Baker both claimed seniority.

The Pauper Historian

Proving his honesty, Ford was financially destitute when his term ended. Refusing to run for other office, he returned to his father-in-law's farm and spent three years writing a history of Illinois in the vain hope that royalties would support his five children. Then he went to Peoria to practice law, but again met failure, with poor health a contributing factor. His last illness was diagnosed as tuberculosis.

He died November 11, 1850, at Peoria, a month after his wife died of cancer. Anonymous acquaintances paid for their last illnesses and burials. He was first buried in the city cemetery but was later removed to Springdale, where the state erected a monument in 1895. A brief document described as an autobiography said the governor became a Methodist a few weeks before his death.

Thomas Ford's tragedies continued into the next generation. His five children depended on the charity of friends and neighbors. The governor's two sons, believed to be horse thieves, were hanged by Kansas vigilantes.

Before his death, Ford asked U.S. Senator James Shields to arrange for publication of his masterpiece, *A History of Illinois: From Its Commencement as a State in 1818 to 1847*. The book was on sale by 1854. Because of its caustic and outspoken criticism of public men, Shields or the publisher reportedly excised more than half of the manuscript, which is regrettable in view of Ford's personal knowledge of the men and events he wrote about. The surviving chapters tell in detail of his troubles during the two legislative sessions he served as governor. Lyman Trumbull and Stephen A. Douglas, future U.S. senators of eminence, were among those he criticized with questionable fairness. Be it noted, however, that Ford had reason to dislike many leaders of his party. Other writers and other documents also have exposed many, in and out of the legislature, to equally harsh criticism. Errors and misjudgments, if such they be, are more than counterbalanced by the vast amount of information and opinion presented by a scholar who lived in Illinois during the first three decades of statehood and who played a major role in part of the events he wrote about. He has frequently been quoted and cited in this book.

Much of what Ford says about politics, politicians, government, and private citizens is applicable to other time periods and to other states. The governor wrote compactly, forcibly, and precisely. Even if he wrote with cynicism, his book has been recognized as a superior analysis of American politics and one of the most important volumes printed in Illinois before the Civil War.

Home of Thomas Ford's in-laws in rural Brown County where he wrote his **History of Illinois**

9th Governor

Augustus Chaplin French

1808 -1864

1808 — Born August 2 at New Chester (now Hill), New Hampshire
1831 — Admitted to the bar
1832 — Teaches at Little Prairie school west of Albion, Illinois
1837 - 1841 — Serves in the 10th and 11th General Assemblies
1846 — Defeats Whig Thomas M. Kilpatrick for governor
1848 — New state constitution grants greater powers to the governor, sets gubernatorial elections on a schedule coincidental with presidential elections, and makes all state and county offices subject to popular election. French wins a four-year term, making him the first two-term governor.
1858 — Loses election for superintendent of public instruction
1862 — Represents St. Clair County as a delegate to the constitutional convention; voters fail to ratify this constitution.
1864 — Dies September 4

Democrat
December 9, 1846 to January 8, 1849
January 8, 1849 to January 10, 1853

Augustus Chaplin French was a compromise candidate at the Democrats' 1846 state convention, but he became the first two-term governor. As Illinois outgrew its frontier period, French performed a great service by not deviating from Thomas Ford's recipe for slow repayment of the public improvements debt through taxation. Succeeding governors followed his example, and both parties became committed to strict economy and eventual solvency. French himself was a string-saver, a tight-fisted Yankee whose habits of personal economy made it possible for him to educate his orphaned siblings. Stories of his stinginess became legendary.

As for his two consecutive terms as governor, that was a loophole. Like the original Illinois Constitution of 1818, the new Constitution of 1848 limited governors to single four-year terms. It also decreed that state elections should be synchronized with presidential balloting, beginning in 1848. Because it seemed unfair to dismiss the popular incumbent in midterm, he was elected to four more years, for a total of six. He was the only governor reelected until after the Civil War.

From Lawyer to Lawmaker

Born August 2, 1808, at New Chester (now Hill), New Hampshire, he was the oldest of six children of Joseph and Eunice Dickerson French. In 1827, at his widowed mother's deathbed, he promised to rear and educate his siblings, which presumably he did.

About that time, he abandoned his given name, Aram. If he briefly attended Dartmouth College, which he is reputed to have done, officials there have no record of him. His middle name "Chaplin" is also a small source of controversy. It's spelled "Chaplin" in his daughter's family papers, but there are variant spellings.

He read law in the office of a judge at Gilmanton, New Hampshire. In 1831, he was admitted to the bar and promptly headed westward. The next year, as Augustus French, he was in Illinois, teaching at the Little Prairie school west of Albion. By 1833, he was at Paris, four counties northward, and active in politics. The legislature elected him circuit attorney for the Wabash River district. He served as a colleague of Abraham Lincoln and Stephen A. Douglas in the 10th General Assembly and was reelected to the 11th. Douglas' friendship might explain French's political advancement thereafter. He began by volunteering to be the Democratic nominee for lieutenant governor, a bid that was unsuccessful but gave him some name recognition. President Martin Van Buren appointed him receiver for the land office at Palestine, Crawford County. There he lived and had a fairly good law practice, but he was little known in most of Illinois. Ford's *History* says French was a member of a group of "regulators" who took law enforcement in their own hands by whipping and expelling a troublesome band of thieves and counterfeiters.

In 1839, French married Clarissa Kitchell of Palestine, who died two years later after giving birth to a son who died soon after. The future governor in 1843 married Lucy Southworth at West York. They were parents of three sons and two daughters.

The Compromise Candidate Becomes a Six-Year Governor
In advance of the 1846 Democratic convention, no one regarded French as a leading gubernatorial possibility. Cautious and colorless, French resembled his predecessors, Thomas Carlin and Thomas Ford, in that he was neither a political leader nor an administrator. Among six Democratic candidates, he alone came from eastern Illinois, which had been neglected by Democrats. Lyman Trumbull, whom Governor Ford and numerous other Democrats disliked, led on the first ballot, with French second. After the third ballot, the other four candidates withdrew in a stop-Trumbull movement. One story is that Congressman O. B. Ficklin feared that French would run against him in the Wabash River district and promoted him for the governorship without any idea that he would be nominated.

At their first state convention, the Whigs nominated a superior candidate, Thomas M. Kilpatrick of Scott County, who as state senator had been a leader in a movement for public schools and helped Governor Ford pass the debt reduction legislation. The Whigs were unpopular because of the Mexican War, and Kilpatrick did not attempt a campaign. For the first time, more than 100,000 people cast votes in a gubernatorial election, with French receiving 58.2 percent. The highest-ranking Whig winner in Illinois was Abraham Lincoln, the new congressman in the Springfield district.

Two years later, French polled 86.6 percent. In the legislature, the Whig minority was smaller than usual.

The Governor's Conservative Fiscal Policies

French approved enactment of a series of laws that refunded the state's debt, including accrued interest. Thus, he helped establish the state's reputation for fiscal integrity. French corresponded frequently with the state's financial agents in New York and London, and he asked for a constitutional amendment to allow the state to buy its bonds at a discount with tax revenues. Because the public distrusted the legislature and believed the state should not profit from under-par transactions, voters defeated the proposed amendment. In 1851, also at the governor's suggestion, homesteads were exempted from taxation.

The New England-born governor accepted the antibank prejudices of Jacksonian Democrats, who wanted business transacted only with gold and silver coins. In 1848, French was reelected on a platform that advocated outlawing banks and paper money. At the 1849 legislative session, the first under the new state constitution, he announced he would veto any general banking law. Two years later, after election of more bank men from northern districts, the legislature voted to license free or stock banks that could accept deposits and circulate paper money backed by bonds deposited with the state auditor. French vetoed the bill, but the legislature passed it over his veto. In the Senate, Joel A. Matteson of Joliet, a Democrat who would be the next governor, cast the deciding vote on the paper money bill.

In the 1851 referendum, the bank law was approved as a result of strong support from the growing northern districts.

The Governor's Self-Interested Push for Railroads

On French's recommendation, the state sold the Northern Cross Railroad at a 90 percent loss. But this was just one facet of the governor's interest in the state's involvement with the railroad industry.

The governor, a land speculator, actively but unsuccessfully opposed the concept of "state" policy, a provincial belief that Illinois railroads should stay within the state and not serve cities on the other side of its borders, especially St. Louis. He could not influence the legislature, which repeatedly refused to issue a corporation charter for an interstate railroad from Cincinnati through Vincennes to St. Louis. French, who reportedly had a financial interest, joined other opponents of state policy at a mass meeting in Salem. He called a special legislative session at which he recommended enactment of a general law on incorporation of railroads. The legislature insisted on retaining the power to issue charters and fix terminals. The railroad into St. Louis wasn't authorized until French's two terms ended.

Because Cairo, Galena, and Chicago were within Illinois, there was no objection to the north-south Illinois Central line. After Stephen A. Douglas reached the U.S. Senate in 1846, Congress granted 2,595,000 acres to the state. On the governor's recommendation, the land was turned over to eastern capitalists who promptly constructed the world's longest railroad. Under the charter, the governor became an *ex officio* member of the Illinois Central board of directors.

In the developing western country, most governors were speculators who bought heavily at government land offices, often at bargain prices, as a result of acquisition of bounty warrants issued to veterans of the 1812 and Mexican wars. New opportunities developed with the railroad era. French speculated by buying government land. He also had a financial interest in at least one railroad. He presided at a Charleston meeting of incorporators of a railroad that would extend from Springfield to Terre Haute, Indiana. Along its right-of-way, he owned 3,840 acres near Vandalia. Such interests were not unusual and were less obvious than pressure on the legislature to grant special charters to corporations, a practice begun during the Reynolds Administration.

Law and Order and Social Policy

French had little more success than Ford in dealing with lawlessness in Massac and Pope counties, where so-called regulators enforced mob rule. The legislature in 1847 created a district court with venue powers intended to produce unbiased jurors. That law proved ineffective, but the situation slowly improved.

Like several of his predecessors, French recommended better common schools, which the public increasingly supported. The legislature responded by granting local authority to levy taxes through referendums to build schoolhouses and hire teachers. It did not provide state financial support. In his inaugural message, French also said the state should provide for the insane. The legislature established an asylum in 1847 and a school for the blind in 1849, both at Jacksonville.

French did not take sides on the slavery issue when the principle of the Wilmot Proviso, prohibiting human bondage in territory acquired from Mexico, was approved by the legislature in 1849 and disapproved in 1851. He also avoided a controversy when he had an opportunity to appoint a U.S. senator. After the discovery that Irish-born James A. Shields had not yet met citizenship requirements, he called a special session to mark time until Shields was eligible.

The Retired Statesman

Upon French's retirement, Governor Joel Matteson appointed him state bank commissioner. French moved to Lebanon, where he was a law professor and a member of the board of trustees of McKendree College. Twice more he sought public office. In 1858, Newton Bateman defeated French for superintendent of public instruction. In 1862, he was a St. Clair County delegate to a wartime constitutional convention.

French died September 4, 1864, and was buried in College Hill Cemetery in Lebanon.

Courtesy of the Abraham Lincoln Presidential Library

John Hossack II ran a grain and lumber business in Ottawa beginning in 1849 and was one of the first to ship grain to Chicago on the Illinois and Michigan Canal. An abolitionist, he was arrested in 1859 under the Fugitive Slave Act for rescuing a slave and helping him to freedom in Canada. Citizens of Chicago paid his fine and talked of running him for governor.

10th Governor

Joel Aldrich Matteson
1809-1873

1809 — Born August 2 near Watertown, New York

1843 - 1853 — Serves in the Illinois Senate

1847 — Helps pass a bill that allows citizens to turn in certificates of state indebtedness, such as canal scrip, in exchange for state bonds

1850 — Organizes Merchants and Drovers Bank at Joliet

1852 — Wins the governor's office

1855 — Lincoln sways the legislature away from electing Matteson U.S. senator.

1856 — Begins redeeming outdated and/or previously redeemed canal scrip for state bonds

1859 — The scrip scandal begins to unravel.

1863 — Sangamon County Circuit Court rules that Matteson owes the state $253,723.77.

1873 — Dies January 31 in Chicago

Democrat
January 10, 1853 to January 12, 1857

J oel Matteson was a business executive with a great talent for making money legitimately. But his biggest personal accomplishment was avoiding prison after the 1859 exposure of the Great Canal Scrip Fraud, the biggest governmental scandal in Illinois' first century. A never-completed investigation placed a $388,528 price tag on Matteson's fraudulent exchange of 20-year-old scrip for new state bonds. (When the government could not pay its bills, it issued scrip — essentially IOUs — that could be redeemed later.) No one believed Matteson's alibi, but he had political clout. He avoided prosecution by paying back part of the money he said he hadn't stolen.

Matteson, who was the last Democratic governor for 36 years, was an efficient chief executive whom the public admired and trusted. Unlike his predecessors, he was neither a lawyer nor a farmer. Like most of them, he was a land speculator who invested in unsettled areas, confident valuations would keep pace with the tide of immigrants. Primarily, he was a businessman, the owner of several banks, and the promoter and manager of railroads. He made sizable contributions to the economy of a state that needed banks and railroads. Like a few other prominent businessmen, he also had a successful career in politics.

Public speaking was not one of his talents, but he avoided factionalism. He resembled Augustus French, whom he succeeded, in that he advanced few causes and got along well with the legislature.

From Farm Boy to Financier

Joel Aldrich Matteson, the son of Elnathan and Eunice Aldrich Matteson, was born August 2, 1809, on a farm near Watertown, New York. He attended a country school. As a young man, he owned a small store across the Canadian border, attended a seminary, taught school, operated a farm given him by his father, worked on construction of South Carolina's first railroad, and toured as far west as St. Louis. Upon his return home, he married Mary Fish. When he was 25, he migrated to Illinois with his wife and their first child. On the way, he made money by selling a wagonload of boots and shoes.

Matteson made money easily. In the Chicago land boom, he bought the southwest corner of Clark and Washington streets for $200 and doubled his money in a few days. He bought 869 acres of government land in Kendall County. Just before the Panic of 1837, he sold at inflated prices and moved to Joliet. Soon he was a town trustee. He was one of the contractors who dug the Illinois and Michigan Canal.

When Illinois abandoned its grandiose plans for internal improvements, he bought 700 tons of railroad iron and sold it at a profit to the builders of the first railroad in Michigan. He operated a woolen mill that was Joliet's largest industry. He owned a store, founded the first bank, lived in the biggest house, and was elected as a Democrat to the state Senate, where he immediately became finance chairman. Thomas Ford credited the senator with "efficient advocacy" of the debt reduction program.

Matteson had major investments in both railroads and banks. He secretly held 1,000 shares of stock in the Illinois Central company. A private letter to Jonathan Sturges, Illinois Central president, spoke of Matteson as "the very ablest man we have in Illinois," adding that "he considers the prosperity of the state to be in no small way identified with the success of your enterprise — and therefore is willing to do all that he can to assist in its consummation."

With Nicholas H. Ridgely as a partner, Senator Matteson in 1847 paid $21,100 for the defunct Springfield and Meredosia Railroad, the original Northern Cross that was the only 1837 internal improvements road to be completed. With experience in digging the canal, by 1851 he became a grading contractor on the Rock Island and Chicago Railroad. While serving as governor, he helped promote and direct the Joliet and Northern Indiana Railroad. When the line between St. Louis and Springfield failed in 1854, Matteson and W. R. Litchfield of New York acquired it. Matteson served as president for several years. He also acquired a half-interest in the St. Louis packet line.

The Matteson Administration

Several Democrats vied for the 1852 gubernatorial nomination, three from northern Illinois. The strongest seemed to be a Chicago Catholic, Secretary of State David L. Gregg. But religion became an issue. Although Gregg led on the first ballot, Matteson was nominated on the 11th. To signify the importance of the foreign-born, the nomination for lieutenant governor went to Gustave Koerner, the political spokesman for settlers from Germany. Without enthusiasm, the Whigs nominated E. B. Webb of Carmi. The Free Soil Party also nominated a candidate, but Matteson avoided controversies. He was elected with 52.4 percent of the vote. The Democratic platform said nothing about banks, opposed meddling in the affairs of other states, and recommended Stephen A. Douglas for president. It also endorsed the Compromise of 1850, the federal act admitting California to the union as a free state; establishing the Utah and New Mexico Territories with the proviso they could not make slave laws; prohibiting the slave trade in Washington, D.C. (but retaining slavery); and imposing a Fugitive Slave law, making federal officials responsible for recovering slaves.

Matteson's election in 1852 was a victory for northern Illinois Democrats — newcomers who were moderates on the slavery issue and had not inherited their party's anti-bank prejudices. He was well qualified to be governor. As chairman of the Senate revenue committee during the Ford and French administrations, he became an authority on state finance. He cast the deciding Senate vote for legalized banking in Illinois.

The Matteson Administration is remembered chiefly for enactment of an effective common school law, which had attracted support through a series of mass meetings. While Thomas Ford was governor, the secretary of state was designated *ex officio* superintendent of schools. Laws passed in 1849 and 1851 permitted an optional local tax for schools, but in practice they were dead letters. In his inaugural address, Matteson asked for financial support of a comprehensive school system, but the legislature did nothing until 1855. Then the state levied a tax that was distributed to local districts that levied property taxes to operate schools six months a year. The state superintendent of schools was made an elective official whose $1,500 salary equaled the governor's. Matteson appointed Ninian W. Edwards to fill the position until the next election.

Ten years after the legislature and the public accepted the Ford austerity program for debt retirement, Governor Matteson found money for construction of a new prison in northern Illinois and had it located in Joliet, his hometown.

The Mattesons were rich and social. The governor, his attractive wife, and their seven children found that the original governor's house on a small lot at Eighth and Capitol streets in Springfield was inadequate for daily living — to say nothing of frequent parties. At the governor's request, the legislature spent $52,000 to purchase a square block and construct and furnish an Executive Mansion. An unusually elaborate structure for a western state, it was the governor's personal project. When more money was needed, he advanced $10,000 so that construction need not stop until the legislature met again. By late 1855, the Mattesons moved and promptly invited the capital's elite to a ball. When the governor decided to make Springfield his permanent home, he spent possibly $100,000 to build an even larger, more palatial home across from the Executive Mansion. The three-story structure with 14 bedrooms was described as the city's finest residence.

Agitation over slavery, which for some time had been a peripheral issue, increasingly intruded into partisan matters. Matteson, a moderate, was a consensus Democrat interested in the success of his party and in the growth of his state. He preferred the middle ground and, during the uproar that greeted repeal of the Kansas-Nebraska Act sponsored by Senator Douglas, did not take a public position on the issue.

Without openly running, Matteson was almost elected U.S. senator during the 1855 legislative session. He remained aloof during the prolonged deadlock brought about when a handful of Anti-Nebraska Democrats refused to vote either for Abraham Lincoln the Whig or any old-line Democrat. When the anti-slavery group seemed ready to vote for Matteson for senator, Lincoln swung the election to Lyman Trumbull. Lincoln accused Matteson of playing a "double game — and his defeat gives me more pleasure than my own gives me pain."

Lincoln's opinion aside, had the Illinois Constitution permitted second terms, Governor Joel A. Matteson would have been a favorite for reelection. He was popular with voters, who were unaware of fraud.

The Scrip Scandal

Matteson should have known that sooner or later he would be caught.

After his inauguration in 1853, he took custody, in Chicago, of a trunk and a shoebox that contained old records of the State Board of Canal Commissioners. The governor ordered them shipped to him at Springfield, where no one could recall having seen them. The contents included quantities of 90-day scrip, in denominations of $50 and $100, that in 1839 had been used to pay contractors when the canal board was temporarily broke. The total amount issued was $338,554, and all but $316 had been redeemed at the Chicago branch of the state bank.

Bookkeeping was lax; no record of names and dates were kept when the scrip was turned in for redemption. Furthermore, the redeemed scrip had not been canceled. The trunk and box also contained quantities of unissued scrip that had been signed in blank by canal officials. The redeemed and unissued scrip in effect were blank checks, invitations for forgery and embezzlement.

One of the French administration's 1847 refunding bills, which Senator Matteson helped pass, provided that certificates of state indebtedness, including any canal scrip outstanding, could be brought to the Statehouse and exchanged for registered and numbered state bonds at par, plus accrued interest. The governor was the *ex officio* fund commissioner. A clerk he appointed handled the refunding transactions.

In 1856, shortly before his administration ended, Governor Matteson began bringing canal scrip to the clerk for redemption. Many of the bonds thus acquired were deposited with the state auditor as surety for bank notes from the historic State Bank of Illinois at Shawneetown, one of a half-dozen banks he owned or controlled.

Matteson's redemption of the old scrip went unnoticed until the 1859 legislative session. Jacob Fry, who had been a canal official during the Ford and French administrations, learned that an old certificate was in circulation and warned state officials to beware of counterfeiting. Sensational evidence quickly implicated Matteson, who, after leaving office, had stayed in Springfield as a businessman. The embarrassed Democratic majority of the revenue committee, which Matteson once chaired, agreed to an investigation. Orville H. Browning, the future U.S. senator, helped check the records and concluded Matteson's guilt was obvious.

Part of the evidence was circumstantial, but it showed that Matteson had received $223,182.66 in state bonds for scrip that had been in the trunk and box. Some of it had been redeemed 20 years earlier, which meant the state had paid for it twice. Matteson attended the hearings with his lawyers and was allowed to question witnesses. He was not asked to testify, and he made no alibi under oath.

In a letter to the revenue committee, the former governor professed innocence, saying he bought the scrip from strangers whom he could not identify. To preserve his reputation, he continued, he would not keep the controversial bonds, and he would indemnify the state for its losses. In effect, he was willing to pay back money he said he hadn't stolen. The public regarded the letter as a confession of guilt, but the committee dropped the investigation and thanked Matteson for saving it "the necessity of determining many embarrassing questions."

The Republican members of the committee were given permission to pursue the inquiry after the legislature adjourned. The secretary of state, state auditor, and state treasurer, all Republicans, kept the controversy alive by demanding that "a great fraud committed upon the people" be investigated by the Sangamon County grand jury. Prosecutor J. B. White, a Matteson partisan, called witnesses who repeated testimony they gave the Senate committee. Then the jury voted 16-7 to indict the former governor for larceny, reconsidered the action the next day, voted again to indict, reconsidered again, and eventually voted 12-10 not to indict.

The jury then took the unusual step of protesting its own verdict by publishing a 60-page record of its proceedings and a summary of the evidence. It hinted at bribery and jury tampering. Contrary to law, Matteson attended the supposedly secret proceedings. His lawyers were accused of "boldly interfering with the jury to prevent an indictment." The report also criticized the judge, the prosecutor, and the manner in which grand jury vacancies were filled.

An 1861 supplemental report prepared by the revenue committee added $165,346 to the amount embezzled. It found that Matteson cashed some bonds held in the governor's office for special purposes and that on some he had written the names of fictitious payees. That would add forgery to the list of crimes traced to the former governor. The committee decided that faulty record-keeping made prosecution impossible.

The 1859 legislature passed a special law allowing indemnification, but Matteson stalled the case until 1863 when the Sangamon County Circuit Court decreed that the former governor owed the state $253,723.77. Property owned by Matteson and his wife was sold at auction on the courthouse steps for $238,000. Nothing was done about reimbursing the state for the additional $165,346 reported in 1861.

The Former Governor's Financial Fall

For Matteson, financial misfortunes came in a flood. Back in 1850, Matteson organized his first bank, the Merchants and Drovers at Joliet. After he became governor, he acquired five more — at Peoria, Quincy, Shawneetown, Marion, and Bloomington — in which he owned all or most of the stock. For the successor to the historic State Bank of Illinois at Shawneetown, he paid $15,000. Records of the auditor's office indicate that the state bank had the largest note circulation in Illinois. Until 1857, the law required only that bonds of any state be deposited with the state auditor as surety for note issues. Bankers cashed the bond coupons and could pyramid their capital for added profits. As economic conditions fluctuated, they frequently were called upon to deposit additional bonds. As a result, bank owners frequently needed more bonds, especially if they owned multiple banks. R. E. Goodell, the governor's son-in-law and business partner, claimed before the Senate investigating committee the Joliet bank was profitable and that Matteson's banks earned from $50,000 to $100,000 a year. That testimony is suspect, however, because he was trying to prove that Matteson had no need to steal from the state. Matteson's conversion of scrip into bonds had reached a peak about the time he took over the Shawneetown bank. Soon after the scrip fraud, he lost control of the Chicago, Alton, and St. Louis Railroad. By 1861, economic dislocations at the start of the Civil War forced the suspension of his banks.

In foreclosure proceedings, the Matteson mansion sold for $40,000 — less than half its estimated cost. Title was obtained by a son-in-law through a redemption proceeding, and the former governor continued to live there. In 1860, he campaigned in Louisiana and Florida for Stephen A. Douglas. During two of the war years, he made a grand tour of Europe.

On January 31, 1873, three days after his Springfield home burned to the ground, the old governor died in the Chicago home of a daughter.

Matteson family in Paris, France, circa 1862; from left, wife Mary, Clara, Governor Matteson, Lydia, and Belle

11th Governor

William Henry Bissell
1811-1860

1811 — Born April 25 in Hartwick, New York
1834 — Earns M.D. from Jefferson Medical School, Philadelphia
1841 - 1843 — Serves with Lincoln as a representative in the 12th General Assembly
1844 — Earns bachelor of laws degree from Transylvania Law School, Kentucky
1847 — Serves in the Mexican War; becomes a hero in the February 22-23 battle of Buena Vista
1848 — Elected to the first of three terms in Congress
1850 — Accepts a challenge to duel Jefferson Davis
1856 — Elected governor
1860 — Dies in office March 18

Republican
January 12, 1857 to March 18, 1860

Wiliam Henry Bissell set several precedents. He was the first Roman Catholic governor of Illinois and the first to die in office. Bissell, who walked with crutches, was the only governor inaugurated in the Executive Mansion. He also was the first governor to hold a college degree, and among other distinctions, was the only Illinois governor challenged to a duel by Jefferson Davis. They didn't duel, but Bissell's acceptance of the challenge in 1850 made him so popular that six years later, despite a constitutional disqualification and physical handicaps, he was elected the state's first Republican governor. A Mexican War colonel and former Democratic congressman, he committed perjury at his inauguration, and as governor, he turned out to be a poor administrator. Nevertheless, Abraham Lincoln believed Bissell was the only anti-slavery candidate with a chance of carrying Illinois in the critical year of 1856.

In the Republican campaign, Lincoln served as behind-the-scenes strategist and made some 40 speeches. After the election, he acted as the new governor's unofficial legal adviser. Bissell's great contribution was that he provided Lincoln with a home-state power base in 1860. If Illinois had not been a Republican state, Lincoln would have been a less impressive candidate for the presidential nomination.

The Paralyzed War Hero

The son of Luther and Hannah Shepherd Bissell, William was born April 25, 1811, in the obscure town of Hartwick, Otsego County, New York. He taught school, worked on a farm, and studied under a Hartwick physician before entering Jefferson Medical School,

Philadelphia, where he received an M.D. in 1834. He practiced three years at Painted Post, Steuben County, New York, before migrating to Illinois. In an unpublished biography, John F. Snyder, a friend who was a doctor and a historian, says Bissell was headed for Galesburg in 1837 but lost his baggage when a steamboat sank south of St. Louis. He went ashore at Harrisonville, Monroe County, where he found a job teaching school and boarded at the home of a farmer. Bissell married the farmer's daughter, Emily Susan Jones, in 1840, a year after he started a medical practice at Waterloo. She died in 1844, leaving two small daughters. The same year he received a bachelor of laws degree from Transylvania University Law School in Kentucky.

After coming to Illinois, he discovered that he was a talented extemporaneous speaker. One contemporary described his style and diction as "elegant" and his use of satire as "cutting and effective." As a Democrat, he served one term in the legislature, where he met Lincoln. He practiced law at Belleville, was appointed a bank commissioner by Governor Ford, and became a district prosecutor, all before the Mexican War made him a celebrity.

Bissell, who seemed to have an aptitude for command, was captain of a company of Belleville neighbors he recruited at the start of the Mexican War. Because Democratic field officers were in demand, he was elected colonel of the Second Regiment of Illinois volunteers. Attached to General Zachary Taylor's army, he saw action only in the two-day defensive battle of Buena Vista. While under fire his regiment executed a parade-ground maneuver, allowing them to help turn back the Mexican army. On his return to Belleville, he was welcomed as a hero and rewarded with election to Congress in 1848 for the first of three terms.

In Washington, Bissel came to dislike slave-state congressmen. He regarded his Southern colleagues as "insolent, overbearing and bullying beyond all belief," but kept still until James A. Seddon of Virginia (who became the Confederate secretary of war during the Civil War) gave a distorted version of the battle of Buena Vista. Seddon said that Northern troops retreated under fire and that disaster was prevented by the Mississippi regiment commanded by Colonel Jefferson Davis.

Bissell replied with a masterful oration. For almost an hour he tongue-lashed Seddon and other Southerners, whom he accused of plotting secession. Concerning the Buena Vista crisis, he said Davis' regiment was a mile and a half away and that Northern and Kentucky troops, including his own men, turned back the Mexicans. He credited the Mississippians with heroism elsewhere on the battlefield.

The speech made Bissell a folk hero back in Illinois. Davis, a senator from Mississippi, claimed his regiment had been insulted and challenged Bissell to a duel. Northern congressmen customarily refused to settle disputes on the so-called field of honor, but Bissell accepted and stipulated that the two men fight at close range with army muskets loaded with ball and buckshot. Davis backed out by accepting an explanation for the alleged insult that he had previously rejected.

By 1854, an ailment described as rheumatic or neuralgic paralysis prevented Bissell from attending sessions of the House. He had broken with Senator Stephen A. Douglas and the Democratic Party on the slavery extension issue. Douglas was the force behind the pro-slavery Kansas-Nebraska Act that repealed the Missouri Compromise of 1820 and allowed Kansas settlers to decide for themselves whether that state would be slave or free. While Douglas was pushing the bill through Congress, Bissell sent word that, if the issue were in doubt, he would have himself carried into the House chamber on a cot to vote against it. The measure passed the Congress with President Franklin Pierce's approval.

Bissell's career seemed at its end when his second wife brought him back to Belleville in the summer of 1855.

Bissell's Election and Administration

At the start of the 1856 campaign, the politically astute Lincoln believed the Republican candidate for governor must be a former Democrat. In that category, only Bissell had a chance of winning.

When anti-slavery editors met at Decatur on February 22, 1856, to arrange for a nominating convention, Lincoln refused to run for governor but said Bissell would get enough Democratic votes to carry the state. Arrangements for his unopposed nomination were made before the first Republican convention at Bloomington on May 29. In a letter to the editor of the *Alton Courier*, Bissell said he could walk only with "the use of a cane and the aid of a friendly arm" but his health and mental capacity were good. He said he could make campaign speeches but couldn't travel extensively. He was nominated by acclamation.

The Democrats ran Senator Douglas' chief lieutenant, William A. Richardson of Quincy, against Bissell. In speeches and letters, Lincoln argued that votes for the third party Know-Nothing candidates would only help the Democrats. Bissell made at least one speech, possibly one or two more, but there is no record of what he said. At the end of a bitter campaign, Bissell was elected by 4,787 votes, 46.3 percent of the total in a three-candidate field.

Democrats contended Bissell would perjure himself if he took the oath of office. In an effort to stop an epidemic of duels, the Constitution of 1848 required state officials to swear to a special inauguration oath that they had never fought or accepted a challenge to a duel or acted as a second. Of course, Bissell's acceptance of Jefferson Davis' challenge was part of his popularity. The situation embarrassed the leaders of the Republican Party. There is no record that Lincoln, the dominant Republican in Illinois, spoke or wrote about it. However, he did not object to, and presumably he approved of, Bissell's post-election theory that the Illinois Constitution did not apply in his case because the duel acceptance was made in the District of Columbia. That reasoning obviously was faulty because Bissell committed the offense of perjury in Springfield, Illinois, when he took the oath.

For unexplained reasons, the Democrats didn't challenge Bissell's right to hold office. They held small majorities in the legislature, however, and heckled Bissell caustically. In a two-day speech, Representative John A. Logan, a future Union general and Republican U. S. senator, contended Bissell knew he would commit perjury if he took the oath.

Governor Bissell never entered the state Capitol during the three-plus years of his administration. He transacted state business from a second-floor room of the Executive Mansion, where Lincoln frequently called. When the governor signed an 1859 Democratic reapportionment bill he intended to veto, Lincoln telegraphed for Joseph Gillespie, a Whig lawyer at Edwardsville and a personal friend, to "come right up" for a conference that also was attended by Norman B. Judd, the Republican state chairman. Bissell then reversed his action and vetoed the bill with a message that is in Lincoln's handwriting. The return of the bill to the legislature was greeted by a scene of what contemporaries called "great confusion." Lincoln argued and won the case when it was appealed to the Illinois Supreme Court.

Anti-Bissell agitation intensified in 1859 with the discovery that the governor had approved the funding at par of 114 $1,000 canal bonds on which the legislature had placed a ceiling of 28.64 cents on the dollar. The error was discovered in time to prevent loss to the state, but Democrats questioned the governor's honesty and competence, and Republicans found it difficult to defend his credibility.

The Governor Dies

As his health deteriorated, Governor Bissell took little part in state affairs and none in the intensified debate over slavery that reached its peak in the Lincoln-Douglas debates. However, in February 1860, he indicated in a private letter that he preferred Salmon P. Chase of Ohio for the presidency. A month later, on March 17, 1860, Lincoln and other Republican officials called at the Executive Mansion to say farewell to the failing governor. The next day, 10 months before his term ended, Bissell died.

After a state funeral, the first Republican governor was buried with Catholic graveside services. While he was ill in Washington, he had become a Roman Catholic to please his second wife, Elizabeth Kintzing Kane, daughter of Elias Kent Kane, an early U.S. senator from Illinois. His official household as governor included the two daughters of his first marriage and three nieces of his second wife. Religion had not been made an issue in the 1856 campaign. Republicans did not call Bissell's Catholicism to the attention of their predominantly Protestant members, and Democrats likewise did not want to lose the support of Irish immigrants.

The official cause of the governor's death was pneumonia. But according to Dr. John F. Snyder, his health battles had a different cause. "He died of the secondary effects of syphilis — he told me so himself — he contracted in Mexico."

Alton hosted the Illinois State Fair in 1856. The first fair was held in Springfield in 1853, but 12 other cities, including Centralia, Chicago, Decatur, DuQuoin, Freeport, Jacksonville, Olney, Ottawa, Peoria, and Quincy, also hosted. It's been located in Springfield since 1894.

12th Governor

John Wood
1798 - 1880

1798 — Born December 20 in New York
1822 — Builds the first log cabin on a site that was to become Quincy
1837 — Begins service as a state senator in the 10th through 12th General Assemblies
1856 — Becomes candidate for lieutenant governor
1860 — Governor Bissell dies March 18; Wood is qualified as governor on March 21.
1861 — Becomes state quartermaster general for the Civil War effort
1863 — Becomes colonel of the 137th Illinois Regiment of volunteers
1880 — Dies June 4

Republican
March 21, 1860 to January 14, 1861

John Wood, the founder of the city of Quincy and lieutenant governor of Illinois, completed without incident the last 10 months of Governor William H. Bissell's administration. After he took the oath of office at a quiet ceremony on the day of Bissell's state funeral, he did not bother to move to Springfield but generously allowed his predecessor's widow to continue living in the Executive Mansion. Because he wasn't using the governor's one-room office in the Statehouse, President-elect Abraham Lincoln took it over.

Despite the excitement of the presidential campaign and the turmoil over slavery and its expansion, there wasn't much for Governor Wood to do. Historian John Moses said that under the Constitution of 1848, governors often were lonesome for want of callers when the legislature was not in session. Wood anticipated the Civil War by calling attention to the need to reorganize the state militia, about which nothing had been done since the Mexican War.

Wood's Early Years

Wood was a New Yorker, born December 20, 1798, in Cayuga County, the only son of David and Catherine Krause Wood. His father, of Irish blood, was a Revolutionary War captain and surgeon. He also was a linguist who wrote marginal notes in German and French medical texts. At home the family conversed in "Mohawk Dutch," the only language Catherine understood.

The future governor left home around the age of 20 and wandered through Shawneetown to Pike County, where he farmed for two years. He was credited with recognizing the potential of the bluffs along the Mississippi River, where he bought a half section of land. There he founded Quincy, which at one time was the largest city in Illinois. Wood and a companion built the first log cabin there in 1822.

An abolitionist, in 1824 he turned out a large majority in present Hancock and Fulton counties to support Governor Coles' anti-slavery campaign. He initiated the organization of Adams County, served uneventfully in the Black Hawk War, helped promote railroads and a bridge over the Mississippi, and was elected mayor of Quincy several times. He resigned his seat in the state Senate to protest having been instructed to vote against Quincy's best interests on a railroad matter.

In 1835, he built an imposing Greek Revival house. The German craftsmen he hired out of St. Louis to build his house began a wave of German immigration to the area. Local historians estimate that as many as 70 percent of the families in Quincy today can trace their ancestry to immigrants who followed those craftsmen.

In 1826, he married Ann M. Streeter. Of their eight children, one daughter and three sons lived to maturity. His wife died in 1863. Two years later, he married Mary A. Holmes.

The Second Choice Becomes Governor

A rugged man, Wood wasn't the original Republican nominee for lieutenant governor. Because of the importance of the German vote, the 1856 convention at Bloomington nominated Francis A. Hoffman of Cook County, who hadn't been a citizen for the required 14 years. When his ineligibility was noted, Lincoln and other Republican leaders filled the vacancy by nominating Wood.

Lincoln went with Wood because the Democratic candidate for governor, William A. Richardson, also came from Quincy. When as lieutenant governor he presided over the Senate during two legislative sessions, Wood worked harmoniously with the majority Democrats. Wood never ran for state office again.

From Governor to Foot Soldier

Wood had an active and varied career during the Civil War. He was one of five conservative Republicans appointed as delegates to a so-called peace convention at Washington that did nothing. In May 1861, he volunteered for appointment as state quartermaster general and assumed the enormous job of providing food, shelter, and equipment for the dozens of regiments Illinois was sending to the federal armies. Wood had to set up a procurement office that included such essentials as an accounting system. The normal duties of a quartermaster included purchasing, among other items, uniforms, tents, tools, equipment, means of transportation, and fuel. Because no ordnance officer was on duty at Springfield, Wood took over responsibility for supplying arms and ammunition for the first Illinois regiments. When the federal government took over procurement responsibilities, the state quartermaster department was abolished. The adjutant general reported that Wood's department spent $3,714,122 to clothe and equip three-fourths of the first 60,540 soldiers from Illinois.

At the age of 64, Wood went to war as colonel of the 137th Illinois Regiment of volunteers, a 100-day regiment he recruited at Quincy during the manpower shortage of 1863. Stationed at Memphis, the 137th performed picket duty on Hernando Road, where Confederate General Nathan Bedford Forrest's cavalry attacked, causing the loss of seven men, while the colonel was ill at his headquarters.

In his final years, the former governor lost his fortune. In 1873, he told his lawyer, Orville H. Browning, that his extensive property holdings had been mortgaged as security for the debts of his sons. But his financial reversal resulted primarily from the debt on his second new home. Finished in 1864, the octagonal stone house was designed by John Murray Von Osdell, the architect who designed the Executive Mansion, and cost $200,000. The Panic of 1873, a severe economic recession, diminished his wealth and by 1875 caused him to sell his properties to pay his debts. He sold the octagonal house to English and German College for $40,000 and moved back to the Greek Revival house, which he had given to one of his sons.

He died broke on June 4, 1880, after an illness of several years. At funeral services held in Quincy's largest church, a eulogist remembered him as "one of the men who planted civilization in the wilderness."

The Wigwam in Chicago, site of the 1860 Republican Convention that nominated Lincoln

13th Governor

Richard Yates
1815 -1873

1815 — Born January 18 in Warsaw, Kentucky

1831 — Ends studies at Miami University at Oxford, Ohio, to move to Illinois with his family

1835 — Graduates from Illinois College

1843 - 1847 — Serves as representative in the 13th and 14th General Assemblies

1849 - 1851 — Serves as representative in the 16th General Assembly

1850 — Elected to Congress for the first of two terms

1860 — Elected governor

1861 — Abraham Lincoln takes the oath of office to become the nation's 16th president; the Civil War begins on April 12 when Confederate forces fire on Fort Sumter.

1862 — A Democrat-heavy state constitutional convention meets in Springfield; voters fail to ratify the constitution that would cut the governor's term in half and create a Democrat-dominated commission to take over the governor's wartime authority.

1865 - 1871 — Serves as U.S. senator

1873 — Dies November 27

Republican
January 14, 1861 to January 16, 1865

During the Civil War, Governor Richard Yates was the most popular and most controversial civilian on the divided Illinois homefront. Genial, handsome, and an eloquent orator, he excelled as a recruiter of regiments, and his speeches were bugle calls for more men to march southward. Known as the "soldiers' friend," he chartered boats to take doctors, nurses, and hospital supplies to battlefields where the men he had urged to enlist suffered heavy casualties. The role of a war governor is to mobilize his state behind a maximum national effort for victory. Yates did that.

Strongly opposed to slavery, he was a Radical Republican who complained to and about Abraham Lincoln and could not understand why there was any delay in conquering the South. More emotional than intellectual, he never comprehended the complexity of the president's wartime problems, one of which was him.

The governor had his own problems, chiefly with his political opposition: the Peace Democrats and Southern sympathizers who dominated a constitutional convention and the midterm legislature. The governor had no talent for compromise and made no effort at it. He could have appointed a Democrat to Stephen A. Douglas' Senate vacancy; he could have been less of an alarmist and more understanding of the president; and, he could have been a saintly character with many virtues that are invaluable in crisis years. Nevertheless, with Yates as governor of a strategic state, the North won the war.

For charismatic and aggressive leadership, Yates' reward, before the war ended, was election to the U.S. Senate. While there, he was an alcoholic failure who did not deserve, and did not receive, a second term. Nevertheless, the popularity of the wartime governor persisted long after his death. His son, whose chief political asset was that he also was named Richard Yates, was elected governor in 1900.

Yates the Orator, Politician, and Railroad Developer

The first Governor Yates was born in Kentucky on the Ohio River at Warsaw, Gallatin County, on January 18, 1815. He was the fourth of 11 children of Henry and Millicent Yates, cousins from Virginia. He was 16 and enrolled in Miami University in Ohio when his father, recently a widower, moved the family to Illinois in 1831. For a year, the boy attended a log cabin school while his father operated a store at Springfield. Henry Yates then moved 20 miles westward and became a landowner.

The son went on to Jacksonville, the next county seat, his legal residence the rest of his life. In 1835, he was half of Illinois College's first graduating class. He studied law under John J. Hardin and spent a year at Transylvania University Law School in Kentucky. He returned to Jacksonville to practice law, make speeches, and as a Henry Clay Whig serve 10 years as state representative and congressman.

In 1839, he married Catharine Geers, who was small, dark, and fragile. For nine years they lived with her mother, during which time three of their five children were born. Of the three who lived to maturity, the namesake son, the future governor, was the youngest.

Of medium height and somewhat rotund, Yates had an imposing head, thick auburn hair, bright blue eyes, and a friendly manner. "Nature had fashioned him to be admired by the masses," wrote Alexander Davidson and Bernard Stuve, authors of *A Complete History of Illinois from 1673 to 1873*. His strong and flexible voice was adapted to open-air audiences, and Yates, who began as a campus orator, received invitations to speak at Fourth of July celebrations and political meetings. In the great age of Illinois oratory, he was noted for his rhetoric, and he ranked as the equal of William H. Bissell, his predecessor as governor, and Richard J. Oglesby, his successor. Only Robert G. Ingersoll, Owen Lovejoy, and Edward D. Baker were regarded by some contemporaries as the governor's oratorical superiors.

The future governor's law practice was never lucrative, but his son said he made some money as a railroad promoter. Biographers do not credit him with superior intellectual qualities. He is described as convivial, an adjective often applied to heavy drinkers.

A political career was inevitable. At the age of 25, he took an active speaking role in William Henry Harrison's presidential campaign. He was the youngest member of the Illinois House of Representatives, to which he was first elected in 1842, then again in 1844 and 1848. He submitted unfriendly amendments to, but voted for, Governor Thomas Ford's debt management program. At his final session, he was the speakership candidate of the minority Whigs. Gustave Koerner, the German leader who served one term in the House with Yates, said the future governor was "thoroughly anti-slavery" but kept silent about it. Two days before he left the legislature, Yates said that "the earliest impressions of my boyhood were that the institution of slavery was a grievous wrong."

In 1850, Yates was elected to Congress in the old Lincoln district for the first of two terms. Upon the introduction of the Kansas-Nebraska bill — a move to allow Kansas to become a slave state if settlers voted for it — he made a forceful speech against the spread of slavery. He also advocated homestead legislation and was regarded as something of an oddity because he favored women's suffrage.

Returning to Jacksonville, he became president of the Tonica and Petersburg Railroad, which would serve 10 counties in his old congressional district as soon as right-of-way, rails, and rolling stock could be paid for. His job was to raise the money by selling stock to landowners and bonds to counties and townships. To avoid bankruptcy, he discounted mortgages with eastern capitalists. Train service on the road, which eventually became part of the Chicago and Alton Railroad, had not started when he resigned as its president after being nominated for governor.

During his railroad career, Yates refused to run for Congress again but was available for higher office. In 1855, he promised Lincoln he would be a candidate for Senator only "in the event you do not succeed." When the Republican Party held its first convention, Yates was one of 13 vice presidents and made what the official record called a "stirring speech."

The War Governor

Six years after losing his congressional seat and one week before Lincoln won the Republican presidential nomination, Yates became the party's compromise nominee for governor. At the Republican state convention at Decatur, his opponents, both of whom had better ratings in the party hierarchy, were Norman B. Judd of Chicago and Leonard Swett of Bloomington. On the fourth ballot, Swett threw the nomination to Yates, who was regarded as the strongest candidate in important central counties. Lincoln, who had close ties to both Judd and Swett, stayed neutral. So the nod went to Yates, who preferred Edward Bates of Missouri for the presidential nomination.

In November, Yates won by 12,943 votes over Circuit Judge James C. Allen of Crawford County, who became a member of the Democratic peace wing and was elected congressman-at-large in 1862.

At the start of his administration, the new governor was too drunk to deliver his inaugural address. Yates kept the president-elect and other dignitaries waiting a half hour before he, aided by an escort, staggered down the aisle and collapsed in a chair while the House clerk read his long speech. The newspapers printed nothing about the new governor's condition. The speech made clear that Yates was not synchronizing his views with those of Lincoln, who was moving cautiously in an effort to limit the number of seceding states. The Associated Press called it:

> the most decided anti-slavery, anti-compromise and anti-secession document sent to any northern legislature since the beginning of the crisis. Although delivered under the very eye of the president-elect, its tone is so radical as to make it altogether improbable that it has his sanction.

Lincoln had declined when Yates offered to let him read the speech in advance.

Yates, the chief executive of an important state at the start of the nation's greatest crisis, had not borne arms in the Mexican War, had not achieved prominence as a lawyer, had no experience as an administrator, and lacked the full confidence of the president-elect. He did have the backing of several men experienced in state government. After Fort Sumter, Senator Lyman Trumbull, Orville H. Browning, and Gustave Koerner converged on Springfield to help put Illinois on a war footing. They were joined by John A. McClernand, one of the first of the War Democrats. With their help, and with the loyalty of the elected state officials, the Yates Administration performed creditably.

When Fort Sumter was surrendered and the White House called on Illinois to contribute six regiments, the governor enthusiastically began a drive that in four years sent 197,360 men into the Union army. He called the legislature into special session and used the occasion to denounce treason and encourage the enlistment of more regiments than the War Department had asked for. The legislature complied with the governor's request for a $3 million appropriation that violated the state constitution's debt limit but was upheld by the state Supreme Court. He ordered drill teams to Cairo when no other troops were available. He secretly sent a steamboat to bring 10,000 muskets from the St. Louis armory.

For a brief time, homefront harmony seemed possible. Senator Stephen A. Douglas, on a trip requested by the president, reached Springfield during the special legislative session and convinced Orville H. Browning, the former Whig he defeated for Congress, that bipartisanship was vital. Before the General Assembly and later at Chicago, Douglas eloquently pleaded for Democrats to support the war effort.

Douglas' death less than two months after Fort Sumter was a major tragedy, and Browning, his replacement, missed the opportunity to promote homefront unity. Important Republicans urged Yates to appoint a Democrat to fill the vacancy, but Democrats did not encourage activity that might weaken their party's position in future elections. Again, the record is incomplete, but the cautious governor ended the matter by appointing Browning. No one knows what would have happened had he named a War Democrat. As the war developed, a sizable number of Democratic leaders excused their opposition to the Lincoln and Yates administrations by asserting their party should not be dismantled and that the Republican governor had given them precedents for partisanship.

In speeches and proclamations, Yates encouraged the belief that drafting Illinois men would be disgraceful. In the summer of 1862, when Washington called for 52,290 more men and refused to allow credit for previous quota excesses, Yates and other officials spread across the state for a series of mass meetings. They filled the quota in 11 days. The governor soon was quarreling with Lincoln, who protested that Illinois had not accepted the service of a federal officer sent to speed dispatch of new troops to battle zones. Yates retorted that 50,000 men were ready to go as soon as the War Department supplied guns, tents, and other equipment. Lincoln's last word was that there had been "much trouble between officers sent to Illinois and the state government there."

Because Illinois made a better showing than many states, it was exempt from the first two draft calls. Enrollment under the third call was in progress when the war ended. In the fall of 1864, Yates told President Lincoln that a high quota "will not only endanger the peace of the state but will hopelessly defeat us in the coming elections." In his final report to the legislature, Yates boasted the state sent into battle 157 regiments, plus miscellaneous units and 13 regiments of 100-day volunteers.

The governor never hesitated to voice his disapproval of the president's war leadership. He wrote to Senator Trumbull that "if I were Lincoln I would lead enough of the Potomac army to take Richmond —

and this though Washington could not be saved." Homefront radicals applauded in the discouraging summer of 1862 when he wrote an open letter stating that "the crisis demands sterner measures." He urged the president to "summon to the standard of the republic all men willing to fight for the Union. ... Don't waste manpower guarding the property of traitors. ... Use Negro troops. ... Have invading troops forage off the country. ... Mild and conciliatory measures have been used in vain."

Questions of Loyalty

"Old Abe was too slow for me," he told a Brooklyn audience at the end of the 1862 campaign. "I was for the [emancipation] proclamation, for confiscation, for the arrest of rebels and traitors, and for every measure by which we could put down the rebellion."

Yates believed that he was personally responsible for Illinois soldiers, even after they had been mustered into federal service. When heavy casualties had been reported at Fort Donelson and Shiloh, he chartered steamboats and rushed medical aid to the battlefields. During the siege of Vicksburg, the governor socialized with Illinois troops. However, had Illinois drafted replacements for casualties, the original regiments could have been kept at full strength under experienced officers. Yates, for whom the appointment of colonels was a patronage opportunity, preferred to recruit new regiments, which meant that inexperienced units were rushed into battle.

The governor took credit for starting Ulysses S. Grant on his Civil War career. A West Pointer who had resigned from the army, Grant came to Springfield hoping for a command. Yates put him to work as a $2-a-day clerk in the adjutant general's office before appointing him colonel of one of the dozens of regiments from Illinois.

Yates himself had to contend with partisan Democrats whom he considered his homefront enemies. A constitutional convention in 1862 unwisely asserted that it had executive and legislative authority, questioned whether Illinois troops were properly equipped, tried to cut in half the governor's term, and proposed that a commission dominated by Democrats take over the governor's wartime authority. A committee that investigated purchases of uniforms reported that no wrongdoing could be traced to Yates and John Wood, his quartermaster general. In 1861, when the Lincoln Administration took over military purchasing for Illinois troops, Yates resisted, giving the impression that he was profiting politically, if not financially.

He invoked a hitherto unused power to dismiss the 1863 obstructionist legislature. Because the biennial appropriation bills had not been passed, he and the other state officials were forced to borrow money to pay their office expenses for two years. (The same situation existed in Indiana, where Governor Oliver P. Morton ran his state government for two years without legislative appropriations.)

Yates, who was inclined to be hysterical, believed that the Lincoln Administration's arbitrary arrests of civilians were justified but inadequate. "Secession is deeper and stronger here than you have any idea," he wrote to Senator Trumbull. "Its advocates are numerous and powerful, and respectable." In 1862, he asked that a regiment of infantry be sent to Springfield to guard the state government while the constitutional convention was in session. His fears increased amid reports of the organization of pro-Confederate secret societies in areas where there had been a heavy enlistment of loyalists. Yates proposed appointing a U.S. marshal with power to arrest anyone deemed dangerous to the federal government. He called General John M. Palmer back from his command in Tennessee and sent him to ask Lincoln and Secretary of War Edwin M. Stanton to organize four or five regiments for security service in Illinois. The president's response was to ask, "Who can we trust if we can't trust Illinois?"

As the 1864 election approached, Yates and other Radicals lacked enthusiasm for Lincoln and hoped to nominate someone who had taken a stronger stand on slavery. In September, however, the governor told newspaperman Horace Greeley that Lincoln's election was probable, that he knew of no other man who could carry Illinois, and that it would be disastrous to attempt to substitute candidates. In Illinois, Union victories and Democratic criticism of the war helped the Republican campaign.

The Republican victory included majority control of the 1865 legislature, which elected Yates to the U.S. Senate over Congressman Elihu B. Washburne and General Palmer. In his final message to the legislature, he asked for repeal of the 1849 black laws and, in a long review of Illinois' support for the war, he included the text of the 1862 letter in which he urged Lincoln to use more decisive measures against the Confederates.

The Senator Drinks a Little

After Lincoln's assassination, Senator Yates helped convince the widow that burial should be in Springfield. Yates wrote a eulogy in which he confessed error in his criticism of the president:

> I thought he was too slow in calling out men, too slow in arming the freemen, too slow in issuing the Proclamation of Emancipation, but in his own time came, in succession, all those important measures, and the whole world now plainly sees and acknowledges that

Abraham Lincoln always did the right thing in the right way, and at the right time, and at the right place.

The eulogy was never delivered. Yates included tributes to Lincoln in later speeches.

As governor, Yates had asked that slavery be ended by a constitutional amendment. As a radical senator, determined that the South be punished, he wanted former slaves to have the right to vote, regardless of education. He voted to impeach President Andrew Johnson, but there had been doubt whether Yates would be present for the roll call. Near the end of Johnson's trial in "an address to the people of Illinois," he confessed that he was a periodic drinker who once had been a total abstainer for 10 years. "I have never appeared in the Senate except while sober," he wrote to several newspapers. "I have often yielded to temptation and as often have suffered the pangs of unutterable remorse." He apologized, said he had reformed, and swore that he would stay reformed. The *Chicago Tribune* commented that "it would be better taste to reform once without issuing a proclamation than to be continually issuing proclamations and never reforming." To make certain that he did not miss the impeachment roll call, Yates sent to Jacksonville for his wife, who for a month sat in the gallery watching him.

Yates hoped that he might win a second Senate term in 1870 by playing two generals, Richard J. Oglesby and John A. Logan, against each other. Reality closed in, and Yates' farewell to public office was a letter to Governor John Palmer that would not reach Springfield until after his successor had been elected. He regretted his bad habit but wanted credit for his early stands against slavery and for women's suffrage:

> I know not what I can do. I am wedded to politics. I think I will never drink again. I have been a good member of the Senate, done a good deal of work and made a great many speeches, but they are buried because I drank. I have not asked a friend about [reelection to] the Senate because I deserved nothing more from their generous friendship.

General John A. "Black Jack" Logan, who could control his drinking, replaced the one-termer.

Missing the Senate, Yates wanted an appointment to a diplomatic mission or the governorship of one of the western territories. He hoped that President Grant would remember who had made him colonel of the 21st Illinois Regiment. More likely, the president would remember a more recent occasion when Yates had been "uproariously drunk" at a reception given for General and Mrs. Grant by President Johnson. The former senator returned to Jacksonville and waited until the mail brought an appointment as a member of a commission that would disband as soon as it inspected a land grant railroad in Arkansas.

He took the job. On his way back home to an unpromising retirement, he died suddenly in a St. Louis hotel on November 27, 1873. Eulogists at his well-attended funeral recalled only that Yates had been the patriotic homefront leader of Lincoln's state during the difficult years of the Civil War. Fifty years later, his statue was erected on the Statehouse grounds.

Courtesy of the Abraham Lincoln Presidential Library

At the end of the Civil War, a fleet of 102 barges piled up in the LaSalle Basin at the southern end of the Illinois and Michigan Canal, waiting for navigation to open into the Illinois River.

Courtesy of the Abraham Lincoln Presidential Library

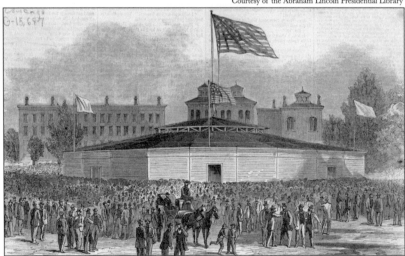

View of the wooden "tent" where the Democratic Convention of 1864 was held in Chicago

14th Governor

Richard James Oglesby

1825-1899

1825 — Born July 25 in Oldham County, Kentucky

1836 — Comes to Illinois as an orphan

1847 — Sees action at the Mexican War battles of Vera Cruz and Cerro Gordo

1849 — Goes to California during the gold rush; comes home with a $5,000 nest egg

1856 - 1857 — Travels to Europe and the Near East

1858 — Makes an unsuccessful run for Congress

1860 — Elected to Illinois Senate; resigns to fight in Civil War

1862 — Critically wounded at the Battle of Corinth in Mississippi; he recovers and returns to battle, but eventually removes himself from the field. He remains with the army until his first gubernatorial run.

1864 — Wins the Republican gubernatorial nomination for governor and defeats James C. Robinson in the general election

1869 — John Palmer becomes governor.

1873 — Becomes governor on January 13; 10 days later, as part of a campaign deal, Republican legislators send him to the U.S. Senate; Lieutenant Governor John L. Beveridge becomes governor.

1873 - 1879 — Serves in the U.S. Senate

1877 — Shelby M. Cullom takes office as governor.

1883 — Cullom resigns the governorship in his second term to become U.S. senator; John M. Hamilton becomes governor.

1885 — Returns to the Executive Mansion

1886 — On May 4, police move to break up a labor rally in Haymarket Square in Chicago. A bomb explodes, injuring and killing several people, including seven police officers. Oglesby commutes to life imprisonment the death sentences of two of several anarchists convicted in the case. Four others are hanged on November 11, 1887.

1899 — Dies April 24

Republican
January 16, 1865 to January 11, 1869
January 13, 1873 to January 23, 1873
January 30, 1885 to January 14, 1889

Richard James Oglesby, whose speeches "waved the bloody shirt" before Union veterans, was elected governor three times and U.S. senator once with a minié ball in his chest and a twinkle in his eye. The wounded general's spread-eagle oratory blaming Democrats for the Civil War and its casualties was a major factor in enabling the Republican Party to extend until 1892 the control of the governor's office, which began in 1856.

One of the most popular politicians of his time, Oglesby was

Illinois' first three-term governor. He won nonconsecutive elections in tough political years: in 1864, when Peace Democrats and Southern sympathizers hoped to deny Lincoln a second term; in 1872, when some of Lincoln's associates joined a coalition of Liberal Republicans and Democrats; and in 1884, when Grover Cleveland became the first Democratic president after the Civil War. The second term ended in 10 days, when the legislature elected Oglesby U.S. senator. His record of three terms stood until James R. Thompson was elected to his fourth term in 1986.

Joseph W. "Private Joe" Fifer, the third man to succeed Oglesby in the governor's chair, praised the affable, portly Oglesby for his "endurance, his bubbling humor, his eloquence, sometimes on the most homely subjects ... his faculty for remembering names and faces." He also remarked on "the spontaneity of the crowds in their response to his presence." The first Adlai E. Stevenson, who almost never criticized a public man, accused Oglesby of using "imagination" in the oratory that classified all Democrats as unpatriotic. He added that in the U.S. Senate, Oglesby was over his intellectual depth in debates about revenue and the tariff.

The expanding bullet that struck him down at Corinth ended a promising career as a battlefield commander but enabled Oglesby to campaign for governor before the war was over. After his promotion to major general and before his recuperation was complete, he made his first "bloody shirt" speech at Springfield. Without distinguishing between Southern sympathizers and loyalists, he shouted that Democrats were guilty of treason and hypocrisy and were obstructing the Lincoln and Yates administrations. He called Democratic legislators a "fire in the rear" of patriotic Union soldiers. Jeriah Bonham, an agricultural editor who attended many meetings, said he never listened to a more eloquent speech. Oglesby could be vehement, passionate, and scornful. He didn't use notes. He depended on the inspiration of the moment. Consequently, his speeches could be very good or very bad.

A popular perennial, Oglesby was a well-to-do man who could afford and was willing, even in his advanced years, to run for office. Despite his three governorships, however, he had a lower political batting average than his two Republican rivals, General John A. "Black Jack" Logan and Shelby M. Cullom, a noncombatant. Logan was serving his third term as senator when death shortened his career in 1888. Cullom was elected governor twice and senator five times. Together they limited Oglesby to one term in the U.S. Senate. After the 1870 election, Oglesby expected to be elected senator to succeed Richard Yates, but Logan had more votes when Republican legislators caucused. The same thing happened in 1878, when Oglesby's Senate term ended. Oglesby again was a loser in 1883 when Cullom was elected senator the first time.

From Orphan to War Hero

Oglesby was born July 25, 1825, in Oldham County, Kentucky, and came to Illinois in 1836 as an orphan. When he was 8 years old, a cholera epidemic killed his parents, Jacob and Isabella Watson Oglesby, two brothers, and a sister. His father, a farmer, had been a militia colonel and had served in the legislature. A wandering uncle took the future governor to Decatur where other relatives lived. The uncle and the boy worked a farm for a year, went back to Kentucky and another farm, to Decatur for a month, and then to Terre Haute, Indiana. A year later, the boy walked to Decatur where two aunts soon sent him to Kentucky to learn carpentry. Two years later, he returned to Illinois and, for three months, attended school for the first time. That summer he raised hemp and converted it into rope. A friend recalled seeing him "plodding through Decatur's streets with the old ox cart." Nothing had trained him for leadership.

In 1844, he abandoned manual labor and took up the study of law in the Springfield office of Silas W. Robbins, where the first volume of *Blackstone's Commentaries* was the first book he read cover to cover. After 18 months, he was admitted to the bar and practiced briefly at Sullivan. "I was never very much of a lawyer," Oglesby wrote a year before his death. "I never studied law."

He did travel extensively. In the Mexican War, as the first lieutenant of the Decatur company, he participated in the siege of Vera Cruz and the battle of Cerro Gordo. He came home in time to make Whig speeches for Zachary Taylor in 1848.

The next journey was to California in the 1849 gold rush. Borrowing $250 for expenses, he joined eight men in driving three six-mule teams from St. Joseph, Missouri, to Sacramento in 95 days. He worked as a miner, teamster, and storekeeper; he repaid the $250, suffered losses in a bank failure and a fire, and was back in Decatur in 20 months with some $5,000 in gold. The California trip, rather than his law practice, was the foundation for Oglesby's wealth.

He doubled his money by speculating in Decatur real estate, but first he went back to Kentucky to keep a boyhood promise and purchase the freedom of Uncle Tim, his father's slave. Oglesby credited his opposition to slavery to his memory of Uncle Tim's sale for $400. Throughout his public career, like Yates, he championed the interests of blacks. At his first inauguration, he said blacks and whites should have the same rights and privileges.

In 1852, Oglesby was a Whig candidate for presidential elector. He formed a law partnership with Sheridan Wait and handled stock subscriptions for the Indiana and Illinois Central Railway. He could afford to make a trip to Europe and the Near East in 1856 and 1857 that would compensate for his lack of culture and formal education. He traveled far and met important people. As he had done in Mexico and California, he wrote letters to hometown newspapers that told about visiting the English Parliament, hunting boar with the Prussian emperor, witnessing the czar's coronation in Moscow, sailing up the Nile River, crossing the Arabian desert, and reciting the Ten Commandments on Mount Sinai. Back home, his well-attended lectures gave him public speaking practice and a wider acquaintance.

Abraham Lincoln and Oglesby were close associates. In 1854, they corresponded about Richard Yates' drinking problem. Two years later, when Lincoln met with anti-Nebraska editors at Decatur to call the first Republican state convention, Oglesby toasted the Springfield lawyer as "our next candidate for United States Senator." At the 1860 Republican convention at Decatur, Oglesby, with an electrifying speech, was responsible for naming Lincoln the "railsplitter candidate." After the battle of Corinth, President Lincoln telegraphed General Ulysses S. Grant that he was "very anxious to know the condition of General Oglesby, who is an intimate personal friend." Several hours before the president's assassination, the governor called at the White House and listened to the reading of four chapters of a Petroleum V. Nasby book. He played a prominent role in arranging for Lincoln's burial at Springfield, served as president of the Lincoln Monument Association, and in 1874, made the dedicatory address at the tomb in Springfield's Oak Ridge Cemetery.

Oglesby missed the Republican Party's founding convention at Bloomington in 1856 but returned from Europe in time to run for Congress and lose in 1858. In 1860, he won his first political office, state senator from the Decatur district. He resigned when President Lincoln called for 300,000 30-day volunteers. Oglesby recruited a Decatur company and went to war as colonel of the 8th Illinois Volunteer Regiment. Until General Ulysses S. Grant replaced him, he was commanding officer at Cairo, the southernmost point then held by Union troops.

As a brigade commander, Oglesby led the attack at Fort Donelson and was promoted to brigadier general. At Corinth, he commanded one of the brigades that stopped the Confederates and then was critically wounded while leading a charge. After six months, he returned to duty and, as a major general who had performed well in two battles, was given command of the XVI Corps. The wound was troublesome, however, and he soon asked to be relieved. Thereafter, he served in Washington as president of courts martial until it was time to resign from the army and run for governor.

Oglesby's First Term

In the selection of an 1864 candidate for governor, Lincoln did not take sides between Oglesby and State Auditor Jesse K. Dubois, who also had been a close friend. Adjutant General Allen C. Fuller, whose record as a homefront administrator was deserving, also was a candidate, and General John M. Palmer, still in uniform, received some votes. Oglesby led on the first ballot and was nominated on the second. As an ardent Lincoln supporter, he was elected by 32,000 votes, with the big Republican counties in the north deciding the outcome. His opponent was Congressman James C. Robinson, who had defeated him six years earlier and had consistently voted for compromise and peace.

The country was prosperous, the Republican legislature supportive, and Oglesby's first term as governor was successful. It also was a time of personal tragedy. His inauguration, a quiet ceremony, was delayed a week because of the governor's grief over the death of his 5-year-old son Dickie. His first wife, Anna White, whom he had married at Decatur in 1859, died in the Executive Mansion in May 1868. She was survived by her husband and two children.

Before the surrender of General Robert E. Lee's army, at the governor's urging, Illinois became the first state to ratify the Thirteenth Amendment that outlawed slavery. Later, the legislature ratified the Fourteenth Amendment that conferred citizenship on black men and women. It also repealed the repressive black laws that in varying forms had existed since statehood. In his official capacity, the governor telegraphed the House of Representatives that "the people of Illinois demand the impeachment of President Andrew Johnson and will heartily sustain our Congress."

Despite shortcomings of the legislature, important action was taken by the peacetime session, which the governor asked to give attention to long-neglected problems of education, development of natural resources, the needs of the poor, and encouragement of the arts and sciences. A referendum was ordered on the calling of a constitutional convention. The first appropriation was made for construction of the new state

Capitol, which was completed in 1888. Oglesby supported the city of Urbana as the location of the new industrial university (now the University of Illinois) and appointed its first board of trustees. The elective office of attorney general was created, and Robert G. Ingersoll, who was Oglesby's close friend and appointee, retained the position after the election. To achieve assessment uniformity, a State Board of Equalization was created, with members elected by districts. A first step was made toward regulation of railroads and warehouses. A law that made eight hours a legal day's work, except for farmers, was enacted at the request of unions but was not enforced. The first voter registration law was enacted.

Oglesby advocated for reform of the overcrowded prison system under which, since 1837, the penitentiary at Joliet was leased to private parties who could profit from the leased labor of convicts. When the lessees lost money under postwar conditions, the privateers surrendered their lease. In the emergency, a special session of the legislature enacted a law for state control of prison operations and appropriated funds to buy machinery for prison industries. Earlier, the logrolling legislature had voted for a penitentiary at Menard and a reformatory at Pontiac.

Masses of special and private bills, sometimes as many as 500 in an omnibus package, were railroaded through without deliberation and with allegations of bribery. As a result, there was increasing sentiment for a new constitution. Chicago traction (streetcar) ordinances became a legislative issue with passage of a bill extending from 25 to 99 years the franchises of horse-car companies that had refused to issue interline transfers. The governor's veto was quickly overridden, after which he gave up and made no further effort to stop the flood of special legislation.

Oglesby's Run for a Short Second Term

When his term ended, Oglesby went back to Decatur and cultivated friendships in Grand Army of the Republic posts. In 1872, he was available when Lincoln's party faced its greatest crisis, a deep split in its ranks. Scandals marred President Grant's first term; economic conditions had turned sour; some people objected to harsh treatment of Southern leaders; and Governor John M. Palmer, who had succeeded Oglesby, had started to act like a Democrat. The Republicans feared future elections would be lost unless former slaves voted in the South. In Illinois, they were alarmed when Democrats and dissenting Republicans held simultaneous conventions on opposite sides of the Statehouse square. For governor, both nominated Gustave Koerner, the German intellectual who had been elected lieutenant governor 20 years earlier by Democrats and then turned

Republican on the slavery issue. The two conventions divided the rest of the state offices. In what seemed an emergency, Oglesby got his second nomination by acclamation.

The Liberal Republican movement collapsed in midcampaign because its presidential candidate, Horace Greeley, was unpopular among Democrats. For second terms, Grant carried Illinois by 57,000 votes and Oglesby by 40,000. It might have been different, at least closer, had Grant been opposed by an Illinois man. Senator Lyman Trumbull, Supreme Court Justice David Davis, and Governor Palmer wanted the nomination. In the future, Trumbull and Palmer would become losing Democratic candidates for governor. Some of the dissident Republicans returned to the mainstream Republican fold, which henceforth had conservative foundations.

At the Republican national convention, Oglesby made an unscheduled speech that focused first on former slaves, who for the first time were voting delegates, and then on the presence in the gallery of Garrett Smith, who before the war had been a prominent abolitionist. Cullom wrote that Oglesby "set the crowd wild."

Oglesby's second term lasted 10 days. During the election, he campaigned for Republican legislators who would elect him to the U.S. Senate. According to plan, the new governor resigned, turned the state over to Lieutenant Governor John L. Beveridge, and replaced Senator Lyman Trumbull in Washington.

Because Oglesby's colleagues did not appreciate his arm-waving speeches, the Senate term was a failure. Like Yates, but unlike Stephen A. Douglas and Trumbull, he contributed little to the discussion of national issues. He dreamed of running for president in 1876, but he found eastern audiences disinterested in the oratory that was effective at Grand Army of the Republic reunions in Illinois. When he sought a second Senate term, the Republican caucus vote was 80 to 26 in favor of John A. Logan, who had been senator from 1871 to 1877.

The Third Term

Twenty years after he first became governor, Oglesby won a third term; this time by 15,000 votes, his closest election. Oglesby's opponent, Carter Harrison, the former and future mayor of Chicago, didn't understand rural Illinoisans, and they didn't understand him. Harrison's political stands drew criticism even in his own party, notably from Congressman William R. Morrison, a downstate Democratic powerhouse.

Because both parties had elected 76 members of the Illinois House, Oglesby's 1884 inauguration was delayed more than two weeks until

Elijah M. Haines, the lone independent, was elected speaker. Haines, who became speaker 10 years earlier under similar circumstances, again presided over a disorderly session that accomplished little aside from establishing a soldiers' and sailors' home at Quincy and appropriating money to complete work on the Statehouse.

On May 4, 1886, police moved to break up a labor rally in Haymarket Square in Chicago. A bomb exploded, injuring and killing several people, including seven police officers. For 10 emotional days after the U. S. Supreme Court refused to intervene in the case, Oglesby was deluged with pleas for and against leniency for several convicted anarchists. Like predecessor governors, he regarded his office as administrative and, hesitating to interfere with judicial findings, he refused to intervene with many death sentences. But there is evidence that he wanted to commute the Haymarket sentences and hoped for public support from Chicago's business leaders. Finally, a day before the executions were scheduled, he commuted the sentences of Samuel Fielden and Michael Schwab, the only anarchists who might be classified as contrite. Another killed himself in his cell with a bomb. Four others were hanged on November 11, 1887.

An economic conservative in public, Oglesby in private criticized corporation heads who called for state protection whenever threatened with violence. When deteriorating economic conditions brought strikes by Joliet and Lemont quarrymen in 1885, and by East St. Louis switchmen and Chicago stockyards employees the next year, he followed precedent and restored order by calling out troops. In factories, work stoppages were frequent, more than half of them involving long working hours.

Retiring to the Rubber Chicken Circuit

During his first year as senator, Oglesby married Emma Keays, the widowed daughter of John D. Gillett, Logan County's largest landowner. In Decatur, they built a handsome Italianate house with seven fireplaces. In it were born the four children of their second marriages. When he left the governorship for the third and last time, Oglesby did not return to Decatur. He and his wife built a house around an old chimney and fireplace remaining from a double log cabin built in 1835 by James Latham, the first settler in Logan County. In 1890, they erected Oglehurst, a more imposing residence on Elkhart Hill.

His final years were active. Republican legislators attempted to return him to the Senate in an 1890 deadlock finally broken when Democrats elected another aging general, John M. Palmer. Oglesby joined four other former Republican governors in a campaign tour in support of John R. Tanner, the 1896 winner. To the end, he was in demand as an entertaining and inspirational speaker. One of his best-known examples of old-style oratory was his impromptu tribute to Indian corn, delivered September 9, 1894, at the Chicago Fellowship Club's harvest home festival.

He died April 24, 1899, at Oglehurst. Funeral services were conducted by an Episcopal bishop at the Gillett family's private chapel. One of his sons, John G. Oglesby, was elected lieutenant governor in 1908 and 1916.

The casket of Governor Oglesby was carried by six of his longtime family servants from the Oglehurst estate to a horse-drawn hearse that led as many as 4,000 mourners to services at the Episcopal chapel a quarter mile away. About half of those attending, including Governor and Mrs. John Tanner and other state officials, arrived on four special trains at the small town of Elkhart north of Springfield. Following the pallbearers is T.J. Abells, commander of the Decatur G.A.R. post, carrying the flag that had draped the casket of Abraham Lincoln.

15th Governor

John McAuley Palmer
1817-1900

1817 — Born September 13 in Scott County, Kentucky

1848 — Serves as a delegate to the state constitutional convention

1851 - 1853 — Serves in the Illinois Senate as an intermittent member of the 17th and 18th General Assemblies

1856 — Presides over the Bloomington convention that establishes the Illinois Republican Party.

1859 — Unsuccessfully runs for Congress

1861 — Is promoted to brigadier general and continues a distinguished Civil War combat career until an 1864 dispute with General William T. Sherman

1864 — Appointed military governor of Kentucky

1868 — Wins the Republican gubernatorial nomination on the first ballot and defeats Democratic Congressman John R. Eden in the general election

1870 — Illinois adopts a new constitution on July 2 requiring all executive officers of the state to run independently; approving successive terms; and granting blacks, but not women, the right to vote.

1871 — An October 8-9 fire destroys three-and-a-half square miles in the heart of Chicago and takes 300 lives.

1872 — Does not seek his party's nomination for a second term as governor because he feels he cannot campaign for the reelection of President Grant

1888 — Accepts the Democratic nomination for governor; loses to Joseph Fifer by 1.6 percent of the vote

1891 - 1897 — Serves as U.S. senator; starts the Gold Democrats faction

1896 — Runs for president as the nominee of the Gold Democrats

1900 — Dies September 24

Republican
January 11, 1869 to January 13, 1873

During a six-decade career of distinction, John M. Palmer was a Republican governor, a Democratic U.S. senator, and an activist in three other parties. Seldom neutral, a man of independence, integrity, and intelligence, he changed political affiliations whenever he was in major disagreement with the party to which he belonged at the time. In an era of political volatility, Palmer was a Democrat, an Anti-Nebraska Democrat, a Republican, a Liberal Republican, a Democrat again, and finally the presidential nominee of the "Gold" Democratic Party.

"I had my own views," Palmer told colleagues in the U.S. Senate near the end of his career. "I was not the slave of any party." He added that, instead of following party doctrine, "I thought for myself and [have] spoken my own words on all occasions."

Much of his life, Palmer was a Democrat, but he left Stephen A. Douglas' Democratic Party in 1854 on the moral issue of slavery and then William Jennings Bryan's Democratic Party in 1896 on the economic issue of bimetallism. He helped Abraham Lincoln found the Republican Party in Illinois. As a major general in the Civil War, he commanded an army corps. One of the best lawyers in the state, he accepted a draft to run for governor.

At the age of 79, because he believed that the nation's economy would be ruined by the Bryan-Altgeld silver policy, he ran for president on the National "Gold" Democratic ticket and thereby contributed to the election of Republican William McKinley.

Palmer could be stubborn, as when he asked to be relieved of his army corps command during a quarrel over seniority. He was inconsistent when he called for the impeachment of President Andrew Johnson, who was following Lincoln's moderate reconstruction policies, and when he criticized Governor John Peter Altgeld for objecting because President Grover Cleveland sent federal troops to keep order in Chicago during the 1894 railway workers' strike. Twenty-three years earlier, Governor Palmer complained to President Ulysses Grant about the unrequested presence of soldiers in Chicago after the 1871 fire. In 1891, when Palmer, as the Democratic candidate, was elected U.S. senator by the legislature, Altgeld supported him in public but secretly tried to get the office for himself.

Palmer's Early Legal and Military Career

John McAuley Palmer was born on September 13, 1817, near Eagle Creek in Scott County, Kentucky. At the age of 14, he was brought to Illinois by his father, Louis D. Palmer, an impoverished Baptist minister who admired Andrew Jackson and hated slavery. A wagon breakdown caused them to settle near Wood River. Two years later, the death of his mother, Ann Hansford Tutt Palmer, forced the breakup of the family. John, who had little schooling but showed an early aptitude for reading, was 18 when his father "gave him his time," an old-fashioned permission for a minor son to leave home. "I have no money to expend for your education," the father said, "but a healthy boy as you are needs no help; you may go tomorrow morning. I give you your time. Don't disgrace me. May God bless you."

John and an older brother Elihu worked at odd jobs for 18 months while they attended Alton College, which opened under the manual labor system and became Shurtleff College. Then the future governor tried coopering, peddled clocks in the Military Tract, and taught school at Canton, where he began to read law in his spare time.

At 21, Palmer studied law in the Carlinville office of John S. Greathouse and lived with Elihu, a learned and eccentric clergyman. Stephen A. Douglas recommended Palmer open an office in Carlinville the year he was admitted to the bar because he was too poor to move to a larger town. He found clients, and in 1842, while living in a log house, he married Malinda Ann Neely, who became the mother of his 10 children. While his law practice slowly developed, he had time to work his way into local political prominence. He was a Democrat by inclination and with Douglas' encouragement, he was elected probate justice of the peace, constitutional convention delegate, county judge, and state senator.

At the 1848 constitutional convention, he advocated free common schools in which sectarian education would be prohibited. He established a reputation for independence and fearlessness. He was called an abolitionist when he opposed a proposal to bar free blacks from Illinois.

In the legislature, he broke with Douglas by opposing repeal of the Missouri Compromise, a pro-slavery measure that would allow Nebraska settlers to determine the question of slavery for themselves. He resigned his seat and was reelected as an Anti-Nebraska Democrat. He led a five-man anti-slavery bloc that triumphed when Lyman Trumbull was elected U.S. senator, the office Abraham Lincoln wanted. Palmer did not turn Republican until the 1856 Democratic state convention endorsed Douglas for president.

Palmer was the obvious choice to preside at the 1856 Bloomington convention at which the Illinois Republican Party was founded. Robust and ruddy, he was a 200-pounder who stood slightly under six feet. As a speaker, he lacked Richard Oglesby's fluency and Richard Yates' ornate language, but his voice was pleasant, his vocabulary accurate, and his fund of information extensive. He reasoned clearly, and his speeches were forcible and convincing. Photographs show him with a beard.

Personal courage was one of his characteristics. On one occasion during a congressional campaign that had been marked by name-calling, he carried a loaded pistol into an opposition meeting and, placing it in cocked position before him, castigated the Democratic Party.

At the 1856 Republican national convention, Palmer placed in nomination for vice president the name of Lincoln, who received 110 votes. At Lincoln's request, he reluctantly and unsuccessfully ran for Congress in 1859. The next year he helped engineer Lincoln's presidential nomination at the Chicago Wigwam convention. He was a Republican elector and, in early 1861, in recognition of his political reliability, was an Illinois delegate to a national peace conference that did not make concessions to the South.

During the Civil War, Palmer simultaneously was a loyal supporter of Lincoln and a Radical Republican who protested arbitrary arrests by the military. In Illinois, his stature as a volunteer officer was exceeded only by that of General John A. Logan. Without Mexican War experience (he raised a company that was not needed), he was one of the first politicians to be given a colonel's commission by Governor Yates.

Before the end of 1861, he was promoted to brigadier general by President Lincoln on the recommendation of Republican congressmen. He quickly demonstrated an aptitude for command, intelligent understanding of the tactical situation, and defensive stubbornness. His 14th Illinois Infantry Regiment began service in Missouri and took part in the capture of Mississippi River Island No. 10. As a major general, he stood fast under repeated assaults at Stone's River and Chickamauga. He was promoted to command an army corps for the Atlanta campaign, but by August 1864, his battlefield career was terminated by a dispute with General William T. Sherman. Palmer had developed a low opinion of West Point officers and protested when General John M. Schofield, whom he considered his junior, was placed over him. Within military channels, he was relieved at his own request. The merits of that dispute are unclear, but Palmer had been hoping he could resign and return to Carlinville, where a son was ailing.

In 1864, Lincoln appointed him military governor of Kentucky, where the population was evenly divided between loyalists and Southern sympathizers. His evenhanded orders, which established the rights of blacks while deferring to Kentucky law whenever possible, involved him in a heated controversy with state authorities. When Palmer was indicted for violating Kentucky's black laws, he announced that if he should be arrested, his second-in-command was under orders to storm the jail. The sheriff did not serve the warrant on him.

Because a black boy had accompanied him home while on sick leave from the army and then became a member of the Palmer household, the general was indicted at Carlinville for violating a black code provision that John A. Logan had introduced in the legislature a decade earlier that prohibited white families from adopting blacks. Palmer was acquitted when he insisted on being tried by a jury.

Palmer was one of the most popular of the military leaders. While he was still in uniform, 75 delegates to the 1864 Republican state convention in Decatur voted to nominate him for governor. Two years later, when the Grand Army of the Republic spread across the North, Palmer, instead of Logan, was the first state commander.

In September 1866, Palmer moved his family to Springfield and became the partner of Milton Hay, who ran one of the state's most prestigious law firms. In fact, Palmer moved in to replace future governor Shelby M. Cullom, who was off to Washington to serve as congressman. Palmer's colleagues had great respect for his legal ability. He was an expert on constitutional law who depended more on fundamental principles than the citation of cases. But the former general did not confine himself to the law, and he never avoided politics and public service.

The Reluctant Candidate Becomes Governor

Palmer had personal reasons for not wanting to be governor. As a lawyer, his income in two months was equal to the $1,500 annual salary fixed by the 1848 Constitution. At home in a large and expandable household were his wife, six children, and two dependent sisters-in-law. Tom, the youngest son, was an epileptic who would die near the end of the governor's term. Susie, the youngest daughter, was blind. Mrs. Palmer, an invalid, in a wartime letter referred to herself as "but a poor, weak woman, not a highly polished wife that likes to cut a dash. But, after all, we have been happy in our own way."

"I am not and do not intend to be a candidate," Palmer insisted in advance of his draft by the 1868 Republican convention. His repeated declaration of disinterest encouraged Attorney General Robert G. Ingersoll, Congressman-at-large S. W. Moulton, and State Auditor Jesse K. Dubois to run for nomination as governor. At the convention, Palmer had a clear majority on the first ballot, accepted the nomination, and won easily over John R. Eden, a Democratic congressman. After the war, Palmer followed the standard Republican practice of "bloody shirt" speeches in which local issues were avoided.

His inauguration speech shocked Republicans and delighted Democrats by taking a strong and unexpected stand for states' rights. The new governor insisted that the U.S. Constitution recognizes that the states have inherent rights and that the federal government is limited to enumerated powers. Since the wartime emergency had passed, he declared that "the states' just authority must be respected by the federal government." With a general demand for control of corporations and regulation of railroads, he told the legislature that abuses must be corrected and rigid economy practiced. Palmer directly challenged the Republican premise that the simultaneous growth of the federal government and business corporations was beneficial to the country.

He was a reform governor who vetoed more than 100 private and special bills at the start of his administration. His 1869 veto messages complained that floods of corrupt legislation gave special privileges to capitalists and promoters and allowed tax money to be spent for personal or private benefit. Typical vetoes, all overridden before adoption of the Constitution of 1870, objected to municipal bond issues that paid for the sites of railroad shops and business firms and to the investment of local tax funds in hotels, coal and insurance companies, and warehouses. The Illinois Supreme Court upheld Palmer's veto of a "tax grab" bill that had wide support in rural communities where tax-supported bonds had been issued to help pay for railroad construction. Counties and other local governments wanted to be relieved of their obligation. Palmer held that taxation should be uniform throughout the state and said that the proposed legislation would be a precedent for unwise bond issues. Vetoed and repassed was the Chicago "lakefront" bill that ceded downtown real estate to the Illinois Central Railroad. That law was repealed in 1873 and the controversy settled by federal courts 15 years later.

His barrage of vetoes called attention to legislative excesses that were ended only by the midterm adoption of the Constitution of 1870.

After the 1871 Chicago fire destroyed three-and-a-half square miles of the city, Palmer showed how nearly $3 million could be appropriated for the city's financial relief. His solution, presented at a special legislative session, was to reimburse the city for money it spent on deepening the Illinois and Michigan Canal. In the fire emergency, Palmer acted promptly to keep informed about the amount of destruction and looting in the burned area. A diplomatic crisis arose when General Philip H. Sheridan, responding to a direct appeal from a local relief agency, detailed four army companies to Chicago in what seemed to be a long-term, law-and-order mission. In the chaotic situation, the protocol of consulting the governor had been overlooked. Palmer protested that the federal government did not have the power to intrude in a situation in which the state had jurisdiction. President Grant courteously avoided the issue, and neither the legislature nor the public supported the governor.

In the spring of 1872, Palmer announced that he could not campaign for President Grant for reelection. Therefore, although he was eligible under the new state constitution, he would not seek a second term as governor. Whether he could have been renominated is uncertain. Palmer's states' rights advocacy was unpopular with old-line Republicans, and Shelby M. Cullom, who would be the 28th General Assembly's speaker of the House, had lined up high-level endorsements to return Richard J. Oglesby to the governor's office.

Before his term as governor ended, Palmer ceased to be a Republican.

At the 1872 Liberal Republican convention at Cincinnati, David Davis had half the Illinois delegation, with the others split between Palmer and Lyman Trumbull. Palmer ordered his delegates to support Trumbull, but the nomination went to Horace Greeley, who President Grant easily defeated. In the Illinois gubernatorial election, the governor supported the Liberal Republican-Democratic coalition candidate, Gustave Koerner.

A Party-Hopping Ex-Governor

A private citizen again, Palmer resumed a law practice in Springfield and briefly was a mugwump — an independent. He denounced monopolies and called the old parties useless when he spoke at a statewide meeting of farmers. However, by 1876 he was a Democratic activist again — but with reservation. He supported Samuel J. Tilden for the presidency, but at the state level the Democrats had formed a coalition with the Greenbackers on a platform that opposed specie payment of the government debt. As a result, Palmer, who was a conservative on monetary issues, did not campaign for Lewis Steward, a coalition-supported Greenbacker who lost the governorship to Shelby Cullom by 7,000 votes.

Samuel Tilden beat Rutherford Birchard Hayes in the balloting in the 1876 presidential election, but Republicans challenged the vote totals from Oregon and claimed that blacks had not been allowed to vote in South Carolina, Florida, and Louisiana. With the electoral college votes from these states, the Republicans could put Hayes in the White House. To avoid a legislative deadlock, Congress appointed a 15-man electoral commission to arbitrate. The national Democratic Party sent Palmer to Louisiana as chairman of a delegation of observers. But the commission was stacked with Republicans, and the necessary electoral votes went to Hayes.

Palmer stuck with the Democrats a while. For 21 ballots at the start of the 1877 legislative session, Palmer was the Democratic caucus choice for U.S. senator. Then he withdrew in a deadlock that resulted in the election of David Davis as an independent. At the 1884 Democratic state convention, Palmer as keynoter espoused the party's platform planks for an eight-hour day and the right of labor to organize, causes that had gained support since the tumultuous 1877 railroad strikes. In 1888, Democrats proposed that Palmer accept their gubernatorial nomination with an understanding that he need not campaign actively. He insisted that an all-out effort be made to carry the state. He criticized Illinois governors as a class, saying they had used the office "as a stepping-stone to other places."

Aggressively denouncing Republican conservatism and taking an early stand for labor and other liberal causes, the elder statesman spoke in 60 counties and came within 12,547 votes of defeating Republican Joseph W. Fifer in the year that Grover Cleveland lost the presidency to Benjamin Harrison.

Palmer then convinced Democratic leaders that he could be elected senator in 1890, if the party endorsed him in early summer on a liberal and pro-labor platform. A two-month deadlock ended with Palmer's election. Democratic candidates who campaigned as Palmer supporters were elected to 101 legislative seats, along with 100 Republicans and three members of the Farmers Mutual Benefit Association.

During the Senate term, which began when he was 75 years old, Palmer opposed the protective tariff and favored the direct election of senators and pensions for Supreme Court justices. He became concerned about inflationist agitation for the unlimited coinage of silver at an arbitrary ratio of 16-to-1 with gold — an idea supported by William Jennings Bryan and Illinois Governor Altgeld. The senator did not object to coinage of silver but believed that gold, being more expensive, would disappear from circulation in the United States and that the national economy could not prosper on a silver basis. He could support the Republican national platform but not McKinley, a high-tariff man. With the quiet encouragement of President Cleveland, Palmer helped organize, wrote the platform for, and became the presidential nominee of the National "Gold" Democratic Party.

At the age of 79, he campaigned in major cities with the vice presidential candidate, Confederate General Simon Bolivar Buckner of Kentucky. Their well-attended speeches denounced bimetallism. While they didn't specifically ask people to vote for McKinley, in an unusually hard-fought campaign they contributed to Bryan's defeat.

After his Senate term, Palmer returned to Springfield. His frail wife died of tuberculosis in 1885. Three years later, he married Hannah L. Kimball, the city librarian. In good health and with a clear memory, he completed two valuable books. His memoirs, *Personal Recollections: The Story of an Earnest Life*, is in considerable part an explanation and justification of the positive stands taken during his long career. Also bearing his name is a two-volume collection of biographies, *The Bench and Bar of Illinois*. He was in demand as a speaker. As one of the last survivors, he attended the 44th anniversary reunion of delegates to the 1856 Bloomington convention. He died in his sleep the night of September 24, 1900.

John Palmer speaks to a crowd gathered to commemorate Knox College in Galesburg as the site of the 1858 Lincoln-Douglas debate. Lincoln was in the legislature in 1837 when it granted the college its charter. In 1860, the college awarded Lincoln an honorary doctorate degree, his first educational degree. Lincoln's son Robert spoke at the 1896 event.

The Chicago Fire of 1871 burned an estimated 18,000 buildings, took 300 lives, and cost almost $200 million. Illinois had been in a severe drought, and Chicago had seen hardly any rain in three months. The governor proposed, and the legislature agreed, to forgive the city its debt in the building of the I & M Canal, effectively providing it with about $3 million in relief funds.

16th Governor

John Lourie Beveridge
1824 -1910

1824 —Born July 6 near Greenwich, New York

1858 —Becomes a delegate to the state Republican convention

1861 - 1866 — Serves in the Union army, mostly in the 8th and 17th Illinois Cavalry

1870 —Elected state senator; serves 18 months in the 27th General Assembly

1872 —Resigns as Illinois congressman-at-large after he is elected lieutenant governor on a ticket headed by Richard J. Oglesby

1873 —Becomes governor on January 23, when, as part of a campaign deal, Republican legislators send Oglesby to the U.S. Senate

1881 —President Chester Alan Arthur appoints Beveridge assistant U.S. treasurer.

1910 —Dies May 3

Republican
January 23, 1873 to January 8, 1877

John Lourie Beveridge, the third and last Civil War general to become governor of Illinois, served all but the first 10 days of the second term of Richard J. Oglesby, who resigned when he was elected U. S. senator. Beveridge, the first chief executive from Cook County, lived in Evanston and practiced law in Chicago. He wasn't well known outside Cook and DeKalb counties, but in 1872, when Republicans briefly needed a more liberal image, he was elected lieutenant governor.

Cold and inclined to be unsociable, he was a temperance advocate who had been a hard-riding cavalry commander. More important, at a critical juncture for the GOP in Illinois, the dry, politically conservative Protestant chose not to follow Congressman John F. Farnsworth, his law partner and comrade-in-arms, into the Liberal Republican Party. A decade after the war over slavery, Lincoln's party was in the process of turning conservative, and Beveridge's reputation as something of a reformer was a political asset when he was nominated for lieutenant governor in 1872. But after he advanced to the governorship the next winter, the time for a reformer had already passed.

Beveridge, a dignified man with a beard and silver hair, never tried to be a backslapper. John Moses, who was both a Republican activist and a historian, wrote that the "temperate life of the new governor and the religious tone of his mind were not such as to recommend him to the favor of saloon politicians. ... He possessed the courage of his convictions and never dreamed of sacrificing principle to popularity."

The Teetotaling Early Years

Born July 6, 1824, on a farm near Greenwich, Washington County, New York, he was the son of George and Ann Hoy Beveridge, who were of Scotch and Scotch-Irish descent. They were such strict Presbyterians that the future governor was 19 before he heard a sermon of another denomination. When he was 18, the family moved to Illinois to a farm near Somonauk in sparsely settled DeKalb County. John, who had received a good common school education in New York, taught school one winter, attended the academy at Granville, and then completed the academic course at Rock River Seminary at Mount Morris.

Rather than burden his parents with the cost of a college education, he went to Tennessee in 1845 with $40 to teach and become a lawyer. Four years later, he returned to his father's home with a wife, a son and a daughter, and 25 cents. Due to an associate's mismanagement, a business venture failed, but Beveridge stayed in Tennessee until his debts were paid. His wife was Helen May Judson, daughter of Philo Judson, pastor of the Clark Street Methodist Church in Chicago. For the next five years, Beveridge practiced law in Sycamore, kept books for businessmen, and did some engineering.

In the spring of 1854, Beveridge moved to Evanston, a new suburb north of Chicago platted by Methodists as a site for Northwestern University, for which Judson was financial agent and business manager. Beveridge became a lay leader of the suburb's Methodist church, a member of the drainage commission beginning in 1855, and secretary of the Evanston Pier Company in 1870. In 1855, he opened a law office in Chicago. He became politically active and in 1858, as a delegate to the Republican state convention, heard Lincoln's "House Divided" speech.

The future governor rose quickly through the ranks of the army during the Civil War. When John F. Farnsworth organized and became colonel of the 8th Illinois Cavalry, Beveridge recruited Company F and was elected its captain. The line officers then elected him the second of three majors. Organized at St. Charles, Farnsworth's "Big Abolition Regiment" was sent east as part of the Army of the Potomac. It paraded before the White House and spent the winter of 1861-1862 on the out-skirts of Washington. Major Beveridge commanded the regiment during much of the summer of 1863. At Gettysburg, two dismounted battalions of the 8th Cavalry fired the first shots of the three-day battle. In 1863, he returned to Illinois and at St. Charles recruited the 17th Illinois Cavalry, which drilled at Alton while guarding Confederate prisoners. He spent the rest of the war as a colonel in Missouri, where he engaged in skirmishes, chased guerrillas, and countered Sterling Price's raid.

Oglesby Opens the Door

When the war ended, Beveridge was given the brevet rank of brigadier general and was sent to St. Louis to preside over military trials. Not until 1866 did he return to his law practice and become involved in the political wars. While his military record was commendable — he had been in several dozen battles and skirmishes — it did not make him conspicuous among the generals and colonels who were volunteering for federal and state offices.

Nevertheless, in seven years Beveridge rose to the governorship. Volunteer officers made good candidates, and in 1866 he was elected sheriff, a two-year office, and state senator four years later for a term that lasted 11 months. When associates of Lincoln, including Farnsworth, began to join the new Liberal Republican movement, Beveridge was rewarded for not following them. Elected to a vacancy as congressman-at-large, he resigned after 11 months when he was elected lieutenant governor in 1872 on a ticket headed by Richard James Oglesby. Oglesby, as part of a deal concocted during the campaign, was elected senator 10 days after inauguration, and Beveridge walked into office.

In the pattern of his time, Beveridge was a caretaker governor devoted to economy and a low profile. Steady progress had been made in paying off the public improvements debt of the 1837 era, and the governors were not expected to find new ways to spend public funds. In his 1875 message to the legislature, Beveridge regretted that Illinois did not practice budgeting.

The Beveridge Administration coincided with former Governor John M. Palmer's return to the Democratic Party, the prolonged and severe Panic of 1873, and the Granger movement that was a political force in Illinois long enough for the legislature to adopt a workable railroad regulation law. His administration began with a setback when the state Senate refused to confirm his nominees for members of the new Railroad and Warehouse Commission. In the 1874 midterm election, Illinois went Democratic for the first time in 12 years.

Beveridge's career paralleled that of Governor Thomas Ford in that he was criticized for failure to cope with prolonged lawlessness in southern Illinois. A "bloody vendetta" started in Williamson County and extended into Franklin and Jackson counties. Governor Palmer had offered a $1,000 reward for the arrest of night riders responsible for murders and whippings. Beveridge was convinced that the state could do little, and nothing happened when he reminded state's attorneys of their law enforcement responsibilities.

The disastrous and long-lasting Panic of 1873 arrived soon after his inauguration. The next year, the governor sent 100 rifles and ammunition to keep order in St. Clair County, where striking white union members, who had been paid four cents a bushel for digging coal, prevented black miners from working for three cents.

Beveridge was the first governor to occupy the executive suite in the unfinished Capitol building, on which construction continued until 1888.

He appointed an African American, John J. Bird of Cairo, as a trustee of the state industrial university that was renamed the University of Illinois.

For three years and 50 weeks, his conservative administration was generally satisfactory, and in 1876, he felt that as a loyal Republican, he deserved election to a full term. The *Chicago Tribune* was persistently hostile, however, and both political parties wanted to steer clear of temperance politics that might close saloons on Sundays, or close them altogether. Elihu B. Washburne of Galena, the minister to France, announced and then withdrew his candidacy for governor. The only other candidate of consequence was Shelby Cullom. The power of incumbency was not operative, and the Republican state convention voted for Cullom 389 to 87.

Retirement in the Private Sector

Out of office, Beveridge returned to Evanston to live. In Chicago, he was a partner in a private banking firm. In 1880, as a Republican national convention delegate, he supported Ulysses S. Grant for a third term. In 1881, President Chester Alan Arthur appointed him assistant United States treasurer at Chicago, an office he held until Grover Cleveland became president. In 1895, the former governor moved to Hollywood, California, where he died May 3, 1910.

Helen May Judson Beveridge

The first Beveridge home in Evanston; a second was built on the same lot. Neither is standing.

17th Governor

Shelby Moore Cullom
1829-1914

1829 — Born November 22 in Wayne County, Kentucky

1857 - 1859 — Serves in the House in the 20th General Assembly

1861 - 1863 — Serves as speaker of the House in the 22nd General Assembly

1862 — Loses an election for state senator

1864 — Begins the first of three terms in Congress

1870 — Loses a bid for a fourth term in Congress

1873 - 1877 — Serves in the House in the 28th and 29th General Assemblies; speaker of the House in the 28th Assembly

1876 — Survives the "Pekin whisky ring" scandal and rounds up enough delegates prior to the state convention to win the Republican gubernatorial nomination; defeats Lewis Steward in the closest general election since Edward Coles won in 1822

1880 — Wins a second term as governor

1883 — Resigns the governor's office to become U.S. senator

1883 - 1913 — Serves as U.S. senator from Illinois

1914 — Dies January 28

Republican
January 8, 1877 to January 10, 1881
January 10, 1881 to February 16, 1883

Shelby M. Cullom was an able, durable, rather colorless, and generally conservative Republican who sat out the Civil War. But he proved to be a better politician than the generals and colonels who for decades were his competitors. He was twice elected governor, resigned that office after six years, and then began a five-term, 30-year career in the U.S. Senate. Earlier service as state representative and congressman gave him a total of a half-century in public office, the last 40 years of which were continuous. When he finally retired, unwillingly, he was 83 years old. Of all of Illinois' governors, only Adlai E. Stevenson and Frank O. Lowden were better known nationally.

Cullom first established his reputation in Washington: He was a conservative who avoided extremes but wasn't always orthodox; he was a dependable Republican on roll-call voting; and he was known for his personal integrity. In the field of government, his greatest achievement was the creation of the Interstate Commerce Commission, the first step toward federal regulation of commerce. As speaker of the Illinois House of Representatives during the Granger era, he guided to enactment a law for state regulation of railroad rates that survived constitutional attacks. In the Senate, he saw that the problem was national and spent his first term creating the climate for passage of his regulatory bill. He was the first chairman of the Senate Interstate Commerce Committee and later held the Foreign Relations Committee chairmanship longer than any predecessor.

A tall and spare man, Cullom was proud to think that he "looked like Abraham Lincoln," who had been a friend of Cullom's father and in whose office the young Cullom had hoped to begin the study of law. Cullom's hair was black, his forehead high and massive, and his clear-cut features expressive. His speeches were convincing rather than oratorical. He was at his persuasive best in face-to-face explanations of his political and legislative plans.

Although Cullom was disappointed three times in his ambition to become president, his political astuteness was exceeded only by Lincoln's. An ego-centered lone wolf, who in his early career had been a well-paid lawyer and later a bank president, he instinctively understood how to get his colleagues to cooperate in solving governmental problems in ways that won public approval. People trusted him, and he had two special talents: He could appear to be favoring both sides of a question, and he could get elected with a minimum of personal effort. Most of the campaigns began with Cullom expecting to lose to generals or colonels who had popular followings at Republican conventions or to Democrats whose optimism increased when economic conditions were unfavorable. And he generally won those elections by narrow margins.

As Republican governor, he distributed state jobs to some Democrats and to spokesmen of Chicago ethnic groups. As senator, he headed a federal patronage organization that loyally and successfully supported him in election after election. Two of its leaders became federal judges. But "Uncle Shelby" seldom tried to influence the nomination of state candidates or to form alliances with other Republicans. The Cullom political machine was unique in that it cared only about Cullom. Between his reelection campaigns, it went into hibernation. Its inactivity encouraged other Republicans to think he could be beaten, but when the senator needed votes, his "federal crowd" efficiently spread the word that the voters should continue to trust the wise and experienced man who was respected and influential in Washington.

From Farm Boy to Congressman

Shelby Moore Cullom was the last of the governors from Kentucky. Born November 22, 1829, in Wayne County, he was the seventh of 12 children of Richard Northcraft Cullom and Elizabeth Coffey, who moved to a Tazewell County farm when Shelby was a year old. The father, an anti-slavery Whig of some prominence, served eight years in the Illinois legislature. On Lincoln's advice, young Shelby read law in the Springfield firm of John T. Stuart and Benjamin Edwards. The rest of his life he lived in Springfield or Washington.

In 1855, he was admitted to the bar, married, and entered politics. His first wife, Hannah Fisher, died within six years, leaving Cullom with two small daughters. In 1863, he married her sister, Julia. In his first campaign, he was elected city attorney. In 1856, he was defeated for presidential elector as a Know-Nothing and elected state representative by a local coalition of Republicans and Know-Nothings. A follower of Lincoln, he lost when he ran for reelection in 1858, but two years later, when the legislature for the first time was controlled by Republicans, he was the young speaker of the House at the opening of the Civil War. There he made a reputation as an efficient and harmonious presiding officer. In the Democratic mid-war sweep of 1862, he was defeated for state senator. Lincoln recognized him with an appointment to a commission that investigated claims involving army purchases at Cairo.

He never wore a Union uniform in the Civil War — and hence wasn't later eligible for membership in the politically powerful Grand Army of the Republic. He never mentioned the reason for his wartime civilian status in his speeches or memoirs. He had been a healthy Tazewell County farm boy. But, as a young man on his way to attend Rock River Seminary at Mount Morris, he became soaked and chilled while leading stagecoach horses through a heavy snowstorm. Thereafter, he was unable to do hard physical work due to a damaged heart. (He nevertheless completed the two-year course at the seminary.) After his death, an associate revealed that the senator — who was speaker of the Illinois House at the start of the Civil War and did not retire from public office until Woodrow Wilson entered the White House — was subject to fainting spells that fortunately never occurred in public.

Starting in 1861, he made money as the law partner of Milton Hay in Springfield. Because he wanted a political career most of all, he gave up a lucrative practice to become a congressman. He accumulated $30,000 and "never saw that much money again." He served three terms in Congress, starting in 1864. There, as chairman of the Committee on Territories, he introduced a bill to outlaw polygamy in Utah. Losing a fourth-term campaign in 1870, he returned to Springfield and briefly was president of the State National Bank. His stature was such that he was chairman of the Illinois delegation to the 1872 Republican national convention, where he placed President Ulysses S. Grant in nomination for a second term with the shortest speech on record, one sentence of 82 words:

> Gentlemen of the convention: On behalf of the great Republican Party of Illinois, and that of the Union — in the name of liberty, of loyalty, of justice, of law — in the interest of economy, of good government, of peace, and of the equal rights of all — remembering with profound gratitude his glorious achievements in the field, and his noble statesmanship as chief magistrate of this great nation — I nominate as President of the United States, for a second term, Ulysses S. Grant.

In the election of 1872, to help block a campaign to move the seat of state government to Peoria, Cullom won a return engagement to the legislature. Again elected speaker, he was primarily responsible for enactment of a law that achieved state regulation of railroad rates. The inflexible Granger laws in other states failed, and the Illinois Supreme Court upset rural voters by invalidating an 1871 law that forbade discrimination by passenger carriers. Cullom, who was a reasonable man, persuaded the legislature to provide that railroads charging more than a fair rate were guilty of extortion but allowed them to prove that their rates were justified.

Cullom was reelected to the House in 1874, but economic setbacks had reduced Republican numbers, and he lost the speakership to Elijah M. Haines, the only independent. He wanted to stay in politics and decided that his best chance was to run for governor.

A Close Win for Governor

For Cullom, winning was seldom easy. Governor John L. Beveridge, a cavalry general, controlled state patronage and wanted a full term. Two other generals, John I. Rinaker and Green B. Raum, were candidates, as were Thomas S. Ridgeway, the state treasurer, and Elihu B. Washburne, minister to France, who had *Chicago Tribune* backing. Before the nominating convention, Cullom's name was involved in a "Pekin whisky ring" scandal. While the other candidates called for his withdrawal, Cullom went before the Republican state committee and angrily denied any wrongdoing, after which the unproved charges were dropped. Cullom's friends contended that the teetotaling Beveridge had tried to inject the Pekin case into the campaign. It was the only hint of scandal ever raised against Cullom.

In a typical Cullom feat, the master politician solved his immediate troubles in advance of the state convention. In an era of increasing Republican factionalization, some of his opponents withdrew. Cullom rounded up more than a majority of the delegates in advance and achieved a first-ballot nomination on a conservative, hard-money platform. At the opening of the fall campaign, many expected that he would lose if Democrats and independents united against him. In 1876, the Democratic gubernatorial candidate was Lewis Steward, a white-haired farmer, manufacturer, and lawyer who had strong rural and independent backing as a result of the economic depression that began in 1873. In the two-man contest, Cullom won by 6,798 votes in the closest election since Edward Coles won in 1822. The result could have been even closer had former governor-turned-Democrat John M. Palmer actively supported Steward.

Despite the depression, which Cullom regarded as the inevitable result of a period of inflation and growth, the newly elected governor believed that the productive wealth of Illinois guaranteed an early return of prosperity. Instead of advocating new programs, he warned against legislative excesses. He regarded state government as a business enterprise dealing with the preservation of order, the enforcement of law, the punishment of lawbreakers, the care of the poor and unfortunate, and the education of the young. At the inaugural ceremony, Cullom devoted much of his message to a discussion of state revenues. He asked that the Illinois and Michigan Canal, largely obsolete in the railroad age, be modernized, extended to the Mississippi River, and ceded to the federal government.

Governor Cullom's first problem involved the railroads, which in the depression were having troubles with receiverships and strikes. Fortunately, the legislature followed his advice and reorganized the state militia, which had fallen into disrepair since the Civil War. Strikes in eastern cities caused considerable damage in the summer of 1877 before mobs in Chicago shut down several roads. Cullom used contingent funds to buy equipment for the untrained National Guard. He reminded the people of the right to assemble peacefully and then issued an ultimatum to the rioters. He asked for help from President Rutherford B. Hayes, who sent six companies of army regulars to the danger spot at Chicago, and peace was restored promptly. At East St. Louis, another trouble spot, Cullom personally took charge. When strikers disobeyed his orders that they allow trains to run, he called in militia regiments and 300 army regulars. There was little trouble at other rail centers in Illinois. The governor restored order without loss of life or damage to property.

Cullom's Second Term

At the 1880 Republican state convention, the governor remained neutral during a bitter factional fight that ended when Ulysses S. Grant was given the endorsement for a third term. Charles B. Farwell, a leader among Chicago Republicans, supported James G. Blaine of Maine. In an anticlimax, six men wanted to replace Cullom, who needed state patronage to win second-term renomination on the fourth roll call. Former Governor Richard J. Oglesby started and finished in second place. In the November campaign, he had two opponents: former Senator Lyman Trumbull ran as a Democrat, and Alson J. Streeter ran as a third party candidate. Cullom was reelected with 50.6 percent of the vote.

Thirty-four years after Thomas Ford retired as governor, Cullom announced at the start of his second term that Illinois was debt-free. Through the frugality of eight governors and 17 legislatures, the state paid the last cent of, and interest on, the $16 million liability incurred in the visionary era when legislators believed that profits from state banks could pay for state-owned railroads. Governor Ford correctly predicted that the state's population would expand so rapidly that the debt could be retired by a relatively small tax. A tax on the Illinois Central Railroad itself and the post-war currency inflation helped, but the main factor in debt retirement was the growth of farming and commerce in the post-frontier decades.

Afraid to run for a third term as governor in 1884, Cullom set his sites on the U.S. Senate. The opportunity came when his party won control of the 1883 legislature. A deadlocked legislature sent independent Supreme Court Justice David A. Davis to the Senate in 1877. But there was no way he would be reelected by the 1883 Republican legislature. Farwell, who wanted a Chicago senator (meaning himself), Oglesby, and two other downstate generals were the 1883 Republican candidates, but the party powerbrokers were unable to agree which one should have their united support. At the Republican caucus, Cullom won on the fifth ballot. In advance, he submitted a legal brief contending that, regardless of the 1870 Constitution, he had the right to switch offices in midterm.

The Grand Old Senator from Illinois

Before the U.S. Supreme Court in 1886 held that states could not control interstate commerce, the deliberate-minded Cullom concluded that some federal control was essential if railroads were to be regulated. Only the Illinois Granger law, drafted by Cullom when he was in the Illinois House in 1873, established a degree of flexibility that met judicial approval. Given that track record, he accepted the chairmanship of the Committee on Commerce, an unattractive assignment in the senatorial hierarchy, and presided at a series of regional hearings at which carriers, shippers, and the public were consulted. The bill he introduced included the Illinois theory that the basic evil was unjust discrimination in rail rates but that some discrimination, such as long- and short-haul situations, might be proper.

In the U.S. Senate, Cullom needed all of his negotiating talents to guide to final passage in 1887 a law that created the Interstate Commerce Commission. Experts were provided to deal with transportation problems as they arose. Congress did not give the commission power to fix rates, and the burden of proof rested with the injured shipper, but those defects were gradually corrected.

The first-term senator built his political machine around John R. Tanner, a state senator from Clay County who soon went on the federal payroll as United States marshal for southern Illinois. A genius in political organization, he was Cullom's chief political operator until the end of the century, when their ambitions clashed. Cullom's "federal crowd" included judges, prosecutors, court officials, postmasters, and revenue collectors in every county and district. Sol R. Bethea of Dixon and J. Otis Humphrey of Springfield, influential lawyers, were key figures whose awards were appointments to the federal bench. W. A. Northcott, who became lieutenant governor, also was a key figure in the Cullom machine.

Tanner and the other federal employees soon proved their effectiveness, but they failed three times to get their leader an Illinois favorite-son endorsement for the presidency. In 1888, when first terms ended for Cullom and President Grover Cleveland, Joseph Medill of the *Chicago Tribune* favored Walter Q. Gresham for president. Cullom never announced that he wanted his name presented to the party's national convention, which nominated Benjamin Harrison for president. Cullom settled for a second term in the Senate. For the only time in his long career, he was nominated without opposition. When the legislature met in 1889 with Republican majorities, the senator stayed in Washington knowing that in Springfield, Tanner had his reelection well under control.

Early in 1894, he went so far as to say that he wouldn't turn down support for the presidency, but Illinois Republicans wanted James G. Blaine of Maine. With John P. Altgeld in the governor's office, Cleveland in the White House, and the country in an economic collapse, the prospect seemed hopeless; but, out of a sense of duty, Cullom campaigned loyally for his party's legislative candidates. When the election went Republican, several others, including Medill, became interested in going to the U.S.

Senate, but Tanner kept the factional confusion under control. Only one other name was presented to the caucus when Cullom won a third term with apparent ease.

Cullom was 66 years old before his presidential ambitions finally died. He hoped that the 1896 boom for William McKinley would collapse, but Charles G. Dawes, newly arrived in Chicago, prevented it. Tanner, who wanted his own political career, was elected governor. In 1900, Tanner could have had a second term with Cullom's support, but he announced his candidacy for Cullom's seat in the U.S. Senate instead. Tanner made maximum use of gubernatorial patronage, but he withdrew just before the Republican state convention. Three congressmen, including Joseph G. Cannon of Danville, also were interested in the Senate but failed to unite. The outlook seemed uncertain when the legislature met, but the Cullom forces had quietly obtained written pledges from a majority of the members. A byproduct of that campaign was an increased interest in replacing boss-controlled conventions with a direct primary system.

In Washington, the senator had accumulated enough seniority to trade the Interstate Commerce Committee chairmanship for that of the Foreign Relations Committee. His experience in that field included the chairmanship of a committee on Cuban relations during the Civil War and the chairmanship of a special committee that drafted the system of government of the Philippine Islands as a United States territory.

In 1906, Illinois partisan battles were renewed in an effort to send Richard Yates, son of the Civil War governor, to the U.S. Senate. Yates, who won the governorship in 1900 as a dark horse in a factional war, lost it in 1904 but believed that he had high-level promises that would allow him to replace Cullom. Again there was a great fracturing of alliances, and the senator had the support in Cook County of Congressman William Lorimer, a Republican wire-puller, and some allies of Governor Charles S. Deneen. Yates, who had lackluster campaigning talents, conceded defeat before the 1907 legislative session opened. One of Yates' difficulties was that Cullom again was backed by his long-time Republican colleagues.

Cullom, who was the dean of the Senate in years of service and the second-oldest senator, vacillated about retirement but finally decided that he would try for a sixth term in 1912. He was concerned about public reaction to his 1911 votes: first to acquit William Lorimer, who had been accused of buying a Senate seat by bribing legislators, and then for a second Senate investigation of the allegations concerning his new colleague. Cullom eventually announced that he would permit his name to be entered for the first time in a U.S. Senate primary election.

Under a new law, the primary was advisory only, but the senior senator said he would abide by the voters' choice.

Cullom's "federal crowd" found that primary campaigning was both expensive and required new techniques. Cullom's time-tried issue, that he deserved another term because of experience, wasn't enough. He finished second behind Lawrence Y. Sherman, a former speaker of the Illinois House who also looked something like Lincoln. In mid-summer, after he cast a soul-wrenching vote to unseat Lorimer, Cullom announced that he was retiring. He did not ask the 1913 legislature to elect him a sixth time, and thus kept his word to abide by the primary's outcome.

Two days before he left the Senate, as a final honor, his colleagues made him special resident commissioner to supervise construction of the Lincoln Memorial at Washington.

Cullom, the last surviving member of the Lincoln funeral party, lived another year. He died January 28, 1914, and was brought back to Springfield for burial in Oak Ridge Cemetery.

Courtesy of the Abraham Lincoln Presidential Library

Julia Fisher Cullom

18th Governor

John Marshall Hamilton
1847-1905

1847 — Born May 28 near Richwood, Ohio
1870 — Admitted to the bar
1877 - 1881 — Serves as a senator in the 30th and 31st General Assemblies
1880 — Wins nomination for lieutenant governor when incumbent Andrew Shuman falls
victim to partisan infighting
1883 — Assumes the governorship on February 16 when Cullom resigns to become U.S.
senator
1884 — Is overlooked as a gubernatorial candidate as the troubled Republican Party nominates
the tried-and-true Richard Oglesby for his third term as governor
1886 — Is an unsuccessful candidate to fill the slot of deceased U.S. Senator John A. Logan;
turns his attention to his Chicago law practice
1905 — Dies September 22

Republican
February 16, 1883 to January 30, 1885

John Marshall Hamilton was nine months past his 35th birthday when he began serving the final two years of Governor Shelby M. Cullom's second term in 1883. Two years earlier, he was elected lieutenant governor because he was a standpat Republican and, as a young state senator, made a reputation as an able legal draftsman and parliamentarian.

The Learned Politician

The future governor was born May 28, 1847, in a log cabin near Richwood, Union County, Ohio. His father, Samuel Hamilton, was the son and nephew of pioneer Methodist preachers in Ohio. His mother, who had been Mrs. Nancy McMorris, was a Virginian. When John was 7 years old, the family loaded two wagons and made a three-week journey to a farm that had been selected in advance in Roberts Township, Marshall County, in north central Illinois. For John's early education, more credit goes to his mother than to the few months he spent in country schools.

His family opposed slavery, and the boy saved money to buy a uniform to march with a company of Lincoln Wide-Awakes — the first association of young Republicans — in parades in 1860. He wanted to go to war with his drill team, which formed the nucleus of a militia company, but was rejected because of his youth. During the winter of 1863-1864, he attended a Methodist academy at Henry.

Accompanied by 13 neighbor boys, he escaped farm work at the age of 17 by going to Elgin, where he was accepted by the 141st Illinois Volunteers, a 100-day regiment that served uneventfully in southwestern Kentucky. He was promoted to corporal.

Upon discharge, he taught school for a year then entered Ohio Wesleyan University, where he completed the three-year classical course with honors. In 1871, the university awarded him a master's degree. Hamilton thus became the first Illinois governor to hold a graduate degree and was the best-educated in the 19th century.

Hamilton was ambitious to become a lawyer. He moved to Bloomington and studied law in the offices of Weldon, Tipton and Benjamin, whose partners were political activists and future judges. For one year, he also taught Latin at Illinois Wesleyan University in Bloomington. In 1870, he was admitted to the bar. The next year he married Helen Williams, daughter of the professor of Greek at Ohio Wesleyan. They became the parents of a son and two daughters.

As the partner of J. H. Rowell, a future congressman, Hamilton rose rapidly in the law and Republican politics. In 1876, at the age of 29, he defeated a Democratic-Greenback candidate for state senator.

Hamilton immediately took a prominent role in Springfield and earned the friendship of John A. Logan, a candidate for a second term in the U.S. Senate. In a long deadlock, Hamilton voted for Logan on every ballot.

Hamilton had an unusual memory for the statutes and was recognized for his uncommon talent for writing legislation. He was sponsor of the bar association bill that established the appellate court system as a means of reducing the Supreme Court's workload. He successfully handled controversial legislation that created a State Board of Health and reorganized the militia. With only two years' experience, he was made president pro tem of the Illinois Senate in 1879. In that capacity, he helped Logan return to the U.S. Senate over the opposition of Richard J. Oglesby.

The Two-Year Governor

At their 1880 state convention, Republicans fought for three days before endorsing Ulysses S. Grant for a third term as president. Governor Cullom won a renomination contest, but most of the other state officials lost in the factional fighting. One of the casualties was Lieutenant Governor Andrew Shuman, editor and publisher of the *Chicago Journal*, who was replaced by Hamilton. Two years later, when Cullom resigned and was elected senator, Hamilton was quietly inaugurated governor.

In an unusual assertion of executive power, Hamilton reversed the official 1884 election showing that by 10 votes Rudolph Brand, a Democrat, had defeated Republican Henry W. Lemen for state senator in a Chicago district. Affidavits collected by the State Board of Canvassers showed that Lemen won by 390 votes. Under those circumstances, the governor assumed a judicial function and issued a certificate of election to Lemen. As a result, the Senate had a Republican majority.

During his quiet two years in office, Hamilton sided with temperance forces and signed the Harper "high license" bill, soon repealed, that allowed municipalities to suppress the number of saloons by requiring $500 licenses. He also signed the first compulsory education law.

A Life Away from Politics

In 1884, Hamilton wanted election to a full four-year term, but the Republican Party was in trouble and again needed "Uncle Dick" Oglesby at the head of the state ticket. Two years later, the death of U.S. Senator John A. Logan left Hamilton without high-level sponsorship. When he and seven others became candidates for the Logan vacancy, the Republican caucus selected Charles B. Farwell, who became the first senator from Chicago since Stephen A. Douglas and Lyman Trumbull.

Hamilton's future was in the law rather than politics. When his term as governor ended, he went back to Bloomington but soon moved his law practice to Chicago. He died in Chicago on September 22, 1905.

Courtesy of the Abraham Lincoln Presidential Library

"Flying Squadron" campaign for Tanner in 1896; sitting, from left, John L. Beveridge, Richard J. Oglesby, Shelby M. Cullom, John M. Hamilton; standing, from left, John C. Smith, John R. Tanner, James Van Cleve, Joseph W. Fifer, and Lyman R. Ray

19th Governor

Joseph Wilson Fifer
1840-1938

1840 — Born October 28 in Staunton, Virginia
1857 — Family moves to McLean County, Illinois
1863 — Wounded after the fall of Vicksburg
1868 — Graduates from Illinois Wesleyan University
1869 — Admitted to the bar
1881 - 1885 — Serves as senator in the 32nd and 33rd General Assemblies
1888 — Wins the Republican gubernatorial nomination; defeats former Governor and Civil War General John Palmer in the general election
1891 — Illinois women granted the right to vote in school elections; Illinois adopts the secret ballot.
1892 — Renominated for governor by Republicans, but loses to John Altgeld in the general election
1899 — Is appointed to the Interstate Commerce Commission
1900 — Refuses to run for governor
1903 — Reappointed to the Interstate Commerce Commission
1906 — Leaves the Commerce Commission for health reasons
1920 — Serves as a delegate to the state constitutional convention (Voters would reject the convention's proposal in 1922.)
1924 — Fifer's daughter, Florence Fifer Bohrer, is elected the first female state senator in Illinois.
1938 — Dies August 6

Republican
January 14, 1889 to January 10, 1893

A quarter of a century after the Civil War, Joseph Wilson "Private Joe" Fifer acquired his nickname and became governor of Illinois because he had the temerity to argue with a general. The issue was Fifer's $24-a-month pension paid for wounds in the right lung and liver suffered nine days after the fall of Vicksburg. A former state senator from Bloomington, he became an instant celebrity. As a spokesman for the common soldier, he defeated six former officers for the Republican nomination for governor. Then he was elected over former governor and Civil War general John M. Palmer, the state's strongest Democrat. Elevated to the governorship, he was less conservative than the Republican leadership.

For his popularity, Fifer was indebted to General John C. Black, a Danville Democrat who was commissioner of pensions in the first Grover Cleveland administration. In testimony before a U.S. Senate committee and in a letter to a Washington newspaper, Black cited Fifer as a typical Republican politician who did not deserve his pension. Fifer defended his personal honor with a sarcastic and incisive letter that was widely circulated by the Republican press and praised at meetings of the Grand Army of the Republic posts. Offering to compare wounds with the general, he said his pension was paid at the standard rate for common soldiers, but that Black, by a special law, received a pension of $100 a month.

A tall and slender man with black hair, "Private Joe" was a moderate Republican who kept state government on an even keel, did not attempt to be a factional leader, avoided partisanship, and worked well with Democrats.

Young Private Joe

He was born at Staunton, Virginia, on October 28, 1840, the third of five children of John and Mary Wilson Fifer. In 1857, they moved to Danvers, Illinois, in McLean County, where his father, a farmer and mason, operated a brickyard. At the start of the war, he enlisted. When wounded, he refused a discharge and, upon recovery, was assigned to guard a prison boat. After the war, he lived over a downtown store, slept on a straw bed, and did his own cooking and laundry while studying law at Illinois Wesleyan University. While still in school, he was elected tax collector of Danvers Township, which paid a welcome $300 a year. In 1870, a year after being admitted to the bar, he married Gertrude Lewis. The couple had two children.

He was elected Bloomington city attorney and then state's attorney for two terms. In 1880, he went to the state Senate as replacement for John M. Hamilton, the new lieutenant governor. After serving in the Illinois Senate, he went back to his Bloomington law practice. He wasn't well-known outside of McLean County until Black attempted to reduce the pension rolls.

Governor Fifer and the "Little Red Schoolhouse" Issue

The publicity over Fifer's celebrated response to Black caused state Treasurer John R. Tanner to recognize Fifer's potential as a candidate. Tanner lined up the support of Chicago factional leaders. At the 1888 Republican state convention, Fifer was nominated on the fourth ballot over three generals, one colonel, one major, and one captain. The best known of his opponents was another Bloomington lawyer, General John McNulta. In the November election, Fifer won by 12,547 votes over another general, former Governor John M. Palmer.

Fifer conducted the state's business with a staff of three — a private secretary, a stenographer, and a messenger — in the public reception room. He took credit for "enlightened" policies, such as the Australian ballot, which provided that ballots be furnished by the state rather than the political parties. It was a major step toward honest elections and a forerunner of the Progressive movement.

The most controversial event of his administration was enactment in 1889 of a compulsory education law requiring that children in both public and parochial schools be taught reading, writing, arithmetic, history, and geography, all in English, to age 12. There was general dissatisfaction with public education, and Fifer in his inaugural message also asked for a stronger teacher certification law. Written by Richard Edwards, former normal school president who was state superintendent of public instruction, the compulsory school law was enacted with bipartisan support. Complaints soon were heard from German Lutherans who did not want their children educated in English and from Catholics who did not want truant officers coming into their schools. The "little red schoolhouse" became a political issue in Fifer's bid for a second term.

The legislature permitted women to vote in some school elections, outlawed child labor under 13 years (a statute that was not enforced because it contained loopholes), authorized construction of an asylum for insane criminals at Menard, created the Chicago sanitary district, and approved financing for the 1893 World's Columbian Exposition in Chicago. Bills that would have fulfilled some campaign promises to working men and farmers were defeated.

On the convention's first ballot, Fifer beat out four candidates for the Republican nomination for a second term as governor. But Private Joe lost the 1892 general election by 22,872 votes to John Peter Altgeld, another Civil War private. The German-born Altgeld had supported the legislation requiring English-only school instruction in 1889. But by the 1892 campaign, he was blaming Fifer for its passage.

Part of Fifer's legacy to Altgeld was a "basketful of documents" relating to pardon petitions for the remaining men convicted in the 1886 Haymarket bombing case. Fifer received these papers late in his administration, and he planned to give their consideration high priority if reelected. But upon losing the election, he left the matter to Altgeld.

The Old Soldier

During Altgeld's administration, Fifer's Civil War wounds started to become bothersome, and Fifer never campaigned again. He refused to run for governor in 1900. Like many top-level Republicans in an era of political factionalism, he frequently changed allies. At the start of his administration, he appointed Tanner, his original mentor, to the Railroad and Warehouse Commission but soon disagreed with him. He was an enemy of Senator Shelby Cullom in 1891 but his friend the next year. As permanent chairman of the 1900 Republican state convention, he was on Cullom's side against Tanner. One of his closest friends was his predecessor, Richard J. Oglesby, who, when Fifer was in office, had enjoyed a standing invitation to be an overnight guest at the Executive Mansion. Milton Hay, Springfield's leading lawyer, usually joined them in late-night discussions. In his later years, Fifer said nothing about Republican rivalries when he recalled that he enjoyed harmonious relations with other state officers, the legislature, and the public.

He was appointed to the Interstate Commerce Commission by President William McKinley in 1899 and reappointed by Theodore Roosevelt in 1903. Because of his health, he resigned three years later and lived in a tent in his Bloomington yard for several months. In 1918, he took his turn as state Grand Army of the Republic commander. In 1920, his name appeared on the ballot for the last time when he was elected a constitutional convention delegate. His unheeded advice was that the delegates amend the 1870 Constitution but not attempt to replace it.

The badly wounded soldier became an elder statesman who was respected by both parties longer than any other governor. James O'Donnell Bennett, who for four days in 1933 interviewed Fifer for the *Chicago Tribune*, marveled at his memory, lucidity, and knowledge of the classics. He had the respect of later governors, especially Frank Lowden and Henry Horner, who were among frequent callers at the home of the political link connecting two Illinois centuries.

The former governor lived 14 years after his daughter, Florence Fifer Bohrer, was elected the first woman state senator in 1924. When he was 92, both legs were broken when he was hit by an automobile. He was blind, deaf, and crippled before he died on August 6, 1938. He was 97 years old.

Private Joe Fifer in his Civil War uniform; he was wounded at Vicksburg, and his fight with the bureaucracy to be paid his promised $24-a-month pension earned him celebrity and popularity with the common soldier.

This store at Division and Noble in Chicago was headquarters in 1890 for the Kosciusko Guards, a militia made up mainly of Polish businessmen and named after a Polish noble who fought in the Revolutionary War.

Chicago's State Street dressed up for the dedication of the 1893 World's Columbian Exposition; in its six months, nearly 27 million people visited the fair, which made a $1 million profit.

20th Governor

John Peter Altgeld
1847-1902

1847 —Born December 30 in Germany

1875 —Moves to Chicago to begin a career as a lawyer and real estate developer

1884 —Finances his own unsuccessful bid for Congress

1886 —Elected judge of the Superior Court of Cook County by a coalition of Democrats and members of the United Labor Party; on May 4, police move to break up a labor rally in Haymarket Square in Chicago. A bomb explodes, injuring and killing several people, including seven police officers. Governor Richard J. Oglesby commutes to life imprisonment the death sentences of two of several anarchists convicted in the case. Four others were hanged November 11, 1887.

1890 —Assembles a dozen liberal articles and letters into a book, *Live Questions*

1892 —Wins the gubernatorial election

1893 —Grants outright pardons to the three surviving anarchist prisoners convicted in the Haymarket bombing

1894 —A general railway strike from May to July is precipitated by a workers' strike at the Pullman Car Company. President Grover Cleveland sends federal troops to break up the strike, even though Altgeld never asks him for assistance.

1896 —Helps turn the Democratic National Convention in Chicago against President Cleveland; the party nominates William Jennings Bryan for president; Altgeld loses his reelection bid to John R. Tanner.

1899 —Loses his bid for mayor of Chicago

1900 —Is denied delegate credentials to the 1900 Democratic convention at Kansas City

1902 —Dies March 13 in Joliet

Democrat
January 10, 1893 to January 11, 1897

John Peter Altgeld was the first liberal governor of Illinois. The German-born son of peasants was undersized and undereducated, but he possessed a superior intellect and massive ambition coupled with compassion for the underprivileged. Also, he was a master politician. He started with as many handicaps as Lincoln and became the first governor from Chicago, the first foreign-born governor, and the first Democratic governor in 36 years.

Since John M. Palmer, Illinois governors had moved slowly from the traditional conservatism that still characterized not only the Republican leadership but also a large sector of Democratic opinion. Altgeld's hopes for the future required caution in dealing with traditionally conservative lawmakers. For that reason, he was a closet liberal during the first five months of his turbulent administration. But, when all was said and done, Altgeld philosophically turned out to be a governor markedly different from any Illinois had seen in a long while.

Altgeld had several careers. In clear and fact-filled prose, he wrote books that were admired by opinion-makers. Overcoming a slight harelip, he became an effective public speaker. Instead of taking time to develop a profitable law practice, he speculated in Chicago real estate, constructed downtown buildings, and achieved the shaky status of paper millionaire. Downstaters admired his business success when he sought the Democratic nomination for governor. In his unusual campaign for governor, he refused contributions and spent $100,000 of his own money, which no candidate for governor had done before.

The Rise of a Chicago Liberal

The son of John Peter and Mary Altgeld, the future governor was born December 30, 1847, in the village of Nieder Selters, in the Prussian province of Nassau. Three months later, his wagonmaker father took his family to a farm near Mansfield, Ohio. In his boyhood, "Young Pete" was required to work as hard as a man, without wages but with paternal beatings. For one winter and two summer terms, he went to a country school. He escaped from farm work briefly during the Civil War by enlisting in a 100-day regiment and giving his father all but $10 of his $100 bonus. In eastern Virginia, where the regiment served uneventfully, he caught "Chickahominy fever," a malarial-type infection from which he never fully recovered. When he returned home, his father objected but he went to high school for one term and to a select school for three months, long enough to qualify for a teacher's certificate. At 19, he began earning $35 a month as a teacher. All of it went toward paying for his father's farm.

At 21, free from parental domination and rejected by a girl from a prosperous family, he tramped westward. In Kansas, he worked as a railroad section hand until the recurrent fever sent him to a hospital. When partially recovered, he wandered into northwestern Missouri. At Savannah, Andrew County, he found a teaching job and began a white-collar career. He read books, was admitted to the bar, and demonstrated a capacity for getting people to like and help him. Trying his hand at politics, he controlled the local Democratic convention. Endorsed also by the local Grange, he was elected county prosecutor.

He stood a half-inch more than five-feet-six. He had uneven features and unruly hair, but he grew a neatly trimmed Vandyke beard and bought comparatively expensive clothing, signs that he was ambitious to advance in the world. For Altgeld, one year as county prosecutor was enough. In 1875, four years after arriving in Savannah, he resigned.

With the $100 he earned from the sales of his law books, he took a train to Chicago, a city of strangers.

Altgeld opened a law office and slept in it until he became solvent. Lacking time to practice liberalism, he cultivated the acquaintance of important men who helped him find clients. As soon as he saved $500, he began buying and selling real estate. Two years after his arrival in Chicago, he went back to Mansfield, Ohio, and married Emma Ford, a school teacher. He was a lawyer with corporate clients, but chiefly he was a businessman who erected commercial and office buildings. His big ambition was to own a tall building that would be one of Chicago's showplaces. (But not until the early 1890s did he erect the Unity Block, 12 stories high, at what is now 127 North Dearborn Street.)

In English and German, Altgeld made liberal speeches to available audiences. By 1884, he collected enough important friends to run for Congress in a heavily Republican district. Minority parties in such situations did not discourage volunteer candidates, especially if they financed their own campaigns. In defeat he was impressive: He polled more votes than a more prominent Democrat had two years earlier. While he campaigned, he wrote and published, apparently at his own expense, his first book, *Our Penal Machinery and Its Victims*. It blamed crime on urban conditions and denounced the judicial system that was more concerned with learned precedents than with justice for the young defendants who were filling jails. The book established Altgeld's credentials as a liberal and widened his acquaintance. One of the lawyers to whom he sent autographed copies was young Clarence Darrow, thereafter his admirer and friend.

Altgeld continued his part-time career as a writer of essays that he submitted to editors and of letters mailed to officials and opinion-makers. One of the first, printed by the *Chicago Evening Mail* in 1886, urged that strikes be settled by arbitration. It marked his first public stand on the side of labor and appeared a week before the bombing in Haymarket Square that broke up a meeting called to protest police brutality. In 1890, he assembled a dozen articles and letters into the first edition of a new book, *Live Questions*, of which *Our Penal Machinery and Its Victims* took up the final 174 pages.

"The Little Dutchman" had friends in a short-lived United Labor Party that, in a coalition with Democrats, elected him judge of the Superior Court of Cook County in 1886. Meanwhile, he did not join the 60,000 Chicagoans who signed clemency petitions for the professed anarchists who were later hanged for the Haymarket bombing.

Altgeld's service as a judge was marked not so much by liberal stands as by instances of questionable personal ethics. In 1891, he sent Darrow to Springfield when the legislature again deadlocked in a Senate election. He tried to sway votes away from the eventual winner, John M. Palmer, the Democratic Party's endorsed candidate and thereafter Altgeld's enemy. The judge sued the city of Chicago on a claim that one of his properties had been damaged by a change in the street grade. He was fined $100 for writing a contemptuous letter to three appellate court judges. In a spirit of revenge, he spent $5,000 to help defeat Mayor John Roche.

The Progressive Administration

After five years as a judge, he resigned and ran for governor with support that ranged from upper-crust liberals to the ranks of Germans and labor. Downstate Democrats, who hadn't been enthusiastic when Chicago Mayor Carter Harrison ran for governor in 1884, did not object to "the man with a barrel," who paid for his own campaign.

His downstate opposition was divided, and Altgeld, running as a law-and-order candidate, was nominated on the first ballot at the Democratic state convention. In early summer, far in advance of the traditional campaign season, he began an energetic tour, during which he charged that Republicans had mismanaged state government. Repeatedly, he displayed unusual finesse in putting his opposition on the defensive. He blamed his opponent, Governor Joseph W. Fifer, for the 1889 compulsory education law that Altgeld himself helped pass but that turned out to be unpopular among Lutherans and Catholics. Altgeld's campaign style was to work hard and to answer every opposition charge with a counter charge of his own.

Spending his own money helped him take on the protective coloration of apparent conservatism. In the past, both parties were equally conservative. There was some variation at the leadership level, however, and the governors tended to be less conservative than other party leaders. For example, Palmer, who was a conservative governor, had turned pro-labor and anti-corporation after he returned to the Democratic Party. Among Republicans, Beveridge was something of a progressive, although hardly a liberal, and Fifer was elected as a friend of the working man and common soldier. While Altgeld sought to broaden his base of support, he did not rush espousal of liberal causes.

With Democrats leading the state and national tickets, Altgeld defeated Fifer by just under 23,000 votes. On his coattails the Democrats elected legislative majorities.

However, instead of taking a vacation, the governor-elect overtaxed his strength by accepting invitations to establishment dinners and receptions. Exhausted physically and suffering from a bad cold, against his doctor's wishes he went to Springfield for an overcrowded swearing-in ceremony that resembled Andrew Jackson's presidential inauguration in 1828.

Obviously ill, Altgeld arrived at his inauguration on Fifer's arm and could read only the opening paragraphs of his inaugural speech. The long and rather innocuous inaugural message contained good advice in vague terms that would not alarm members of the establishment. The new governor mentioned the possibility of inheritance and corporation taxes but hardly endorsed them and referred vaguely to municipal ownership of utilities. He also pointed out the need for a constitutional convention. (The Senate, but not the House, agreed with him.) The message lamented that an "ever increasing proliferation of boards and commissions, each dealing with an isolated problem" added to governmental complications. Because there was no centralized supervision of state funds, the governor called it "a notorious fact" that custodians of public funds, state treasurers among them, pocketed the interest on bank balances. (Both of those situations would not receive corrective action until the next century.)

That evening, he attended part of a reception at which the crowd was so large that Adlai E. Stevenson, the vice president-elect, could not squeeze into the room. Then Mrs. Altgeld insisted that her husband go to Asheville, North Carolina, to rest, and Altgeld missed more than a month of the legislative session. Speaker Clayton E. Crafts, a Chicagoan, ran the House of Representatives without too much attention to the absent governor's wishes.

As a candidate for governor in 1892, Altgeld followed Democratic custom and complained about high taxes under Republican administrations. Once in office, however, he abandoned the emphasis on economy, and he did not hesitate to spend treasury surpluses and raise the state levy on property. As part of his progressive administration, he increased appropriations for the University of Illinois and encouraged its expansion in the fields of medicine and science. He was responsible for the opening of normal schools at DeKalb and Charleston, hospitals for the insane at East Moline and near Peoria, and the home for soldiers' widows at Wilmington. One of his appointees, Florence Kelley, a protégé of Jane Addams, rigidly enforced a labor law requiring inspection of factories. The law also limited employment of women to eight hours a day and strengthened an earlier child-labor statute. Regulation of insurance companies was strengthened.

However, common school education took a step backward under Altgeld. Four years earlier, he supported the Fifer Administration's compulsory education law. In his campaign of 1892, Altgeld switched sides and made opposition to the legislation his chief issue among Germans and Catholics. In office, he made good on an unwise pledge to the voters and signed the repealer. The Altgeld Administration did nothing to increase school financing.

Altgeld's Financial and Physical Woes

Financial scandals in his administration embarrassed the governor. Harry Barnard's biography, *Eagle Forgotten: The Life of John Peter Altgeld*, says that an audit — brought about by the 1894 discovery that Treasurer Rufus N. Ramsey was some $300,000 short in his accounts — uncovered $50,000 worth of Altgeld's promissory notes that were part of the state treasury. Altgeld apparently borrowed the money to help with his Unity Block development project in Chicago. The governor's friends were reported to have covered up the transaction and repaid the $50,000.

Altgeld's physical and financial condition deteriorated during his governorship. Hard work and mental stress were punctuated by occasional illnesses. During his second year in office, he was diagnosed as having multiple sclerosis. The Unity Block, a financial albatross, suffered from absentee management, and the governor lost his status as a paper millionaire. (Unable to meet bond payments, he would lose the building in an 1899 foreclosure.)

To attest to Altgeld's personal honesty, there is evidence that he rejected a bribe that would have ended his personal financial troubles and saved the Unity Block. Author Harry Barnard is convinced that Charles T. Yerkes, the key figure in the Chicago traction industry, offered the governor from $100,000 to $1 million if he would sign legislation to extend maximum streetcar franchises from 20 to 50 years. (Edward F. Dunne, who became the next Democratic governor, told of congratulating Altgeld, then out of office, for turning down $1 million. He says that Altgeld replied that the amount was a half-million.)

The Haymarket Pardons and the Pullman Strike

The turning point in Altgeld's career came as a result of the fallout of the 1886 Haymarket bombing case. In the early months of his administration, Altgeld ignored requests that he free the three anarchists who had not been hanged for the bombing. Many prominent men favored clemency, and many thought public opinion would accept their release on grounds of mercy. The governor studied the trial record and collected *ex parte* information about police brutality at the rally. On June 26, 1893, without advanced notice, he granted pardons.

His courageous but belligerent 18,000-word justification of the decision made him the most hated man in Illinois. In complete detail, he criticized the judge, jury, prosecution, and police, especially Judge Joseph E. Gary and Police Inspector John Bonfield. Later generations believed Altgeld acted properly when he held that the trial six years earlier was unfair, the jury packed, and the judge prejudiced. In 1893, however, the pardon was a public relations disaster. The public, which hysterically feared a reign of terror by bomb-throwing foreigners, believed criticism of the judge and police was the equivalent of attacking law and order. The newspapers, with the *Chicago Tribune* in the lead, began a vilification of the governor. Outside of liberal and labor circles, John "Pardon" Altgeld's reservoir of goodwill dried up.

Altgeld, who had told friends he would do justice to the anarchists whatever the consequences, could have released them without passing on guilt or innocence. Instead, with a display of venom, he shortened his career and handicapped the Democratic Party. An explanation might be that Judge Gary had just written for *Century* magazine an article belittling the anarchists and their defenders.

The governor's unpopularity increased as a result of his 1894 quarrel with President Grover Cleveland over the unrequested use of federal troops in the American Railway Union's strike. Like the governor, socialist union organizer Eugene V. Debs, who called the strike, sympathized with the starving residents of the company town owned by George M. Pullman, the sleeping car manufacturer. Like predecessor governors, Altgeld called out state troops to maintain order during strikes at Lemont and elsewhere. He insisted, however, that they must not be used as strikebreakers. The president sent army units to Chicago, although Altgeld, at the request of Mayor John P. Hopkins, had dispatched two brigades of National Guardsmen. Altgeld protested the action as well as the Justice Department's use of injunctions to break the rail strike. He was accused of siding with strikers who were acting in open violation of the law, triggering a new wave of vilification that was not limited to Illinois newspapers.

Politically Undone, Altgeld Flexes His Muscles

Nationally, the 1894 midterm election showed a Republican trend that in Illinois was increased by anti-Altgeld sentiment. By margins of 130,000, Republicans were elected state treasurer and superintendent of public instruction. Both houses of the new legislature had strong Republican majorities, and Shelby Moore Cullom was elected to a third term in the U.S. Senate. The minority Democrats did not offer Altgeld as their choice for senator.

His personnel record was mixed. More than his predecessors, Altgeld closely supervised administrative agencies. Believing that good government required frequent turnovers, he arbitrarily fired a number of top-level officials, including the eminent Frederick H. Wines, who for years had been secretary of the State Board of Public Charities. One downstate editor called Altgeld a poor judge of men who was inclined to consider party loyalty more important than personal integrity. On the other hand, he signed a bill, a forerunner of the Progressive movement, that permitted some municipalities to adopt civil service.

Though it destroyed his electability, the Haymarket pardon did not terminate Altgeld's political influence, and the 1896 Democratic national convention at Chicago was the setting of his greatest triumph. A populist whose political career began as a Grangerite prosecutor in rural Missouri, he was a bimetallist who wanted to increase the supply of money by coining silver at a ratio of 16-to-1 with gold. Unlike John Palmer, Grover Cleveland, and prominent Chicago Democrats, he believed that the gold standard was a chief cause for widespread poverty. He opened the convention with an eloquent attack on the gold standard. In firm control, he wrote the platform that repudiated Cleveland by taking stands for free coinage of silver, a tariff for revenue only, and a federal income tax, and against government by injunction. In an obvious reference to Altgeld's quarrel with Cleveland, the platform denounced federal interference in local affairs. No longer would Democratic and Republican conventions support duplicate economic policies.

For the Democratic presidential nomination, Altgeld reluctantly backed William Jennings Bryan, whom he had rebuffed a year earlier. As chairman of the Illinois delegation, he cast its vote four times for Richard P. Bland of Missouri, a veteran congressional worker for free silver. On the fifth ballot, he yielded to home-state pressure and voted for Bryan, who at 36 had a silver tongue but had not matured as a politician. If he had not been foreign-born — and thus constitutionally ineligible — the governor might have been a strong candidate for the nomination. Altgeld declined to support Vice President Adlai E. Stevenson for the presidency.

Altgeld neglected his own reelection campaign, which he realized was hopeless, and worked valiantly for Bryan, who in Illinois received

9,733 fewer votes than the unpopular governor. With 43.7 percent of the gubernatorial vote, Altgeld lost by 113,381 to John R. Tanner, a conservative Republican.

In private life, he joined Clarence Darrow's law firm. Still head of the Democratic Party in 1897, he dictated that the second Carter H. Harrison be the candidate for mayor of Chicago. It was an error, for after the election Harrison joined the party's gold wing. Two years later, an outcast from leadership, Altgeld ran for mayor as an independent. Sizable crowds turned out for his speeches, but he finished third. He was denied delegate credentials to the 1900 Democratic convention at Kansas City, which endorsed Altgeld policy by renominating Bryan on a liberal platform. In Illinois, he made speeches for the Democratic ticket.

"The Little Dutchman" never stopped being spokesman for the underdog. He died March 13, 1902, in Joliet of a cerebral hemorrhage several hours after a speech advocating Boer independence from the British in South Africa.

Governor Altgeld with his staff at Camp Lincoln, which in 1895 hosted a first-in-the-nation open-air military mass that drew a crowd of 10,000 people, including the governor and his wife

21st **Governor**

John Riley Tanner
1844-1901

1844 — Born April 4 in Booneville, Indiana

1863 — Enlists in the Union Army

1881 - 1885 — Serves as senator in the 32nd and 33rd General Assemblies

1886 — Elected state treasurer; serves 1887 to 1889

1894 — Manages the midterm election campaign that elects Republicans by unprecedented
majorities

1896 — Defeats Altgeld for governor

1898 — A special session of the legislature makes more than 12,000 Illinoisans available for the
war with Spain.

1900 — Covets Cullom's U.S. Senate seat; he is denied it, and the Republicans run Richard
Yates in the gubernatorial election.

1901 — Dies May 23

Republican
January 11, 1897 to January 14, 1901

Tall, virile, and amiable, John R. Tanner was a six-foot-two-inch 200-pounder with a dark complexion and long hair. He was a master of the complexities of organizing political factions, and got great practice by organizing Shelby M. Cullom's political machine. He parlayed his connections into a term as governor. And then he committed political suicide by challenging Cullom, his patron, for his seat in the U.S. Senate.

The Young Organizer

The fourth generation John Tanner was a country boy from southern Illinois, where he was taken soon after his birth in a log house near Booneville, Indiana, on April 4, 1844. He grew up on a farm near Carbondale, with an education limited to country schools. His mother, Eliza V. Downs, was the daughter of a Baptist preacher. His great-grandfather John Tanner was killed in the Revolutionary War, and his grandfather was killed by Indians in Kentucky. His father died in a Confederate prison camp. The future governor enlisted with the Union in 1863 and served in Sherman's army from Kentucky to Georgia.

After the war, he bought 60 acres in Clay County, where he farmed, sold fruit trees and real estate, ran a sawmill, and took up Republican politics at the age of 26. In a Democratic county, he was elected sheriff and circuit clerk. At 30, he began long service as a member of the Republican state central committee. He was elected state senator in 1880 at the start of Cullom's second term as governor. When Cullom became U. S. senator, the invaluable Tanner went on the federal payroll as marshal for southern Illinois. At the start of Grover Cleveland's Democratic administration, he stayed in politics by being elected state treasurer. When Tanner disagreed with Governor Joseph W. Fifer, who appointed him to the state Railroad and Warehouse Commission, Cullom arranged for his appointment as assistant U.S. treasurer at Chicago.

As Republican state chairman, Tanner managed the midterm campaign that, in the wake of Governor John Peter Altgeld's Haymarket pardons, elected Republican candidates by unprecedented majorities. In 1896, he was the Republican's best hope to limit Altgeld to one term. The five living former Republican governors — Richard J. Oglesby, John L. Beveridge, John M. Hamilton, Cullom, and Fifer — formed a "flying squadron" that campaigned for Tanner. Oglesby did it reluctantly, but party tradition required that rivalries be forgotten during campaigns. Tanner's winning majority, 113,381 votes, was sensational.

The Ornate Administration

Republicans, who wanted to replace the Democrats Altgeld had appointed, immediately flooded the governor-elect with job applications. The governor's office received more than 3,000 letters in two weeks, and swarms of patronage seekers stood in line all day to see him.

Tanner's first wife, Lauretta Ingraham, died in 1887, leaving two children. The celebration of election to the governorship included the announcement of his engagement to Cora Edith English, a Springfield socialite who was 20 years his junior. The wedding, 11 days before the inauguration, was Illinois officialdom's brightest and possibly most expensive social event. Some of the invited guests were unable to crowd into St. Paul's Episcopal Church. Wedding presents, many of them accompanied by job applications, included a trunk of solid silver tableware (348 pieces) and a Landau carriage and team of matching horses. For the first time, festoons of electric lights were part of the state Capitol's lavish decorations. The Tanners lived in a hotel for several months while the Executive Mansion was remodeled and redecorated.

The governor, addicted to pomp and circumstance, reviewed a long parade before the elaborate inauguration ceremony, which was followed by a dinner and a ball. At formal events during the next four years, he was accompanied by his personal staff, one man from each congressional district. They were known as "sunburst colonels" because of the elaborate gold braid on their tailor-made uniforms.

Soon after his inauguration, Tanner signed a controversial bill, similar to one Altgeld had vetoed, that permitted the Chicago City Council to grant 50-year franchises to street-car companies. Chicago newspapers and assorted reformers then turned public sentiment against the governor, who found that no one listened to his explanation that financing of some corporations, including utilities, required long-term bond issues for which 20-year franchises were inadequate. The utility companies, which were essential to the growth of cities but not yet under governmental regulation, were forced to pay tribute to venal politicians. In the uproar, the unused 50-year franchise law was repealed in two years. There is no record that Tanner profited personally when he signed the bill.

Like Altgeld, Governor Tanner refused to allow state troops to be used as strikebreakers. Governor Shelby Cullom in 1877 called out the militia when mine owners asked for protection during strikes. Twenty-one years later, Cullom's protégé sided with union members who were striking at Virden and Pana. He blamed mine owners for violence and said that the laboring man's right to strike "is as dear to him as the capitalist's millions." When 12 men were killed and 40 wounded at Virden, Tanner sent troops to the railroad station to prevent the unloading of Alabama black men — presumably potential strike breakers — who were guarded by private detectives hired in St. Louis. He said the train would have been stopped at the state line had he known that a private army was on board. He earned the gratitude of labor at the expense of rural support.

As a conservative Republican, Tanner stood for economy. He borrowed money to retire the treasury deficit and reduced the state's property tax rate. In the wake of the Haymarket controversy, he sponsored creation of a pardon board of three members to review clemency applications. He approved a bill that outlawed the hiring of out-of-state strikebreakers. Like most postwar Republican governors, he wanted but didn't get Chicago police placed under a state board. His solution for local tax troubles was to have property assessed quadrennially at one-fifth value. A judicial reorganization abolished the Ottawa and Mount Vernon divisions of the Supreme Court, which thereafter met only in Springfield.

The legislature, in special session in 1898 at the outbreak of the Spanish-American War, gave the governor full power to raise men, munitions, and money as needed. The governor's call for troops produced more regiments than could be used.

Political Suicide

Governor Tanner's dual positions, as a key member of Cullom's organization and as the head of his own faction, turned out to be incompatible. When harassed by heavy criticism, he needed someone to blame for his troubles. Republicans were shocked when he severely criticized the senator and then ran against him. The state payrollers and the "federal crowd" fought over the nomination of legislators and the election of delegates to the 1900 Republican state convention. Before it was over, the great campaign manager conceded defeat without consulting William E. Lorimer, the only congressman who supported him. Cullom, who had no objection to his lieutenant's gubernatorial ambitions, said Tanner could have been reelected in 1900 had he remained loyal. Why the governor split with the senator is one of the mysteries of Illinois political history. Lorimer, the British-born son of a minister, was frequently blamed, often with apparent justification, for whatever went wrong. The frequent shifting of alliances encouraged multiple candidacies and deadlocks that helped give Illinois politics a bad name.

When Tanner left office, he was broken politically and physically. He had been handicapped in his last campaign by an illness that was diagnosed successively as gastritis, neuralgia of the stomach, and gallstones. Four months after he returned to private life, he died in his Springfield hotel suite on May 23, 1901. His funeral was as impressive as his inauguration. An estimated 30,000 passed before his casket in the Statehouse rotunda. His grand mausoleum is in Springfield's Oak Ridge Cemetery, where Abraham Lincoln's is.

Courtesy of the Abraham Lincoln Presidential Library

Crowd near the Capitol awaiting the funeral cortege of former Governor John Tanner

The Tanner Cadets, a youth drill organization formed in response to the patriotic fervor of the Spanish-American War, was made up chiefly of boys from prominent Springfield families. Shown here in 1898 in their summer dress uniforms in front of the Executive Mansion, the cadets appeared frequently in parades and other patriotic occasions. The Tanner Cadets disbanded at the end of the governor's term, then reformed as the Yates Cadets.

Tanner lay in state in the Capitol rotunda. Crowds were estimated as large as Lincoln's in 1865.

22nd Governor

Richard Yates
1860-1936

1860 — Born December 12, a month after his father's election to the governor's office
1892 — Loses his bid to be congressman-at-large
1894 — Elected Morgan County judge
1900 — Emerges from the Republican convention as its dark horse nominee; wins the general election by more than 60,000 votes
1904 — Is not renominated for governor
1908 — Runs in the gubernatorial primary and loses to incumbent Governor Charles Deneen
1912 — Runs in the gubernatorial primary, finishes fourth in a field of seven
1919 - 1933 — Serves as congressman-at-large
1936 — Dies April 11

Republican
January 14, 1901 to January 9, 1905

The second Richard Yates, the first governor of the 20th century, lived in the past, the stirring times of the Civil War when his father, the patriotic orator for whom he was named, was Republican governor and then a U.S. senator. Father and son had the same assets — charisma and the ability to electrify an audience. Unfortunately for the son, who was the first Illinois-born governor, he was a peacetime chief executive without a martial stage on which to perform. He had no interest in the developing Progressive movement that sought to disturb the status quo with governmental reforms, regulation of business, and improvements in the lot of the common man. Generally, the postwar governors were less conservative than the legislatures and the Republican leadership, but the second Yates was an exception.

As chief executive, he had no program of his own and left no imprint on Illinois government. Four times a candidate for governor, he won his first and only campaign in 1900. His participation in a series of deadlocked conventions led to one of the major reforms of the Progressive Era, the direct primary law, the enactment of which was the first order of business when Yates was replaced by a stronger governor. Yates ultimately found his political niche and had a 14-year career as congressman-at-large, an office for which name recognition was a chief qualification. Harold L. Ickes, who at that time was a Progressive worker and seldom was charitable toward conservative Republicans, described Yates as a "weak, easy going nonentity with few ideas, no real purpose and little character."

The Governor's Son

Yates was born in Jacksonville on December 12, 1860, a month after his father's election to the governor's office. He grew up with vague memories of soldiers marching outside the Executive Mansion. As a boy, he sat with his mother in the state Senate gallery while his father mingled with famous men on the floor below. As a teenager, in the genteel poverty of his widowed mother's home, his dream of a military career vanished when President Ulysses S. Grant did not appoint him to West Point. When he reached Whipple Academy, the preparatory school for Illinois College, he made a friend of classmate William Jennings Bryan, the son of an important downstate Democrat. "Oh, dear," Yates' mother once said of Bryan, "I wish you had the energy and iron will of that boy. He will go far." At one time, they considered forming a Bryan and Yates law partnership.

While at Illinois College, Yates won second honors in an interstate oratorical contest. Of slight build, with a pale face and dark eyes, he was a University of Michigan Law School graduate, but he never practiced outside Jacksonville. Before and after law school, with the title of city editor, he was most of the editorial staff of the Jacksonville *Daily Journal*. At every opportunity, he made speeches reminding Civil War veterans and other Republicans that he bore a famous name. He was active in local politics, but his hometown law practice was never important. He was city attorney when he married Ellen Wadsworth; they had two daughters.

In 1892, a Democratic year, Yates was the losing nominee for congressman-at-large, a statewide congressional office. Two years later, he was elected Morgan County judge. In four more years, he was congressional district leader for the William McKinley presidential campaign and made speeches in seven Midwestern states.

He lacked administrative experience, but he could make friends in high places and get patronage jobs from them. Over objections from Senator Shelby Cullom, President McKinley appointed Yates collector of internal revenue for the central Illinois district. At Republican conventions, his downstate followers loyally supported him during long deadlocks.

The Son Becomes Governor

Not yet 40 years old, he was elected governor in 1900. Better known men were among the Republican candidates, but Yates began campaigning as a neutral dark horse and picked up support from Senator Cullom's "federal crowd." When his original candidate seemed to be a loser, Congressman William Lorimer grabbed a Yates banner and stampeded the convention. The result of the third ballot was never announced, and Yates won on the fourth. He was at least presentable, so he was accepted as being preferable to a split in Republican ranks.

For a gubernatorial candidate, the Democrats compromised on an Altgeld follower, Samuel Alschuler of Aurora, who lost to Yates by 61,233 votes, but nonetheless ran more than 15,000 votes better than the Bryan-Stevenson presidential ticket.

Yates, a spoils politician, had no trouble with the standpat legislature, and it would have no trouble with him. He opened his inaugural address with an unprecedented confession of ignorance and inexperience: "At this time my knowledge of state affairs is so limited that it would be discourteous to attempt to convey that limited knowledge to the legislature." After 1902, he was for civil service reform, which had been endorsed by both parties, but he avoided a leadership role on this and other issues. He did nothing about paving roads, which would increase rural taxes and mean that more autos would kill chickens and scare horses. In his autobiography, Yates said his administration was "a prosaic affair" that "could really be summed up in one word — economy." He signed bills that permitted municipal ownership of street railways and restricted prison industries. A new child-labor law made Illinois the first state with a 48-hour work week for children. He vetoed a bill for centralized auditing of state agencies.

The governor complained to downstate followers that he was being unfairly criticized by the Chicago newspapers, which complained that the governor made state employees do campaign work and contribute to a slush fund. Like John Tanner, he had a personal staff of "sunburst colonels" who rode behind him in parades. One of his proudest moments occurred during the McKinley inauguration parade. As Yates, in top hat and frock coat, rode past the reviewing stand, his trick horse saluted by lowering one knee to the ground.

Wrangling for Patronage and Power

In 1904, Yates attained some prominence by being the first western Republican to declare for the nomination of Theodore Roosevelt at the national convention in Chicago. But by that time, the governor knew he had no hope of a second consecutive term as governor. At the Republican state convention, downstate backing gave him the lead over six rivals for 58 ballots between May 13 and June 3. He lost his only Chicago power base when Congressman Lorimer defected to another candidate. When Yates convinced himself that he couldn't get the votes to win, he decided to throw his support to State's Attorney Charles S. Deneen of Cook County. He thus denied the nomination to Frank O. Lowden, who finished second on the earlier ballots.

Deneen handily won the 1904 general election. But the two soon became political enemies. Deneen remained neutral when Senator Cullom came up for a fifth term in 1906. Yates, who thought that Deneen promised to support him, unsuccessfully challenged Cullom in one of the bitter campaigns for which Republicans were notorious in that era. Two years later, Yates failed to prevent Deneen's second-term nomination. When Yates ran for governor again in 1912, Deneen was first and Yates fourth in a primary field of seven.

After he moved out of the Executive Mansion, Yates lived in a large house in Springfield and divided his time between the chautauqua lecture circuit and patronage jobs, which he found to be scarce during the Deneen and Lowden administrations. Briefly, he was an assistant attorney general. Edward F. Dunne, a Democratic governor, appointed him a minority member of the state utility commission, in charge of telephone companies. Then in 1919, he became a conservative congressman-at-large. He lost in the 1928 primary but was given the nomination when the man who defeated him died before the election. Finally defeated in the 1932 Franklin Delano Roosevelt landslide, he nevertheless polled more votes than any other Illinois Republican. He ran and lost one more time. In 1933, after voting against repeal of Prohibition during the lame duck session of Congress, he was an unsuccessful candidate for delegate to the convention that ratified the Twenty-first Amendment.

He retired to Harbor Springs, Michigan, where he died April 11, 1936, while writing his memoirs.

Courtesy of the Abraham Lincoln Presidential Library

Ellen Wadsworth Yates (center), daughters Dorothy, age 8, and Catherine, age 12

Governor and Mrs. Yates have readied themselves and the Executive Mansion for a Christmas party in 1902. Staff members are not identified.

George Kennedy drives a team with George Eells hitched to a jackass to settle an election bet in Winslow in Stephenson County. The bet was that Eells, a Frank Lowden supporter, would pull a cart carrying Kennedy with a sign saying "Two of a Kind" if the town went for Yates in the 1904 primary election. Had the town gone with Lowden, Kennedy would have been in harness.

23rd Governor

Charles Samuel Deneen
1863-1940

1863 — Born May 4 at Edwardsville

1893 - 1895 — Serves in the House of Representatives in the 38th General Assembly

1897 — Begins a two-term stint as a state's attorney; wins convictions of a state treasurer, several bankers, and prominent people

1904 — Wins the gubernatorial nomination as a compromise candidate on the 58th ballot; beats Democrat Lawrence B. Stringer in the general election; one of his triumphs is legislation establishing primary races that determine party slates for the general election.

1908 — Defeats Democrat Adlai E. Stevenson to win a second term as governor

1909 — General Assembly approves a law limiting the legal workday for women to 10 hours.

1910 — After several attempts, the General Assembly approves a direct primary law that is upheld by the courts.

1911 — The "mother's aid" law provides funds for dependent and neglected children; Illinois gets its first Workmen's Compensation Act, the forerunner of the state's modern workers' compensation laws.

1912 — Gets the Republican nod for a third term and remains loyal to the Republican Party though a Progressive faction breaks away; the Progressive Party nominates its own gubernatorial candidate and splits the general election vote so that Democrat Edward F. Dunne wins with a little more than 38 percent of the vote.

1925 - 1931 — Serves in the U.S. Senate

1940 — Dies in Chicago on February 5

Republican
January 9, 1905 to January 18, 1909
January 18, 1909 to February 3, 1913

Charles S. Deneen was one of the state's strongest governors. A mildly liberal reformer who headed the respectable faction among Chicago Republicans, he championed much of the Progressive movement's legislative program but would not be its candidate when he sought a third term in 1912. In number and importance, the legislation and administrative advances for which he is credited exceed those of Governor John P. Altgeld, the Democratic hero of the 1890s.

Deneen, who had been a vigorous state's attorney in Cook County, rose to the governorship on a groundswell of complaints about municipal corruption and corporate domination of government that culminated in formation of the Progressive Party and Theodore Roosevelt's unsuccessful presidential campaign of 1912. The first two-term governor since Shelby Cullom, Deneen was the first of three reform governors who overlapped the Progressive movement and remade the face of Illinois government between 1905 and 1921. He was succeeded by Edward F. Dunne, a former Democratic mayor of Chicago, and Frank O. Lowden, a civic-minded Republican. In a period of intense factionalism in both parties, these men had the same goal — better government. But they acted independently of each other. Deneen and Lowden cooperated at times but were political rivals for two decades.

A cold, cautious man, Deneen didn't know how to engage in political small talk with the Democrats and the conservative Republicans who made his leadership difficult. Effective, unpopular, and durable, Deneen could, nevertheless, count considerable accomplishments. His honesty was never questioned, and the "jackpotters" who sold their votes in the legislature detested him.

The Republican Prosecutor

The future governor was the son of a Latin professor at McKendree College, grandson of a Methodist minister, and the great-grandson of a territorial legislator who opposed slavery. He was born May 4, 1863, in Edwardsville, where his mother, the former Mary Ashley, lived with a sister-in-law until Adjutant Samuel H. Deneen returned from the Civil War to his home in Lebanon. Young Deneen graduated from McKendree and taught in downstate and Chicago schools before getting a degree from Union College of Law in Chicago. He was married in 1891 to Bina Day Maloney of Mount Carroll. One of their four children was born in the Executive Mansion.

In Chicago, he lived within the congressional district of William Lorimer, the "blond boss" of the West Side Republicans. With Lorimer's backing, he became a state representative, attorney for the sanitary board, and a member of the Republican state central committee. Starting in 1897, during two terms as state's attorney, he won convictions of a state treasurer, several bankers, and others of prominence. By 1900, Lorimer and Deneen were dominant powers in Cook County Republican politics. Deneen terminated their alliance before he ran for governor.

The Progressive Governor

In 1904, Chicago Republicans, who wanted the next governor to come from the city, had two strong candidates: Deneen and Frank O. Lowden, who helped create an unusually long deadlock at the state convention. Because Governor Richard Yates and others who opposed Lowden couldn't agree on anyone else, Deneen won nomination on the 58th ballot. He named his personal friend Roy O. West, a Chicago lawyer who later became President Calvin Coolidge's secretary of the interior, to be Republican state chairman. Running with the popular Theodore Roosevelt, Deneen was elected by a 2-to-1 margin over Democrat Lawrence B. Stringer of Lincoln.

Deneen appealed chiefly to middle-class and professional voters. Charles E. Merriam, a Progressive who might have been elected Chicago's mayor in 1911 had the governor supported him, wrote that Deneen's standards of integrity and competence were "quite superior" to those of competing politicians. He was a straight-laced Methodist who rode a day coach to his inauguration, served nothing stronger than lemonade in the Executive Mansion, and invited popular evangelist Billy Sunday to hold a prayer meeting there. He abolished the personal staff of "sunburst colonels" who had paraded behind Governors Tanner and Yates.

The new governor, who owed his nomination to boss-controlled convention politics, endorsed primary elections and civil service, both high items on the Progressive agenda. "Our state needs a compulsory primary law," he said at the opening of his inaugural address. Four years later, he won his longest fight when the Illinois Supreme Court finally approved a law, the fourth enacted at his insistence, that gave the nomination of candidates to the voters in primary elections.

Espousing another Progressive crusade, Deneen, at his first legislative session, used the power of his office to place employees of the 17 welfare institutions under civil service. When the perverse legislature omitted an appropriation for the new Civil Service Commission, the governor allocated $14,000 from contingency funds.

The unusual success of his extensive legislative program reflected the governor's campaigning ability and persistent refusal to accept conservative rebuffs. He did not hesitate to call special legislative sessions, and time after time, he stumped downstate counties and Chicago wards, appealing for public support and eventually getting his bills passed. Excluding old-line conservatives, he had a sizable segment of public opinion on his side. The Municipal Voters League elected a majority of the Chicago City Council, and at a 1904 referendum, the statewide vote was 4-to-1 for selection of candidates by the voters instead of by convention delegates.

Dunne, his Democratic successor, commended Deneen in his autobiography for supporting legislation needed by Chicago. He specifically mentioned replacement of the justice-of-the-peace system with a municipal court, abolition of township government in the metropolis, construction of the municipal harbor and pier, and authorization for the council to fix electric and gas rates.

The Deneen Administration made significant changes in state government. Management of welfare institutions was centered in a five-member State Board of Administration, replacing 17 local boards that were a major source of political patronage. Inmates of county homes and local almshouses were transferred to state institutions. A state highway commission with a salaried engineer began propaganda for paved roads. Motorists were required to register their cars and pay $2 for identification plates; the money went into a road fund. The nation's first "mother's aid" law provided funds for dependent and neglected children. Workmen's compensation and occupational diseases laws were enacted, women were limited to a 10-hour workday, and mining laws were modernized. The board of health was authorized to distribute diphtheria antitoxin. Suburban and downstate municipalities received permission to adopt a commission form of government. A local option law was passed with Anti-Saloon League support. State school appropriations, which had been $1 million a biennium since 1872, were doubled. More money was provided for the University of Illinois.

The governor was a hard-nosed administrator. During a race riot in Springfield, he called out the National Guard and ordered the state's attorney to convene a grand jury. At Deneen's request, Attorney General William H. Stead forced the Illinois Central Railroad to pay additional taxes on its gross receipts. State agencies were required to deposit all collected funds into the state treasury.

The reformer governor had enemies in both parties. When the 1904 deadlock was broken, Yates believed that Deneen had given at least an implied promise to support him in the future for the U.S. Senate. Two years later, however, the governor remained neutral when Yates ran against Cullom and lost. In the 1908 primary, held under a primary election law that was later invalidated by the courts, Yates lost again when he sought revenge by running against the governor. In the 1908 election, William Howard Taft carried Illinois handily for president, but the popular Adlai E. Stevenson, the former vice president, came within 23,164 votes of defeating Deneen for governor. Democrats claimed that the election had been stolen in Chicago wards controlled by Mayor Fred A. Busse, leader of another Republican faction. Win or lose, Illinois governors traditionally run poorly in second-term campaigns.

A Second Term Troubled by Partisan Politics

The unstable factionalism in both parties made Deneen's second term especially complex. He faced diplomatic problems involving his legislative program; Old Guard elements considered it improper for a political leader to support the reform program of the puritanical Progressives. Deneen controlled the Senate, but House Speaker Edward D. Shurtleff was reelected by a conservative Democratic coalition. U.S. Senator Albert J. Hopkins of Aurora won an advisory primary but had few supporters in the legislature. After months of maneuvering, during which Deneen refused to be "kicked upstairs" to the U.S. Senate, another bipartisan coalition elected Lorimer to succeed outgoing Senator Albert J. Hopkins. (In two years, Lorimer was expelled from the Senate after investigations in Washington and Springfield turned up evidence of graft and payoffs in the legislature.)

Progressive sentiment was at high tide in 1912. Deneen had six opponents in the Republican primary but was nominated for a third term by 152,997 to 64,168 votes over Len Small, a future governor who ran second. Deneen willingly voted for Theodore Roosevelt at the Republican's national convention. When President Taft was renominated and the Roosevelt forces bolted to form the progressive Bull Moose Party, Deneen, out of party loyalty, refused to be the Progressive candidate for governor. He had endorsed the federal income tax amendment and had been primarily responsible for enactment of much of the Progressive program. However, after considerable debate, the new Progressive Party split the general election vote by running Frank Funk of Bloomington for governor. Funk was a virtual unknown in Chicago. As a result, Democrat Edward F. Dunne won the crowded general election with a little more than 38 percent of the vote. Deneen finished second and Funk third. Whether Deneen could have been elected as a Progressive is doubtful. In that case, the conservative Republicans no doubt would have entered their own candidate, again giving Dunne the advantage.

Senator Deneen

After he returned to his Chicago law practice, Deneen remained a political force, but his leadership was handicapped by Governor Lowden's greater popularity. On occasion they cooperated, but they never attempted a political partnership of non-machine Republicans. In 1916, Deneen cautiously supported Morton D. Hull, a wealthy Chicagoan, for governor, but Lowden was nominated. During the Lowden Administration, Deneen and Roy O. West kept their faction alive and won a few Cook County and Chicago offices.

In 1924, the former governor was elected U.S. senator with the help of William Hale Thompson, who especially hated the incumbent, Medill McCormick, a former Progressive leader. In the Senate, where his legal ability and integrity were respected, Deneen supported President Calvin Coolidge on the World Court and other issues. As the Republican Party declined in influence during the 1920s, Deneen was accused of dealing with Roger Sullivan, the rising Democratic leader, in some campaigns. In 1930, with 38 percent of the vote in a field of three candidates, he was defeated for renomination by Ruth Hanna McCormick in a campaign scandalous for its heavy spending.

Deneen was practicing law when he died in Chicago on February 5, 1940.

Courtesy of the Abraham Lincoln Presidential Library

The Deneen family in the Executive Mansion; clockwise from left, Dorothy, Bina Day Maloney Deneen, Charles Ashley, and Frances holding Bina, the first baby born to a seated governor

Courtesy of the Abraham Lincoln Presidential Library

The house in Edwardsville where Charles Deneen was born; it belonged to state Senator Andrew W. Metcalf. Child unknown

Governor Deneen with barnstorming pilot Charles F. Willard; at left is Octave Chanute, an air flight pioneer and mentor to Orville and Wilbur Wright. On July 14, 1910, in Decatur, Willard had made the best flight recorded in Illinois at that time, six miles at 600 feet.

Campaign headquarters for candidates at Republican convention in Chicago, 1904

24th Governor

Edward Fitzsimmons Dunne
1853-1937

1853 — Born October 12 in Waterville, Connecticut
1895 — Elected to a vacant circuit judgeship
1905 - 1907 — Serves as mayor of Chicago
1907 — Turns the mayor's office over to Republican Fred A. Busse after losing the general election
1912 — Wins election to the governor's office with a little more than 38 percent of the vote after a Progressive faction splits from the mainline Republican Party and nominates its own candidate, dividing Republican votes in a multi-candidate race
1913 - 1917 — Sets in motion infrastructure improvements, such as the push for paved roads and governmental restructuring recommendations from the governor's commission on efficiency and economy
1916 — Loses gubernatorial general election to Frank O. Lowden, who is helped by a reunified Republican Party; leaves public life
1937 — Dies of heart disease in Chicago on May 24

Democrat
February 3, 1913 to January 8, 1917

The only mayor of Chicago who became governor of Illinois was Edward F. Dunne, a personable and idealistic Irishman who led the Democratic Party's reform wing when Republicans were split by the Progressive movement. A disciple of John Peter Altgeld and supporter of William Jennings Bryan, he was a progressive at heart, the second Democratic governor since the Civil War, and the second Catholic governor (Bissell was the first). His four productive years as governor coincided with and complemented the first term of Woodrow Wilson's presidency.

As mayor from 1905 to 1907 and governor from 1913 to 1917, Dunne failed to achieve his major ambition to provide municipal ownership of street railway and utility companies. His campaign on the issue did pay dividends in the creation of a state utility commission that regulated privately owned companies.

He was the connecting link between Charles S. Deneen and Frank O. Lowden, Republican reform governors, both of whom were his superiors as administrators and leaders of the legislature. One of his accomplishments was creation of the legislative Efficiency and Economy Committee, whose wide-ranging recommendations he backed. Only a few of them were approved by the foot-dragging Republican legislature during the Dunne Administration. Lowden continued the drive for governmental reorganization with triumphant success.

An Irish Boy Becomes His Honor

Edward Fitzsimmons Dunne was born in Waterville, Connecticut, on October 12, 1853, the son of P. W. and Delia M. Lawler Dunne. Two years later, the family moved to Peoria. He attended Trinity College in Dublin, Ireland, for three years, but did not graduate because of his father's business reverses. Back in Peoria, he worked in his father's mill and began the study of law. In 1876, he went to Chicago and graduated the next year from Union College of Law. Five years later, he married Elizabeth J. Kelly. Intelligent, friendly, and good-looking, he entered successful law partnerships. Active in political and legal circles, he came under the influence of Governor Altgeld. In 1895, he was elected to a vacant circuit judgeship.

While the Hearst newspapers beat their drum, Dunne rode the traction [streetcar] issue into the mayor's office. Drawing on information obtained during a European trip in 1900, he argued that gas and electric rates were lower in cases where foreign and American cities owned their own plants. When Mayor Carter Harrison equivocated, Judge Murray F. Tuley, a senior member of the bench, proposed that public ownership forces unite and agree on Dunne as their candidate. With Hearst's help, Dunne was endorsed by most wards, nominated when Harrison stepped aside, and elected by 25,000 votes over a Republican who favored franchise-operated utilities.

Although referenda showed that he had public backing, the "hopelessly hostile" city council ignored his messages on municipal ownership and, after considerable stalling, adopted ordinances that he vetoed. "The so-called bosses of my own party were decidedly opposed to municipal ownership and quietly helped the utility corporations beat me," he remembered. When the traction companies finally agreed to sell, the mayor asserted that the settlement did not protect Chicago's interests. The council overrode his vetoes. Meanwhile, a Deneen Administration law allowed the city to reduce gas, electric, and water rates. The mayor took satisfaction that he had erased the city's treasury deficit, added 1,000 policemen, doubled saloon license fees, and enforced building ordinances. High-quality appointments included Walter L. Fisher as special traction attorney, Jane Addams as a member of the school board, and James Hamilton Lewis as corporation counsel. "Honest service had been rendered to the city," he said. "Graft and crookedness had been driven from the city hall."

In 1907, the traction issue again frustrated Dunne. He was renominated by Democrats after defeating Carter Harrison in an advisory primary, but he lost by 12,000 votes to Republican Fred A. Busse.

Dunne believed that he could have been reelected had he made deals with river ward leaders. He said Democratic leaders cooperated in raising a $600,000 slush fund that was used against him and that he had been offered bribes to change his stand on municipal ownership and to let brothels stay open another year.

Some contemporaries said he had tendencies toward "starry-eyed" idealism. But in his history/autobiography, Dunne admitted that he simply lacked "political finesse" and had made some mistakes in the mayor's office. Five years later, he found that being governor was more enjoyable.

The Roads and Public Utilities Governor

Split opposition enabled Dunne to win both the 1912 gubernatorial primary and election. He saw signs that the Republicans were weaker, one of them being Adlai E. Stevenson's strong race for governor in 1908. Chicago votes helped his nomination over two downstaters, Samuel Alschuler of Aurora, who was backed by former Mayor Harrison, and Congressman B. F. Caldwell of Springfield, the choice of Roger Sullivan, who within a few years would be the dominant Democrat in Illinois. Party ranks closed in the fall campaign, in contrast to the Bull Moose split among Republicans. Against Deneen, he used a "jackpot government must go" slogan — jackpotism being popular lingo for the sale of public office. Dunne charged that the Republican governor was part of a corrupt conspiracy in Springfield. Deneen protested that the charge was "shameless and untruthful." Dunne was elected with 38.1 percent of the vote.

Dunne and his wife, the former Elizabeth J. Kelly, were the parents of 13 children. Nine lived to help overcrowd the Executive Mansion, into which Mrs. Dunne moved extra beds.

In his inaugural message, which was delayed three weeks by a speakership fight, the former mayor emphasized his views on municipal ownership. He was successful in the creation of a public utilities commission with power to control the financing, service, and rates of privately owned companies. (In a case of questionable judgment, he appointed former Governor Yates a minority member.) One feature of the reform law outlawed granting of railroad passes to politicians and other prominent men. Another Dunne law authorized cities to operate their own utility plants.

The drive for paved roads moved forward under Dunne, who campaigned downstate with a hired car and chauffeur. He proclaimed April 15, 1913, as "road day" and asked able-bodied men to contribute their labor to the elimination of mudholes. Surrounded by state officials in overalls, the governor used a silver-plated shovel at Mooseheart to start the improvement of the Aurora-Elgin highway. Checks for one cent each went to 1,300 volunteers who showed up. As part of a prison reform movement, he offered to commute one-fourth of the sentences of honor prisoners who worked on roads. At Grand Detour, Ogle County, 51 convicts spent the winter cutting through a hill and grading one mile. Responsibility for work on major routes was shifted from townships to counties by a law that gave increased powers to a bipartisan state commission that supervised the work of highway superintendents in each county. The state was to assume half of the cost and take over maintenance. Only Vermilion and Cook counties made extensive use of new bonding powers.

Dunne started the state reorganization drive that Governor Lowden would finish. Since statehood, Illinois' problems had been met by the creation of myriad agencies, which were usually inadequate and, at times, conflicting. Except that they appointed the governing officials and received reports from them, the governors had little control over the agencies. Some progress was made in the last half-century, especially by Deneen in the welfare field, but, in general, centralized accounting did not exist. The decentralized system provided autonomous patronage rolls and kept governors from becoming too powerful.

On Dunne's strong recommendation, the legislature created an eight-member Efficiency and Economy Committee, which engaged professor John A. Fairlie of the University of Illinois as chief of staff. The governor endorsed its report, which called for consolidation of state agencies, including those under other state officials, into 10 departments. Intensive lobbying was not his style, however, and the legislature was more attentive to fears of many state employees who believed their jobs would be eliminated. At the end of the Dunne Administration, reorganization bills of consequence that had passed provided for uniform reports and established the Legislative Reference Bureau with responsibility for preparing a biennial budget.

By a one-vote margin in the House of Representatives, Dunne failed to win enactment of legislation by initiative and referendum, which was one of the top items on the Progressive agenda. Dunne also wanted action on the long-delayed plan to open the Illinois Waterway to barge traffic, but federal officials and Henry T. Rainey, a downstate congressman, refused to approve a channel of only eight feet. Dunne also unsuccessfully urged the abolition of capital punishment.

Dunne applauded major steps forward for women's suffrage. Illinois became the first state east of the Mississippi River to allow women to vote for presidential electors and some local officials.

Retirement

Most Progressives closed ranks with the Republicans by 1914, when Republican Lawrence Y. Sherman defeated Harrison in the first popular election of a U.S. senator. The next year, the controversial William Hale Thompson became mayor of Chicago. Dunne worked hard in a dull campaign for a second term as governor but lost to Frank O. Lowden.

Dunne never ran for public office again. The former governor remained an elder statesman. Frequently, he spoke in major cities on the municipal ownership issue. Irish ethnic groups sent him and Frank Walsh of Montana to the Paris peace conference to plead for independence for Ireland. With Clarence Darrow, Dunne convinced Cook County Democrats they should oppose ratification of the 1922 state constitution. At the 1932 Democratic national convention, he was an early supporter of Franklin D. Roosevelt. After a long illness, he died in Chicago of heart disease on May 24, 1937.

The wedding party of Governor Dunne's daughter Eileen and W. J. Corboy pose on the steps of the Executive Mansion in 1915.

25th
Governor

Frank Orren Lowden
1861-1943

1861 —Born January 26 in Sunrise City, Minnesota

1896 —Marries Florence Pullman, daughter of George M. Pullman, the sleeping-car millionaire

1904 —At the Republican state convention, backed by Congressman William Lorimer, Lowden makes a strong showing for the gubernatorial nomination; he loses the bid when, after 58 ballots, Governor Yates throws his support to Charles S. Deneen.

1906 - 1911 — Serves in the U.S. House

1916 —Defeats Dunne in the governor's race

1917 —Passage of the Civil Administration Code reforms Illinois government.

1918 —Pushes a $60 million bond issue, to be paid off by increased automobile license fees, to pave Illinois' roads

1920 —An Illinois constitutional convention convenes in Springfield; voters would reject its recommendations in 1922; Lowden refuses to consider a second term as governor and loses an Illinois preferential primary for president

1943 — Dies of cancer on March 20 in Tucson, Arizona

Republican
January 8, 1917 to January 10, 1921

Governor Frank O. Lowden, a farm boy turned millionaire, deserves major credit for enacting the Civil Administrative Code of 1917, which reorganized Illinois government in the interests of efficiency and economy and was one of the two most important laws ever put forth by the state legislature. In long-term effect, it was equaled only by Governor Thomas Ford's 1843-1845 debt retirement program that saved frontier Illinois from bankruptcy.

The governor didn't make all the changes he wanted in state government, but his biographer, William H. Hutchinson of the University of Chicago, concluded that the Lowden reforms exceeded those of any other state to that time. Credit goes to the governor for vigorous and persistent backing of his program and for skillful handling of the legislature and patronage. Before or after, no Illinois governor has had more success in getting legislative support at critical times.

An activist, Lowden was both a conservative Republican who believed government should operate on business principles and an administrative reformer who backed many of the Progressive movement's goals. He launched Illinois on a program to pave roads through bond financing, obtained referendum approval for a constitutional convention, and, during World War I, rallied the Illinois homefront in full support of the Woodrow Wilson Administration. He actively supported suffrage for women but was neutral on the constitutional amendment for Prohibition.

In addition to the governorship, Lowden had several careers. His interest in government and politics developed while he was a brilliant young Chicago lawyer. He was financially successful before he married Florence Pullman, the daughter of George M. Pullman, the sleeping-car millionaire. He left his law practice and moved from the "silk stocking" Second Ward to downstate Illinois. As the "Squire of Sinnissippi," the owner of a model farm on the Rock River, he demonstrated ways to increase the productivity and income of American farmers.

From Iowa Farm Boy to Millionaire Farmer

Frank Orren Lowden was born in the obscure town of Sunrise City, Minnesota, on January 26, 1861, the son of Lorenzo O. and Nancy Elizabeth Bregg Lowden. He was 7 when his farmer-blacksmith father, who had been a Granger, Greenbacker, and Democrat, moved to a farm in Hardin County, Iowa. The boy worked on a farm and attended a Quaker academy at New Providence. Money loaned by a Quaker enabled him to attend the University of Iowa. There, his brains, energy, good looks, and personality forecast success. He graduated as class valedictorian and taught one year at Burlington, Iowa. Then Wirt Dexter, general counsel of the Chicago, Burlington and Quincy Railroad, gave him a clerkship in his Chicago law office. Lowden became valedictorian at Union College of Law and was admitted to law practice in 1887.

Within a few years after Dexter's death, Lowden headed a firm with corporate clients. In addition to a general practice, he helped arrange the merger of corporations of which he became a stockholder and director. He was one of the financiers of the Coliseum, which was donated to the city. Lowden probably was the wealthiest Illinois governor.

In 1896, he married Florence Pullman, whom he met on an ocean liner two years earlier. Endowed with tact, as well as her father's intellect and firmness, she fully supported Lowden's political career. Their marriage produced four children. Lowden managed or was a director of some of his father-in-law's enterprises after Pullman's death in 1897.

As a member of the Civic Federation's political action committee, he worked for primary elections. He resigned as president of the Second Ward Republican Club when it resisted his anti-patronage proposals. During the John Tanner Administration, he backed a futile effort to combine local governments within Chicago. The title of colonel, by which Lowden was deferentially addressed in later years, refers to his role in the Spanish-American War; he was lieutenant colonel of a National Guard regiment that was not called into federal service.

An active role in the William McKinley campaign of 1900 gave the congenial Lowden a statewide acquaintance among Republican leaders. William Lorimer, the West Side Chicago boss, recognized him as a superior candidate and offered to run him for U.S. senator in 1902. Lorimer's support put Lowden in the midst of Republican factional entanglements. And his public image was not helped when he bought and developed his farm on the Rock River near Oregon in Ogle County. The "squire's" manorial style did little to guarantee popularity among farmers, just as the Pullman millions could be a liability among city dwellers.

In 1904, as a Lorimer-backed candidate for nomination as governor, he opposed Governor Richard Yates, State's Attorney Charles S. Deneen, and three other candidates. In a deadlocked convention, Deneen, his rival for the support of the more respectable element among Chicago Republicans, finally won. As a consolation prize, Lowden became Republican national committeeman. Two years later, he was elected to a congressional vacancy. In Washington he was interested in agriculture, the tariff, and natural resources. He led a successful fight to upgrade the State Department's consular service. After slightly more than two terms, he retired from Congress.

In the Bull Moose Party split of 1912, Lowden proposed the compromise under which Republican convention delegates were elected by congressional districts. As a district delegate, he voted for his friend Theodore Roosevelt, but in the campaign, as a traditional Republican, he supported President William Taft. Later, he was influential in getting the Progressives to return to the Republican Party.

The Governor Who Reformed the Government

As a harmony candidate who could unite Chicago and downstate, Lowden won the governorship in 1916. In the primary, he was endorsed by, among others, William Hale "Big Bill" Thompson and Fred Lundin, who had succeeded Lorimer as the "Great Manipulator" of Chicago politics. Lowden had the impossible task of not affronting the Chicagoans while simultaneously showing downstaters he was not a City Hall puppet. In the primary, he polled 54 percent of the vote over two other millionaires, Morton D. Hull of Chicago, who was Charles Deneen's man, and Frank L. Smith of Dwight.

In the fall campaign, Governor Edward F. Dunne pointed to Lowden when he charged that corporations controlled the Republican Party. Lowden, who pledged to introduce business methods in government, asserted that Dunne had raised taxes and administrative costs alarmingly. With the party reunited, Illinois again was a Republican state and Lowden carried 79 counties.

Before the legislature convened, Lowden announced he would not run for a second term and that his top priorities were administrative reorganization and calling a constitutional convention. His inaugural address stressed that Illinois had entered an industrial age and political reforms must follow economic and social changes. The reorganization bill, drafted under the new governor's supervision, abolished some of the 125 controversial state agencies and reorganized the others into nine departments, each headed by a director responsible to the governor, whose power to make appointments was greatly increased. Budgeting and accounting were centralized. Unlike Dunne, Lowden avoided political complications by not interfering with lesser state officials, each of whom was an ambitious and jealous political power.

In the first weeks of his administration, Lowden was applauded nationally for putting Illinois into the front rank of modern states with the passage of the Civil Administrative Code. For several decades a few hesitant steps were taken toward modernizing state government, and Dunne, the preceding governor, had sponsored a centralization bill that the legislature ignored. Lowden's program was passed by both houses in 12 days with only two negative votes. Fourteen other states copied the Lowden blueprint, and, in some features, so did Congress when it created the Bureau of the Budget.

Only after the code passed did Lowden give attention to the requests of Republican legislators who wanted the right to name some of the men who would fill the reduced number of patronage positions. He went outside Republican ranks when the directors of the new code departments were appointed. The nonpolitical head of the new public welfare department was Charles H. Thorne, retired president of Montgomery Ward and Company.

Lowden wanted a new constitution with a flexible revenue article that would centralize the state's tax structure, permit an income tax, and abolish township assessors. The legislature in the 1917 session and the voters in 1918 approved calling a convention that met in futility for two years beginning in 1920. The controversial constitution it drafted was approved by Lowden and Deneen; opposed by Dunne, Thompson, and Len Small, the man who succeeded Lowden; and rejected in 1922 by the voters.

The Deneen and Dunne administrations laid the foundation for a hard-road system, but cement was being poured too slowly to suit Lowden. His solution was to finance 4,800 miles of pavement with a

$60 million bond issue, to be paid off by increased automobile license fees rather than by real estate taxes. The bond issue, first advocated by the Illinois Highway Improvement Association, was approved in a 1918 referendum. In order to have a backlog of public works jobs for returning veterans, Lowden did not sell bonds during the war, but he ordered the public works department to go ahead with surveying, grading, and bridge construction. As a result, the Small Administration was able to make an early start at cement pouring.

Where Governors Deneen and Dunne failed, Lowden negotiated an agreement with federal officials that allowed construction to start on the Illinois Waterway between Lockport and Utica. Support for the waterway, a major public works project, began soon after the Panama Canal opened. Barge navigation was the main objective, but some hydroelectric power was produced.

In 1919, Lowden openly supported ratification of the 19th Amendment that gave women the right to vote. In another reform, the 1919 legislative session created a three-member tax commission, appointed by the governor, to replace the elected State Board Equalization, which beginning in 1869, met once a year to adjust corporate assessments. The governor also prevailed upon the legislature to abolish more than 500 private banks that had never been under state supervision.

Before his term ended, Lowden had the support of John H. Walker, president of the state labor federation, and Frank Farrington, president of the miners union. He successfully sponsored a workmen's compensation law that required employers to report accidents in hazardous occupations. Twice the legislature failed to reduce from 10 to eight hours the maximum working day for women in industry. The legislature did not approve an administration request for a commission to study economic and industrial aspects of race.

To increase state pride on the 100th anniversary of Illinois statehood, the Lowden Administration constructed the Centennial Building to house expanding departments and provided for the publication of a scholarly six-volume set of Illinois histories.

In World War I, Lowden's patriotic leadership was wholehearted. When five Illinois congressmen voted against the declaration of war, the General Assembly, at Lowden's request, called upon Illinois to forget partisanship and give the Democratic administration in Washington shoulder-to-shoulder support. He called for public support of such activities as bond sales, food conservation, thrift measures, and Red Cross drives.

Lowden had some difficulties. When a strike hindered coal

production in the upper Mississippi River valley, Lowden considered taking over the mines, but his legal authority was questioned. He used troops to prevent strike violence and restore order when mobs in East St. Louis and Chicago attacked blacks who came from the South to meet manpower demands. Mayor Thompson permitted the Chicago situation to get out of control before asking the governor to send the National Guard.

Lowden found it impossible to work with Mayor "Big Bill" Thompson who persistently belittled the governor's programs. No wonder the ever-ambitious Thompson was turned down in 1918 when Chicago for the first time asked for financial aid from the state treasury. The final break came at the 1920 Republican state convention, where the mayor wanted downstate delegates to approve an isolationist Cook County platform. Lowden called it radical, socialistic, and demagogic, and declared that the mayor was unworthy of being Republican national committeeman. On a vote to table Thompson's platform, Lowden won 1,110 to 631.

Frustrated Presidential Ambition

Lowden refused to reconsider his decision to be a one-term governor. He ran for president, but in the 1920 Illinois preferential primary he lost Chicago by 30,000 votes. In other farm states, his campaign for delegates was disappointing, in part because of the political ineptness of his manager, Secretary of State Louis L. Emmerson. At the opening of the convention in Chicago, Lowden was embarrassed when opponents claimed Emmerson bribed two Missouri delegates. For nine ballots, the convention was deadlocked by Lowden, U.S. Senator Hiram Johnson of California, and another cadidate. The nomination went to Warren G. Harding. Had he been supported by Thompson's Chicago delegates, Lowden might have been the presidential nominee in a landslide year.

In the 1920 primary, Lowden's candidate for governor was John G. Oglesby, who had served two terms as lieutenant governor but lacked the campaigning ability of his father, the Civil War general and three-term governor. Lowden's other candidates were nominated, but Oglesby lost to Thompson's candidate, Len Small, the winner of the general election. In 1924, Lowden refused to be a favorite-son candidate for president because he would have to support Small for a second term as governor. When he was offered the vice presidential nomination, Lowden refused in a message read to the Republican convention.

In 1928, he was the popular choice of Midwestern farmers who objected to President Calvin Coolidge's vetoes of farm policy bills. Without enthusiasm, Lowden was a candidate for the presidential nomination but had no chance of winning over Commerce Secretary Herbert Hoover. Thereafter, as the rural depression of the 1920s spread to urban America, Lowden's national role from Sinnissippi Farm was to raise a respected voice in advocacy of governmental assistance for farmers.

In his final years, he was distressed that Illinois violated the spirit of the Lowden code by creating autonomous boards and commissions. Lowden died of cancer on March 20, 1943, in Tucson, Arizona.

Governor Lowden spoke to a crowd on the banks of the Mississippi River in Chester in August 1918 as part of a celebration to mark the state's centennial.

26th Governor

Lennington Small
1862-1936

1862 — Born June 16 in Kankakee

1901 - 1905 — Serves in the Illinois Senate in the 42nd and 43rd General Assemblies

1905 - 1907 — Serves as state treasurer

1912 — Loses the Republican gubernatorial primary to Governor Charles Deneen

1917 - 1919 — Serves as state treasurer

1920 — Defeats Lieutenant Governor John G. Oglesby (son of three-time Governor Richard J. Oglesby) in the Republican gubernatorial primary; defeats Democrat James Hamilton Lewis in the general election

1921 — Is indicted on charges that he ran a money laundering scheme during his days as treasurer; is acquitted but may have tampered with the jury

1922 — Voters fail to ratify a new state constitution that many believe would give too little representation to Cook County and that would provide for the imposition of a state income tax.

1924 — Wins a second term as governor; Oscar E. Carlstrom, his candidate for attorney general, wins as part of a Republican sweep.

1927 — Loses civil suit in money laundering scheme resulting in a judgment of more than $1 million

1928 — Loses the Republican gubernatorial nomination to Louis Emmerson

1932 — Wins the Republican nomination for governor, but loses the general election to Democrat Henry Horner

1936 — Dies May 17

Republican
January 10, 1921 to January 12, 1925
January 12, 1925 to January 14, 1929

The inauguration of Governor Len Small in 1921 abruptly ended the 16-year Deneen-Dunne-Lowden reform era in Illinois government. A farmer from Kankakee, Small was one of the great American road builders. He also was the downstate Republican partner of William Hale "Big Bill" Thompson, the notorious Republican mayor of Chicago. Small's election gave the ambitious Thompson a share of political spoils in Springfield, as well as major control of those in Chicago. During the next eight scandalous years, machine politics triumphed over the cause of good government. Small, who scoffed at the complaints of reformers and metropolitan newspapers, never deviated from Thompsonism.

Early in the automobile age, Small pulled Illinois out of the mud and gave it one of the nation's best hard road systems. The 7,000 miles of 18-foot-wide pavement he constructed in eight years were badly needed, well engineered, economically built, and highly political. Each county got its share of the pavement if it voted for Small and his legislative candidates. In Small's second term, LaSalle County ran short of paved roads; not coincidentally its state senator, Thurlow G. Essington of Streator, had opposed the governor in the 1924 Republican primary.

From Farm Boy to State Treasurer

All his life, Small's home was at the edge of Kankakee. He was born on the farm of his parents, Dr. Abram Lennington and Calista Currier Small, on June 16, 1862. How long he attended Northern Indiana Normal School and a business college official biographies do not say, but he didn't need a formal education in his chosen fields of politics and agriculture. He taught school briefly, and he boasted that his first wages were invested in Kankakee County farmland. At 21, he was secretary of the State Board of Agriculture; later he became its president. Soon he was a county supervisor, which led to long service as secretary of the Kankakee Interstate Fair. He became clerk of the circuit court and a member of the Republican state committee. The Kankakee State Hospital was his political fiefdom as a result of appointments by Governors John Tanner and Richard Yates II to its board of trustees. (In fact, his name was first tied to scandal when, in 1902, Small's patronage employees were allegedly coerced into making political contributions to the Yates campaign.)

In 1883, he married Ida Moore, a schoolteacher and the daughter of a neighboring farmer. (Stricken by apoplexy, she died the day the jury acquitted Small in a 1921 trial on misappropriation of funds.) Their two sons and son-in law would be prominent appointees in his gubernatorial administration.

Small's given name was Lennington, but after his election as state senator in 1900, he shortened it to Len. At the end of his first term as treasurer, President William Howard Taft appointed him assistant U.S. treasurer at Chicago. He was a Republican county chairman who didn't mind making political deals with the Democrats, if he had to, and he played the patronage game well. In the 1912 primary, as Senator William Lorimer's candidate for governor, he finished second to Governor Charles Deneen in a field of eight. He was a conservative Republican who never supported Progressive causes and whom farmers especially regarded as a kindred spirit.

In 1916, Small was again elected state treasurer and apparently used the office for personal gain. In fact, after each of his terms as treasurer, laws were passed to tighten the regulation of treasury funds. In 1907, the Deneen Administration required that all public money received by the treasury be deposited in state banks. When Small left the treasury in 1919, the Lowden Administration ordered that banks bid for state treasury deposits.

Small prospered during his long political career, and at the time of his gubernatorial inauguration, he owned a model farm, a bank, and Kankakee's daily newspaper.

Pavement, Patronage, and Political Corruption

Small was lucky when he ran for governor again in 1920. Frank O. Lowden, who had presidential ambitions, was popular and could have been renominated over any opposition. Small's campaign manager was Fred Lundin, a one-time congressman who called himself the "Poor Swede" and was credited with masterminding Thompson's two elections as Chicago mayor. Governor Lowden supported the uninspiring lieutenant governor, John G. Oglesby, the son of the Civil War general and three-time governor. In a four-man primary field, Small won, but only by 7,902 votes. Lowden men were nominated for the other state offices. In November, the Warren G. Harding landslide gave Small a big margin over Democrat James Hamilton Lewis.

Lewis was a hard campaigner who took issue with Small's questionable record as state treasurer and his close affiliation to Chicago Mayor Thompson, who specialized in patronage and political favors and who fostered the environment in which "Scarface Al" Capone thrived. But Small's political machine carried him to victory. Downstaters wanted the road projects he promised, and Thompson paved his way in Chicago.

Small's inaugural address emphasized the economic value of hard roads, but otherwise largely echoed the platform Thompson used in Cook County.

The Small Administration effected several popular measures during his eight-year term in office. A state bonus for war veterans was financed by a $55 million bond issue. State aid to schools was placed on an equalization formula designed to help weaker districts. The state conservation department was created, and pari-mutuel betting on horse races was legalized. Also, electrocution replaced hanging for capital punishment.

But Small's lasting contribution to Illinois' infrastructure was more concrete. The Lowden Administration's $60 million road bond issue, advance engineering work, and right-of-way purchases enabled Small to start road-building quickly. He rejected the first bids, which averaged nearly $40,000 a mile for 18-foot cement pavement, and announced that under normal conditions costs could not exceed $30,000 a mile, including grading, culverts, and some bridge work. By 1924, his admin-istration had reduced the cost to $27,000. Year after year, he set new national records as a road builder. When he ran for a third term in 1928, Small could boast that "Illinois leads the world . . . and its 7,000 miles of completed concrete pavement exceed the mileage of any other state in the Union." To fund the roads, he won a 1924 referendum approval of a new issue of $100 million in bonds. The 1927 legislature enacted a two-cent-a-gallon tax on gasoline, to be divided between the state and counties. (But after five months and $200,000 in collections, the tax was held unconstitutional.)

Using a $20 million bond authorization that also had been inherited from Lowden, Small pushed construction of locks and dams on the waterway between Utica and Starved Rock. Designed to bring to the Midwest some of the benefits of the Panama Canal, the waterway project was part of Mayor Thompson's efforts to get national attention. The mayor, who in 1918 lost a race for nomination as senator, seemed to consider himself presidential material.

But the good the governor did couldn't erase his penchant for graft and nepotism.

Given the skeletons in his closet, Governor Small made a huge political error at the end of the 1921 legislative session when he made deep cuts in Lowden-backed Republican Attorney General Edward J. Brundage's appropriation bill. The attorney general, who was one of the mayor's factional rivals in Chicago, retaliated by indicting Small for conspiracy and embezzlement of interest money during his second term as treasurer. Small had deposited state funds in the Grant Park Bank, a long-dormant private bank in suburban Kankakee, and then loaned the laundered money to Chicago meatpackers. From them he collected interest at standard commercial rates as high as six percent. He reimbursed the state at call money rates of two or three percent. He did not account for the difference. Brundage brought the governor up on charges in Sangamon County in July 1921. Tried at Waukegan in 1922 under a change of venue, Small denied wrongdoing and testified that he paid the state more interest than all preceding treasurers. The criminal trial ended with an acquittal verdict. Historian Donald Tingley reports that the verdict may have been the result of jury tampering. (After the trial, four jurors received state jobs.)

Brundage then charged Small in a civil suit. When the evidence about the interest money was resubmitted in that trial, the judgment went against the governor. The Illinois Supreme Court upheld a master-in-chancery ruling that he owed the state $1,025,434. In 1927, a friendlier attorney general, Oscar E. Carlstrom, cut the figure to $650,000 and stipulated that Small had not received any interest illegally. Small had been instrumental in electing Carlstrom in 1924.

Patronage, which got Small where he was, also played a part in bringing him down. He appointed his son, Leslie Small, to head the Department of Purchases and Construction, which controlled highway construction for the state. A.E. Inglesh, the new administrative auditor of the Department of Finance, was the governor's son-in-law. Before Small's administration was over, Leslie had a trial date to answer charges related to rigging state highway contracts.

When the state Public Utilities Commission would not ratify Mayor Thompson's streetcar program for Chicago, Small replaced it with a Commerce Commission with duplicate powers but a compliant membership. When Will Cloven, superintendent of paroles and pardons, resigned after he was accused by two grand juries of selling paroles, he was promptly placed on the commission payroll. In 1926, Small appointed Commerce Commission Chairman Frank L. Smith of Dwight to a short-term Senate vacancy caused by the death of Senator William McKinley. Smith had already won his own Senate seat in the 1926 election. But the Senate refused to seat Smith for the elected or the appointed position after an investigation revealed that he had received a $125,000 campaign contribution from Samuel Insull, a utility magnate. The Senate saw the conflict of interest in the Commerce Commission chairman's accepting contributions from a utility owner, even if the governor did not.

The Machine Goes Bust

Small found it difficult to hold his power base together when his cronies started to lose influence and fight among themselves. A succession of scandals in Chicago soon made "Big Bill" an embarrassing partner. Fred Lundin, who wanted credit for the mayor's election-day majorities, broke off relations when Thompson appointed his private secretary as chief of police. Small retained Lundin for his own machine by giving him control of patronage of Chicago's West and North Side parks. Faced with graft charges and lawsuits, Thompson retired from the mayor's office in 1923.

William Lorimer, a political harmonizer who had been in an eclipse since the U.S. Senate unseated him in 1912 when it declared he won an illegal election, returned from South America and patched up relations between Small and Thompson. In 1927, Thompson won another term and returned to City Hall. The mayor, who planned to back Carlstrom for governor in 1928, instead supported Small for a third term. Chicagoans, traditionally tolerant about letting politicians have a free hand, became fed up with Capone-style gangsterism and Thompson's loose talk. In the Republican primary, in both Cook County and downstate, Small ran behind Secretary of State Louis L. Emmerson, who in the November election won the difficult job of dealing with the city's accumulating financial problems.

Between 1912 and 1936, the optimistic Small was a candidate for governor six times. In 1932, he led a field of eight Republican primary candidates but was the big loser in the first Franklin Delano Roosevelt-led Democratic landslide. In that campaign, Thompson and Small made a flamboyant barge cruise, stopping at Illinois cities along the Illinois and Mississippi rivers.

Small died May 17, 1936, a month after Thompson backed him as the Union Progressive candidate for governor.

Governor Small and Sioux Chief Return of the Scouts before a performance with the Hagenbeck-Wallace Circus in Springfield, 1927

A section of State Route 13, which runs from Old Shawneetown to Centreville in the Metro East area, in the early 1900s; the first mile of rural cement road in the United States, paid for with private funds, was laid near Malta in DeKalb County as part of the Lincoln Highway.

Window display in Lincoln for a 1927 road hearing; during Governor Small's eight-year tenure, the state built 7,000 miles of 18-foot pavement and lifted people out of the mud.

27th Governor

Louis Lincoln Emmerson
1863-1941

1863 — Born December 27 in Albion

1912 — Loses bid for the Republican nomination for state treasurer

1917 - 1929 — Serves as secretary of state, winning elections in 1916, 1920, and 1924

1924 — Republican caucus leaders discourage Emmerson's bid for the gubernatorial nomination.

1928 — Defeats Small in the Republican gubernatorial primary and wins the general election

1929 — The October 29 stock market crash marks the beginning of the Depression; the governor calls four special sessions of the General Assembly to help ease the economic crisis and establishes relief commissions and a state income tax that is later declared unconstitutional.

1932 — Chooses not to run for reelection

1941 — Dies on February 4 in Mount Vernon

Republican
January 14, 1929 to January 9, 1933

Louis L. Emmerson was elected governor a year before the arrival of the Great Depression. A conservative Republican from southern Illinois, he defeated Governor Len Small in the 1928 primary and was an easy winner in the landslide election that put Herbert Hoover in the White House.

Emmerson had a good record as secretary of state, an office of high exposure to which he was twice reelected. His loyalties were to Lowden, rather than to the Small-Thompson branch of his party. His private honors included the top Illinois office in the Masonic Lodge. He was a courageous executive who tried to cure the financial hangovers of the almost-bankrupt Cook County government. But he couldn't foresee the Depression, which became his biggest burden. To cope, Emmerson appointed special relief commissions, summoned the legislature into multiple special sessions, and advocated a state income tax, which the Supreme Court ruled unconstitutional.

From Store Clerk to Secretary of State

Tall and angular, with protuberant ears, Emmerson was a small-town boy from the Wabash valley. At Albion in Edwards County, he was born to Presbyterian and Republican parents, Jesse and Fannie Saurdet Emmerson, on December 27, 1863. His father was a farmer and village official. His grandfather, Alan, was a cobbler from the state of Virginia who arrived in Albion in 1818 with the Beckwith-Flower colony of English settlers. He served with AbrahamLincoln in the legislature.

Young Lou, whose formal education ended with graduation from high school, played the tenor horn. After a concert at nearby Grayville, he met Anna Mathews, whom he married in 1887. (There is some disagreement over the name of his bride, however. Her name is given as Anna in *Who's Who in America*, on information presumably provided by her husband. Obituaries and other documents have variations, such as Ann Eliza, Eliza Ann, Ann, and Annie.)

He then moved to Mount Vernon to take a job as a furniture store clerk. He had previously clerked in stores in Albion and Sullivan, Indiana. At Mount Vernon, his home for the rest of his life, he became a partner in a general store and later opened a furniture store. An undated clipping from the *Mount Vernon Register-News* says that in 1898 he "graduated in embalming under Prof. Sullivan of St. Louis." (Small city furniture retailers frequently doubled as undertakers.) As time passed, he became one of the county seat's leading citizens, active in the Presbyterian church and several lodges. He was an alderman and school board president. He helped organize the Third National Bank, was its treasurer, and its president for 28 years.

As a Republican, he was county chairman, briefly a member of the State Board of Equalization, and a trustee of the Menard penitentiary by appointment of Governor Charles S. Deneen. In 1912, he ran unsuccessfully for nomination as state treasurer but was a delegate to the first of 10 Republican national conventions he attended. For the first of three times, he was elected secretary of state in 1916, defeating Lewis G. Stevenson, the son of a vice president and father of a future governor. As secretary of state, Emmerson reduced administrative expenses and sponsored new securities and corporation laws.

Despite inexperience in national politics, Emmerson in 1928 was manager of Frank O. Lowden's presidential campaign. In that capacity, he gave $2,500 checks to two St. Louis politicians who later became convention delegates. That situation enabled Lowden's opponents to claim improper use of campaign funds. But the governor never lost confidence in Emmerson.

The Governor of a State in Economic Crisis

In 1924, Emmerson wanted to run against Governor Len Small but was turned down at an elimination caucus of Republican leaders. That November, he polled the highest vote among state candidates when he was elected secretary of state for the third time. Four years later, his chief competition was Attorney General Oscar Carlstrom, who finally withdrew. In the primary, backed by Lowden and Deneen, he carried Cook County as well as downstate and finished 539,793 votes ahead of Governor Small. His Democratic opponent in the general election was Floyd E. Thompson of Rock Island, a young chief justice of the state Supreme Court who had no chance, while Secretary of Commerce Herbert Hoover won the presidency over Governor Al Smith of New York.

The new governor, facing a Republican legislative majority that included Small holdovers, postponed patronage appointments until the 1929 session ended. In a departure from the preceding administration, he disregarded many patronage requests and recalled some officials who served under Lowden. Emmerson set a precedent when he appointed a woman as assistant director of public welfare. A woman and a black man were named to the parole board.

His wife replenished the silverware and china in the Executive Mansion. He constructed 2,000 miles of pavement to complete the Lowden-Small program and sponsored a three-cent-a-gallon gasoline tax, one-third of which went to the counties. This time, it was upheld by the Supreme Court. In his first year in office, he launched a $2.5 million building program at welfare institutions.

In the largely sectional split over Prohibition, Emmerson was a downstate supporter of the Anti-Saloon League. In spite of a 1930 public policy referendum, he vetoed a bill to repeal the Illinois law that prohibited the sale of intoxicants and gave search and seizure powers to enforcement officials.

Emmerson tackled the streetcar problem that had been a Chicago issue for a third of a century. Under his leadership, the legislature adopted a franchise law that the metropolitan newspapers had opposed when it had Small-Thompson sponsorship. Former Governor Edward F. Dunne testified in opposition, but the ordinance was approved by the Chicago City Council and by a large majority in a 1930 referendum. The difficulty remained, however, as the surface and elevated lines still were unprofitable.

Even before the Depression, Chicago government was on the verge of bankruptcy. At Mayor Thompson's request, the state tax commission ordered a reassessment of Cook County real estate that delayed tax collections. They were two years behind schedule and a $40 million loan on tax anticipation warrants was necessary. Emmerson insisted that reckless extravagance by city officials was responsible and complained that Cook County had not paid its share of the state property tax for two years.

Massive unemployment was Emmerson's biggest problem. In October 1930, he called a conference of influential Chicagoans and proposed that governmental activity be limited to providing institutional building and road construction jobs. To coordinate private funds and distribute them through charitable organizations, he appointed the Governor's Commission on Unemployment and Relief. In Chicago, money raised by the Association of Commerce and the Council of Social Agencies was gone before spring.

The 1931 legislature, dominated by downstaters, limited itself to making townships rather than counties responsible for poor relief. When for the fourth time the governor summoned a special session, he asked it to reorganize the metropolitan assessment machinery and to provide state funds for the impoverished. He accepted administrative responsibility by appointing an Illinois Emergency Relief Commission. Backed by Lowden, he proposed a state income tax and increased tobacco and motor vehicle levies. The legislature provided the necessary two-thirds majorities, but the graduated income tax was held unconstitutional because it violated uniformity requirements. For Cook County, a $17 million relief bond issue was enacted without a requirement that it be approved by referendum.

As a stockholder, Emmerson personally suffered in the Depression's wave of bank failures. He gave up the presidency of the Third National Bank in Mount Vernon but was a stockholder in the Ridgely-Farmers State Bank in Springfield. He attended a directors' meeting that, without advance notice, asked State Auditor Oscar Nelson to liquidate the bank. Despite double indemnity liabilities that reportedly were heavy, he was comparatively well-to-do in retirement.

The Governor Retires

Emmerson was inaugurated 18 days after his 65th birthday, making him older than any of the other governors had been while they were in office. He suffered a minor stroke and, a year in advance, Emmerson announced he would not seek a second term. Age and health would have been reasons enough, but there were additional factors. The Depression made Republicans unpopular in Illinois, and party factionalism intensified during the Emmerson Administration.

Attorney General Carlstrom, who had "wet" leanings, believed that in 1928 he had been promised Emmerson's support. However, the retiring governor favored Omer N. Custer of Galesburg, a newspaper publisher, businessman, and believer in Prohibition, for the gubernatorial nomination. When Small won the primary, the retiring governor, who had been grand master of the Masonic Lodge in Illinois, quietly passed word that he favored Henry Horner, the Democratic candidate who also was a 33rd-degree Mason.

His final message expressed pride in state employees who, at his suggestion, contributed a day's pay a month to the relief of the needy through two winters. "Probably in no similar period since the Civil War has there been so much financial distress," he commented. Urging rigid economy and revision of the tax laws, he condemned "profligate" borrowing to meet current needs and government encroachment on private business. A conservative to the end, he said he was "unalterably opposed to the dole system."

Most of his retirement was spent in his Mount Vernon home. He died there on February 4, 1941.

Governor Emmerson and family at the Executive Mansion with President Herbert Hoover, who was in Springfield in June 1931 to rededicate Lincoln's Tomb after an extensive restoration

28th
Governor

Henry Horner
1878-1940

1878 — Born November 30 in Chicago
1897 — Receives law degree from Kent College of Law
1899 — Passes the bar; begins practice with Frank Whitney
1914 — Elected judge of probate court
1932 — Wins the Democratic gubernatorial nomination and defeats former Governor Len
Small in the general election
1935 — Asks that the sales tax be raised to 3 percent and that utility bills also be taxed; the
General Assembly passes the Old Age Security Act to give state aid to the elderly.
1936 — Defeats Chicago Democratic machine candidate, Dr. Herman N. Bundesen, in a costly
and bitter primary; defeats Republican C. Wayland Brooks in the general election
1940 — Dies in office on October 6

Democrat
January 9, 1933 to January 4, 1937
January 4, 1937 to October 6, 1940

No Illinois chief executive had a more difficult administration than Henry Horner, the Depression governor. With a humanitarian's compassion, an extrovert's personality, and a marathoner's determination, he prevailed upon the reluctant legislature to support taxes and bond issues for unemployment relief. The first Jewish governor, he was a former Chicago judge, an administrator in the Progressive tradition, and a proud man who decided he would not be pushed around by the mayor of Chicago. Somewhat out of character, the first two-term Democratic governor since before the Civil War fought the Chicago political machine by becoming a successful, vindictive political boss. He literally worked himself to death. He was the second Illinois governor to die in office.

Horner's long-term legacy to Illinois government was revision of the revenue system: substitution of the retail sales tax for the inadequate property levy that was the state's chief support. His predecessor's income tax was invalidated by the Supreme Court; only with a sales tax could the state pay its share of unemployment relief. After Horner twice forced the legislature to enact sales tax laws, the people grumbled about the extra pennies they paid. Chicago Mayor Edward J. Kelly believed that "High Tax Henry" was a loser.

However, Horner's triumph in the 1936 primary, followed by election to a second term, established the governor's political independence.

Judge Horner, the "Professional Honest Man" of the Ticket

Horner, who never married, was the first governor who was a native of Cook County. He was born into an established German-Jewish family in Chicago on November 30, 1878. When Horner was 5 years old, his mother divorced his father, Solomon A. Levy, a business-man, because he abused her. She resumed her maiden name, Dilah Horner, and insisted that her son's name also be changed to Henry Horner II, after his grandfather. With a degree from Kent College of Law, Horner began practicing in 1899 with Frank A. Whitney, the son of Henry Clay Whitney, a friend of Abraham Lincoln's and a collector of Lincoln memorabilia. Horner moved into a bachelor apartment where he too collected Lincoln material. He assembled a 5,000-volume Lincoln library that he willed to the State Historical Library. The collection is now in the Abraham Lincoln Presidential Library and Museum

An attractive young candidate for underdog Democrats, Horner was elected judge of the Probate Court of Cook County in 1914. For 18 years, he made certain that widows and orphans got a square deal in estate settlements. At the same time, he broadened his acquaintance among important families. For Cook County Democrats, he was what ethnic politics expert John M. Allswang calls a "professional honest man," a candidate whose name made ballotmates more acceptable.

The Taxing Concerns of Governor Horner

Throughout his judicial career, Horner was politically subservient to Roger C. Sullivan, George E. Brennan, and Anton J. Cermak, who in succession dominated Chicago Democratic politics. Mayor Cermak, also county chairman, wanted to run for governor in 1932 but estimated his election was unlikely because he was defeated for senator four years earlier. Because Jews were a major element in Cermak's political coalition and prominent campaign contributors favored Horner, the mayor backed Horner in the primary. Horner defeated Michael L. Igoe, the hero of the Chicago Irish, and State Democratic Chairman Bruce A. Campbell of Belleville. Horner captured 50.4 percent of the total, with 397,499 votes, while Igoe and Campbell received 255,527 and 134,972, respectively. Then in the first Franklin D. Roosevelt landslide, Horner was elected easily over former Republican Governor Len Small.

At his inauguration, the affable Horner asked for nonpartisanship in facing the financial and social problems of the Depression. His immediate troubles were mostly caused by Cermak, who objected when the governor appointed personal friends to sensitive positions. One was Ernest Lieberman, who was put in charge of highway contracts. To placate Cermak, Horner appointed Dr. Frank J. Jirka, Cermak's son-in-law, as state health director. However, Horner filled positions with people suited to the jobs, including some Republicans. That upset Cermak and downstate patronage chiefs like John Stelle.

Less than two months after the inauguration, Horner gave the eulogy at the funeral for Cermak, who had been assassinated in Florida. Horner helped with legislation that enabled the city council to fill the vacancy. The Irish returned to power when Edward Joseph Kelly got the job and shared leadership with Patrick A. Nash, the Democratic county chairman.

Horner's troubles continued as the new mayor, like Cermak, tried to control the governor's office. Kelly established a close relationship with President Roosevelt, who preferred to deal directly with big city mayors and came to admire the election night majorities in Chicago. Horner soon found that he was being bypassed by Harry L. Hopkins, director of the Emergency Relief Administration, when decisions were made about the distribution of federal funds.

Repeatedly, the legislature, which only met from January to June every other year, was reconvened for emergency action. After the regular session of 1933, there were four special sessions. Nevertheless, Washington complained that Illinois was contributing less to relief financing than other high-unemployment states. In the year ending August 1, 1933, the federal government contributed 99 percent of the $68 million spent for relief in Illinois. A $20 million bond issue floated with difficulty by the Emmerson Administration was exhausted. Horner raised $30 million with another issue, but the money was gone within a year.

Horner, who considered Depression victims his personal as well as his official responsibility, fathered the Illinois sales tax out of necessity. During his first legislative session, in which Democrats were in the majority but downstate Republicans were especially balky, he drove a 3 percent sales tax through the legislature. The Supreme Court promptly invalidated it because motor fuel and sales of farm produce were exempted. After corrections were made and the rate was reduced to 2 percent, Horner tried again. The bill passed a week before the end of June, after which two-thirds majorities would have been required. This time, the Supreme Court concurred.

In 1935, Horner asked that the sales tax be raised to 3 percent and that utility bills be taxed. The legislature complied after state funds were exhausted, Hopkins shut off federal funds, and the governor pleaded that the jobless faced starvation. With increasing rates and a broadened base, the tax became the foundation of the revenue system for a third of a century, until it was coupled with a state income tax.

Horner gave tax relief to homeowners and farmers by canceling the annual meeting of the *ex officio* board that traditionally levied the state property tax, effectively suspending the tax and lowering bills. The board was later abolished.

The idealistic Horner was loyal to the Democratic Party and its social philosophy, but like many others, he had reservations about Roosevelt's court-packing proposal permitting the executive to control the judiciary. In spending programs for the unemployed, he was closer to Progressive Harold L. Ickes than to Hopkins. He also held back from embracing the "blue eagle" of the short-lived National Recovery Administration, which was invalidated on the ground that it would put private business under governmental dictation.

Synchronizing with New Deal innovations, Illinois adopted old-age pension and unemployment insurance legislation. Horner tried but failed to settle mine union warfare. The rising national prominence of United Mine Workers leader John L. Lewis nullified any negotiating power the governor had. Horner had somewhat more success in helping the state's teachers. Chicago teachers were paid only in scrip and tax anticipation warrants for a year. The special legislative session Horner called in early 1934 passed a bill to temporarily divert one-third of the state motor fuel tax to the school fund, with half going to Chicago.

The Fight for Reelection

A political "wet," Horner signed a repealer of the Illinois prohibition law and presided at the state convention that ratified repeal of the Eighteenth Amendment in December 1933. He wanted legal liquor sales to be regulated by a state law that would keep political influences out of saloons. Kelly caused a deadlock in the legislature by insisting upon local control. Eventually, they compromised, but other conflicts between the governor and the mayor kept arising. Because of rivalry between City Hall and the governor's office, the legislature awarded enforcement of the new driver's license law to the secretary of state.

The final break with the Kelly-Nash Democrats came late in 1935. Without advance notice, Horner, on public policy grounds, vetoed a bill giving Chicago a new revenue source by permitting the city council to license off-track betting. In the mayor's view, the veto proved that the governor was a bluenose. On December 9, in the presence of President Roosevelt, who was in Chicago for a farm speech, Kelly called Horner a "one-termer." Roosevelt offered Horner an appointment to a federal judgeship if he would step aside.

The mayor's candidate for governor in 1936 was the city health commissioner, Dr. Herman N. Bundesen, whose subservience to the Chicago organization was undoubted. Bundesen wore spats and had written a book on baby care, characteristics that downstaters did not regard as qualifications for the governorship.

On the other hand, in the 1936 primary race, Horner made a spectacular transformation from the unpopular sponsor of the sales tax into a hero. Thoroughly angry, Horner announced his second-term candidacy with organized support in only three Chicago wards. Making political bossism his chief issue, he scathingly denounced Mayor Kelly and Cook County Democratic Chairman Nash. Charging wholesale vote fraud in Chicago, he befriended Cook County Judge Edmund K. Jarecki, who also was dropped from the Democratic ticket. In Illinois political history, the 1936 Democratic primary rates as one of the most bitter and most expensive. Thomas B. Littlewood, Horner's biographer, estimates that $3 million, an enormous sum in pre-television elections, was spent on the two candidates in their mudslinging campaign. As a byproduct, Horner's primary strategy gave Republicans a precedent for future campaigning against "Kelly-Nash bossism."

Thus, Horner cast himself as a popular underdog who wouldn't take orders from the party bosses, a message that played especially well with downstaters. His unexpected talent as an organizer and propagandist blossomed and, with Republicans helping, Horner carried every down-state county and eight Chicago wards, beating Bundesen 820,313 to 659,221. The victory was personal, for the other statewide nominations went to incumbents who ran on the Kelly-Nash slate. Horner tried to defeat all but Secretary of State Edward J. Hughes and Attorney General Otto Kerner, who had personal followings.

After the primary, Horner remained angry. At the request of the League of Women Voters, he changed his position and called a special session, which, over City Hall protests, enacted permanent registration of voters in Cook County. He vetoed a bill to allow Chicago to use sales tax money to pay part of local relief costs. The continuing feud alarmed the White House, but surface harmony was restored, and in November, the Democrats carried Illinois again. Horner got his second term by defeating Republican C. Wayland Brooks by a little more than 385,000 votes. Democrats Roosevelt and Senator James Hamilton Lewis won their races by larger margins than Horner did, and some observers suspected that Kelly trimmed the governor's vote totals.

Determined to purge his enemies from party leadership, Horner resumed the Democratic warfare in 1938 by running Scott W. Lucas, his tax commission chairman, for U. S. senator. The downstate incumbent, William H. Dieterich, stepped aside and the Chicagoans countered with Michael L. Igoe, a former legislative leader. Lucas won the primary and the general election.

A Crusade Cut Short

Horner's next political steps might have been a third-term campaign for governor in 1940 and/or an effort to turn Mayor Kelly out of office in 1943. Had he succeeded, the political history of Illinois would have some different chapters. But two days before Lucas's election, the overworked governor suffered a coronary thrombosis. Thereafter, his office (when he was not wintering in Florida) was his bedroom in the Executive Mansion, reached by a one-man elevator. He conducted state business through a "regency" of administration officials, although under the Illinois Constitution, Lieutenant Governor John H. Stelle was acting governor when Horner was out of the state. At one point, he returned from Florida just in time to appoint James M. Slattery, his Commerce Commission chairman and campaign manager, to succeed Senator James Lewis, who died (conveniently) just as Horner was about to cross into Illinois. Lieutenant Governor Stelle might easily have appointed Patrick Nash.

The incapacitated governor gave up his third-term ambitions. Because he hated Stelle almost as much as he hated Kelly, he refused to resign and turn the state over to the lieutenant governor. Nevertheless, so that Democrats could have a united front in the 1940 campaign, he consented to a harmony ticket. Kelly and Nash came to Springfield but never rode the elevator upstairs. They allowed Horner to dictate the important decisions. He blackballed Stelle (who ran in the primary anyway) and named Harry B. Hershey of Taylorville, his insurance director, to be the candidate for governor.

In order to retain his official powers, Horner refused to leave the state again. The last months of his life were spent in a rented mansion on the lakefront. At the age of 61, the man who had guided Illinois through the Depression died on October 6, 1940. He had lived long enough to see Hershey defeat his lieutenant governor for the 1940 Democratic gubernatorial nomination.

Governor Henry Horner, second from left, with Amelia Earhart, at Springfield Airport, October 19, 1934; others pictured, from left, are Illinois State Register *editor V.Y. Dallman, Supreme Court Justice Norman Jones, L.P. Bonfoey and State Treasurer John C. Martin.*

Governor Horner gathered an extensive Lincoln collection, which began with a book, Life on the Circuit with Abraham Lincoln, *written by Henry Clay Whitney, a friend of Lincoln's.*

29th Governor

John H. Stelle
1891-1962

1891 — Born August 10 in McLeansboro
1916 — Graduates from Washington University Law School
1917 - 1919 — Serves in the Army; sees combat action in World War I
1934 — Wins election to the state treasurer's office
1936 — Wins the lieutenant governor's race on the Nash-Kelly Democratic slate
1940 — Runs in the primary and loses after Governor Horner refuses to endorse him
1946 — Serves as national commander of the American Legion
1962 — Dies July 7

Democrat
October 6, 1940 to January 13, 1941

John H. Stelle was the downstate chum of the Chicago political machine headed by Mayor Edward Joseph Kelly and Democratic Cook County Chairman Patrick A. Nash. The alliance with the Nash-Kelly Democrats helped him in the divisive political warfare of 1936. That year, Stelle advanced from state treasurer to lieutenant governor.

But the alliance also drew the wrath of Governor Henry Horner, who did everything he could to make sure Stelle would never be governor, including seeing to it that Stelle would not win the 1940 gubernatorial nomination. In the end, however, it wasn't enough. Horner worked himself to death, and Stelle served out the remaining 99 days of Horner's second term.

The Doughboy Who Entered Politics

Stelle was born at McLeansboro August 10, 1891, the last of seven children of Thompson B. and Laura Blades Stelle. His great-grandfather had been an early settler and his grandfather a farmer and Civil War soldier. His father owned 2,000 acres of farmland, operated a department store, and practiced law. The future governor attended high school and Western Military Academy before he played professional baseball for several seasons without reaching the major leagues. In 1913, Stelle married Wilma Wisehart of Shawneetown. Together they would have two sons.

He graduated from law school at Washington University and was admitted to the bar in 1916. The next year, he enlisted and attended the first officers training school at Fort Sheridan. After 17 months in the U.S. Army, during which he was gassed and wounded, he returned home with the rank of captain.

Stelle was a fourth-generation resident of Hamilton County. There he was a lawyer who operated a 769-acre farm but gave major attention to successful business ventures, which included oil and racing horses. He helped organize and was president of the Cahokia Downs racetrack across the Mississippi River from St. Louis, and became the most influential downstater in the horse racing circles of his day. At McLeansboro, he owned a creamery and manufactured brick and drain tile. He owned a coal company at Evansville, Indiana, and a glazed structural tile plant at Brazil, Indiana.

He was a member of the Methodist church and several lodges. He was very active in the American Legion. From the end of World War I until a few years after World War II, the Legion was a major political organization, much like the Grand Army of the Republic had been after the Civil War. He attended the Legion's organizing conference at St. Louis. Broad-shouldered and virile but an indifferent speaker, he became one of the group's kingmakers, helping shape its policy and select the top officers.

Ambitious for a political career, he cultivated friendships among Legion leaders in Chicago. In the 1930 campaign, he headed a committee that helped veterans on the Democratic ticket. One of the candidates he worked to elect was Edward J. Barrett, a political unknown. When Barrett was elected state treasurer, Stelle went to Springfield as assistant treasurer. After the next election, Barrett was state auditor and Stelle his right-hand man. In 1934, Stelle was nominated and elected state treasurer.

The 99 Days

In the 1936 primary, Kelly and Nash slated Stelle for lieutenant governor. Kelly and Nash were feuding with Governor Horner, who had a slate of his own. In the Democratic primary, the Kelly-Nash gubernatorial candidate, Dr. Herman N. Bundesen, lost every downstate county; Stelle carried only his home county, but votes in Chicago nominated him over Horner's candidate, Attorney General John E. Cassidy of Peoria. Horner and his lieutenant governor rarely saw eye-to-eye on political matters, and two years later, Stelle did not support Scott W. Lucas, who was Horner's winning entry for U.S. senator.

The ailing Horner might easily have resigned during the long illness that haunted his second term. But he refused because he did not want Stelle as his successor. When it became obvious that Horner could not himself seek another term as governor, he conferred with Kelly and

Nash on a Democratic "harmony" ticket. Horner insisted that Stelle not appear on the slate, and so named Harry B. Hershey of Taylorville, his insurance director, to be the candidate for governor.

But Stelle ran for governor in the 1940 Democratic primary anyway. He joined Benjamin S. Adamowski and Edward J. Barrett in a challenge to the harmony ticket, with Adamowski running for U.S. senator and Barrett for auditor.

During his illness, Horner began running state business through a "regency" of administration officials, even when wintering in Florida. Stelle made this practice a primary issue. He called it "Nudelmanism" after regency member Samuel Nudelman, Horner's finance director. Stelle believed government by regency was improper. The lieutenant governor should assume leadership when the governor is unavailable or incapacitated. He also believed administration officials were making decisions that only the governor or acting governor could make. If there was a constitutional issue of executive disability, it received little support because Horner was a popular hero. No one on the rogue Democratic ticket won the primary.

Stelle was working in a wheat field on his farm when he learned of Horner's death on October 6, 1940. He was inaugurated in a brief ceremony in his old office and proclaimed a 10-day period of official mourning. Later, a large number of Horner partisans were discharged.

Those who thought Horner a hero automatically thought Stelle a villain. Critics whispered scandal when the Executive Mansion, dingy after eight years as the residence of bachelor Governor Horner, was redecorated and the new first family sent dinner invitations to McLeansboro neighbors and Springfield friends. The *St. Louis Post-Dispatch*, which watched the Stelle Administration closely, reported that a "tremendous amount of equipment, coal and other merchandise" was bought. Rumors of irregularities were never documented. Milburn P. Akers, who had been part of the Horner regency, blamed the men around Stelle and wrote, "If John Stelle was ever off base, he was never tagged."

War clouds were growing more ominous as the new governor denounced appeasement, appointed draft boards, set up an emergency defense council, and created a reserve militia to take the place of the National Guard, which had been called into federal service. As he went out of office, he told the legislature that the state police and the parole board should be taken out of politics. He asked his friends to cooperate with Dwight H. Green, the incoming Republican governor who had defeated Hershey in the general election.

The Legionnaire

At the end of World War II, Stelle was one of the American Legion leaders who drafted the Servicemen's Readjustment Act of 1944, commonly called the GI Bill of Rights, and lobbied it through Congress. His turn to be national commander came in 1946. From that position, he criticized General Omar N. Bradley, who headed the Veterans Administration after the war. Bradley, who had refused to build a veterans hospital at Decatur, charged that Stelle "deliberately obstructed" his office.

Out of office and back at McLeansboro, Stelle frequently raised his voice as a southern Illinois Democrat who had Republican friends in high places. In 1952, he turned his back on Adlai E. Stevenson's bid for the presidency and made speeches for Dwight D. Eisenhower. In Illinois and Indiana, he supported the winning Republican candidates for governor.

Stelle died on July 7, 1962, at Barnes Hospital, St. Louis, of acute leukemia.

Courtesy of the Abraham Lincoln Presidential Library

Governor Stelle with his grandson John Paul Stelle and his daughter-in-law in the governor's farmhouse in McLeansboro; the photo was taken when he was serving as lieutenant governor.

John H. Stelle

Courtesy of the Abraham Lincoln Presidential Library

Governor Stelle rides a mule presented by Sam Plant of Murphysboro. Plant, who is holding the halter, allegedly stole a mule from Stelle in France during World War I. Active in the American Legion, Stelle led a team of Legion officials who in 1943 drafted the main features of the GI Bill of Rights and shepherded its successful passage through Congress.

Courtesy of the Abraham Lincoln Presidential Library

Governor Stelle, second from left, at his McLeansboro farm; his son Russell is on the left, and his son John Jr. is second from right. The other men are identified only as neighbors.

219

30th Governor

Dwight Herbert Green
1897-1958

1897 — Born January 9 at Ligonier, Indiana

1917 — Leaves Wabash College to serve as an Army aviator; as a second lieutenant, spends the war in California teaching others to fly

1920 — Finishes his undergraduate degree at the University of Chicago

1922 — Earns his law degree from the University of Chicago

1925 — Takes a job in Washington as an attorney for the IRS

1931 — Plays an instrumental part in building and presenting the tax evasion case against Al Capone

1939 — Defeats former Mayor William Hale "Big Bill" Thompson in the Republican Chicago mayoral primary, but loses the general election to Mayor Edward J. Kelly.

1940 — Defeats Democrat Harry B. Hershey to win the governor's race

1941 — The United States declares war on Japan December 8; on December 18, the General Assembly convenes a special session to prepare Illinois for war; 670,000 Illinoisans would serve in World War II.

1944 — Squeaks by Democrat Thomas J. Courtney to win a second term

1945 — World War II ends.

1947 — A coal dust explosion kills 111 miners in Centralia. Green aides had solicited campaign contributions from mine owners while ignoring the coal miners' warnings about unsafe conditions.

1948 — Fails to get the vice presidential nomination and is badly beaten by Democratic challenger Adlai Stevenson in the governor's race

1958 — Dies February 20

Republican

January 13, 1941 to January 8, 1945

January 8, 1945 to January 10, 1949

Governor Dwight H. Green made his reputation as the prosecutor who sent "Scarface Al" Capone to prison. As for politics, his early specialty, the denunciation of Chicago Democratic leaders on the "Kelly-Nash bossism" issue, enabled the conservative Green to win reelection during World War II. While he was governor, Republicans extended their control to all state offices, the legislature, the Supreme Court, and half of the Cook County offices. But then Green's ambitions for either a third term — or maybe the vice presidency — fell flat.

An amiable blond with classic features and compact frame, Green was perhaps the most handsome of Illinois governors. He tried to be noncontroversial as he shared Republican leadership with U.S. Senator C. Wayland "Curly" Brooks, a golden-voiced World War I marine, who also was first elected in 1940 and roundly defeated eight years later. Brooks was an isolationist favorite of Colonel Robert R. McCormick of the *Chicago Tribune*. In anti-Roosevelt campaigning, Green balanced the public's patriotism against its dislike of regimentation. While patriotically supporting the two-ocean war effort, he criticized the federal agencies that regulated homefront activities during the Depression and the war.

Green established the precedent that Republican governors cooperate with Democratic mayors for the good of Chicago. Once in office, he stopped denouncing Mayor Edward J. Kelly by name. Early in his second term, he invited the mayor, to whom he had talked only at public gatherings, to lunch at the Executive Mansion. Together they solved a problem that had perplexed noncooperating governors and mayors for a half-century. To the surprise of those downstaters who believed his warnings about Democratic bossism, he and the mayor jointly sponsored legislation that created the Chicago Transit Authority and put streetcar, elevated lines, and the new subway under public ownership, which had been Governor Edward F. Dunne's recurring dream.

Thus ended five decades of agitation about traction franchises. As part of the bipartisan program, the mayor appointed four members of the Chicago Transit Authority and the governor appointed three. The Republican Administration enacted housing and terminal authority bills City Hall wanted.

Green's example of state-metropolitan cooperation became a model for the William G. Stratton, Richard B. Ogilvie, and James R. Thompson administrations.

The Prosecutor Who Brought Down Capone

The future governor was born on January 9, 1897, at Ligonier, Indiana. He was the son of Harry and Minnie Gerber Green. A 1948 campaign biography said that his grandfather came from Germany and that his father had been a farmer. For two years, "Pete" Green went to Wabash College in Crawfordsville, Indiana, where he played quarterback and third base before he enlisted at the age of 20 and applied for assignment as an Army aviator. As a second lieutenant, he spent the war in California teaching others to fly at Mather Field, Sacramento.

After the armistice, Green resumed his college education, for one quarter at nearby Stanford and then at the University of Chicago, where he finished his undergraduate work in 1920 and obtained a law degree in 1922. While studying, he did apprentice work in the office of Roy D. Keehn, a family friend who was the Hearst counsel in Chicago. Green's wages came from the Chicago papers, where he was a reporter for the *Examiner* and wrote a legal column.

In 1925, U.S. Senator Charles S. Deneen got him a job in Washington as an attorney for the Internal Revenue Service. The next year, he married Mabel Victoria Kingston and in a few months took her to Chicago, where their two daughters were born. He was the only tax specialist on a staff assembled by District Attorney George E.Q. Johnson to investigate Prohibition-era hoodlums. He prepared the income tax case on which Capone was indicted and did most of the work of presenting the evidence to the jury in 1931.

When Capone went to the Atlanta federal penitentiary, Green's reward was appointment by President Herbert Hoover as the U.S. attorney in the Chicago district. The Senate's Democratic majority failed to confirm him, but he held the office for three years during the Roosevelt Administration until the faction-split Illinois Democrats agreed upon a successor. Meanwhile, orders came from Washington to prosecute Samuel Insull and his brother Martin, whose expansive utility and transportation empire had failed. (Samuel Insull had at one time controlled Commonwealth Edison, Peoples Gas Company, the Public Service Company of Northern Illinois, the elevated railways in Chicago, and utilities in St. Louis and Indiana.) Although the Insulls were unpopular, Green regarded the mail fraud case as weak and requested the help of special prosecutors. His judgment was vindicated when the jury quickly acquitted the Insulls.

In the 1939 mayoral primary, Chicago Republicans needed an attractive candidate to run against former Mayor William Hale "Big Bill" Thompson, who was trying for a comeback. Barney Goodspeed, treasurer of the Republican National Committee, raised a $100,000 fund and recruited the young former prosecutor, who had a law office in the Chicago Loop. Green won easily and then, with only $50,000 for campaign expenses, faced Mayor Edward J. Kelly. The Capone prosecutor ran as a reformer, and his speeches promising clean government were patterned after Governor Henry Horner's 1936 and 1938 denunciations of Chicago politicians. Kelly was reelected, but Green carried 14 wards and polled 43 percent of the vote, an unusual showing for a Republican in Chicago.

Governor Backtracks on Reform

In 1940, Green was the bright hope of Republicans who wanted to extend gains made two years earlier. As a candidate for nomination as governor, he opposed Richard J. Lyons, a Lake County legislator who was backed by the *Tribune*. Green won the primary 618,025 to

457,643. Running against Harry B. Hershey of Taylorville, whom Democrats had nominated at Horner's request, Green promised to reduce taxes and work to reform state welfare institutions. He accused Kelly-Nash Democrats of tolerating crime and gangsters, and he charged there had been corruption in the way Horner's campaigns had been financed. Green was the strongest Republican vote getter in the strong Republican race of 1940. The only winner on the Democratic state ticket was Edward J. Hughes, the veteran secretary of state.

In advance of his inauguration, Green's appointment of Leslie P. "Ike" Volz as his executive secretary signaled that he did not plan a reform administration. The official explanation was that the governor, a political newcomer, needed someone who understood the background of Republican factionalism. Volz, who in 1915 was Fred Lundin's secretary, had been an insider in the "Big Bill" Thompson-Len Small era.

The war in Europe stimulated the economy, and the Green Administration opened with a tax cut, reducing Horner's sales tax from 3 percent to 2 percent. Part of the revenue loss was recouped by the state's first tax on cigarettes — two cents a pack — and increases in beer and liquor taxes. Although the Depression wound down, relief was still a major expense. At Green's request, the 1941 legislature created a permanent Public Aid Commission to replace the Emergency Relief Commission that since 1932 had allocated state and federal funds to local agencies.

With the approach of Pearl Harbor, Green steered a middle course between Senator C. Wayland Brooks, who opposed the draft, and U.S. Rep. Everett M. Dirksen, who in 1941 changed positions and announced support of President Franklin D. Roosevelt's policies. When hostilities began, the governor followed the example Governor Frank Lowden set in the previous war by appointing a state council of defense and calling the legislature into special session to put Illinois on a war footing. He worked hard, traveled the state tirelessly, and spoke to innumerable groups concerned with war bond sales, victory gardens, and civil defense.

Green generally had the cooperation of the legislature, which had Republican majorities. In the House, if there was trouble in passing an administration bill, he could usually rustle up some votes from a handful of downstate Democratic members who were grateful for patronage favors. After tackling the Chicago transit problems, he turned his attention to downstate roads. Hundreds of miles of all-weather farm-to-highway roads that were previously impassable for weeks at a time were constructed in 1946 and 1947. Nevertheless, the Republican legislature showed its independence several times. At the opening of the 1945 session,

Green demonstrated his political ineptness when he announced, without consulting the leadership, a preference for T. Mac Downing of Macomb for president pro tem of the state Senate and Hugh Green of Jacksonville for House speaker. House Republicans fumed but complied. The senators figuratively thumbed their noses by putting Edward E. Laughlin of Freeport in the leadership post. Green, who had been elected on a pledge to remove the sales tax from food, could not get the required two-thirds approval of a constitutional amendment. The legislature also denied his request for a "gateway" change that would make the amending process easier.

When the first bill for a fair employment practice commission appeared in 1943, the governor avoided a stand by appointing an inter-racial commission, without power to act against discrimination. Two years later, all labor groups supported fair employment bills, but for nearly 20 years the legislature refused to pass them.

As is traditional for Illinois governors, Green ran poorly in his 1944 second-term campaign. He and his Democratic opponent, Cook County State's Attorney Thomas J. Courtney, lived in the Edgewater Beach apart-ments on the lakefront. Courtney, an early riser, went to bed thinking he had been elected. Green, who stayed up until southern Illinois reported its vote, knew differently. His winning margin was 72,271.

A year after World War II victory celebrations, demobilization had not been completed and meat shortages caused griping. In 1946, Republicans won half of the Cook County offices and increased their majorities in the legislature and the congressional delegation. Green and his advisers assumed it was a personal endorsement and expected to keep on winning. To them, Illinois no longer was a doubtful state, and any of the governor's shortcomings as an administrator did not seem important.

Unfulfilled Veep and/or Third-Term Ambitions
Green's reputation took a ding, however, when a coal dust explosion killed 111 men in a Centralia mine in 1947. Green's aides solicited the mine owners for campaign contributions and ignored repeated warnings from the coal miners that the mine was unsafe. The state belatedly accepted federal rules on mine ventilation, and the mine company was fined $1,000 for negligence.

Green in 1948 dreamed of becoming the vice presidential nominee in what promised to be a Republican year. To ensure the solid support of the Illinois delegation to the national convention, he announced his third-term candidacy for the governorship. Lieutenant Governor

Hugh W. Cross, who thought it was his turn to run, upset the surface harmony by announcing that he would oppose Green. The *Tribune* then reported that Warren Wright, a perennial candidate, also would run. Because he would have no chance in a three-man race, Cross withdrew. So did Wright, leaving Green unopposed for the nomination.

Through Old Guard contacts, Green was appointed temporary chairman of the convention. That provided an opportunity to stampede the convention with a rousing keynote oration. The governor, though never a spellbinder, could speak convincingly from a ghostwritten text he hadn't seen before. Close friends passed the hat and paid an easterner to write a latter-day imitation of William Jennings Bryan's 1896 "Cross of Gold" speech. Each of the contributors was allowed to see the speech in advance. Each took the liberty of revising some of the ghostwriter's rhetoric. As delivered by Green in a sweltering hall, it was a typical anti-New Deal speech. The delegates didn't listen closely, and the vice presidential nomination went to Governor Earl Warren of California.

Harry Truman wasn't a strong top of the Democratic ticket (indeed he barely won the 1948 presidential election), and Green expected election to a third term. He campaigned as an experienced executive who merited appreciation by the voters, and he derided Democratic challenger Adlai Stevenson as a striped-pants diplomat. Republicans were overconfident because of their 1946 victory and because Mayor Kelly had been forced to retire.

They didn't count on how effective the "egghead" Stevenson would be in attacking the governor's record. Stevenson was as persistent and effective as Green had been eight years earlier in his disapproval of Kelly-Nash Democrats. He kept talking about the Centralia mine disaster, accused the Republicans of a permissive attitude toward gambling and slot machines, pointed out that scores of newspaper reporters were on the state payroll without doing any work, and disapproved of Attorney General George F. Barrett's indictment of a St. Louis reporter who was investigating evidence that the Shelton gang was expanding its activities from southern Illinois into the Peoria area. Green lost the general election by half a million votes.

Away from public office, Green opened a law practice in the Loop and became a Republican elder statesman. He died of lung cancer on February 20, 1958.

Mabel Victoria Kingston Green

Governor Green

Governor Green, right, at Republican Day at the Illinois State Fair, 1946; from left, Mabel Green, Robert R. McCormick, publisher of the Chicago Tribune, *and Maryland McCormick*

31st Governor

Adlai Ewing Stevenson
1900-1965

1900 —Born February 5 in Los Angeles

1916 —Learns that his father has lost the election for secretary of state

1918 —Enters Princeton as a freshman and an apprentice seaman

1919 —Discharged from the Navy

1922 —Receives B.A. from Princeton

1926 —Earns law degree from Northwestern

1928 —Marries Ellen Borden; the couple will have three sons, including Adlai Stevenson III, who will run for governor in 1982 and 1986.

1933 —Works on the legal staff of the Agricultural Adjustment Agency, one of President Franklin Delano Roosevelt's New Deal agencies

1935 —Is elected president of the Chicago Council on Foreign Relations

1941 - 1944 — Serves as special assistant to the secretary of the Navy

1945 - 1946 — Takes a position at the State Department and participates in conferences leading to the foundation of the United Nations

1947 —Serves as an alternate U.S. delegate to the United Nations

1948 —Defeats Governor Dwight H. Green by more than 570,000 votes

1949 —Divorces Ellen Borden; secures passage of a bill that puts the Illinois state police under civil service

1951 —Orders police raids against illegal gambling; gets a highway construction program through the legislature

1952 —Accepts a draft to run against Dwight D. Eisenhower in the presidential race; carries only nine states

1956 —Runs again against Eisenhower for president but fares even worse than he did in 1952

1960 —Loses the Democratic nomination for president to John F. Kennedy

1961 —Is passed over as President Kennedy's secretary of state

1961 - 1965 —Serves as U.S. ambassador to the U.N.; advises Kennedy during the Cuban missile crisis and publicly supports President Lyndon Baines Johnson's Vietnam policies

1965 —Dies of a heart attack in London, England, on July 14

Democrat
January 10, 1949 to January 12, 1953

Adlai E. Stevenson was the most nationally prominent of all modern Illinois governors, and it's certainly impossible to give his career its proper due in just a few pages. However, a look at his work in Illinois shows why four years as governor propelled him to two presidential nominations. His landslide election in 1948, followed by reform efforts in Illinois government, brought invitations to appear before influential out-of-state audiences. There, his witty, articulate speeches coincided with the Democratic Party's search to replace Harry Truman in the White House.

In Springfield, demonstrating that executive experience is not necessarily a requisite for the governorship, he was fairly successful with his ambitious legislative program. He practiced fiscal as well as personal economy, preferring to spend more on schools and the unfortunate. When his term was over, his presidential supporters could claim that he had improved the moral climate of state government. His failures could be blamed, in part, on Republican legislators to whom the nonorganization Democrat was a political threat they did not understand.

The Rise of an "Egghead"

Adlai Ewing Stevenson II was born February 5, 1900, in Los Angeles, California, where his father was assistant manager of William Randolph Hearst's *Examiner*. His mother was Helen Louise Davis, whose family owned the *Bloomington Pantagraph*. Important Bloomington names were in his pedigree. On the Republican side was a maternal great-grandfather, Jesse W. Fell. A Quaker, Fell was Bloomington's first lawyer and was the friend who suggested Abraham Lincoln debate Stephen A. Douglas.

The Democratic Stevensons came from Kentucky. The first Adlai E. Stevenson, the governor's grandfather, supported Lincoln's opponents in 1864. Later, he was elected to Congress as a Greenbacker and Democrat. A gregarious man, he became Grover Cleveland's assistant postmaster general assigned to getting rid of some 40,000 Republican postmasters. He was elected vice president on the Cleveland ticket in 1892 and was defeated as William Jennings Bryan's running mate in 1900. In 1908, he came close to beating Charles S. Deneen for governor. Lewis G. Stevenson, the governor's father, also had political experience but at a lower level. He was the vice president's secretary and, in the Dunne Administration, parole board chairman and secretary of state by appointment. In 1916, as a candidate for a full term as secretary of state, he led the losing Democratic ticket. At other times, he managed 49 Midwestern farms owned by his family and Arizona copper mines owned by the Hearst estate.

After attending Choate prep school, earning his undergraduate degree from Princeton, studying law at Harvard, and earning his law degree at Northwestern, Adlai Stevenson II began a public service career that often took him to the nation's capital. He married Ellen Borden, a wealthy socialite, in 1928. They divorced in 1949. They had three sons, Adlai III, Borden, and John Fell. Adlai III became a state representative, state treasurer and U.S. senator but lost twice in bids for governor.

In 1933, Adlai II joined the legal staff of the Agricultural Adjustment Agency, a New Deal agency formed by President Franklin Delano Roosevelt. His work grew in responsibility and included a trouble-shooting post with Navy Secretary Frank Knox, the publisher of the *Chicago Daily News* and Alf Landon's running mate in 1936. He also participated in economic missions abroad for President Roosevelt and assisted two U.S. secretaries of state — Edward R. Stettinius, Jr. and James F. Byrnes — during the time the United Nations was being organized. He served as an alternate U.S. delegate to the United Nations in 1947.

Stevenson Becomes a Candidate

Every few years Stevenson returned to an intermittent law practice and local leadership of the Chicago Council of Foreign Relations. Thus he had the status of a public-spirited Chicagoan. At a time when both parties were in disrepute in Illinois, he aspired to a seat in the U. S. Senate. A group of friends started to explore the possibility of an independent campaign in the 1948 Democratic primary.

Former U.S. Secretary of State Byrnes provided a breakthrough when he told Jacob M. Arvey, the new mastermind of Illinois Democrats, that Stevenson was qualified to be senator or ambassador. Arvey was a practitioner of the Democratic theory that it is better to win an election with a reform candidate than to lose with an organization man. He had maneuvered Mayor Edward J. Kelly out of Chicago City Hall and replaced him with Martin H. Kennelly, a businessman with a good government image who had never been aggressive in politics. The Democrats needed two more clean faces to run against Governor Dwight H. Green and U.S. Senator Charles Wayland "Curly" Brooks. Already campaigning for governor was Paul H. Douglas, a University of Chicago economics professor and an ex-Marine with a Purple Heart for wounds received in combat in the Pacific. But he had been an independent Chicago alderman, and the Democrats didn't want him in Springfield. Arvey made an offer: If Stevenson would run for governor and Douglas for senator, both would have the party's support. Stevenson accepted after a period of private agonizing.

Despite his Washington career, the candidate was a stranger to the electorate. Republicans derided him as an "egghead." Nevertheless, Stevenson campaigned before small audiences, accusing Green of eight years of mismanagement. The result was a landslide repudiation of the incumbent. President Harry Truman carried Illinois by a little more than 33,000 votes, Douglas by a little less than 408,000, and Stevenson by 527,067 votes, a record at the time.

Governor Faces a Conservative Legislature

With a plea for nonpartisanship, contending that party differences at the national level had nothing to do with state and local issues, Adlai Stevenson was inaugurated before a conservative legislature. With Paul Powell as speaker, Democrats had a small majority in the 1949 House. Otherwise, Republicans controlled both legislative branches during the Stevenson Administration.

Green and Stevenson were the last Illinois governors until the late 1980s without severe budgetary problems. The Democrat inherited a wartime treasury surplus and spent it, following gubernatorial custom, on education, welfare, and other pressing governmental needs. To modernize Len Small's hard roads, in 1951 he proposed highway use taxes to support a $100 million, 10-year program. The legislature allowed a two-cent gasoline tax increase, to five cents a gallon, and a $28 million increase in truck license fees. The next legislature canceled part of the truck fees.

Stevenson wanted a new constitution, with or without an income tax. The Senate, always happy to be uncooperative, refused to vote for a convention. To the Republican contention that changes should be made piecemeal by individual amendments, the governor responded with a challenge to join him in supporting a "gateway" amendment and a "blue ballot" procedure that increased prospects for ratification. Opposition then ceased and the gateway, adopted in 1950, rated as a major achievement and helped pave the way for a successful constitutional convention 20 years later.

The legislature accepted the governor's proposal to reorganize the state police, which Green had used as a political agency. He enlarged the force, giving Democrats half the positions, and installed a merit system. But Stevenson failed to put the conservation department under a commission.

Stevenson asked that Illinois follow the example of President Truman, who had appointed Herbert Hoover to survey the organization and procedures of the federal government. Again the legislature agreed, and Walter V. Schaefer, a Northwestern University law professor who had been the governor's chief legal adviser, was appointed chairman of a "Little Hoover" commission. In the first survey of state government since enactment of the Lowden code in 1917, Schaefer's group did not attempt a top-level reshuffling but submitted several core recommendations, many of which were adopted by the legislature. Under the governor's sponsorship, Schaefer was elected to the Illinois Supreme Court. There his career was as distinguished as those of better-known staff members who later went to Washington.

Other appointees included J. Edward Day, future postmaster general; Carl McGowan, who became judge of the U.S. Court of Appeals in Washington; and William McCormick Blair, later ambassador to Denmark and the Philippines. Among Cabinet posts, Democratic politicians were interspersed with professionals. Richard J. Daley, later mayor of Chicago, was the first revenue director. Fred K. Hoehler, who had headed the Chicago Community Fund, took over the public welfare department when promised that he could disregard patronage demands of politicians.

Stevenson was the first governor to ask for a fair employment practice law and to place his prestige behind the Chicago Crime Commission's effort to improve law enforcement. Both failed. Taking an unpopular stand, he vetoed an American Legion-backed bill requiring that people on public payrolls swear a noncommunist oath. Earlier he was accused of being "soft on communism" for giving a deposition that Alger Hiss had a good reputation for integrity, loyalty, and veracity when Stevenson knew him in 1933 and later in 1949.

His own administration's scandals embarrassed the governor. James W. Mulroy, his campaign manager and executive secretary, resigned by request when it was discovered that as an insider he had bought Chicago Downs racing stock at five cents a share. Charles W. Wray, superintendent of foods and dairies, was fined for taking a $3,500 bribe to allow the sale of horsemeat as beef.

During his eighth month as governor, Stevenson announced with regret that on grounds of incompatibility, he and his socialite wife of 20 years, the former Ellen Borden, were separating. "I do not believe in divorce but I will not contest it," he announced.

With Republicans out of power and Kennelly an inactive mayor, Stevenson had no problems with Chicago City Hall. A lucid writer and engaging speaker, he depended upon rhetoric to sway public opinion and seldom became involved in Democratic problems.

The Presidential Campaigns and the U.N.

Given Stevenson's convincing victory in 1948, some in the Democratic Party had early in his term pegged him as a presidential candidate. Not only did Stevenson appear to be a vote getter, he had extensive interest and experience in foreign policy. But by January 1952, Stevenson had already announced that he wanted another four years as governor. That month, President Truman met Stevenson in Washington and asked him to be the Democratic nominee for president. Stevenson balked; he refused to have his name entered into primaries, though by February Stevenson for President committees had already formed without him. The media was persistent. In March, Stevenson was interviewed on *Meet the Press* and again confirmed that he was not a candidate for president but for governor of Illinois. In a written statement in April, Stevenson said there was "unfinished work in Illinois" and that he "could not accept the nomination for any other office this summer." But Stevenson supporters at July's Democratic national convention in Chicago refused to let this be the final word. Indiana Governor Henry F. Schricker placed Stevenson's name in nomination saying, "There are times when a man is not permitted to say no." The delegates agreed, and Stevenson could not say no. After accepting the presidential nomination, Stevenson intervened with the Democratic state committee to insure that his successor nominee for governor was Lieutenant Governor Sherwood Dixon, rather than Secretary of State Edward J. Barrett.

The Republicans nominated Dwight D. Eisenhower as their presidential candidate in 1952, and the "egghead" ran a distant second to the war hero in the election. He was decidedly less reluctant to run against Eisenhower again in 1956. Still, his image could not match Ike's. At one 1956 campaign event a woman is reported to have called out, "You have the vote of every thinking person," to which Stevenson replied, "That's not enough, madam. We need a majority." In the general election, Stevenson faired worse than he had in 1952. Stevenson sought the Democratic nomination in 1960, but this time the nod went to John F. Kennedy.

Stevenson wanted President Kennedy to name him secretary of state, but Kennedy chose Dean Rusk instead. Stevenson served as U.S. ambassador to the United Nations for the Kennedy Administration and continued into the Lyndon Johnson Administration. The former governor died of a heart attack July 14, 1965, on a London street.

A supporter of Stevenson's presidential bid; Stevenson lost twice to Dwight Eisenhower.

Candidate Stevenson and his wife Ellen cast their votes at Half Day, the polling place nearest their farm home in Libertyville.

Governor Stevenson, second from right, with top Democrats after his nomination as the presidential candidate; from left, Lieutenant Governor Sherwood Dixon, Secretary of State Edward Barrett, Senator Paul Douglas, President Harry Truman, and daughter Margaret

32nd Governor

William Grant Stratton
1914 - 2001

1914 — Born February 26 in Ingleside

1934 — Graduates from the University of Arizona with a degree in political science

1941 - 1943 — Serves as Illinois congressman-at-large

1943 - 1945 — Serves as state treasurer

1945 - 1946 — Becomes a lieutenant in the U.S. Navy and serves in the South Pacific

1947 - 1949 — Serves a second term as Illinois congressman-at-large

1948 — Loses the general election race for secretary of state

1951 - 1953 — Serves a second term as state treasurer

1952 — Defeats Lieutenant Governor Sherwood Dixon to win his first term as governor

1956 — Asks for Auditor Orville E. Hodge's resignation after he learns Hodge has been embezzling state money; wins his second term as governor

1960 — Loses the gubernatorial election to Otto Kerner

1965 — Is acquitted of income tax evasion charges stemming from the way he spent some of his campaign funds

1968 — Receives only 7 percent of the vote in the Republican gubernatorial primary

1997 — Co-chairs a task force that recommends the state "define inappropriate expenditures and prohibit personal use" of campaign contribution money

2001 — Dies March 2 in Chicago

Republican
January 12, 1953 to January 14, 1957
January 14, 1957 to January 9, 1961

William G. Stratton was a hands-on administrator who, more than any other governor before him, was an authority on Illinois and its governments, state and local. During the 1940s and 1950s, he held statewide office 16 years — two terms each as governor, state treasurer and congressman-at-large. He called himself a progressive Republican, and he combined a political scientist's concept of what Illinois needed with a politician's understanding of what the legislature and the people would accept. Before 1952, when he was elected governor, he had expert knowledge of the power structures in Springfield, Chicago, and Washington, D.C.

Elected before his 39th birthday, he didn't look like a typical governor. Almost boyish in build, he lacked the fluency of a platform orator, and his voice was pitched a little too high. Nevertheless, he was a strong governor. Important bills cleared the legislature rather easily, some with bipartisan support. Few administrations accomplished more.

Stratton was personally responsible for the Illinois toll highway system and for the first legislative reapportionment since 1901. Among other initiatives, his cooperation with metropolitan officials made possible the expressways inside Chicago. He persuaded the legislature to let large and small municipalities bolster their finances with a sales tax. Stratton bond issues financed major building programs for universities and mental hospitals. He advocated judicial reform and civil rights.

Politics as a Family Business

The governor came from a politically active Republican family in Lake County. William Grant Stratton was born February 26, 1914, in Ingleside, and was taught to read and write by his mother, Zula Van Wormer Stratton, who had been a schoolteacher. His father, William J. Stratton made his way upward as supervisor, county chairman, and deputy warden during the future governor's formative years. In the Small Administration, he was chief game warden and the first state director of conservation. In 1928, he took Louis L. Emmerson's place as secretary of state. The Depression and Franklin D. Roosevelt ended the older Stratton's office-holding career.

Young Bill learned campaign techniques while touring the state with his father. He was 8 years old when, during a trip to the Capitol, he sat in Governor Len Small's chair. He attended public schools five years before entering high school at age 12. He was a political science major at the University of Arizona, graduating at the age of 20.

After graduation, he married Marion Hook of Gurnee and landed a trainee job with Northern Illinois Public Service Company. He bought a 10-room Victorian house in Morris that had been built in 1869 by Lieutenant Governor Lyman B. Ray.

In 1940, at age 26, his chief political asset was his late father's name. (William J. Stratton had died two years earlier.) Without campaign funds, he was one of 14 candidates for two Republican nominations as congressman-at-large. He polled the highest vote in the June primary and November election. When the new Congress met, he was the youngest member of the House of Representatives. At the end of his term, he returned to Illinois. In 1942, at only 28, he was elected state treasurer.

Stratton wanted to be secretary of state, the office his father had held. But in 1944, Governor Dwight H. Green blackballed his candidacy for that office. According to Stratton biographer David Kenney, Green apparently was afraid Stratton would defer to his friend Senator Charles Wayland "Curly" Brooks on patronage choices and shift party power away from the governor. Stratton ran anyway, but lost in the primary to the slated candidate, Arnold Benson, by nearly 100,000 votes. Then he volunteered for service as a U.S. Navy officer in the South Pacific, which gave him politically valuable status as a war veteran. In 1946, he shocked liberals by defeating Emily Taft Douglas, the new congress-woman-at-large. In 1948, Green Republicans did not oppose him for secretary of state, but it was a Democratic Party year. President Harry Truman defeated Thomas Dewey; Adlai Stevenson beat Governor Green; and Paul Douglas replaced Curly Brooks in the U.S. Senate. Stratton lost to Edward J. Barrett, another veteran. Two years later, as a candidate for state treasurer, Stratton defeated six Republicans in the primary and Michael J. Howlett in the election.

In 1949, while out of office, Stratton divorced his wife. The next year, after election as state treasurer, he married Shirley Breckenridge of Chicago, who was nine years younger and had been divorced three years earlier. Two daughters of this first marriage lived with them. A second-marriage daughter was born in 1962.

Stratton's First Term as Governor

In early 1952, Stratton was convinced that he could unseat Governor Adlai E. Stevenson. Many Republicans, however, did not believe he would be their party's candidate. Only one ward committee-man in Chicago supported him. Most of the others lined up behind William N. Erickson of Evanston, chairman of the Cook County Board, who in midcampaign withdrew because he was indicted in a ghost pay-rolling scandal. The race then seemed to be between Park Livingston of Hinsdale, president of the University of Illinois Board of Trustees, and Richard Yates Rowe of Jacksonville, who had been secretary of state by appointment. A fourth candidate was James Simpson, former Lake County congressman. To their surprise, Stratton was nominated with 57 percent of the vote. By July, Stevenson had dropped out of the governor's race to accept his party's draft to run against Dwight D. Eisenhower in the presidential election. In November, Stratton carried 92 counties and was elected by 227,642 votes over Stevenson's stand-in, Lieutenant Governor Sherwood Dixon.

At his inauguration, Stratton announced he would give major attention to highway and building construction projects. The first step in rebuilding Governor Len Small's hard roads was to widen U.S. Route 66, the diagonal route connecting Springfield with Chicago and St. Louis. Funds for the project came from the Stevenson Administration's increases in the gas tax and auto licenses. Stratton also used bond issue financing for multi-lane construction in northern Illinois where traffic volume and land values were beginning to rise. Before his second term ended, he took credit for 7,057 miles of new roadways and 638 bridges, many of which received financial help under the federal interstate highway program.

At his request, the legislature created the Toll Highway Commission, which issued bonds to buy rights-of-way and build 187 miles of expressways in northeastern Illinois. To speed up construction, which was finished in 1958, contractors were limited to 10 miles of work each. Stratton also made possible the early completion of the expressway system radiating from the Chicago Loop. Cook County had voted a $70 million bond issue in 1950, but work didn't start because funding was incomplete. As soon as the 1952 election returns were in, Dan Ryan, president of the Cook County Board, asked for help with an expressway program that Governor Stevenson had vetoed. Stratton cooperated and, with the legislature's approval, the city, county, and park districts used their distributive shares of the gas tax to service a $245 million bond issue. In dollars spent, if not in miles paved, Stratton built more roads than Len Small. Forecasting a future bond issue, in 1959 he said financial troubles of mass transit systems were Illinois' greatest weakness.

In his first term, Stratton accomplished the first reapportionment of the legislature since 1901. Using the full prestige of his office, he won approval of a constitutional amendment that made population the basis for districts from which House members were elected. The act gave downstate permanent control of the Senate, whose 58 districts were geographically based. In the next decade, geographically based districts were held unconstitutional in one of the U.S. Supreme Court's one-man, one-vote decisions.

With determination, Stratton sponsored bond issues and financed major construction projects at state universities and welfare institutions. The bonds were important to the development of the new Chicago Circle and Edwardsville campuses and to the existing universities at DeKalb, Macomb, and Charleston. With funds from the mental health bond issue, Governor Otto Kerner would build a series of zone centers.

Downstate followers of Paul Powell, the Democratic speaker of the House of Representatives, provided the added votes needed to increase the sales tax by a half cent. It was the only major tax increase during Stratton's two terms. Determined that Illinois should remain a low-tax state, the governor opposed a state income tax. At the start of his second term, he asked, without success, that the legislature approve a constitutional amendment for more flexible taxing authority.

In 1956, the media began printing rumors about the spending habits of Orville Hodge, the Republican state auditor of public accounts, who was quickly going through his appropriation. Investigation revealed Hodge was embezzling state money — to the tune of $1.5 million. The governor asked for and received Hodge's resignation.

The Second Term

Illinois governors usually have trouble with second term candidacies, and, in the wake of the Hodge scandal, things shouldn't have been so easy for Stratton. But the political fallout from the Hodge case took an odd political turn. The 1956 Democratic candidate for governor was Cook County Treasurer Herbert C. Paschen. The Hodge investigation led to Paschen's organization. He had deposited county funds in banks connected to the Hodge embezzlement. The kicker, however, was the revelation that Paschen kept an "employees' welfare fund," supposedly for flowers for funerals and such, sustained by banks in which county funds were deposited. The fund's books showed that most of the payouts went to Democratic Party people and affairs. The Democrats replaced Paschen with Richard B. Austin, a judge of the Superior Court whose handicap was that he had never campaigned in downstate Illinois. In the second Eisenhower landslide, Stratton was reelected by 36,877 votes, and with stronger Democratic candidates available, cynics wondered whether Richard J. Daley, the new Chicago mayor and Cook County chairman, didn't prefer to work with Republican governors.

In his second term, Stratton pushed for judicial reform, as he had in his first term. When the legislature, following orders from Daley, blocked a proposal to take selection of judges out of politics, the Stratton Administration achieved partial reform by establishing a new office of court administrator, authorizing the Supreme Court to reassign judges, and putting justices of the peace on salaries.

During the centennial of the Lincoln-Douglas debates, Stratton broke with conservative Republican opinion downstate and with much of the business community by speaking out against racial segregation. In Quincy, he said that "legal discrimination is the stepchild of slavery." Speaking at Charleston, he said that a "divided set of social attitudes cannot survive." His bill to create a fair employment practices commission was killed by the Republican Senate in 1959.

The governor, who believed prosperity required a harmonious business-labor climate, displeased conservative Republicans by supporting part of the legislation sought by union leaders. "This man is a friend of ours," Joseph Germano, district chairman of the steelworkers union, told the United Steelworkers Political Action Committee in 1959. Stratton gained nothing politically. He was booed while addressing the 1960 AFL-CIO state convention, which endorsed only Democratic candidates.

Life Out of Office

Stratton's political successes were personal rather than organizational. At times he was resented by county chairmen, most of whom he had placed on state payrolls. He did not hesitate to dominate party affairs, but he seemed disinterested in developing an organization. At times Stratton allowed Republicans to have an "open primary," meaning he did not endorse any candidates. In 1954, he did not interfere with the nomination of Joseph T. Meek, a conservative who was no match for U.S. Senator Paul H. Douglas. In 1958, his candidate for state treasurer, Louis E. Beckman of Kankakee, was defeated in the primary by Warren E. Wright, who lost the general election.

Like Deneen, Small, and Green, Stratton ran for and lost a third term. He won the Republican primary. But then his political good fortune ran dry. Unlike 1952 and 1956, the Democrats' chosen candidate did not leave the race. In the fall election, the voters didn't care whether he had done a good job for eight years. Overwhelmed by Democrat Otto Kerner, Stratton was the biggest Republican loser that year.

The governor's political philosophy was that Illinois was a swing state that could be carried by Republican candidates if they had good issues but that the issues could change during a campaign. He also believed that a candidate couldn't win if his name wasn't on the ballot. In 1968, the year Richard B. Ogilvie was elected governor, Stratton made his last campaign. As the third candidate in the Republican gubernatorial primary, he received 7 percent of the vote.

In 1964, Stratton was indicted on charges of violating income tax laws. At the end of an expensive trial, he was acquitted on tax evasion charges that centered on political contributions. The government did not claim that state funds had been mishandled. Senator Everett M. Dirksen, the climactic defense witness, testified that a governor, unlike legislators, has ceremonial duties that are official in part and for which use of unrestricted campaign fund contributions is justified. In the Stratton case, the U.S. Tax Court later ruled that the Internal Revenue Service should not assess a tax on outright unrestricted gifts.

In 1968, Stratton abandoned campaigning, sold the Morris house, moved to a Lake Shore Drive apartment, and started a successful career as a Chicago businessman. Starting as a vice president of Canteen Corporation in 1968, he became a director in 1981. Retiring when he turned 70, he took up banking, eventually becoming a vice president of the Associated Bank of Chicago. From the sidelines, he continued his interest in the Republican Party. Meanwhile, he was actively involved in business, charitable, and educational causes, including the presidency of the Mental Health Association of Greater Chicago and the Rotary Club of Chicago. He served as board chairman of the Chicago and Illinois Restaurant Association.

He also made his expertise available to the study of public policy and politics. In 1987, he served as a co-chairman of Governor James R. Thompson's "Committee of 800" to help seek a tax increase. Ten years later, he and former U.S. Senator Paul Simon chaired the Illinois Campaign Finance Task Force, a nongovernmental body. One of the recommendations of the task force's final report was for state law to "define inappropriate expenditures and prohibit personal use" of campaign contribution money. One of his last assignments was as a member of the Illinois Civil Service Commission, appointed by Governor George Ryan in 1999.

Stratton died in Chicago on March 2, 2001.

Courtesy of the Abraham Lincoln Presidential Library

Governor Stratton and Austin Wyman, chairman of the Illinois Toll Highway Commission, break ground to begin building the state's toll road system, which now covers 274 miles.

33rd Governor

Otto Kerner
1908-1976

1908 — Born August 15 in Chicago

1930 — Graduates from Brown University

1934 — Receives a law degree from Northwestern University

1934 — Joins the Black Horse Troop of the Illinois National Guard

1942 - 1946 — Transfers from the guard to a mobile artillery unit in World War II; after the war, he rejoins the guard and remains active for several more years.

1947 - 1954 — Serves as U.S. attorney

1954 - 1961 — Serves as Cook County judge

1960 — Defeats Governor Willima G. Stratton in the general election

1963 — Vetoes a Republican redistricting bill when a bipartisan commission fails to agree on a plan; all Illinois House candidates appear on a yard-long 1964 state ballot.

1964 — Defeats Charles Percy to win a second term as governor

1967 — Is appointed by President Lyndon B. Johnson as chairman of the National Advisory Commission on Civil Disorder

1968 — Resigns as governor to become a judge in the Chicago U.S. Court of Appeals; Lieutenant Governor Samuel H. Shapiro becomes governor.

1973 — Is convicted of bribery, conspiracy, income tax evasion, mail fraud, and perjury in relation to Illinois race track stock deals

1974 — Enters the Federal Correctional Institution at Lexington, Kentucky

1975 — Is released from prison

1976 — Dies May 9

Democrat
January 9, 1961 to January 11, 1965
January 11, 1965 to May 20, 1968

Otto Kerner, a popular but indecisive governor, would have been a strong candidate for a third term in 1968 if he had not resigned to accept an appointment to the U.S. Court of Appeals, the nation's second-highest tribunal. Six years later, he was in a federal prison, convicted on all counts in a conflict of interest case involving state supervision of race tracks.

Proud, handsome, and naive, Kerner never could admit that he had made a mistake. Perhaps his biggest error in judgment was his trust and confidence in Theodore J. Isaacs, his friend, financial adviser, campaign manager, revenue director, and prisonmate. He never repudiated Isaacs, who also corrupted the state division of printing, the financial institutions department, and the Illinois Supreme Court.

A Judge Goes to the Governor's Office

Of Bohemian parentage, Kerner had ties to one of Chicago's East European ethnic groups. Born in Chicago on August 15, 1908, he was the son of Otto and Rose Barbara Chmelik Kerner. The father, a close associate of Mayor Anton J. Cermak, had been alderman of Cermak's ward, attorney general, and, on Governor Henry Horner's recommendation, a member of the State Court of Appeals, where his record was commendable.

Kerner had an Ivy League education, a degree from Brown University followed by a year at Trinity College, Cambridge University, in England. He was admitted to the bar after graduating in law from Northwestern University in Evanston in 1934, the year after Cermak was assassinated in Florida. He married the late mayor's daughter Helena. Later, when Helena developed a drinking problem, the public sympathetically approved his solicitous care of her.

While getting a start in a law practice, he joined the Black Horse Troop of the Illinois National Guard and was promoted to captain before the guard was federalized at the start of World War II. Most of his overseas service was with artillery regiments in Africa and Sicily. At the end of the war he was a lieutenant colonel. His final National Guard rank was major general.

Near the close of the Truman Administration, the post of U.S. attorney for the Northern District of Illinois was open to a Democrat who didn't seem too close to City Hall. Kerner, who hadn't yet settled into a law practice, caught the eye of Cook County Board Chairman Jacob M. Arvey, who recommended him for the job. During seven years as federal prosecutor, Kerner didn't prosecute anyone of political consequence.

Having proved his reliability, in 1954 Kerner was the Democratic nominee for county judge. He appointed Isaacs, whom he met in the army, attorney for the Chicago Election Commission. Meanwhile, the voters agreed with Kerner's compassionate handling of child welfare and mental health cases. He had the largest Cook County vote when he was reelected in 1958.

Finances, Civil Rights, and the Yard-Long Ballot

The urbane and courteous Kerner in 1960 again was the Democratic man of the hour. Stephen A. Mitchell, who had been Adlai E. Stevenson's choice for Democratic national chairman in 1952, criticized City Hall slatemaking, saying it discouraged Democratic voting, and announced that he was an anti-organization candidate for nomination as governor. So did state Treasurer Joseph D. Lohman, who had been a University of Chicago criminologist and parole board chairman. The ward organizations backed Kerner who was nominated overwhelmingly.

In the fall campaign, Kerner did not resign the county judgeship. Among downstaters, he pretended to be a political independent to whom Richard J. Daley was unimportant. Supported by independents and some Republicans, Kerner ran well in the suburbs and downstate. A short man with a military bearing, he had a sincere manner and an ironclad memory. As governor he would show that he didn't know how to compromise with the legislature, and he never fully understood the complexities of state government, but the people loved him. Kerner beat Governor William G. Stratton by well over 500,000 votes.

The governor remained "independent" in the sense that he never tried to be a Democratic leader; but after his inauguration he deviated on only a few Chicago City Hall policies. He insisted that a constitutional amendment to reorganize the judiciary must continue the system under which judges were nominated at party conventions and elected on partisan ballots. During the 1961 legislative session, bar leaders who had wanted selection of judges taken out of politics gave in and let Daley have his way when the state Constitution was amended.

The Kerner Administration was not immune from the budgetary squeezes that arose partly because of the money drain caused by increasing public aid costs. At Kerner's inauguration, he said increased revenues were essential. In 1961, he got the state sales tax raised a half cent and a new tax on hotel and motel rooms. But often Kerner's fiscal planning decisions were postponed, and his policy objectives were muddy.

Kerner saw the need for a more flexible revenue article in the state Constitution and appointed a commission to make recommendations, but he let months pass before giving it funds and appointing legislative leaders as members. Observers were baffled about what he wanted. The governor omitted the revenue article matter from an early winter special session call. It could be done in the spring, he said. As time passed, he denounced Republican legislators as being incompetent, irresponsible, and politically motivated. Stratton, the two-term Republican he had defeated in 1960, criticized the indecision, saying governors should accept final responsibility for budgeting and devote full time to improving official relations with the legislature.

Kerner's position on an income tax frequently shifted until his 1964 campaign for a second term. When hard-pressed by Charles H. Percy, the Republican nominee, Kerner announced flatly that Illinois didn't need an income tax. He kept asking for increases in existing taxes, some of which the legislature approved. He was turned down when he wanted part of a gas tax increase diverted to general revenues. In 1967, he got higher sales, cigarette, utility, and corporation taxes, and a one-cent gas tax increase for highways.

Perhaps his biggest flip-flop was in 1962 on public aid financing. Under budgetary pressures, and without consulting the Public Aid Commission, he arbitrarily cut $91 million from its biennial appropriations request for $613 million, half of which came from the federal government. To avoid a special session, he ordered a 10 percent cut in individual grants. The commissioners, including Auditor Michael J. Howlett and Finance Director James A. Ronan, refused. Kerner caved in, presumably due to pressure from Daley. Instead of administrative cuts, the governor agreed the commission should have more caseworkers. The legislature provided additional money in controlled amounts and insisted that Illinois, like 31 other states, put ceilings on individual grants.

During the controversy, C. Virgule Martin, a Chicago State Street merchant, resigned in protest as commission chairman and was replaced by Arnold H. Maremont, an industrialist friend of Kerner. When Maremont said Republican senators were "anti-Negro," the majority refused to confirm him. The commission soon was replaced by the Department of Public Aid, created in 1963.

On the positive side, to maintain Illinois' standing as the leading export state, Kerner led trade missions to Europe in 1963 and to Japan in 1965. In 1967, he succeeded in a drive to locate at Weston, DuPage County, the Atomic Energy Commission's high-energy accelerator. The state appropriated $30 million for the 6,800-acre site. With bipartisan support, the Board of Higher Education and the Junior College Board were created and land acquisition authorized for Governors State University and Sangamon State University, the latter of which became the University of Illinois at Springfield.

During his first year in office, Kerner achieved creation of the Fair Employment Practices Commission, which had been killed by the state Senate since 1945. Still, the Senate turned down three of his appointees. When the legislature refused to approve an open occupancy law, he achieved the goal through an executive order prohibiting discrimination in the sale and rental of real estate. An earlier order prohibited discrimination by indivduals licensed by the state.

The governor had a strong record on civil rights. In 1967, he was appointed by President Lyndon Baines Johnson to the chairmanship of the National Advisory Commission on Civil Disorders. Its report denounced racial discrimination, declaring that America had become "two societies, one black, one white — separate but unequal."

Census data from 1960 triggered the process of redistricting. But things didn't go smoothly. In 1963, the House Republican leadership approved a redistricting bill strictly along party lines. After the legislature adjourned, Kerner vetoed the bill, and then, in accordance with the state Constitution, appointed a 10-member bipartisan commission to draw new districts for the Illinois House. When the commission failed, the next step was a statewide at-large election for the Illinois House. Thus, in 1964, every ballot in the state contained the 236 names of all the candidates for the legislature (118 names from each party). The nearly yard-long ballot of that year came to be known as the "bedsheet ballot." Democrats won a two-thirds majority, but it did Kerner little good. The Senate in the 1960s was dominated by Republicans.

Despite setbacks, the governor planned to run for a third term, but in February 1968 decided not to seek reelection. One month later, President Johnson nominated Kerner to the Seventh Circuit U.S. Court of Appeals. Lieutenant Governor Samuel H. Shapiro succeeded him as governor.

The Judge Goes to Jail

However, Kerner's ultimate fate was set in motion during his second-term campaign in which he defeated Charles H. Percy by more than 175,000 votes. The campaign was endangered by a scandal involving Theodore J. Isaacs, who quickly resigned as its manager. Percy was ineffective in exploiting Isaacs' role as counsel of the Cook Envelope Company, which sold large quantities of envelopes to the state. (Isaacs stonewalled an investigation until after the 1964 election.) Later it was stipulated in Sangamon County Circuit Court that he organized the company after the 1960 election and owned a half-interest in it. Indictments for conspiracy, collusion in bid-rigging, and defrauding the state were dismissed on technical grounds.

Meanwhile, Isaacs resigned as revenue director, though he maintained backdoor contacts that embarrassed his successor. He became counsel for the Civic Center Bank and Trust Company in the Chicago Loop, which previously had been unable to obtain a charter from Joseph E. Knight, Kerner's director of the Departmet of Financial Institutions. Isaacs secretly controlled a bloc of bank stock, which influential people, including Knight, could buy at cut-rate prices and sell at a profit.

In 1969, after Kerner left to become a judge, a special commission headed by Frank Greenberg, president of the Chicago Bar Association, began looking into bank stock transactions. The commission's report forced the resignation of two Illinois Supreme Court justices. Nothing happened to Isaacs as a result of the bank stock investigation.

Marjorie Lindheimer Everett, the dominant figure in Illinois racing, had secretly dispensed her race track stock in the same manner as Isaacs did the bank stock. Judge Kerner's troubles began when Internal Revenue Service agents wondered why Mrs. Everett on her 1966 income tax return claimed a capital loss on a stock sale. U.S. Attorney James R. Thompson, a future governor, investigated the complicated case and found that Mrs. Everett had secretly issued track stock to then-Governor Kerner and Isaacs at bargain-basement prices and that both men profited when they sold the stock back to her. In return, she received special treatment from the state. Kerner had appointed her friends to racing boards, given her tracks the racing dates she requested, signed legislation she desired, and fired a harness-racing chairman who insisted that a competing track deserved consideration.

In 1973, Kerner and Isaacs were convicted of conspiracy, income tax evasion, mail fraud, and making false statements on income tax returns. Kerner also was found guilty of perjury and making false statements to revenue agents. A special panel of the Court of Appeals called the transactions bribery and found that Kerner and Isaacs each gained nearly $150,000 from dividend earnings and the sale of stocks for which they paid about $15,000.

On the witness stand, Kerner projected an aura of untouchability that did not impress the jury. After the trial, he insisted that, while he might have been indiscreet, criminal intent was not involved. He said his troubles with the Republican prosecutor were in retaliation for President Richard Nixon's failure to carry Illinois in 1960. Kerner appealed his conviction with only partial success. He resigned from the federal bench in 1974 and entered the Federal Correctional Institution at Lexington, Kentucky. In 1975, he was released after being diagnosed with lung cancer. He had been a pack-a-day smoker.

Kerner's last public appearances were at a series of testimonial dinners given by his admirers. He died May 9, 1976, in a Chicago hospital, two months after removal of a cancerous tumor from his right lung.

**Governor Kerner gives a corsage and a kiss to Mrs. Kathryn
Lange, 88, of Belleville on Golden Age Day at the Illinois
State Fair. She was the oldest among Belleville women
visiting the fair. She called him the "handsomest" governor.**

**Governor Kerner lends a hand to University of Illinois football All-American Jim Grabowski in
a butter churning exhibition at the Illinois State Fair.**

34th Governor

Samuel Harvey Shapiro
1907-1987

1907 — Born April 25 in Estonia

1908 — Shapiro family moves to Kankakee

1929 — Graduates from the University of Illinois Law School

1933 — Is appointed city attorney for Kankakee

1936 — Wins election as state's attorney

1940 — Loses his bid for reelection to state's attorney

1947 - 1949 — Serves in the Illinois House in the 65th General Assembly

1951 - 1961 — Serves in the Illinois House in the 67th through 71st General Assemblies

1960 — Wins election as lieutenant governor

1964 — Is reelected lieutenant governor

1968 — Takes the oath of office on the heels of Kerner's resignation in May; Vietnam War protesters clash with police in Chicago during the Democratic national convention in August; loses the gubernatorial race to Richard B. Ogilvie in November.

1976 — Endorses Secretary of State Michael J. Howlett in the gubernatorial Democratic primary instead of incumbent Governor Dan Walker

1981 — Votes to break the tie on the commission that redraws the legislative district map, which helps Democrats gain control of both chambers of the General Assembly for a decade.

1987 — Dies March 16

Democrat
May 21, 1968 to January 13, 1969

Samuel H. Shapiro, a smiling specialist in soft-sell politics, knew how to work with Republican legislators and was a successful governor during the last eight months of Otto Kerner's second term. With a background of 14 years in the House of Representatives and more than seven as lieutenant governor, he quietly obtained the cooperation of Republican legislators in solving temporarily the financial problems Kerner left behind when he resigned to become a judge of the U.S. Court of Appeals.

From the Baltic to Illinois State Government

Shapiro was the second foreign-born and the second Jewish governor. He was born April 25, 1907, in Estonia near the Baltic Sea, but he could not remember the name of the village. Tillie Bloom Shapiro brought her first son to Kankakee when he was a year old. Her husband, Joseph Shapiro, a Polish bootmaker, had established a shoe repair shop there.

A violinist, young Sam paid for most of his education by playing with dance orchestras, starting in his high school years. The job paid four dollars an hour and led to the presidency of the local musicians' union. After high school, he enrolled at St. Victor College in Kankakee and then transferred to the University of Illinois, where he got good grades and was president of his fraternity while working as a shoe sales-man and soliciting business for a photographic studio. He graduated in law in 1929.

For a legal and political career, the young Democrat went back to Republican Kankakee, the home of former Governor Len Small. At the approach of the Depression, he became the junior partner of J. Bert Miller, a leader of the local anti-Small Republican faction, and helped Democrats take over half of the county offices. In 1933, Shapiro was appointed city attorney. Three years later, he was elected state's attorney with a higher vote than Franklin D. Roosevelt received for president. Shapiro married Gertrude Adelman in 1930. She met Shapiro at a dance in Kankakee when he was state's attorney. Her parents came from Latvia and Lithuania. In 1940, a Republican year in down-state Illinois, he came within 176 votes of a second term.

During his reelection campaign, Shapiro convened a special grand jury that indicted Archie L. Bowen, director of the Department of Public Welfare in Governor Horner's Cabinet, for malfeasance in con-nection with a typhoid epidemic at Manteno State Hospital. Bowen, a tight-fisted and unpopular administrator, under Horner's orders had enforced economy and stopped political appointments at state institu-tions. Shapiro accused him of "palpable omission of duty." After the first trial ended with a hung jury, Bowen was convicted in a bench trial, fined $1,000, and removed from office. The Supreme Court reversed the conviction on the ground that the prosecution had not shown that the epidemic was caused by polluted drinking water.

Shapiro, who was overweight and a fraction under the five-foot, six-inch requirement, became a U.S. Navy officer in World War II by dieting severely and performing back-stretching exercises before his physical. Assigned to anti-submarine warfare intelligence and then to a court-martial staff, he finished the war as a lieutenant.

In the legislature, to which he was elected in 1946, he cosponsored legislation to raise standards of mental health institutions. The Research Foundation for the Mentally Ill named him "Mr. Mental Health," and a Republican administration renamed the Kankakee State Hospital for him. In Democratic factionalism, Shapiro sided with his party's Chicago leadership against downstate followers of Paul Powell. He had been secretary and state treasurer of the Young Democrats of Illinois and had been prominent in Jewish organizations.

In 1960 slatemaking, he became the party's candidate for lieutenant governor and twice was elected on the ticket headed by Kerner. He represented the administration on numerous occasions. By Kerner's appointment, he was chairman of the state mental health commission and headed a commission on mental retardation.

Taking the Governor's Seat

When he was inaugurated governor, with Kerner presiding, Shapiro called for mutual cooperation with the legislature and said he would not retreat from Kennedy, Johnson, and Kerner policies. Although the new governor did use the larger executive office on the second floor of the Statehouse, he didn't much change his lifestyle. On a busy day, legislators could easily find him eating a hot dog while standing at a lunch counter near the legislative halls.

Kerner had left the state in a financial bind. Faced with a flood of major and minor bills during the fiscal emergency, the legislature needed Shapiro's calming influence. At the start of his abbreviated administration, he told House and Senate leaders that fund transfers and belt-tightening would make additional taxes unnecessary for a year. He got their agreement to borrow $60 million from gasoline tax funds, enough to keep state government operating until the next General Assembly met. The emergency bill came up for Senate passage when Shapiro was in Cincinnati attending a governors' conference. W. Russell Arrington, the Republican president pro tem who was acting governor, "worked the floor" to get the necessary votes. Kerner had never worked closely with Arrington and other Republican leaders.

In an era of protest, citizens expressing their right to free speech often clashed with police trying to keep order. When the legislature insisted on passing a stop-and-frisk bill designed to clarify police authority to question suspects, Shapiro worked out a compromise he could sign. Kerner had vetoed the first stop-and-frisk legislation.

The Election of 1968

The announcement that Kerner would become a federal judge came in time for Shapiro to take his place on the Democratic slate in the 1968 primary. To give him campaign exposure at the Democratic national convention in Chicago, he had a spotlight role as chairman of the rules committee, and he opened the nominating process to minorities. Before the convention, which was plagued with dissent over the Vietnam War, he mobilized 5,649 National Guardsmen to join Chicago police in keeping order in the streets.

Kerner's delayed resignation and Hubert Humphrey's controversial presidential nomination hurt Shapiro's campaign for a full term as governor. The 1968 Republican ticket was strong, headed by Richard M. Nixon for president and Senator Everett M. Dirksen, who would win his fourth term. But Shapiro, a comparative stranger in much of downstate Illinois, carried 14 counties and came within 127,794 votes of defeating Republican Richard B. Ogilvie. Paul Simon, Shapiro's running mate, was elected lieutenant governor by 96,421 votes.

Two days before his term ended, Shapiro complied with Mayor Richard J. Daley's wishes by appointing 10 Democrats and one Republican to judicial vacancies. The unexpected action was invalidated by the Supreme Court.

Although he did not hold a major elective office again, Shapiro, as an elder statesman, did occasionally have a role in state politics. He did not comment when the Ogilvie Administration sponsored a state income tax. But later he said that, had he been elected to a full term, he would have tried to meet appropriation increases by broadening the sales tax. In the 1976 Democratic primary, he endorsed Secretary of State Michael J. Howlett instead of incumbent Governor Dan Walker. After the 1980 census, when the legislature deadlocked on reapportionment, Shapiro was named the ninth — and tie-breaking — member of a bipartisan commission to remap legislative districts. As a result of the map he drew, Democrats had control of both houses of the General Assembly throughout the 1980s, starting with the 1982 election.

The former governor for several years was a senior partner in the Chicago law firm of Friedman, Koven, Shapiro, Salzman, Koenigsberg, Specks, and Homer. Meanwhile, he kept his Kankakee home and three-man law office there. When the 79-year-old former governor failed to appear in court on March 16, 1987, police went to his home and found that he had died of natural causes during the night. Gertrude, his wife of 47 years, had died four years earlier. They were childless.

Democratic leaders with Governor Shapiro; from left, Paul Simon, Shapiro's running mate in 1968, who won the election to serve with Republican Governor Richard Ogilvie; Secretary of State Paul Powell; Attorney General William Clark; Governor Shapiro; Auditor of Public Accounts Michael Howlett; and Revenue Director Francis Lorenz.

Governor Shapiro checks out groceries at a Springfield supermarket; such meetings almost gave him enough votes to overcome a strong Republican ticket headed by Senator Everett Dirksen.

35th
Governor

Richard Buell Ogilvie
1923-1988

1923 — Born February 22 in Kansas City, Missouri

1944 — Drops out of Yale to join the Army; a tank commander, he is wounded in France.

1947 — Graduates from Yale

1949 — Graduates from Chicago-Kent College of Law

1954 - 1955 — Becomes an assistant U.S. attorney

1958 — Becomes a special assistant to the U.S. attorney general in charge of a new Midwest office to combat organized crime; his work helps lead to the income tax evasion conviction of mobster Tony "Big Tuna" Accardo (which was later reversed by the Court of Appeals).

1962 — Wins election as Cook County sheriff

1966 — Wins election as Cook County board president

1968 — Defeats Democratic Governor Samuel H. Shapiro; the lieutenant governor is Democrat Paul Simon, marking the first time the two top offices are from different parties.

1969 — Pushes through a bill creating the state's first income tax; creates the Bureau of the Budget and the Department of Corrections

1970 — In June, Illinois passes an Environmental Protection Act and establishes the state's Environmental Protection Agency.

1970 — The constitutional convention adopts a new state Constitution in September; voters ratify it in December. The new Constitution shifts elections of statewide officers to nonpresidential election years, requires that the governor and the lieutenant governor be elected as running mates, gives the governor the power to reorganize state agencies, and gives the governor the power to amend portions of bills approved by the legislature.

1972 — Creates the Illinois Department of Transportation; loses the governor's seat to Dan Walker

1988 — Dies on May 10

Republican
January 13, 1969 to January 8, 1973

Short on charisma but long on executive ability, Richard B. Ogilvie made major administrative and fiscal reforms in Illinois and Cook County governments. A hard-working, tough-minded Republican, Ogilvie insisted that the legislature enact an income tax. This was an issue most governors would have avoided, but the state needed it. He was defeated when he ran for a second term. Still, among Illinois governors, he rates as one of the statesmen.

One of Ogilvie's political handicaps was his stern look, the result of a war wound. Pragmatic rather than philosophical, he ran for office not out of public demand but with a conviction that he could do a better job in Cook County as sheriff and president of the county board of commissioners, and in Springfield as governor.

War Hero, Sheriff, Board President

Richard Ogilvie was born February 22, 1923, in Kansas City, Missouri, the first of two sons of Kenneth S. and Edna Mae Buell Ogilvie. For his public career, he credited his mother, whom he described as a strong-minded woman who believed hard work and determination could overcome obstacles. Kenneth Ogilvie, a casualty insurance executive, moved the family to Evanston, where the future governor lived seven years starting in 1930, and then to Rockville Center and Port Chester, New York, where he graduated from high school in 1940. He attended Yale University.

Because of bad eyesight, at the start of World War II he was rejected by the Army, Navy, Marines, and Army Air Corps, but the Army Enlisted Reserve Corps accepted him. Two years later, Sergeant Ogilvie, a tank commander near the French Swiss-German border, was hit on the head by fragments from an exploding shell. Months of hospitalization and plastic surgery preceded his discharge in 1945 with a Purple Heart, two battle stars, and a permanent facial scar.

He returned to Yale as an American history major and planned a teaching and coaching career. Instead, he went to Chicago-Kent College of Law under the GI Bill of Rights and helped Charles H. Percy and William J. Scott, fellow students, revive the Young Republican organization in Cook County before he graduated in 1949. In 1950, he was admitted to the Illinois Bar and married Dorothy Shriver of Oak Park. They had one daughter, Elizabeth, and lived in Northfield.

He intermittently interrupted a Chicago legal career to become involved with law enforcement. After five years with Lord, Bissell and Brook, he became an assistant U. S. attorney. Back in a year, he became a partner in the firm. In 1958, he left his law practice to become a special assistant to the U.S. attorney general in charge of a new Midwest office to combat organized crime. He won the conviction of Tony "Big Tuna" Accardo, syndicate chief and one-time associate of Al Capone, in a complex income tax case that was reversed by the Court of Appeals in a split decision. At the end of the Eisenhower Administration he became a partner in Hackbert, Rooks and Pitts.

In 1962, for the first time, Ogilvie was a candidate for election. Running for sheriff of Cook County and asserting that the office needed upgrading, he was the only Republican elected in the countywide race. In the sheriff's office he replaced patronage with civil service and initiated professional training for his police force. Gaining the public's attention, Ogilvie sent his new force on 1,800 raids. The Chicago Crime

Commission said the office had never been more effective in suppressing organized crime and rackets. During a racial disturbance in Dixmoor and a civil rights march in Cicero in 1966, Ogilvie took personal command in tense situations and prevented full-scale rioting.

In 1966, Ogilvie was elected president of the Cook County Board of Commissioners by 172,320 votes, the biggest margin among Republican winners of local office. He put civil service regulations into effect and left 2,000 jobs vacant. He increased competitive bidding on highway projects and supported election reforms. Improved billing procedures were credited with a $7 million increase in Cook County Hospital revenues.

The Governor Takes a Tough Stand for Taxes

Midway in his term as county board president, Ogilvie announced he would be a candidate for governor in 1968. Chicago Republicans protested that 600 patronage positions would be forfeited because his successor would come from the board's Democratic majority. In the Republican primary, he finished 46,823 votes ahead of John Henry Altorfer, a Peoria businessman, with former Governor William G. Stratton far behind.

In the general election, he polled 127,794 more votes than Governor Samuel H. Shapiro. Paul Simon, a Democrat, was elected lieutenant governor, the first time the two top offices had gone to men from opposing parties. In the interest of governmental harmony, Ogilvie and Simon agreed to forgo partisanship. When Ogilvie was out of the state, Simon, who was then acting governor under the 1870 Illinois Constitution, did not attempt to take partisan advantage.

During the campaign, he and Shapiro, who was completing Otto Kerner's second term, avoided the subject of possible tax increases. Ogilvie, contending that the state's executive machinery was outmoded, warned that the state's financial situation was critical, but talked hopefully about an easy solution in which the federal government would share its revenues with the states.

After his inauguration, he surveyed the treasury's income prospects and the increasing demands for money. As he had feared, the revenue gap had become critical during the eight years of the Kerner and Shapiro administrations. He decided it could be closed only if Illinois supplemented the retail sales tax, which had been the chief revenue source since the Depression, with a tax on corporate and personal incomes. Other industrial states had income taxes, but the Illinois Supreme Court in 1932 had ruled that the 1870 Constitution prohibited them.

Rather than drastically curtail state expenditures, Ogilvie decided to stake his prestige as an incoming governor on enactment of an income tax law. He hoped constitutional problems would be solved by taxing individuals and corporations at a flat rate, rather than the graduated rate used by the federal income tax system. He proposed a 4 percent tax on corporate and individual incomes to finance increases in school, welfare, and other appropriations as well as to bring under control the costs of public aid that had been troublesome since the second Stratton term.

Most governors would have broken the bad news gently and started a public relations campaign, but during his first weeks in office Ogilvie proved that he was not a politician. In speeches, interviews, and meetings with opinion-makers, the new governor never mentioned the possibility of an income tax, which had been recommended by a revenue study commission appointed by Shapiro the year before. The day before his biennial budget message was scheduled, Ogilvie told legislative leaders, metropolitan newspaper editors, and others of his plans on an off-the-record basis. Not until noon on April 1 did the public learn that he wanted an income tax coupled with large increases in spending. The word spread quickly, and that day Republicans lost some local elections.

Because of Ogilvie's determination and willingness to compromise, the administration bill was enacted three months later in the closing hours of the 1969 legislative session. There were revolts in both chambers in both parties. Downstate Democrats insisted personal incomes be taxed at a lower rate than corporations. Mayor Richard J. Daley, who liked an Ogilvie income-sharing provision giving local governments one-twelfth of the revenue on a no-strings-attached basis, won additional concessions. The final compromise taxed corporations at 4 percent and individuals at 2.5 percent. On the final roll calls, Democrats made certain the tax bills passed and Republicans would be held responsible. Earlier in the session, new or increased levies on beer, cigarettes, and hotel receipts also had been approved. Local governments were given an additional quarter-cent of the sales tax.

Of course, the constitutionality of the income tax was immediately challenged. But the state Supreme Court unanimously upheld it. Thus, the court reversed its 1932 position on the tax, an opinion obviously informed by 40 years of social changes. As a result of the increased revenue, Illinois was spared a near-shutdown of government such as Pennsylvania and some other states underwent. The income tax, and the favorable ruling on its legality, removed what could have been an insurmountable obstacle from the agenda of the constitutional convention that met midway through the Ogilvie Administration.

The convention prepared a new constitution that was ratified by the voters in 1970. It became effective the next year and replaced the state's 100-year-old third constitution.

Reshaping State Government

Ogilvie's reforms extended into the state's executive and legislative branches. He asked that annual budgeting replace the increasingly unsatisfactory system in which the General Assembly appropriated funds for two-year periods. The legislature, which for several decades had met frequently in special sessions to consider requests for deficiency appropriations, followed his advice and shifted to an annual-session basis before the Constitution of 1970 mandated the change.

Another Ogilvie law established a Bureau of the Budget within the governor's office and gave the executive direct control of the budgetary process. As a result, a legislative commission that traditionally made final budgetary decisions went out of business, and the director of the budget bureau, responsible only to the governor, became the second most powerful official in the executive department. Its first director was John McCarter, who was conspicuous among the young and bright staff members brought into state government. One of his assistants was Robert Mandeville, who became budget director for Governor James R. Thompson.

From the governor's office, Ogilvie continued to make administrative reforms in Cook County government. He prevailed upon the legislature to consolidate the Cook County and Chicago jails and put them under a merit system, and to modernize the county's budgetary and administrative systems. Other Ogilvie proposals, to which City Hall Democrats had stronger objections, were blocked in the House of Representatives. They would have reorganized the city health department, required state licensing of building inspectors, and consolidated Chicago and suburban elections. Downstate Republicans blocked an administration effort to provide a state subsidy for the Chicago Transit Authority.

To improve the state highway system, the governor sponsored a 1.5-cent increase in the gasoline tax and creation of a highway trust authority with bonding power. He created the state's Department of Transportation with William F. Cellini, Jr. as its first director. The state's 24 adult and youth correctional facilities were put under a newly created Department of Corrections. The state's law enforcement machinery was reorganized. In education, the state school aid formula was changed from $400 to $520 per pupil. The governor also signed a bill to permit silent prayer in public schools. In June 1970, six months before the federal government took action, Illinois became the first state to approve an Environmental Protection Act and establish an Environmental Protection Agency. He won approval of a $750 million antipollution bond issue to enable local governments to improve sewage facilities.

Even with the infusion of more income, revenue problems persisted. Because tax rates had been shared with local governments and because the legislature dictated other compromises, revenues were less than expected. Costs of government kept increasing, and the budget bureau soon had to order cuts in spending requests. Meanwhile, the legislature could not resist the temptation to appropriate more than the treasury could afford. That problem grew worse in following administrations.

Income Tax as Political Suicide

Politically, the governor wanted the Republican Party to be competitive in Chicago as well as downstate and believed he should be its leader. But the backlash of the income tax hurt the party. Democrats carried the 1970 off-year election.

Naturally, the income tax was the chief issue in Ogilvie's campaign for a second term in 1972. In the general election, many thought the governor would face his lieutenant governor, Paul Simon. Simon had Democratic organization backing for the governorship, but an aggressive maverick named Dan Walker took the nomination away from him. Ogilvie, who in midsummer was several points behind in the polls, focused on the nonrevenue changes he had made in Chicago as well as downstate. He had additional handicaps, including an unpopular ban against leaf burning ordered by the state Environmental Protection Agency. The governor had given free rein to the EPA and its Pollution Control Board and paid for it when voters took their anger out on him. On election day, he lost by 77,494 votes.

After an absence of 12 years, Ogilvie returned to the practice of law in Chicago and, like William G. Stratton, demonstrated that a former governor can have a future in private life. He became managing partner of the venerable firm of Isham, Lincoln and Beale, of which Robert Todd Lincoln had been a co-founder. As the court-appointed receiver of the bankrupt Chicago, Milwaukee, St. Paul, and Pacific Railroad Company, he restored solvency by drastically cutting mileage. His executive ability also was recognized with an appointment to take charge of an incomplete addition to McCormick Place.

In the role of an elder statesman, he sought to strengthen Republican tickets in Cook County, but he declined opportunities to run for mayor of Chicago. In the 1976 presidential primary, he took a public stand for President Gerald Ford's reelection when Ronald Reagan, who was born in downstate Illinois, also was a candidate. Ford carried Illinois that year.

Ogilvie earned millions of dollars as a trustee of the Chicago, Milwaukee, St. Paul and Pacific Railroad Company, reorganizing the bankrupt line and saving more than a thousand jobs. He also was appointed trustee for the Chicago, Missouri, and Western Railway. In the 1980s, an era known for consolidations, Ogilvie surprised the legal profession by arranging the merger of Isham, Lincoln and Beale with the larger, younger, and more aggressive firm of Reuben and Proctor. When conflicts arose, Isham, Lincoln and Beale dissolved and the former governor became a partner with the firm of Wildman, Harrold, Allen and Dixon.

On May 9, 1988, while working in his downtown Chicago office, Ogilvie suffered a heart attack. He died the next day after undergoing quadruple coronary bypass surgery. His body was cremated, and his ashes were placed at Rosehill Cemetery in Chicago.

Courtesy of the Abraham Lincoln Presidential Library

Governor Ogilvie at work in his Executive Mansion office

36th Governor

Daniel Walker
1922-

1922 — Born August 6 in Washington, D.C.

1940 - 1942 — Serves in the U.S. Navy

1945 — Graduates from the Naval Academy; serves two more years in the Navy

1950 — Graduates from Northwestern Law School; works on the staff of the Illinois Commission to Study State Government, then becomes law clerk for U.S. Supreme Court Chief Justice Fred Vinson

1951 — Is recalled to the Navy to serve in the Korean conflict, but soon is released from service to take the civilian post of deputy chief commissioner of the U. S. Court of Military Appeals in Washington, D.C.

1952 — Joins Governor Adlai Stevenson's staff

1953 - 1966 — Works for a law firm that would come to be known as Hopkins and Sutter

1960 — Is rejected by Democratic Party slatemakers in a bid for Illinois attorney general

1968 — Is chosen by the National Commission on the Causes and Prevention of Violence to investigate the confrontations between Chicago police and Vietnam War protesters during the 1968 Democratic National Convention in Chicago

1971 — Begins to walk the state in a campaign to win the Democratic primary for governor.

1972 — Defeats Lieutenant Governor Paul Simon for the Democratic gubernatorial nomination; defeats Governor Richard Ogilvie in the general election

1973 — Signs a bill in December that creates the Illinois State Lottery

1976 — Loses the Democratic gubernatorial primary to Secretary of State Michael J. Howlett, who loses the general election to James R. Thompson

1988 — Goes to prison to begin serving a seven-year sentence in connection with misusing funds from his failed First American Savings and Loan Association of Oak Brook

1989 — Is released from prison and and returns to California

2007 — Publishes his seventh book, a memoir of his life

Democrat
January 8, 1973 to January 10, 1977

Daniel Walker was confrontational, brilliant, ambitious, and tragic. He left a $120,000-a-year post as a corporation lawyer, and, as an underdog, was elected governor in 1972.

Walker played the role of a big-city populist turned giant killer to win the governorship, first by upsetting Lieutenant Governor Paul Simon in the primary and then by beating Governor Richard B. Ogilvie in the general election. Unique in Illinois, Walker was an adversarial governor. Scornful of compromise, he downgraded the importance of the legislature and managed by using the "me-versus-you" tactics that had brought him courtroom success. For the four years of the Walker Administration, hostility and dispute were the orders of the day. Walker and Chicago Mayor Richard J. Daley were constant adversaries, especially when Walker tried to wrest control of the state Democratic Party from "His Honor." For his part, Daley expressed regret early in the Walker Administration that Republican Ogilvie wasn't serving a second term. Had Walker not challenged Daley's leadership, he could have had a long political career. Instead, he squandered his opportunity by waging a power struggle that had more to do with personality than ideology.

Young Walker

Dan Walker was born August 6, 1922, in Washington, D.C., the son of a U.S. Navy chief petty officer who soon retired and moved to a truck farm outside San Diego, California. Dan Walker left farming after graduation from San Diego High School as class valedictorian. He enlisted in the naval reserve, went to sea on a destroyer, finished third in a competitive examination open to all seamen, and in a year was attending classes at the Naval Academy at Annapolis. Graduating in 1945, he spent two years on fleet duty and then became a resident of Illinois by resigning his commission and entering Northwestern University Law School. In the class of 1950, he was editor in chief of the *Law Review*.

In 1947, while he was a law student, Walker, a Methodist, married Roberta Dowse, a Catholic whose grandfather had been a state representative from Lake County and whose great-uncle had been an early president of the Chicago Board of Education. They reared seven children in Deerfield before divorcing in 1977. In 1978, Walker married Roberta Nelson, executive director of the Illinois Epilepsy Association. She divorced him in 1988. He married Lily Stewart in 1996.

After law school, Walker showed up in Springfield as a staff member of Governor Adlai E. Stevenson's "Little Hoover" commission on governmental reorganization. Soon he was in Washington, D.C, with a prestigious appointment as law clerk to U.S. Supreme Court Chief Justice Fred M. Vinson, but before his year was over, the Navy recalled him for Korean War fleet duty. He returned to Washington after release from active duty to serve as deputy to the chief commissioner of the U.S. Court of Military Appeals, a civilian review body. In 1952, he resigned to join Stevenson's staff in Springfield. Instead of working in the political headquarters — Stevenson had been drafted to run for president against Dwight D. Eisenhower — he learned the routine of state government by going to the Statehouse as an administrative aide.

Next, Walker became a Chicago lawyer, a litigation specialist who became partner in the firm of Hopkins, Sutter, Owen, Mulroy, Wentz and Davis. Walker had Democratic political ambitions but no desire for apprenticeship with the City Hall organization. In the role of an outsider who was concerned about the quality of government in Springfield during the Stratton Administration, he founded and was chairman of the Committee on Illinois Government. When it went out of business in two years, he organized and was president of the Democratic Federation of Illinois, which hoped to mobilize young, college-educated, and idealistic amateurs as a reform element. Mayor Richard J. Daley, who saw it as a potential challenge, smothered the group.

In 1960, Walker appeared before Democratic slatemakers and asked to be chosen for attorney general. William G. Clark, a legislator who later became chief justice of the state Supreme Court, had more influence with Democratic powers, and so Walker was not slated.

After his rejection, he played a minor role as the secretary of Businessmen for Kennedy during JFK's presidential campaign. That year he became vice president and general counsel of Marcor, Inc., the holding company for Montgomery Ward and Company, which put him in the $100,000-plus salary bracket. The corporation had no objection to his civic and political activities, and he served as president of the Chicago Crime Commission and, by Governor Otto Kerner's appointment, as the last chairman of the Illinois Public Aid Commission.

Any possibility of career help from Mayor Daley ended when he accused the Chicago police of violence and rioting instead of keeping order during the 1968 Democratic National Convention. *Rights in Conflict*, a report he compiled for the National Commission on the Causes and Prevention of Violence, gave Walker coast-to-coast attention.

Walking into the Executive Mansion

A year before the 1972 primary, he gambled his nestegg and became an anti-organization candidate for governor. In a low-budget, off-season campaign, he acquired name recognition and a downstate education by walking the length of the state, 1,197 zigzag miles from Brookport to South Beloit and into Chicago in 116 days. To show that he was a man of the people, he slept in farmhouses. Speeches struck populist themes — "government is out of touch with the people" and "patronage has got to go." He promised to hold the line on taxes and spend more on education.

Walker, who 12 years earlier had asked Democratic slatemakers to endorse him for attorney general, berated Simon for running against him with their support. As a major issue, the argumentative Walker insisted that Simon, who had commented about future school financing possibilities, planned to increase the income tax.

For his nomination by 40,293 votes, the independent candidate also was indebted to meddlesome Republicans. The Supreme Court recently had legalized crossover voting, and Republicans had no contests in their own primary. Without realizing how many others had the same idea, Republicans who didn't want Simon to be nominated by too large a majority couldn't resist casting their ballots for his opponent.

Walker boycotted his party's national convention and never during his race for the governor's seat did he mention George McGovern, the controversial Democratic presidential nominee. To get support in Chicago, he made obligatory appearances at Democratic ward rallies. Continually, he reminded the voters that Ogilvie was responsible for the income tax. He won the general election by 77,494 votes.

The Governor Without a Party

Executive combativeness marked the next four years. To distance himself from the legislature, he took the oath of office in bitter weather outside the Statehouse. In a brief speech, he posed as the only honest man in town and proclaimed that lesser men should go elsewhere. When he said, "the free ride is over," Republicans interpreted it as an unwarranted insult to Ogilvie, the retiring governor. He neglected the face-to-face conferences that could develop friendly relations and roll call support, and the Walker Administration soon ostracized Lieutenant Governor Neil Hartigan, one of Daley's ward committeemen. This, of course, further distanced the powerful Chicago Democrats. One Democratic faction, mostly downstaters, was loyal but others in ad hoc alliances with Republicans overrode vetoes and refused to confirm several appointments. Thus his legislative power base was small. In fact, the legislature treated him as a minority governor.

Walker's executive ability was such that he could clear his desk in an hour, which left the rest of the day for politicking. In campaigns and in running the state, his right-hand man was Victor de Grazia, who was rated a political genius. They were better at collecting enemies, however, than in rallying supporters. After his involuntary retirement from the governor's office, Walker said he should have spent more time with legislators and other establishment members instead of trying to build up a grassroots following, but he still blamed Daley for their confrontations.

One of the Walker-Daley battles delayed creation of the six-county Regional Transportation Authority that took over bus, elevated train, and subway service in the Chicago area. Chicago leaders and Republican legislators wanted something done about the servicing and financial problems of the old Chicago Transit Authority, but during the 1973 regular session the governor failed to submit his own program and enter into negotiations. Walker finally participated during a special session that met in October. He contended Daley wanted financial grants set at an unreasonably high level as a precedent for later state aid requests for other programs.

Walker kept firm control of executive departments and made final decisions for the Bureau of the Budget. Because he had campaigned against Simon and Ogilvie on the income tax issue, he had no choice but to cut spending drastically during a period of tight economic conditions nationally. Some help came with enactment of a state lottery that was a secondary but nevertheless important revenue source.

The administration seemed to be dollar honest, but critics accused the governor of having an ethical double standard. In the 1972 campaign, Walker had challenged Ogilvie to issue an executive order requiring businesses that had contracts with the state to reveal their campaign contributions. In office, he found legal excuses for not following his own preaching. Under media heckling, he finally issued the executive order, which a court invalidated. He took credit for enactment of a financial disclosure law that covered state officials; his own campaign finances were confused by the formation of two committees and by long delays in making incomplete reports. In his final campaign, state workers were solicited for contributions, something Walker promised never to do.

Loss, Tragedy, and Hope

The Democratic fight for the 1976 gubernatorial nomination was the roughest since the Henry Horner-Herman N. Bundesen Democratic primary of 1936. Full of national ambition, Walker entered a full slate of candidates for delegates to the Democratic national convention. In this way, Walker aspired to replace Daley as leader of the Illinois delegation. If he could take his own delegates to the convention, he would be on equal terms with Jerry Brown of California and Jimmy Carter of Georgia as presidential possibilities. The primary, however, focused more on Walker's bid for a second term. Daley's candidate for the job was Secretary of State Michael J. Howlett, who, in addition to support from the mayor, had a large downstate following as a result of long service as auditor and secretary of state. The City Hall organization, which hadn't realized Simon was in trouble in the 1972 primary, fired up precinct workers on behalf of Howlett. Near physical and financial exhaustion, Walker concentrated on the suburbs and downstate. This time, liberals and independents in Chicago did not endorse him.

Howlett was nominated, and only two of Walker's candidates won.

Involuntarily retired before his 55th birthday and hopeful that he again could hold high office, Walker formed a multi-city law firm based in Oak Brook with branches in Chicago, Springfield, Moline, Peoria, Kankakee, and Mount Vernon. That ambitious project soon failed. Before he entered politics he had shown business ability — Marcor had wanted the head of its law department to switch to an executive office — and he saw moneymaking opportunities outside the law office. For the former governor, however, nothing seemed to work out. Among other investments, he bought into banks in Illinois, Arkansas, and Florida.

Promising to "cut Jim Thompson down to size," in the late summer of 1981 he announced that he was a candidate for governor. Two months later, he withdrew after Adlai E. Stevenson III received the Democratic endorsement.

He became chairman and chief executive officer of the First American Savings and Loan Association of Oak Brook, which he and his second wife acquired in 1983. Four years later, it was declared insolvent by the Federal Home Loan Bank Board. A federal grand jury had determined that Walker, contrary to conservative practices, had engaged in a rapid-growth program that included insider trading and high-risk commercial lending. Prosecutors said he had received $1.4 million in fraudulent loans.

The former governor elected not to stand trial. On the eve of his 65th birthday, he pleaded guilty to bank fraud, misapplication of bank funds, and perjury. "I have deep regrets and no excuses," he announced. He had hoped to avoid a prison term, but on November 19, 1987, U.S. District Court Judge Ann Williams said he had "placed himself above the law" and had used First American as "a personal piggy bank, a personal kitty" to keep his businesses afloat and to finance a lifestyle that included ownership of a yacht. Walker was sentenced to seven years in prison to be followed by five years probation and ordered to pay $231,609 restitution to First American. On January 4, 1988, the former governor surrendered to authorities at the Federal Prison Camp in Duluth, Minnesota, a minimum-security facility. He was released in 1989, after serving a year and a half of his sentence.

After he left prison, he completed his community service by helping the homeless in Virginia Beach, Virginia. He then moved to San Diego and continued to work with the homeless. Walker, who retired to Escondido where he lives with his wife Lily, published his seventh book in 2007, a memoir titled *The Maverick and the Machine: Governor Dan Walker Tells His Story*. His next book, titled *Veto!*, is a novel about casino gambling and politics in Illinois.

Daniel Walker

Governor Walker stops to rest during his 1,197-mile walk from southern Illinois to Chicago.

Governor Walker takes part in the nation's bicentennial celebration during an event held at the Old State Capitol in downtown Springfield.

37th
Governor

James Robert Thompson
1936 -

1936 — Born May 8 in Chicago

1956 — Enters Northwestern University Law School after three years of undergraduate work at the Navy Pier campus of the University of Illinois and at Washington University

1959 — Begins work at the Cook County state's attorney's office

1964 — Becomes an assistant professor at Northwestern University Law School

1971 — Becomes U.S. attorney for the Northern District

1971 - 1975 — Wins convictions against many political figures, including former Governor and U.S. Court of Appeals Judge Otto Kerner; Chicago Alderman Thomas E. Keane; and Cook County Clerk and former state Treasurer, Auditor, and Secretary of State Edward J. Barrett; joins Winston & Strawn in private practice

1976 — Wins election as governor, limited to a special two-year term to enable future gubernatorial elections to fall in years that don't coincide with presidential elections

1977 — Signs a bill that allows the death penalty for people convicted in any of 16 categories of murder

1979 — Signs a bill, to take effect in 1980, that makes the minimum drinking age 21

1980 — The Cutback Amendment, a ballot proposition approved by the voters, eliminates the system of electing three representatives from each Illinois House district. With the 1982 elections, the House is reduced by one-third.

1983 — Proposes and the legislature approves a temporary increase in the income tax

1984 — Creates the Department of Alcoholism and Substance Abuse and the Department of Employment Security

1985 — A flooding Illinois River turns 22 downstate counties into disaster areas.

1986 — Wins his fourth campaign for governor; candidates for the right-wing Lyndon LaRouche Party win upset victories in the Democratic primary for lieutenant governor and secretary of state; Democratic gubernatorial candidate Adlai Stevenson III runs in the general election on the Solidarity Party ticket to avoid being on the same ticket with the LaRouche-backed candidates.

1989 — The legislature approves a temporary, two-year increase in the state income tax.

1990 — Illinois legalizes riverboat gambling; the first boat goes into operation in 1991.

1991 — Leaves the Executive Mansion after having decided not to run for reelection or seek another elected office

2002 — Becomes a member of the so-called 9/11 Commission

2005 — Leads Winston & Strawn team that defends former Governor George Ryan

2006 — Resigns as chairman of Winston & Strawn, the Chicago law firm he rejoined in 1991, but remains as attorney

Republican

January 10, 1977 to January 8, 1979

January 8, 1979 to January 10, 1983

January 10, 1983 to January 12, 1987

January 12, 1987 to January 14, 1991

James R. Thompson was Illinois' longest-serving governor. After 14 years in executive office, including one two-year term, he accepted a lucrative partnership in Winston & Strawn, one of Chicago's most prominent law firms.

A tall man at six feet, six inches, "Big Jim" was spectacular on the political stump. With no prior electoral experience, he made his first run for governor at the age of 40 and managed to poll 64.7 percent of the vote, an Illinois record at the time for a contested election. Though Thompson had little contact with much of Illinois before that campaign, he built name recognition and a solid reputation as U.S. attorney for the Northern District by successfully prosecuting several dozen Chicago politicians, including a former governor.

In early 1990, the last year of his fourth term, he surpassed the tenure of Ninian Edwards, who was appointed territorial governor for nine years before he was elected to a four-year term.

Unlike his predecessor, the confrontational Dan Walker, the pragmatic Thompson was a master of the negotiated compromise and a specialist in getting along with most Democrats. A spontaneous speaker, he was gregarious, media-savvy, and informal.

Thompson clearly enjoyed being with people and being governor. He was an avid parader, and he often showed up at the Illinois State Fair in a T-shirt to skid down the giant slide — with his dog on one occasion. He once rode a horse in the Capitol.

As a politician, he was durable. When he took office in 1977, Gerald Ford was president and Chicago Mayor Richard J. Daley had been dead only three weeks. When he left office, George H. W. Bush was president and Richard M. Daley was about to run for his second term as mayor of Chicago. His greatest obstacle throughout four terms was a lethargic economy.

A Corruption Buster

Jim Thompson came from Chicago's unglamorous West Side. Born during the Depression, on May 8, 1936, he was the oldest of four children. His parents, J. Robert Thompson and the former Agnes Josephine Swanson, never got involved in politics. DeKalb County natives, they lived in a middle-class neighborhood near Garfield Park. The hard-working father, who had been a farm boy, qualified for the University of Illinois College of Medicine by going to night school for nine years at Lewis Institute and working days as a laboratory technician. During an accelerated medical course, he supported his family as a morgue attendant. Thompson was 8 when his father graduated and became a pathologist at

Municipal Tuberculosis Sanitarium, where he practiced medicine at night by making house calls and giving insurance examinations. Eventually the family moved to Oak Park.

The precocious oldest son, who skipped two years of elementary school, became addicted to reading magazines for political news. And in grade school he decided he would become a politician.

Because the West Side was changing, Thompson's parents decided he would spend his high school years at North Park Academy, a private school on the Northwest Side. Aiming for a law degree as a prelude to a career in politics, he enrolled at the University of Illinois branch on Navy Pier and specialized in history and government. Later, while his father was on Army duty in St. Louis, Thompson transferred to Washington University. After the family moved to Oak Park, he was a deacon in a Presbyterian church and taught a Sunday school class. Two of his siblings became lawyers and the other a geology professor.

At Northwestern University School of Law, which he entered in 1956, Thompson came under the influence of Professor Fred E. Inbau and was the first student to address a prosecutors' workshop. At the time, most law students were pro-defendant activists, but Thompson, a hard worker and a good speaker, gained a reputation by taking the side of law enforcement. After graduation in 1959, though he had no political sponsor, Thompson became head of the appellate division for Cook County State's Attorney Benjamin S. Adamowski, a Democrat turned Republican. In 1964, Thompson would make his mark by arguing for the state before the U.S. Supreme Court — and losing on a 5-4 decision — in *Escobedo v. Illinois*. The case was the first to test the constitutional limits of the police in obtaining confessions. Speaking before police groups in other cities, Thompson predicted that additional decisions would extend the legal protections of defendants in police custody.

Thompson did not lose his job when Democrat Daniel P. Ward became state's attorney. However, he left the state's attorney's office to become an assistant professor of law at Northwestern University. While there, he co-authored three casebooks on criminal law. He returned to Republican politics in 1969 as chief of Attorney General William J. Scott's criminal division, but he did not stay long. Before his 35th birthday, Thompson became assistant U.S. attorney for the Northern District of Illinois, and on November 29, 1971, the U.S. attorney for the Northern District. He was sponsored for the post by U.S. Senator Charles H. Percy, a moderate Illinois Republican. In the 18 months Thompson worked as assistant U.S. attorney, staff in the prosecutor's office doubled, thanks to President Richard Nixon's Omnibus Crime Bill of 1970.

Thompson knew Chicago politics well, and he promptly convened a series of grand juries that ignored whatever unspoken agreements had protected the city's top-level political figures. And he began winning convictions. Judge Otto Kerner, who had left the governor's office to take a post in the U.S. Court of Appeals, went to prison, as did Thomas E. Keane, Chicago's most powerful alderman. County Clerk Edward J. Barrett, who had been state treasurer, state auditor, and secretary of state, was permitted to serve his bribery sentence at home because of poor health. Mayor Richard J. Daley's former press secretary, half a dozen aldermen, several legislators, suburban politicians, policemen, and employees of the politically sensitive election commission and assessor's office also were convicted. Some were Republicans, but most were part of the Democratic organization headed by Daley.

Thompson made the final call on the Kerner prosecution. The grand jury indicted the judge on 19 counts. Thompson appeared in the courtroom as chief prosecutor. When he cross-examined Kerner and made the final argument to the jury, Thompson's future was at stake, for an acquittal would have brought a backlash of sympathy for the urbane former governor. Indeed, the defense criticized Thompson's methods. He was one of the first federal prosecutors to obtain convictions by grants of immunity to reluctant witnesses. Nevertheless, a special panel of Court of Appeals judges from outside Illinois upheld the conviction of Judge Kerner for income tax fraud, conspiracy, perjury, and mail fraud.

By 1975, Thompson was the best-known Illinois Republican. Under pressure to be a candidate for major office, he astutely declined to run against Richard J. Daley for mayor of Chicago. Soon he announced his candidacy for governor and began handshaking among downstaters and assembling a campaign staff. He spent six months as a part-time attorney on the payroll of Winston & Strawn, where he engaged in the private practice of law for the first time.

Thompson's weakness during that first campaign was that, having begun at the top, he knew little about the machinery and problems of state government. And he had never seen most of downstate. Nevertheless, the young prosecutor easily triumphed over a conservative businessman in the 1976 Republican primary. In the fall election, his opponent was Secretary of State Michael J. Howlett, a popular, experienced state official who had eliminated Governor Dan Walker in the Democratic primary. Howlett tried to exploit Thompson's lack of experience, but the tactic failed. The Republican conceded that he needed on-the-job training, but he was a quick study. He had an excellent memory for names and faces, and he was a better speaker than Howlett. Further, the Democrat had been slated for governor by Richard J. Daley — he even looked somewhat like the Chicago mayor — enhancing Thompson's image as a fresh face and enabling him to capitalize on his reputation as a corruption-buster. With the support of independents and some Democrats, "Big Jim" polled nearly two-thirds of the vote and won by 1,390,137 votes.

Cracking Down on Crime and Boosting the Economy

Two issues remained in the forefront throughout Jim Thompson's 14-year tenure: public safety and the economy.

Early in his first term, the former prosecutor focused his attention on the state's criminal justice system. In particular, he called for stiffer mandatory sentences for certain crimes. Indeed, during his administration, the emphasis in criminal justice policy throughout the country shifted from rehabilitation to punishment. Thompson won a new Class X category of felony for such serious crimes as attempted murder, rape, and armed robbery, which carried the penalty of minimum sentences and, for third-time offenders, imprisonment without possibility of parole. And during his first year in office, he signed legislation to reinstate the death penalty. Shortly before he left the Executive Mansion, the state carried out the first Illinois execution in 28 years.

The get-tough-on-crime policies carried a stiff price tag. Thompson's administration built more prisons than at any other time in state history. Yet there still weren't enough. In the first decade of Thompson's tenure, 24,000 offenders were convicted under Class X. When he left office, 120 offenders were sitting on Death Row. Illinois' prisons were bursting at the seams, and even some of the most ardent law-and-order proponents began to reassess the impact of Class X and mandatory minimum sentencing.

Nevertheless, Thompson's stance on criminal justice was popular, and he was well-positioned for his second campaign. His first term lasted only two years because the state shifted statewide elections to nonpresidential years. Perhaps for that reason, voters were especially disposed to renew the young governor's lease on the Executive Mansion. He also may have been helped by the attention-getting, but nonbinding Thompson Proposition, which asked voters whether they thought property tax rates should be controlled. And possibly they were drawn to images of Samantha Jayne, the second baby born to a state's first family and the first in 72 years. The governor's only child was born in the midst of that second campaign. Thompson had courted and married lawyer Jayne Carr of Oak Park during his first campaign. Whatever the reasons, he scored his second landslide. He beat his Democratic opponent, State Comptroller and former state Superintendent of Public Instruction Michael Bakalis, by 596, 550 votes, or 59 percent of the total.

Thompson's second term was marked by a deep recession and structural shifts in the economy. Older industrial plants were shuttered, and jobs were forever lost in the so-called "Rust Belt" of the Midwest. Illinois' overall jobless rate soared 5 percent in seven years to a high of 11.2 percent in 1984. Between 1979 and 1983, the state lost a quarter of its manufacturing jobs. Throughout the '80s, the Thompson Administration energetically implemented strategies to lure and keep businesses. Striving to improve the export economy by promoting Illinois products abroad, he opened overseas trade missions. His frequent trips to Japan and Europe also promoted Illinois as a site for industrial investments. The best-known and most controversial success in luring such investment was an agreement to locate Diamond-Star Motors in the central Illinois community of Normal. Meanwhile, he convinced homegrown companies such as Sears, the state's largest private-sector employer, to stay in Illinois. It was an era when businesses were driving hard bargains with many governors, often demanding tax breaks and infrastructure development, even cash incentives. Thompson was determined to be a player in the competition for jobs and revenue. A high-profile case involved the Chicago White Sox. The team threatened to leave the state unless it received a publicly financed stadium. On June 30, 1988, in the final hours of the legislative session, the governor wrangled votes out of Republican legislators to pave the way for the new Comiskey Park. Nevertheless, critics argued such deals weren't always as advantageous for the state as advertised. By the '90s, incentives and so-called smokestack chasing had bottomed out. Yet Thompson was prescient in positioning Illinois for the coming global economy.

Thompson was forward-thinking as well in envisioning history, art, and culture as a way to boost the economy. He launched the Art-in-Architecture Program, which set aside one-half of one percent of all public building construction costs for art to be displayed in public buildings. He established the state's artisan shops, where artists could sell their work. And he pumped dollars into historic preservation.

But in the mid-'80s, he devised his boldest, certainly his biggest, economic development plan and dubbed it Build Illinois. The program provided $2 billion in new bonding authority for capital improvements throughout the state, including construction of the new State Library. Certainly no one could dispute Thompson's love of anything involving bricks and mortar, especially if it could be sold as a jobs program, but critics charged taxpayers would bear the debt for decades.

Third Run Is a Narrow Victory

In his final two campaigns, good luck helped Jim Thompson defeat the strongest Illinois Democrat, Adlai E. Stevenson III, who had left the U.S. Senate after 10 years because he believed the governorship was more challenging. In 1982 and 1986, Thompson was fortunate that Stevenson, unlike his father, was a dull speaker with negative charisma. The governor chose to run as a friend of the taxpayer, a man who had enforced economy and made tax increases unnecessary.

Still, in Thompson's third bid for office, polls in the summer of 1982 showed he was running a poor second. By October, the situation had reversed, and the governor looked like an easy winner. The pollsters, however, had not realized that many of Chicago's black voters, overwhelmingly Democratic, were in revolt against their party's white leadership and would turn out en masse as a warm-up for the mayoral election of Harold Washington the next winter. Thompson, who had expected to win easily, had to wait 20 days before the State Board of Elections certified he won by 5,074 votes. It took two months and a 4-3 Illinois Supreme Court decision denying a recount before Stevenson conceded. Two landslides had been followed by the closest gubernatorial election in Illinois history.

In 1986, Secretary of State Jim Edgar and Lieutenant Governor George Ryan were available to run for governor, but Thompson did not retire. Stevenson, whom Democratic leaders still considered their best candidate, was given a clear track in the primary. Whether under normal circumstances he might have been elected on his second try will never be known. With Illinois House Speaker Michael J. Madigan as his manager, the former governor's son began an aggressive campaign that ran into unexpected trouble in the primary. The post-Daley Democratic leadership concentrated on renominating Cook County candidates and ignored a slate entered by Lyndon H. LaRouche Jr., an extremist. When the nominees for lieutenant governor and secretary of state turned out to be disciples of LaRouche, Stevenson refused to run with them. During a difficult summer, he resigned the Democratic nomination for governor and became a futile candidate of an ad hoc Solidarity Party.

Thompson worked hard and was elected to his fourth term, not by a landslide but with a respectable plurality of almost 400,000 votes. He carried 13 Chicago wards, two more than he had four years earlier. In four elections, he had polled 57 percent of the vote and won by an average plurality of 597,742 votes.

Costs Climb and So Do Taxes

Thompson won his last two elections by claiming that state

finances were sound. But after each of those campaigns, the governor decided the state treasury was tapped out.

Shortly after the 1982 election, a lame-duck legislature gave Thompson unprecedented authority to cut appropriations by 2 percent for the rest of the fiscal year. When the new General Assembly was seated, Thompson asked for $1.9 billion in new revenue in the form of higher income, liquor, gasoline, and highway user taxes. The legislature agreed to some of those increases. In 1983, the state faced an immediate $300 million budget gap because the recession-plagued economy played havoc with the initial state revenue estimates. Thompson proposed a temporary increase in the income tax rate; the legislature agreed to it. Likewise, booming maintenance costs for the extensive highway system had depleted the fund designated for the state's roads. That problem was solved by a deal that increased the gasoline tax and tied downstate road improvements to a state subsidy for Chicago-area transit. Thompson had taken the initiative in urging two Chicago mayors to recognize that economic health depended on workforce mobility. At the same time, the governor's advocacy of a special sales tax for the collar counties jeopardized his popularity in that Republican stronghold. Meanwhile, the governor found extra dollars for elementary and secondary schools and for colleges and universities, though not enough to satisfy the educational community.

After his 1986 reelection, Thompson again asked for new taxes in quantity. His requests totaled $1.6 billion, which was more than he had any chance of getting. The Democratic response in the House, dictated by Speaker Madigan, was negative. Traditionally, the legislature plays a spendthrift role by passing appropriations that have to be vetoed. But under Madigan, the House for the first time took charge of the budgetary process and dictated that taxes would not be raised. After the stalemated session adjourned, the governor responded with a 4 percent cut in spending and vetoes totaling $363 million. Reminiscent of Governor Deneen 80 years earlier, Thompson in speeches and interviews appealed to the public and warned that the state faced a lowered bond credit rating and possible bankruptcy. He triumphed in the fall session of the legislature when Madigan tried to override vetoes of $62.5 million in school spending. In the final showdown in the Senate, Thompson won with the support of Philip Rock, the Democratic Senate president. Then, in 1989, in a surprising turnabout, Madigan, with Rock's help, rammed another temporary income tax hike through the General Assembly. Thompson signed the measure, which earmarked new revenue for education and local governments. That surcharge was made permanent during the administration of Thompson's successor, Jim Edgar.

Political Summitry

Through most of his tenure, Thompson faced a Democrat-controlled legislature. In fact, Republicans controlled only one chamber, the House, in only one two-year span: 1981 to 1983. From the start, Thompson had a Democratic Senate to work with, but from 1978, Senate President Phil Rock was generally helpful with the administration's major legislation.

However, partisan control of the legislature became particularly pointed in light of the "Cutback Amendment" and the redistricting precipitated by the 1980 Census. The state constitutional amendment was triggered, in part, because the 1978 lame-duck legislature voted itself, the governor, and other officials pay raises. Thompson vetoed the measure, but the General Assembly immediately overrode the veto. Angry voters in 1980 approved a ballot proposition that changed the way representatives were elected to the Illinois House. Under the state Constitution, each district sent three members to the House, two from the majority party and one from the minority party. The amendment doubled the number of House districts, but dictated that only one member would represent each district. Thus, starting with the 1982 election, the House was reduced by a third and the minority party could not automatically be assured of having a third of the House seats. The 1980 U.S. Census spurred redistricting on the grounds of shifting demographics. Partisan control of the Illinois House and Senate was very much up for grabs. The situation was settled only when the luck of the draw in a lottery gave Democrats a majority on a deadlocked redistricting commission.

Thompson's style meshed well with the challenges that cropped up in the early years of the legislative reorganization. In and out of the legislature, the governor specialized in summit conferences when faced with critical problems. Generally they were effective. Key agreements, for example, were hammered out pertaining to Chicago schools and unemployment insurance. When, in 1980, Chicago schools faced a financial crisis, Thompson called board members, bond experts, and other officials to the Executive Mansion and didn't let them leave until an agreement had been reached. And, from his middle-ground stance, the gregarious Thompson maintained contacts that helped him bring labor and business together on insurance for unemployed workers.

Like other recent governors, Thompson was in Chicago much of the time. He was the first to move into the modernistic State of Illinois Center, which was designed to his wishes. Traditionally, Republican governors have worked well with Chicago's Democratic mayors, but Mayor Harold Washington, who sat out a 1987 deadlock between the governor and the General Assembly on taxes, was less cooperative than

Michael Bilandic and Jane Byrne had been. The governor considered Washington partly responsible for his administration's failure to bring a 1993 World's Fair to the lakefront.

The Changing Rules of the Game

Throughout the era encompassing Thompson's public career, reform movements and court decrees chipped away at political parties' abilities to reward loyalty through jobs. Earlier, in a case involving the city of Chicago, public workers were protected from political firings. Then, in the final months of his tenure in the governor's office, the U.S. Supreme Court extended the principle to political hiring. The high court ruled in 1990 in *Rutan v. Illinois* that government hiring based on political affiliation is an unconstitutional abridgment of free speech. Thompson said he would comply with the court's decision, but he argued that a governor could not function without some party patronage.

Yet modern-era officeholders were already turning to no-bid contracts as a way to reward friends, and the term "pinstripe patronage" was coined during the Thompson Administration. Thompson argued that he took personal responsibility for approving some no-bid contracts to ensure that state business was rotated among capable companies and bond houses. And he argued that only a small fraction of those contracts went to friends.

Though Thompson struggled with the changing rules on patronage, he supported legislation in 1983 granting government employees and teachers collective bargaining rights.

National Ambitions

Thompson's administration remained scandal-free. Prompt public apologies were effective in nullifying such mistakes as the questionable acceptance of four Krugerrands from a labor leader and a midnight veto of a legislative pay raise bill on the understanding that it would be quickly overridden. This impressive durability in a big and diverse state attracted national attention, but his career was intrastate. So in 1990, after serving four terms and more years than any other Illinois governor, Thompson decided not to run for a fifth term. Instead, he put an end to his political career and returned to Winston & Strawn in Chicago.

In 2002, President George W. Bush named him to the National Commission on Terrorist Attacks Upon the United States, the so-called 9/11 Commission. In 2006, he resigned as chairman of Winston & Strawn, but remained with the firm. He oversaw the team that defended former Governor George Ryan in his corruption trial.

Governor Thompson won his first election with 64.7 percent of the vote, a record at the time.

Governor Thompson, wearing the number of Chicago Bears' running back Walter Payton, at the State Fair with daughter Samantha and wife Jayne.

Governor Thompson surveys areas flooded by the Illinois and Fox rivers in March 1985 that left four people dead, displaced 2,400 and cost an estimated $11,000,000 in damages.

Flooded towns included Chillicothe, Liverpool, Meredosia, Peoria and Rome.

Governor Thompson, center, shares a laugh with other state leaders, Lee Daniels, left, Jim Edgar, George Ryan and Michael Madigan.

Governor Thompson and Arkansas Governor Bill Clinton

38th Governor

Jim Edgar
1946-

1946 —Born on July 22 in Vinita, Oklahoma

1968 —Receives bachelor's degree in history from Eastern Illinois University

1968 —Accepts a legislative internship sponsored by the University of Illinois; works for Senate Republican leader W. Russell Arrington

1968 - 1974 — Serves on the staffs of Senator Arrington and House Speaker W. Robert Blair

1974 —Makes an unsuccessful bid for the Illinois House

1974 - 1976 — Works for the National Conference of State Legislatures in Denver and as an aide to legislative leaders

1977 - 1979 — Serves in the 80th and 81st General Assemblies

1979 —Leaves the General Assembly to work on Governor James Thompson's staff

1981 —Is appointed secretary of state to fill out the term of Democrat Alan J. Dixon, who was elected to the U.S. Senate

1983 - 1987 — Serves his first full term as secretary of state

1987 - 1991 — Serves his second full term as secretary of state

1990 —Defeats Democrat Neil Hartigan to become governor

1993 —A rainy summer floods 500,000 acres of Illinois causing $1.5 billion in property and crop damage

1994 —Defeats Democrat Dawn Clark Netsch to win a second term as governor

1995 —Mayor Richard M. Daley receives authority over Chicago schools.

1997 —Decides not to run for reelection

Republican
January 14, 1991 - January 9, 1995
January 9, 1995 - January 11, 1999

Jim Edgar was the right governor at the right time. Cautious and credible, he moved into the Executive Mansion in the after-shock of the high-spending '80s and in the wake of an administration given to grand gestures. After 14 years of "Big Jim" Thompson, Illinoisans chose a governor who was comparatively dull, yet popular throughout his two terms. Though he risked raising the subject of taxes during his first campaign, voters believed his promise of fiscal discipline. And after delivering on his pledge not to surprise them, they reelected him by the second-widest gubernatorial margin in state history. Only Governor Thompson's 1976 campaign netted a greater margin of victory.

Throughout much of his career, the downstate Republican showed a knack for good timing. He was appointed to his first statewide office and moved up the political ladder to Illinois' top elected post, where he was instinctively suited to solving the state's growing financial crisis. The national economy had weakened, and Illinois was living beyond its means when Edgar, a moderate with a modest approach to governing, was elected Illinois' 38th chief executive. He immediately moved to trim spending and reduce a stack of unpaid bills. He won the first permanent increase in the state's income tax and pushed successfully to cap the growth in local property taxes. Edgar's decisions to cut social entitlements, beef up jobs programs, and overhaul the state's welfare agency were in tune with Washington's move to limit social supports. And his emphasis on smaller government pilot projects and expanded citizen and corporate involvement reflected the tenor of the downsized '90s.

Though he quickly earned a reputation as "Governor No," Edgar increased funding for higher education throughout his eight years, pumped money into early childhood programs, and steadily boosted state spending for primary and secondary schools. And, as a capstone on his career, he negotiated with lawmakers a guaranteed level of funding for each elementary and secondary student, meaning the state's poorest schools would be assured additional dollars.

But this governor's greatest strength was his greatest weakness. A born administrator, he was naturally suited to managing the state's day-to-day affairs but less comfortable with the give-and-take of an increasingly partisan legislature and less successful when it came to mobilizing public support and cajoling lawmakers into taking political risks. As a result, Edgar failed in an 11th-hour bid to convince lawmakers to find a politically palatable way to shift the locus of school funding away from property wealth. Lawmakers did agree, for the first time, to set and then provide the dollars to fund a minimum foundation level of spending on each elementary and secondary student and allow that foundation level to increase over three years. They also agreed to guarantee funding for those increases. To cover the costs, they cobbled together a package of minor tax hikes. Yet, faced with another election, they would not risk fundamental property tax reform aimed at solving for the long term the inequities in education finance. Edgar was forced to settle for half a loaf, though, as his supporters argued, a fairly substantial one.

As befitting his temperament, Edgar's tenure was marked by incremental programmatic changes. Nevertheless, he balanced the books and restored the state's credit rating without a general tax increase. And that, as he had promised it would be, was his legacy.

But as the national economy boomed and the state's bank account grew, Edgar decided to step down. His health was a likely concern. He had suffered heart trouble for several years, and family was almost certainly a consideration. So, at 52, Edgar accepted an appointment as a Distinguished Fellow with the University of Illinois' Institute of

Government and Public Affairs, where he lectured. He also accepted a three-month fellowship at the John F. Kennedy School of Government.

Edgar faced a $1 billion debt on his first day as governor. On his last day, he left a $1 billion cash balance for his successor.

At the Center of Attention

Jim Edgar showed an early aptitude for politics, an early preference for the Republican Party, and an early streak of stubborn independence.

His parents, Cecil and Betty Edgar, were not active partisans in their small east-central Illinois community of Charleston, but at the least they considered themselves Democrats. No one in the immediate family showed the slightest interest in becoming a politician.

Edgar's interest in public service might have seemed unusual to his rural Illinois neighbors but not to his cohorts. He was born in Vinita, Oklahoma, on July 22, 1946, during the post-World War II baby boom. His parents had moved there shortly after the war so that Cecil could find work with Betty's family. But his parents had moved back to Coles County by the time Edgar was a toddler. He came of age during John F. Kennedy's presidency, a time when public service became a calling to many in his generation. Once again, Edgar chose his own path. He was a political moderate and a devout Baptist. He didn't smoke or drink. Before he graduated from Eastern Illinois University in his hometown, he became a husband and a father — and student body president. Years later, even his toughest critics would call this governor tenacious.

The Family's Fortunes Change

Jim Edgar was the youngest of three boys, raised by a single mother. The family's fortunes changed the year Edgar turned 7. Cecil was killed in a head-on automobile crash. Betty found work in town, first with the federal agriculture department, later at Eastern Illinois University. Edgar learned to be frugal.

While he attended Eastern, working toward a degree in history, he met a fellow student, Brenda Smith, from the southern Illinois town of Anna. They married and had two children, Brad and Elizabeth.

After receiving his bachelor's degree in 1968, Edgar considered law school, but decided to accept a legislative internship sponsored by the University of Illinois. Interns worked for legislators in Springfield. The position paid a small salary, but it also promised an invaluable practical education in politics.

Edgar was assigned to work with Senate Republican Leader W. Russell Arrington. Nothing could have prepared him for the experience of the next few months. Arrington hailed from suburban Evanston, and Edgar recalled some 30 years later that the senator was "a moving force, the likes of which we have never seen around here." In Arrington, the future governor found his first political mentor. And he got a ringside seat at what he later called the legislative "session of all sessions."

Edgar's job in 1969 was to sit next to Arrington on the chamber floor with the bill analysis book and keep the senator posted on staff recommendations. As it happened, during the closing days of that spring session, lawmakers created the state's first income tax. While they were at it, they approved an increase in the gasoline tax and a license plate fee. Republican Governor Richard Ogilvie had asked Arrington to sponsor the bill, knowing it would be politically risky. And because the package was negotiated off the floor by the governor, Chicago Mayor Richard J. Daley, and legislative leaders, the actual vote took little more than half an hour, belying the revolution that had taken place and the revolution yet to come.

Edgar's own career would be affected by that vote. But at the time, he remembered, he was simply impressed. "I thought that was the way government was always supposed to act. It all happened quickly." By the end of his internship, he was "an Illinois Republican, locked in" and committed to state government. Most important, Ogilvie and Arrington were moderate Republicans. Edgar had worried about taking that assignment with Arrington, fearing the leader would be too conservative. But Arrington turned out to be the most "progressive guy in the legislature," Edgar said. "He really believed that if there was a problem, the General Assembly stayed until they got it solved."

He remained on Arrington's staff for two years. But when the Senate leader got sick and left the legislature, Edgar went to work for House Speaker W. Robert Blair. The Park Forest Republican turned out to be another party powerhouse. During Edgar's time on his staff, Blair handled legislation creating the Regional Transportation Authority to oversee mass transit in Chicago and the surrounding suburbs.

In 1974, Edgar decided it was time to strike out on his own, and he made an unsuccessful run for state representative from Charleston — his only electoral loss. Edgar faced two opponents in the primary: one the incumbent and the other favored by the Coles County Republican Central Committee. Edgar came in a close third. He said he learned two important lessons. "One is that you can always lose. And two, I never wanted to lose again."

Edgar subsequently went to work for the National Conference of State Legislatures in Denver, giving him an opportunity to visit other states. But in 1976, he ran again for a seat in the Illinois House. The 1974 campaign had given him a chance to build name recognition and party support. This time he won.

The Frustrations of a Backbencher

At age 30, Jim Edgar took a seat in the legislature, representing the 53rd House District, including his hometown of Charleston. The experience turned out to be an eye-opener. After serving on the staffs of Republican leaders in both legislative chambers, Edgar was suddenly a freshman backbencher in the minority party. He cut a low profile throughout his two-and-a-half years, though he garnered attention for an unsuccessful proposal allowing school districts to opt for a local income tax.

While he served in the House, Edgar backed another proposal that would have a significant impact on policy during his years in the Executive Mansion. He voted for one of Governor James R. Thompson's first initiatives to toughen criminal sentencing. Dubbed Class X, the law established longer sentences for certain crimes.

Among the more politically controversial proposals Edgar supported while in the House was a pay raise for lawmakers and other state officials. In fact, Edgar supported the hike during his 1978 campaign for reelection, and he was one of the few downstate legislators to vote for it in the post-election veto session before the new General Assembly was seated. Thompson vetoed the measure by auto pen while on vacation, in plenty of time for lawmakers to overturn the veto. Thompson apologized to the public, and he and lawmakers renegotiated the raises. But the damage was done. That vote would spark public anger and, as a result, a citizen initiative was approved in 1980 that eliminated multimember districts and reduced the membership in the House, beginning in 1983.

Some five months later, Thompson offered Edgar a job as his legislative liaison. So, near the beginning of his second term, he left the legislature to go to work in the executive branch of state government. As Thompson's top lobbyist, Edgar helped negotiate temporary relief for the financially troubled Chicago schools. The state provided a bridge loan and created a panel to monitor finances. But the problems of that school system, the state's largest, were far from over. Edgar would face them again during his own administration.

In late 1980, Democrat Alan Dixon was poised to leave the secretary of state's office to take a seat in the U.S. Senate. According to the state Constitution, Thompson was in a position to name a replacement until the next election. Handed such a boon for the Republican Party, this was not a decision the governor would take lightly.

Good-looking, straight-arrow, and conscientious, Edgar had an instinct for administrative detail. In many ways he was unlike his flamboyant boss. Thompson was a quick study who loved to party. He was fond of wearing T-shirts, even in the Capitol. Edgar was just as likely to march in a parade in a suit and tie. He was compulsive and disciplined. And he preferred a quiet evening at home. While the outgoing Thompson was at his best when moving through crowds, Edgar was stiff in public. Thompson was an orator. Edgar was not. But he was unlikely to turn out to be an embarrassing pick for Thompson. "Throughout his public career," Thompson said in announcing Edgar's appointment, "his actions and his work have been in the best tradition of public service."

An Activist Secretary of State

At age 34, Edgar became the youngest secretary of state in the 20th century. In his first statewide executive office, he had the chance to call the shots. He led the fight to close loopholes in Illinois' drunk driving law, won the long-running battle to require insurance for all Illinois drivers, launched literacy and organ donor programs, modernized the state's securities laws, and oversaw construction of a new state library.

But Edgar's first weeks on the job may have been his toughest. He discovered he had inherited a license-selling scandal in his Chicago office, as well as an army of Democratic activists, some of them guilty of doing political work on state time. Edgar created an inspector general's office, then quickly settled on a public cause: traffic safety.

The issue was personal as well as political. Though there was never any indication alcohol had been involved in his father's death, Edgar said the accident made him realize the seriousness of traffic fatalities. He began by pushing to strengthen the state's 1972 drunk driving law. Edgar had been on Blair's staff when lawmakers approved the law, which he called a compromise so the state would qualify for federal funding. Edgar argued arrests and convictions were actually declining while that law was in effect. He championed provisions to abolish the waiting period for the Breathalyzer test, eliminate a second test, and double the penalty for driving drunk. After those provisions took effect in 1982, Edgar began to promote quick suspension of driver's licenses with judicial review for drunk drivers, which also was signed into law.

Edgar won an even tougher fight for mandatory insurance. In the early 1980s, nearly a quarter of all registered motorists in Illinois had no insurance, according to the state insurance agency. The insurance industry, however, argued such a law would be unenforceable. Political opponents argued it would impose undue hardship on poor motorists.

Nevertheless, Illinois got in line behind 31 other states, starting with a temporary program that was later made permanent.

His other major accomplishment was completion of a new state library. Thanks to Thompson's Build Illinois program and Edgar's willingness to support and administer a new tax on the sale of used cars, the $30 million library was built on his watch.

Edgar was elected to the office on his own in 1982, winning big during a tough Republican year, and he was reelected in 1986 by what was at that time the largest plurality of any statewide candidate in Illinois history. That year, *U.S. News and World Report* named him one of 30 "rising stars of American politics."

Edgar quickly learned to use the office to build good will throughout the state, including among African Americans and Hispanics, two potential constituencies his party had ignored, if not alienated. And he positioned himself to grab a higher rung on the political ladder. He was sitting in the St. Louis airport in 1989 when aides told him to call the governor. Thompson said he was going to announce that he was not running for a fifth term. "And it's your turn," Thompson said. "The governorship is yours, if you can get elected."

A No-Surprises Governor

Jim Edgar was the second secretary of state to move up to the governorship, and the first governor elected to succeed a member of his own party in 62 years.

Yet, while he and Thompson were moderate Republicans, they couldn't have been more different. No doubt calculating that his mentor's popularity had lost some of its edge after 14 years, Edgar set about early to highlight those differences. He was ready and willing to enforce spending limits, and he wouldn't mislead voters before election day. "I don't want the people of Illinois to be surprised by anything I do after the election, and they won't be," he said on Governor's Day at the Illinois State Fair in the summer of 1990.

In fact, Edgar established an agenda for his entire two-term administration during that first 15-month campaign and his first six months in office. He remained strikingly consistent on the key points throughout his eight years as governor, the major exception being apparent shifts over the years on proposals to reform school finance by swapping higher state taxes for lower property taxes.

Edgar's agenda included restoring the state's fiscal integrity while providing additional financial support for education and early childhood programs. It also included capping rising property taxes in the high-growth suburban counties surrounding Chicago and making permanent a temporary income tax surcharge. On election night, Edgar would say that his victory proved a candidate can be honest about taxes and still win.

Taxes quickly became the central issue in that first race for governor. On the day he launched the campaign, Edgar told reporters the two-year state income tax surcharge should be made permanent for schools. "If that tax ended in 1991, that would mean we would pull $350 million away from schools. And I really don't want to be part of any attempt to pull the financial rug out from under our schools."

The state's income tax had not been permanently increased since 1969, when Edgar watched its creation while working as an intern for Arrington. But in 1989, a temporary surcharge was instituted by the Democrat-controlled legislature. It increased the individual rate from 2.5 percent to 3 percent. The corporate rate was increased from 4 percent to 4.8 percent. The $756 million raised by the increase was split, roughly, between the state's schools and local governments, though some of those dollars were used to cover the cost of doubling homeowners' property tax deductions on individual returns.

The surcharge was set to expire six months after the new governor was sworn in, but calling for an extension during the campaign was politically risky. Nevertheless, Edgar's assessment was that most antitax sentiment was aimed at the local property tax, which covered roughly 60 percent of the costs of elementary and secondary schools. His stance on the income tax secured him the backing of educators and organizations, including some representing minorities, that believed the extra dollars benefited their constituencies.

He defeated Democrat Neil Hartigan by a narrow vote margin that was credited, to some extent, to Edgar's believability on the issue of taxes. Though, to his benefit, Edgar also had built good relations with African Americans and Hispanics while he served as secretary of state. Hartigan, meanwhile, did poorly in the Chicago black communities.

Beyond the surcharge, Edgar believed he would need to concentrate his energies on the spending side of state finance. The day after the election, he began to calculate how many millions would need to be cut.

He de-emphasized so-called smokestack chasing, an economic development strategy employed throughout the country in the 1980s. In the competition for job producers during that decade, governors offered incentives to corporations to stay or relocate in their states, including tax breaks and infrastructure development. Thompson used incentives in negotiating controversial and costly arrangements with Diamond-Star Motors and with Sears. Yet economic circumstances were different in

Thompson's era. Corporations played hardball, and no state wanted to be the first to blink. By the time Edgar took office, smokestack chasing was becoming passé, and he shifted his focus to education and to improvements in the state's infrastructure. Indeed, Edgar's approach to economic development, which looked unfavorably on subsidies for sports stadiums or gambling, was at the heart of a long-running feud between the Republican governor and Chicago's Democratic mayor, Richard M. Daley. Throughout Edgar's tenure, the two would clash over airports, sports stadiums, and land-based casinos.

But at the center of Edgar's economic program was his belief in preventive social services. He argued, for example, that health care prevention programs for poor people would save money in the long run. In fact, spending on entitlement programs was the fastest-growing portion of the budget. The state had become a $1 billion deadbeat, and Edgar faced a mountain of overdue bills from doctors and others who provided services for low-income Medicaid recipients. While the new governor said he expected to see spending increases in the departments of Corrections and Children and Family Services, he would not rule out cuts in social welfare programs.

Spending Cuts and Tax Caps

His first full day on the job, Edgar called for cuts in spending to close a projected $300 million budgetary gap. Due to declining sales tax revenues, the actual deficit turned out to be double that amount in his first fiscal year. The recession would last into the next two years. It would take much of Edgar's first term for the state to pull itself out of the fiscal hole. But Edgar, with the support of his party's leaders in the General Assembly, made a good start that first legislative session.

Against the wishes of Democratic lawmakers, Edgar did away with General Assistance for welfare recipients in his first budget and replaced it with Earnfare, a program that required recipients to work. Despite Democratic opposition, Republicans won the day on property tax caps for the collar counties in the Chicago metropolitan region. Cook County got caps later. And later still, downstate counties got the option to impose caps through referendum. More important, Edgar won an immediate permanent boost in the education portion of the income tax surcharge, and formula changes for distributing the rest of the surcharge revenue that were designed to benefit the state's coffers in the short run and local governments' in the long run. The higher individual and corporate rates were ultimately made permanent.

That first legislative session, complicated by the effort to remap legislative districts, ran into overtime. But after the dust cleared, Edgar was declared a winner. Even Democratic House Speaker Michael Madigan called the new governor "tenacious."

Nevertheless, a number of problems lay ahead. Social service costs continued to rise, the result of a combination of the slowing economy, expanding federal mandates in Medicaid spending, a move by the Edgar Administration to recalculate Medicaid payments, and court decisions affecting child welfare and mental health programs. Edgar and lawmakers executed such maneuvers as short-term borrowing to solve an immediate cash flow problem and new taxes on hospitals and nursing homes to close a budgetary gap.

Yet Edgar never deviated from an overarching approach to governing: a downsized role for the public sector. Further, Edgar, like many moderate Republicans in the '90s, was disposed to look to citizens to solve some social problems. He launched Project Success, for example, a program to use schools to link existing social services with the people who need them. Such an effort, he argued, could be started by government, then picked up and expanded by communities. He began during his second year with pilot programs in six districts. Another example was Edgar's successful effort to get the legislature to authorize community-based charter schools that could operate outside many of the rules and regulations of the education bureaucracy. When critics charged that he lacked vision, Edgar responded that he didn't define vision by spending money. To this governor, smaller government was better government, and private initiatives would have the advantage of holding down costs. He believed, for instance, that better prenatal care for poor mothers and preschool programs for their children could save millions in health care, education, welfare, and prison programs. During his two terms, he pumped hundreds of millions of new dollars into those programs, nearly doubling funding for preschool education.

Prepared for Disaster

Jim Edgar faced two unforeseen crises that first term. The first came in the form of a flood, one of the worst in state history. In the spring and summer of 1993, the Mississippi and Illinois rivers jumped their banks and inundated the western section of the state, putting 16,000 residents out of their homes and 10,000 workers out of their jobs.

Edgar mobilized as if for war, which, in a sense, it was. From a makeshift command center in Springfield, and in his element as a manager, Edgar put the resources of the state to work fighting the floodwaters. When critics asked why he couldn't muscle his agenda through the legislature in the same way, the governor responded that with a flood he could make decisions and simply send the bill to lawmakers, and they would pay it. Political controversies proved more difficult to manage.

Edgar's second crisis was personal. In the summer of 1994, he underwent emergency quadruple heart bypass surgery. It wasn't the first time he had been hospitalized for heart trouble; he had already had an angioplasty. And it wouldn't be the last. In 1998, he was hospitalized after experiencing chest pains while working out. But Edgar's response to his health problems were characteristic. He threw himself into a heart-healthy diet and exercise regime. After bypass surgery, he signed the fiscal 1995 budget in his hospital room and hit the campaign trail.

Using Taxes as a Political Hammer

In fact, Jim Edgar wiped out his Democratic opponent in his second campaign for governor. He faced Chicago liberal Dawn Clark Netsch, the state's comptroller and a former state senator who won only one county in the fall election. Edgar maintained, probably accurately, that Netsch lost the race when he began running ads that summer reminding voters the Democrat was against the death penalty and portraying her as unwilling to talk about her stance on crime and taxes. But the lingering perception is that Netsch lost that race because she called for a large increase in the income tax. Edgar's stance on education spending during that campaign constitutes the starkest inconsistency in his career and helped poison the political well against reform during his second term.

Netsch did propose an increase in the income tax to provide $1 billion for schools and another $1 billion in property tax relief. She called for an additional $500 million for a graduated personal income tax exemption. But her point was to suggest a way to end inequities in school spending, something Edgar had debated throughout his entire career. Yet in the context of this campaign, he hammered Netsch for calling for a 42 percent increase in the income tax rate. At the same time, he refused to endorse a proposed constitutional amendment requiring the state to bear half the cost of funding schools, arguing the measure would not accomplish what it intended.

Once his second term was secured, though, Edgar established a high-profile commission, chaired by former University of Illinois President Stanley Ikenberry, to examine the subject of education finance reforms. The commission served a political purpose as well. It gave the governor cover on the subject of taxes. Citing the panel's report, Edgar called for reforms that bore some resemblance to Netsch's plan.

Reflecting during his final weeks in office, Edgar said he did not see an inconsistency. Rather, he argued, a tax swap wasn't politically feasible at the time of his reelection. The suburban Republican legislative leadership, particularly Senate President James "Pate" Philip, wouldn't support reforms in school finance until changes had been made in Chicago schools. Suburban lawmakers saw nothing to gain from sending state dollars to poor schools in other parts of the state. Philip, who tended toward colorful rhetoric, had long argued that giving more school money to Chicago amounted to sending good money after bad. Still, Edgar failed at using the substantial persuasive powers of his office.

When the Ikenberry Commission issued its report, Edgar endorsed its recommendations, which called for generating $1.9 billion through tax increases and spending cuts, as a way to revamp what he termed the "unfair and uneven" way in which the state funded elementary and secondary schools. Those dollars would have provided $1.5 billion in property tax relief and left an extra $400 million to spend on schools. The report further recommended that $4,225 per year was the minimum level that could be spent to achieve a quality education for each child. Edgar hit the airwaves, using his own campaign funds, to promote the plan. Still, it went nowhere in a General Assembly whose members were skittish about approving any legislation with the word tax in it.

So Edgar changed his approach. He suggested reforms without offering specifics that might box lawmakers in. Indeed, lawmakers in some districts were beginning to get heat for doing nothing to support education, and, late in 1997, they agreed to some of the reforms. They funded a foundation level for school spending, and they hiked taxes on cigarettes, telephones, and riverboats to come up with extra cash. Overall, more than $500 million would go to the state's poorest schools through the year 2001, even if projected revenues were to fall through — a seismic shift in school finance in Illinois. Another $1.5 billion was designated for school construction and repairs.

Edgar and lawmakers also managed to put the capper on Chicago school reform in 1995 by vesting authority over Chicago's schools in Mayor Daley. In short order, Daley restructured the bureaucracy in that school district, put the budget in the black, and established peace with the teachers' union for the first time in years.

Social Welfare Spending

Even before the federal government set limits on welfare, Edgar began in his first term to trim the rolls. In his second term, he established a new Department of Human Services, an effort to streamline the social services delivery system. His critics argued the state was more concerned about moving folks off the rolls than keeping them in jobs. Nevertheless, Edgar was no hard-edged conservative. Early in his tenure, he supported moves to end penalties against families when fathers stayed in the home and when recipients took part-time or temporary jobs. He also backed a successful measure that required teenage welfare mothers to finish their education and to live at home.

In his final year in office, Edgar launched KidCare, an insurance program for minors from low-income families. That spring, lawmakers appropriated dollars to expand the program.

Scandals and Fights

Edgar's administration was not free of scandal. One of his friends and fundraisers, Robert Hickman, was convicted in connection with a lucrative tollway land deal while he served as executive director of the Illinois State Toll Highway Authority. And in 1997, Edgar was called to testify in an unrelated federal trial involving improper payments in a $12.9 million state computer services contract with Management Services of Illinois Inc. The founders of the company, hired to ferret out Medicaid overpayments, were among his biggest campaign contributors. Prosecutors won convictions against the contractors and two administrators in Edgar's Public Aid department by arguing the state employees had accepted cash and gifts in exchange for giving the contractors favorable treatment. Edgar was not accused of wrongdoing, but he ended up being the first sitting Illinois governor in 75 years to testify in a criminal trial. He argued that his aides turned evidence over to authorities as soon as it was discovered. That same summer, Edgar issued an executive order banning most gifts to state employees under his command and requiring more state contracts to be competitively bid.

Edgar's relationships with some of the state's most important public officials were strained throughout his eight years in the Executive Mansion. He got off on the wrong foot with Chicago Mayor Richard M. Daley almost immediately. The decision, shortly after he took office, to abrogate a pact providing state money for Chicago's mass transportation system left Daley and his aides believing this governor could not be trusted. City officials argued the dollars had been promised by the state; legislative Democrats overrode the governor's cuts, but Edgar's response that the agreement wasn't binding likely caused lasting political damage. Further, the governor entered into a political tiff with the state Supreme Court, in particular Republican Justice James Heiple, over a decision in the so-called Baby Richard case, a matter involving the question of parental rights versus the best interests of the child.

Edgar also had a difficult relationship with leaders of his own party in the legislature, House Minority Leader Lee A. Daniels and Senate President James "Pate" Philip, who thwarted Edgar at virtually every turn. Philip refused to advance the governor's plan to shift the tax mix to fund schools. In the last weeks of the governor's tenure, Philip and other Republican senators made a show of voting down more than 100 of Edgar's appointments to boards and commissions.

Despite the challenges and controversies, Edgar judged his second term to be easier and more fun. The economy was going great guns, the state was building a surplus, and the frugal governor was able to loosen the state's purse strings. Edgar and legislators agreed to double the individual exemption on income taxes, and the governor decided to put a few dollars into bricks and mortar, including $10.4 million in planning money for a Lincoln presidential library in Springfield and $30 million for a new Department of Natural Resources building.

Stepping into Private Life

Illinois state government moved into the modern era during Edgar's 30 years in public service.

On paper, Illinois' governor had more power when Edgar moved into the Executive Mansion. For the most part, though, Edgar was not as successful as some at using this bully pulpit. Certainly, tough economic times made it more difficult for Edgar to offer local projects in exchange for legislative approval of his own agenda. Court decisions diminished his power to hand out jobs. And the policy differences between the moderate downstate governor and the more conservative suburban Republican leadership in the legislature served to weaken his hand.

Yet, there also were stylistic differences in the way Edgar played the game. Ogilvie took a hands-on approach to getting the income tax, and Thompson thought nothing of showing up in one chamber or the other. But Edgar was not much given to camaraderie behind the scenes. It could be fairly argued that he rarely ventured beyond the forum provided by annual State of the State and budget messages.

Still, Edgar remained popular with the voters to the end. True to form, his timing was good. He had, he said when announcing his decision not to seek reelection, always wanted to go out on top.

He was approached to run for the U.S. Senate and was nearly convinced to run again for governor against Rod Blagojevich in 2006 but decided not to return to elected politics. He continued to chair the Abraham Lincoln Presidential Library Foundation and raced thoroughbred horses.

Governor Edgar is well guarded by Emy and Daisy while working in the Executive Mansion in 1994.

Governor Edgar drives one of the first cars fueled by E-85, an ethanol mix.

39th Governor

George Ryan
1934 -

1934 —Born February 24 at Maquoketa, Iowa

1954 - 1956 —Serves in the U.S. Army, including 13 months in Korea

1961 —Receives bachelor's degree in pharmacy from Ferris State College in Big Rapids, Michigan

1968 - 1973 —Serves on Kankakee County Board of Supervisors

1973 - 1983 —Serves in the Illinois House of Representatives, including two terms as House Republican leader and one term as speaker of the House (1981-1983)

1983 - 1991 —Serves as lieutenant governor under Governor James R. Thompson

1991 - 1999 —Serves as Illinois secretary of state, taking a leading role in cracking down on drunk drivers, streamlining the efficiency of driver's license facilities around the state, receiving national attention for his efforts at promoting organ donation, quadrupling funding for workplace literacy grants, and using his position as state librarian to develop a comprehensive network of library services

1994 —Is elected to a second term as secretary of state by winning 100 of Illinois' 102 counties

1998 —Runs virtually unopposed for the Republican Party nomination for governor and outdistances Democrat Glenn Poshard to be elected Illinois' 39th governor; makes Illinois history by choosing state Representative Corinne Wood as his running mate. She became the first female lieutenant governor in Illinois.

1999 —Gains legislative approval of a $12 billion public works program, the largest in the state's history, financed by tax and fee increases; leads a humanitarian mission to Cuba, becoming the first sitting governor in four decades to visit the island nation

2000 —Issues a moratorium on executions after 13 prisoners on Death Row were proven to be wrongfully convicted

2001 —Announces he will not seek election to a second term, in the face of a growing federal investigation of his administration

2003 —Issues a blanket order in his last days in office, commuting the death sentences of 164 Illinois Death Row inmates to life imprisonment without parole; the day before, he pardoned four Death Row inmates on grounds of innocence and commuted the death sentences of three other inmates to 40-year terms. In December, he is indicted in the federal Operation Safe Road probe of state worker corruption.

2006 —Is convicted by a federal jury of 18 counts of criminal misconduct, including racketeering conspiracy, and sentenced to six and a half years in prison; he appeals; he loses pension.

2007 —U.S. 7th Circuit Court of Appeals upholds conviction; goes to prison as continues appeals.

Republican
January 11, 1999 - January 13, 2003

G eorge Homer Ryan Sr., the last Illinois governor elected in the 20th century, was a gruff master of old-line politics during his long public career. The ultimate insider, he had the political savvy to achieve much during his one term as governor. But in the end, his conviction for widespread corruption brought personal disgrace and left his Republican Party in shambles.

True to predictions, Ryan as governor parlayed the expertise gained during 26 prior years in state government, including a term as speaker of the Illinois House of Representatives, into success at securing broad-scale programs. However, he faced the likelihood of a badly tarnished legacy, the result of a six-and-a-half-year prison sentence after a federal court jury found him guilty of 18 counts of racketeering conspiracy, tax and mail fraud, and lying to Federal Bureau of Investigation agents. That negative image could be tempered somewhat by the national and international attention accorded Ryan when, in 2000, he put a moratorium on the death penalty until he could be sure the system worked properly. On January 11, 2003, his last Saturday in office, Ryan commuted the sentences of 164 Death Row inmates to life imprisonment without parole. The day before, Ryan pardoned four Death Row inmates on grounds of innocence and commuted the death sentences of three other inmates to 40-year terms.

The evolution of Ryan from an advocate of capital punishment to an outspoken opponent by the time he left office was not the only detour from the conservative pattern of his political life. In raising taxes to finance infrastructure improvements, maintaining a chummy relationship with Democratic Mayor Richard M. Daley of Chicago, and following other paths unacceptable to hard-shell conservatives, Ryan governed as a pragmatic middle-of-the-roader. His stewardship of the state emphasized consensus over partisanship. Yet when he left office, Illinois was saddled with a budget shortfall that was fueled by a cooling economy exacerbated by the terrorist attacks on September 11, 2001. That deficit was projected at $1.2 billion for Ryan's last budget, fiscal year 2003.

Ryan wanted to be remembered favorably as a governor who could get things done for the betterment of Illinoisans. He might well have succeeded had he not become enmeshed in one of the most serious public scandals in Illinois history.

A Product of Kankakee

Ryan was the third Illinois governor — along with Republican Lennington Small and Democrat Samuel Shapiro — tied to Kankakee, an industrial and mercantile city located some 60 miles south of Chicago. He was born February 24, 1934, in Maquoketa, Iowa, but was raised in Kankakee, where his father Thomas Ryan was assigned by his employer Walgreen Co., the retail drugstore chain. In 1948, when George was in high school, Thomas Ryan opened his own independent pharmacy in Kankakee.

In the years that followed, George worked at the family pharmacy and served in the Army, including a stint in Korea. He married his high school sweetheart, Lura Lynn Lowe, in 1956, a marriage that produced six children, including triplet daughters. He attended Ferris State College — later Ferris State University — in Big Rapids, Michigan, where he received a degree in pharmacy in 1961. Four years later, when engaged again in the operation of the family business, George ran the successful campaign of his brother and fellow pharmacist Tom Ryan for mayor of Kankakee. George landed a seat on the Kankakee County Board of Supervisors in 1968 and went on to serve as the board chairman before being elected to the Illinois House in 1972.

Unlike some legislators, George Ryan was already a seasoned and skilled politician by the time he arrived in Springfield. The politics of Kankakee that honed his maturation was of the bricks-and-mortar brand — a system in which Ryan cut deals to get things done, took care of loyal followers, and expected fidelity in return. It was a grounding that served him well in the Illinois House, where he quickly earned high marks on both sides of the aisle for his command of legislative machinery and grasp of bread-and-butter issues. Few were surprised when he rose to serve as House GOP leader from 1977 to 1980 and speaker in 1981 and 1982.

A Statehouse Veteran before Becoming Governor

Ryan was a major player during most of his 26 years in the Statehouse before his election as governor in 1998. After a decade in the House, he served eight years as lieutenant governor under Governor James R. Thompson and then eight years as Illinois secretary of state.

As House speaker, Ryan garnered much attention and bolstered his conservative credentials by spearheading opposition to ratification of the proposed Equal Rights Amendment to the U.S. Constitution. Proponents placed much of the blame on him for the refusal of the Illinois legislature to cast enough votes for approval of the amendment, which was not adopted nationally. Less noticeable was his role in a bipartisan accord to reform unemployment insurance and in a successful move to repeal the state inheritance tax, which was replaced with an estate tax system that applied to fewer people.

In 1982, when Governor James R. Thompson was seeking a third term after having won in 1976 and 1978, Ryan was Thompson's running mate and was elected lieutenant governor. He held the post for eight years — a period in which, like many of his predecessors, he was relegated to a politically low profile. Once again he steered away from conservative doctine and supported a ban on assault weapons. His statewide visibility greatly increased after 1990, the year in which he was elected to replace Jim Edgar as secretary of state. Republican Edgar was elected governor that year.

As secretary of state, Ryan used his two terms to build a largely positive image that would serve him well in his campaign for governor in 1998. He was widely recognized for his anti-drunk-driving efforts, which included passage of legislation to reduce the legal blood-alcohol limit. He used television ads to successfully promote organ donations, making his awareness program a model for other states. As state librarian, a title he held by virtue of being secretary of state, he pushed the use of new technologies for a comprehensive network of library services, which included sharing resources among 3,200 school, public, academic, and special libraries. Along the way, he dispensed favors and jobs in the patronage-rich office to Democrats as well as Republicans.

However, while Ryan was secretary of state, federal authorities made the first arrests in an investigation, dubbed Operation Safe Road, into the exchange of commercial driver's licenses for bribes at secretary of state facilities. It would be the continuation and broadening of the probe into other areas while Ryan was governor that led to criminal charges against a number of his key operatives and eventually against Ryan himself.

A Fast Start as Governor

Ryan launched his bid for governor by pulling no punches about his mastery of Illinois' political system, including his deal-making prowess, which he argued would be a major asset in addressing the state's problems. Some Democrats sought to undermine his campaign by calling attention to the federal investigation, charging that Ryan bore ultimate responsibility for the deaths of six children of the Reverend Duane "Scott" and Janet Willis. The six were killed in a fiery crash in 1994 when debris from a truck driven by a man later found to be improperly licensed in Illinois struck the family's van. Weathering the criticism, Ryan rode a well-orchestrated, abundantly financed campaign to victory over his poorly funded Democratic opponent, U. S. Representative Glenn Poshard of southern Illinois.

He made political history by choosing Corinne Wood as his running-mate. An attorney from Lake Forest, she was serving her first term as a state representative when Ryan selected her for lieutenant governor. She was not the first female candidate for governor or lieutenant governor in Illinois, but she became the first woman elected to one of those positions.

Taking office in January 1999 as the state's 39th governor, the 64-year-old Ryan got off to a whirlwind start. The crowning achievement in Ryan's first year was his guidance through the House and Senate of a $12 billion public works program. Named Illinois FIRST, an acronym for "Fund for Infrastructure, Roads, Schools and Transit," the program took aim at deteriorating roads and bridges, long delayed highway construction, worn-out mass transit operations, unfunded school construction needs, necessary cleanups of urban environmental hazards, and upgrades of sewer and drinking water systems. A wheeler dealer, Ryan couldn't stop himself from authorizing pork-barrel projects that ranged from $25,000 for a Jack Benny statue in Waukegan to $10,000 for a stained glass window in a Naperville parking garage.

He also could take credit for tougher gun safety laws, health maintenance organization reforms benefiting patients, and sweeping gambling revisions that included authority for an unused casino license to move to Cook County, additional support for the horse racing industry, and a green light for riverboat casinos to dock permanently. He was behind the legislature's sign-off on stronger environmental protection requirements for large livestock farms, on an initiative to provide $160 million over four years for open land acquisition by the state, and on improved habitats for Illinois fish and wildlife. He supported or called for numerous programs to buttress funding for adoptions, child advocacy centers, and other kid-friendly programs.

Ryan's successes came with a split legislature. In 1999, only the Senate had a GOP majority, meaning on major issues Ryan had to sway House Democrats led by Speaker Michael J. Madigan of Chicago. That he did so further bolstered Ryan's reputation as a leader who could overcome the acrimonious partisanship that often paralyzes the legislature.

There were few sectors of Illinois, including elementary and secondary education, that did not receive more dollars from Ryan's efforts during his first year in office. Abetting his massive spending programs was a robust economy and a budget surplus inherited from his predecessor, the more fiscally restrained Governor Edgar. Even so, paying for Ryan's projects required lawmakers' approval of increased state borrowing and a variety of fee and tax increases — violations of a campaign pledge. Ryan did attempt to curtail spending in the wake of the 2001 recession and the 9/11 terrorist attacks, which together severely undercut the state's revenues. In the fall of 2001, Ryan sought legislative approval for across-the-board authority to cut spending, but Speaker Madigan declined to support Ryan's proposal. In the spring of 2002, Ryan vetoed $565 million in spending, including $546 million in general funds appropriations, from the fiscal year 2003 budget the legislature sent him in May, then summoned lawmakers to a special session in June to consider the cuts. Senate Republicans — the majority — stood with Ryan, and only

$55 million of the vetoes, including $42 million in general funds, were overridden. According to state comptroller records, general funds appropriations for fiscal year 2003 totaled $22.3 billion, more than $1 billion less than the $23.4 billion general funds appropriations for fiscal year 2002.

The productivity of Ryan's first go-around with the legislature was not matched in the remainder of his governorship — although that period contained some significant, even dramatic, actions by Ryan.

Before the end of his first year in office, he obtained federal approval to lead a delegation on a humanitarian mission to Cuba, becoming the first sitting U.S. governor in four decades to visit the Communist-ruled island. His moratorium on executions came early the following year. It also was in 2000 that he angered the conservative wing of his party by vetoing a bill that would have limited public funding of abortions in the state.

On another front, negotiations in late 2001 between Ryan and Mayor Daley led to an agreement to expand Chicago's O'Hare International Airport — again in contrast to a 1998 campaign promise by Ryan not to support expansion. The same year, he negotiated passage of legislation providing $3.5 billion in financing incentives to spur new power generation in the state and help the struggling Illinois coal industry. In 2002, Ryan signed a bill banning state and local government employees from soliciting campaign contributions from individuals or businesses they regulated, a measure that would have discouraged some of the wrongdoing uncovered in the licenses-for-bribes scandal.

Buried by Corruption

Relentlessly shadowing every phase of Ryan's governorship were the seemingly weekly disclosures of corruption during his days as secretary of state and governor. The intensity of the already fertile federal inquiry was magnified in early 2001 with the naming of Patrick J. Fitzgerald, an aggressive prosecutor of terrorists and top criminals in New York, as the U.S. attorney for the Northern District of Illinois.

Before Fitzgerald's arrival, Operation Safe Road had gone from indicting mainly low-level bureaucrats and clerks to snaring bigger fish. The most notable was Ryan confidant Dean Bauer, a onetime inspector general in Ryan's secretary of state office, who pleaded guilty to obstructing justice in the bribes-for-licenses investigation. He was sentenced to a year and a day in federal prison.

Hounded by the inquiry and plagued by polls showing his unfavorable standing with the electorate, Ryan announced in August 2001 that he would not seek a second term as governor. However, there was no escape from the heat of the probe. Moving far beyond driver's license fraud, prosecutors hit close to home in April 2002 with the indictment of Scott Fawell, Ryan's chief of staff when he was secretary of state and the manager of Ryan's campaign for governor. Fawell, a member of a prominent political family in DuPage County, was charged and later convicted of political racketeering for diverting state employees and property to help elect Ryan and other Republicans and for fixing state contracts, directing cover-ups, destroying evidence, and lying to a grand jury. He was sentenced to more than six years in prison.

Indictments of other cronies in Ryan's inner circle of former legislators and influential lobbyists followed in 2002 and 2003. Charges against them included steering contracts to businesses that agreed to pay kickbacks, tax fraud, money laundering, and bribery. Throughout it all, Ryan insisted that he not only received no money from these activities, but that he was unaware that these individuals had betrayed him by using their clout with Ryan to profit through extortion or other nefarious schemes. Prosecutors deemed otherwise, though, and on December 17, 2003, a little under a year after leaving the governorship, Ryan was indicted on 18 counts of tax fraud, racketeering conspiracy, and other crimes on which he would stand trial. The counts arose out of allegations that he took payoffs, gifts, and vacations in return for government contracts and leases during his years in public office. Indicted at the same time was Ryan friend Larry Warner, a Chicago businessman and lobbyist. Warner already had been indicted once in the probe for allegedly steering contracts for kickbacks. This time, Warner was charged in 12 counts, including mail fraud and extortion.

By this juncture, Ryan was a figure of remarkable contrast. Well before his indictment, he had become a political pariah even to many of his fellow Republicans. On the other hand, his position on the death penalty made him a revered figure to many. A University of Illinois law professor nominated Ryan for the Nobel Peace Prize. Others believed Ryan's highly publicized stance on the issue was designed in part to detract attention from the protracted investigation and to provide him an enduring legacy.

Following a lengthy trial lasting nearly seven months, federal jurors in Chicago found Ryan and Warner guilty on all counts. At the same time Ryan was sentenced to six and a half years in prison, Warner was sentenced to nearly three and a half years. In May 2007, Ryan lost his appeal to keep his state pension of approximately $197,000 a year. The Circuit Court of Cook County upheld Attorney General Lisa Madigan's opinion that Ryan must forfeit all benefits he received from his service in state government. Further, the U.S. 7th Circuit Court of Appeals upheld Ryan's conviction. His conviction put Ryan on a short list of ex-governors convicted of crimes linked to their service in public office. Governor Otto Kerner, a Chicago Democrat, was nailed for profiting from decisions he made while in office in the 1960s. Earlier in the 20th century, Governor Len Small was found guilty in civil court of embezzling state funds. Governor William Stratton, a Republican who was Kerner's predecessor, faced a criminal charge of converting campaign money to personal use. However, he was acquitted. (Governor Dan Walker served time in prison for a conviction on bank fraud unrelated to his term in office.)

The Ryan scandals were not without repercussions. Even before his indictment and conviction, the negative fallout from the Operation Safe Road investigation left the Republican Party dispirited and vulnerable at the state level. Voters revealed their displeasure by electing Democrat Rod Blagojevich governor in the November 2002 general election, thereby ending 26 years of Republican control of the state's highest office through Thompson, Edgar, and Ryan. Democrats also emerged from the election holding all state offices except treasurer, which Republicans lost in the next election.

On a broader scale, Ryan and his cohorts provided one more chapter in Illinois' dark history of political corruption. Editorial writers and others lamented that, whether justified or not, in comparison to other states Illinois would continue to be viewed after the Ryan era as a haven for officeholders who exploit the public trust for personal gain.

Ryan reported to prison in Oxford, Wisconsin, on November 7, 2007, but planned to appeal to the U.S. Supreme Court.

Courtesy of George Ryan

Governor Ryan and wife Lura Lynn met with Cuban President Fidel Castro during a five-day humanitarian mission, the first visit by a sitting governor since the island nation's revolution four decades earlier. State officials took $2 million in food, clothing, and medical supplies.

Courtesy of Brent Hanson, Illinois Information Service

Governor Ryan held a dedication ceremony in November 2002 for the Abraham Lincoln Presidential Library, which, with the opening of the Museum in April 2005, has become the most visited presidential library in the nation, surpassing 1 million visitors in January 2007.

40th Governor

Rod Blagojevich

1956-

1956 — Born December 10 in Chicago.

1979 — Graduates from Northwestern University in Evanston with a bachelor's degree in history

1983 — Receives a law degree from Pepperdine University in Malibu, California

1992 — Is elected to the Illinois House of Representatives, where he would serve two terms

1996 — Is elected to the first of three terms in the U.S. House of Representatives

2002 — Is elected Illinois' 40th governor, ending 26 years of Republican control of the governor's office

2005 — Wins approval in the General Assembly of his All Kids program to guarantee every child access to health care

2006 — Gains second term as governor, with Democrats sweeping control of all Executive Branch offices; federal prosecutors continue investigations into allegations of "endemic hiring fraud" in his administration

Democrat
January 13, 2003 - January 8, 2007
January 8, 2007 -

The election of Rod R. Blagojevich as governor ended a 26-year hold on the office by Republicans. The Chicago Democrat, a son of a Serbian immigrant, pledged to bring fresh air to Illinois government. Yet some of his administration's actions showed the politics-as-usual he decried as a campaigner weren't over.

Blagojevich did put a stamp on the governorship that was all his own. He was fond of large-scale initiatives, including new programs designed to promote health care. But some of his proposals achieved mixed success, especially those aimed at combating the budgetary shortfall he inherited. In striving to get what he wanted, Blagojevich could be earthy, even glib. His style resonated with voters, but aroused resentment among legislators and other officials. Unconventionality was his trademark, a fact underscored by his refusal to move his family from Chicago to Springfield.

Blagojevich, a political unknown outside his hometown prior to his campaign for governor, entered office as a self-styled populist, much in the vein of the previous Democratic governor, Dan Walker. Professing, as did fellow attorney Walker, to be attuned to the needs of "the people," Blagojevich at times mirrored his Democratic predecessor by challenging longtime legislative prerogatives, undercutting the state bureaucracy, and ducking the Statehouse press corps. Unlike Walker, though, Blagojevich was no stranger to elective office or to Springfield before winning the governorship in 2002. He served two terms in the Illinois House of Representatives before his election in 1996 to the first of three terms in the U.S. House of Representatives.

As part of his pledge to bring a new perspective to the governor's office, Blagojevich, who was 45 years old when first elected, surrounded himself with a youthful brain trust led by non-Illinoisans. Yet, a prolific fundraiser, he and his administration were a throwback, awarding contracts and state jobs to contributors and other supporters. His administration's practices in hiring ignited investigations, including a federal inquiry that became public in the latter part of Blagojevich's first term.

A Character Out of the American Dream

Blagojevich's early life might constitute a chapter in the story of the American Dream. He was born December 10, 1956, on Chicago's Northwest Side, the younger of two sons of Rade and Millie Blagojevich. Rade emigrated from Serbia after World War II; Millie was a U.S. citizen of Serbian descent. While Rod was growing up, his father worked at a steel plant — a point noted with pride by the governor, who stressed that his father's labor was a great inspiration in his own move up from modest circumstances. His mother had a steady job as a Chicago Transit Authority worker. To help his family make ends meet, and to save money for college, Rod held many jobs in his early years — from shoe shiner and pizza deliverer to dishwasher on the Alaskan pipeline system. In his spare time, he became a Golden Gloves boxer.

A product of Chicago Public Schools, Blagojevich graduated in 1979 from Northwestern University in Evanston with a bachelor's degree in history and went on to earn a law degree in 1983 from Pepperdine University in Malibu, California. Returning to Chicago, he engaged in the private practice of law and served as an assistant state's attorney in Cook County, a position that enabled him to prosecute domestic abuse and weapons violations. It was his experience in dealing with gun crimes that helped foster his advocacy of tougher sentencing laws and stronger gun controls in his later political career.

Blagojevich married Patricia (Patti) Mell, a daughter of Richard Mell, a veteran Chicago alderman and powerful North Side ward boss. As a result, Blagojevich was forced throughout his years in elective office to defend his independence by downplaying the supportive role of his father-in-law's ward-based political army. Blagojevich and his wife have two daughters, Amy and Annie.

Climbing the Political Ladder

Blagojevich kept a low profile during his decade in the Illinois House and Congress prior to becoming governor. An exception came in 1999 when, underscoring his Serbian ancestry, he accompanied the Reverend Jesse Jackson to Belgrade in the former Yugoslavia to negotiate the release of three captive American soldiers.

His career in elective office was launched with a successful bid for a seat in the Illinois House in 1992. During his four years in that legislative body, he was one of the first state lawmakers to push for a truth-in-sentencing law, requiring the most violent offenders to serve 85 percent to 100 percent of their sentences.

Subsequently, during his three terms in the U.S. House, in which he represented a district centered on Chicago's Northwest Side, he continued to concentrate on public safety issues. Among other proposals, he called for a ban on civilian sales of long-range military sniper rifles, sought legislation requiring gun show promoters to carry out background checks on gun purchasers, helped secure dollars for tracing guns found at crime scenes, sponsored legislation giving the states more than $1 billion to prepare for bioterrorism attacks, and backed an airport security plan making screeners in most airports federal employees. Always active on education issues, he lined up funding for after-school tutoring programs.

Predictably, Blagojevich pledged during his campaign for governor to give priority to education funding and law enforcement. His goals also included more dollars for health care and economic development initiatives.

Blagojevich's bid caught many by surprise, especially residents of downstate. In that region, he had virtually no name recognition. Further, he had a hard-to-pronounce ethnic surname, which isn't con-sidered a political plus in parts of Illinois south of Chicago. Nevertheless, the political winds blew in his favor. Major shortcomings surfaced for former Illinois Attorney General Roland Burris and Paul Vallas, former chief executive officer of Chicago Public Schools, both of whom opposed Blagojevich for the Democratic nomination for governor in the 2002 primary election. Vallas ran a minimal campaign downstate, and Blagojevich was able to bankroll a series of television ads outside Chicago that helped convince many Democrats he was a viable alternative to Centralia native Burris, who was not well-heeled. Blagojevich also had the best organized campaign, as well as the endorse-ment of his party's county chairmen's association. He won, in large measure, because of a strong showing downstate.

Blagojevich went on to victory in the November general election, in which his Republican opponent, Jim Ryan, the Illinois attorney general and another former boxer, was handicapped by a lethargic campaign and a party seriously weakened by the scandals engulfing the departing governor, George Ryan.

The election was opportune for Blagojevich in that it also returned control of the Illinois Senate to Democrats. Thus, he entered executive office with both chambers of the General Assembly in his party's hands, normally an ideal situation for any governor.

Dealing with the General Assembly

The governor's relations with lawmakers were never entirely smooth, however. Self-assertive and combative, Blagojevich promised to restore Illinoisans' trust in government by "changing the old way of doing business" at the Statehouse. Opinions differed on the extent to which he succeeded. Some admired his insistence on sticking to his campaign pledge not to increase major state taxes, on reducing the number of state employees, and on pushing for special programs to help the state's most vulnerable residents, especially children and senior citizens. Critics held that Blagojevich was a governing lightweight with a showy façade, a politician who preached ethical reforms while rewarding allies. And they charged him with fiscal irresponsibility by saddling future taxpayers with increased debt through his attempts to alleviate the state's financial woes in the short term.

Critics also questioned his decision to reach outside the state for key members of his inner circle. Bradley Tusk, only 29 years old when he was named Blagojevich's deputy governor, was a former assistant to Republican New York City Mayor Michael Bloomberg. Blagojevich's first chief of staff, Lon Monk, a former sports agent from California, was his law school roommate. Still, John Filan, Blagojevich's first budget director, was an Illinoisan with a financial background in the private and public sectors. The team displayed competence in helping Blagojevich through the ups and downs of his initial four-year term.

In judging governors, political scientists put considerable weight on the degree of their success with the General Assembly. On this, Blagojevich achieved a passing grade in his first term. But it wasn't easy to accomplish. Though blessed with Democratic majorities, Blagojevich contributed to a testy relationship with many lawmakers, including some in his own party. It didn't help when he derided legislators as spending like a bunch of "drunken sailors" for threatening to restore his spending cuts. Further, lawmakers embarrassed Blagojevich by forcing him to sign "memorandums of understanding" because they didn't trust that he would follow through on his verbal budget commitments. Despite these rough spots, including a nearly eight-week legislative overtime in 2004, Blagojevich developed a generally productive relationship with Democratic lawmakers by the conclusion of his first term. That relationship unraveled in the first year of Blagojevich's second term, however, as he aggressively pushed an unpopular proposal to overhaul business taxes.

He had much to show for his first year in office, though. Despite a tight budget, he secured additional classroom spending, an increase of $250 per pupil in general state aid for elementary and secondary students. Millions more went to provide preschool for 25,000 children. Throughout his first term, he insisted on increased outlays in these areas. But he did not achieve his campaign promise to raise per pupil spending by $1,000 in his first four years.

He won expansion of state-linked health insurance programs designed to provide comprehensive coverage for 20,000 additional youngsters and 65,000 working parents in the initial year alone. And he got a green light on his initiative to make prescription drugs more affordable for older Illinoisans and individuals with disabilities through his program authorizing the state to negotiate for medicines in bulk and pass along savings of up to 30 percent to enrollees.

Showing his appreciation for the support of organized labor, he signed legislation hiking the state's minimum wage in stages from $5.15 to $6.50 an hour, giving Illinois workers the highest minimum wage in the Midwest. He signed a measure requiring businesses to pay women equal pay for equal work. He helped win passage of Chicago Mayor Richard M. Daley's plan to expand O'Hare International Airport, a project expected to generate 195,000 jobs. And he signed measures making it easier for government and school employees to form unions and allowing senior faculty at each of the three University of Illinois campuses to unionize.

Further, Blagojevich supported sweeping death penalty reforms that banned executions of the mentally retarded, gave defendants more access to evidence, and granted the Illinois Supreme Court more authority to toss out improper verdicts in capital cases. Even with these revisions, though, he chose during his first term not to lift the state's moratorium on executions, explaining he wanted to see sufficient evidence the reforms were working to prevent individuals from being put to death for crimes they didn't commit.

A noteworthy development during Blagojevich's initial year was his victory on ethics legislation. One of the most extensive rewrites of the state's ethics laws since the 1970s, the package created commissions and inspectors general to root out government wrongdoing. Lobbyists and their spouses were banned from serving on most state boards and commissions. Unpaid political advisers to statewide officeholders were required to disclose financial interests.

Blagojevich continued during succeeding legislative sessions to win approval for much of what he wanted. The General Assembly approved a watered-down version of his plan to overhaul the State Board of Education by letting Blagojevich replace most of its members and have more control — steps the governor argued were designed to increase the board's accountability. After decades of failed attempts on gay rights legislation, it was approved at the urging of Blagojevich. He ended political gridlock by signing a measure designed to hold down medical malpractice costs for doctors by limiting the awards individuals can collect in lawsuits. And, after wavering a bit, he put his signature on legislation authorizing municipal officials to ban smoking in public establishments. Later, he went along with legislation giving county officers the same power. In the first year of his second term, he signed a statewide ban. Reacting to coal miner deaths in other parts of the country, he helped push through legislation requiring Illinois mine operators to take additional steps to help ensure the safety of underground miners.

Blagojevich's legislative clout was never more visible than near the end of his third year in office when he won passage of his All Kids plan, a program that aims to guarantee every child in the state access to health care. In his words, the undertaking "will do for our kids in Illinois what our country decided to do 40 years ago for our senior citizens under the Medicare program." Skeptics questioned whether the state could afford the plan, but Blagojevich countered that cuts in other state health programs would provide the dollars.

Budget Maneuvering

Blagojevich took office with a fiscal monkey on his back: a budget deficit that he inherited from George Ryan. Blagojevich, along with his budget transition team, said the shortfall was roughly $5 billion over a two-year period. They based that figure on the projected deficit of some $1.2 billion for fiscal year 2003 — Ryan's last budget — and some $3.6 billion for fiscal year 2004, representing the cost of existing state commitments plus Blagojevich's initiatives in his first budget year. According to the state comptroller's office, Illinois finished fiscal year 2003 with a budgetary deficit of $1.094 billion — the largest in state history — and finished fiscal year 2004 with a budgetary deficit of $410 million.

The Blagojevich team generated controversy as it wrestled each year to produce a spending plan. He moved to find new revenue and reallocate existing state dollars to finance new programs, including expanded health care programs. Achieving these objectives was made more difficult because during his first and second campaigns the governor ruled out hikes in the state income or sales taxes.

Consequently, the administration resorted in Blagojevich's first term to myriad maneuvers to come up with the dollars needed to meet the administration's financial targets. In his first year, the governor pushed to get lawmakers to authorize a $10 billion bond sale to reduce the pension debt and help meet existing financial obligations. He pushed to eliminate numerous tax breaks for businesses and increase many state services fees. He diverted money earmarked for road construction and other special purposes to pay the state's bills. Business and other interest groups protested, but largely to no avail. To help balance budgets toward the end of his first term, he negotiated with Democratic leaders to scale back scheduled payments to the state's five public employee pension systems by $2.3 billion over two years.

Some of the administration's proposals didn't pan out. For instance, it proposed selling the state's James R. Thompson Center in Chicago and auctioning the state's disputed 10th casino license, unconventional schemes that didn't float.

A Dark Cloud

Throughout his first term, Blagojevich received negative attention stemming from a public feud with his father-in-law and his decisions to award jobs and contracts to friends and donors. Blagojevich and his chief of staff Lon Monk were interviewed by federal authorities about allegations raised by Alderman Mell, the governor's father-in-law, that a Blagojevich fundraiser had traded campaign contributions in exchange for state appointments. The governor denied the allegation and lashed out at Mell, who later recanted under the threat of a lawsuit.

More ominous developments, however, put Blagojevich and his administration in a precarious political position. In 2006, Patrick Fitzgerald, the U.S. attorney for the Northern District of Illinois, openly declared in a letter to Illinois Attorney General Lisa Madigan that his office was probing "very serious allegations of endemic hiring fraud" in Illinois government. The letter was made public as Madigan said that she was turning over to federal prosecutors her office's own investigation of state hiring practices.

For his part, Blagojevich said his office and Fitzgerald's were cooperating to uncover violators of the rules.

Along with word that Fitzgerald had credible evidence of hiring irregularities in the administration, another Blagojevich fundraiser, Antoin "Tony" Rezko, was indicted on federal corruption charges at the height of the re-election campaign. A pension board appointee and campaign contributor, Stuart Levine, also pleaded guilty to separate allegations of wrongdoing. And the wife of one of the governor's long-time friends told the *Chicago Tribune* she talked to the FBI about getting a state job around the time her husband wrote a $1,500 check to one of the governor's young daughters. Blagojevich denied anything untoward, first saying it was for one daughter's birthday and later saying it may have been for the other daughter's christening.

Dealing with such controversies was more challenging than dispatching campaign opponents. In the 2006 primary, Blagojevich easily defeated former Chicago Alderman Edwin Eisendrath to win his party's renomination for governor. That fall he won reelection over Republican state Treasurer Judy Baar Topinka but with less than 50 percent of the votes cast.

Though Topinka pleaded with the public to pay attention to reports that raised questions about problematic hiring and an alleged "pay-to-play" atmosphere, the governor argued his ethics reforms had helped ferret out the "bad apples" from his administration. Blagojevich used his enormous fundraising advantage to wage a television ad campaign that relentlessly attacked Topinka, the first woman to be the GOP standard-bearer for governor. He won with merely 49.79 percent of the vote, Topinka came in second with 39.26 percent, and Green Party candidate Rich Whitney garnered 10.36 percent, an unexpected turnout for a third party.

Showdown in a Second Term

Blagojevich often maintained in his first term that he welcomed investigations because they would show his administration conducted business properly. A few months into the governor's new term, the wife of another Blagojevich fundraiser was indicted in Cook County Circuit Court for allegedly using her drug-testing firm to bilk the state for work that was not performed. Blagojevich hailed the inspector general of an agency for uncovering the matter. Yet, it was a news report that disclosed federal prosecutors had subpoenaed campaign records that put the governor on the defensive early in his second term. Instead of addressing the issue head on, as he had other potentially explosive matters during his first term, the governor repeatedly ignored questions about the subpoena from reporters in Springfield and Chicago. The subpoena, and the governor's refusal to talk about it publicly, provided an edgy subtext to the first spring legislative session of his second term.

Yet Blagojevich and the two Democratic leaders, Senate President Emil Jones Jr. and House Speaker Michael Madigan, managed to manufacture plenty of drama of their own in what turned into the longest overtime session in modern Illinois history. Their three-way standoff dragged the session through the summer and past Labor Day. Going in, most observers believed the session was poised to accomplish major changes for the good.

When Blagojevich was sworn into his new term in January 2007, education advocates held out hope it would be the year they would finally realize an overhaul of the state's school funding system, in which wide disparities in per pupil spending are based largely on where students live. Business groups believed it could be the year the state would show discipline in reducing the deficit and the long-term debt in the five public employee pension systems. But the legislative session quickly turned into an intramural war among Democrats.

Early on, Blagojevich changed the tenor of the session when he announced a sweeping health care subsidy plan to be supported by a major tax increase that he hadn't mentioned in his reelection campaign. Blagojevich maintained his pledge not to raise income or sales taxes, but he called for a $6 billion gross receipts tax, basically a tax on business revenues that would be imposed without regard to a company's net income. When that faltered, Blagojevich teamed with Senate President Jones, a Chicago Democrat, to retool the program and, to the surprise of even his harshest critics, increase the overall tax to $7 billion. Speaker Madigan, also a Chicago Democrat, dealt the plan a severe blow when he led the House in a 107-0 vote against the idea, but the governor kept pressing.

Jones and Madigan, who had co-chaired Blagojevich's reelection campaign, wrestled throughout the session on the issue of expanded health care subsidies. Jones was aligned with the governor. Meanwhile, Madigan led efforts to defeat the governor's proposal to lease the state Lottery to pay down Illinois' pension debt and pushed for more modest spending than the governor and the Senate president wanted. As a result, the three Democrats failed to agree on a basic state budget by May 31, which put Republicans in play because their votes were then needed in the House for the three-fifths approval that was required after the deadline.

The legislative session got more chaotic, and the politics more strained, as dozens of rank-and-file lawmakers started showing up for the closed-door budget sessions. The talks were subsequently moved to the Executive Mansion ballroom to accommodate the crowd. But as the governor called multiple special sessions of the legislature, fewer lawmakers saw a point in traveling to Springfield. With the approval of the legislative leaders, more of them stayed away. At times, only a handful attended the sessions at the Capitol, meaning there weren't enough members to conduct official business.

In early August, though, both chambers approved a budget that had been worked out among the four legislative leaders without the governor's input. But Blagojevich used his line-item veto authority to cut $463 million in what he called special interest and pork-barrel spending. Madigan's and Senate Republican Leader Frank Watson's caucuses took the brunt of the cuts. The project money allotted to Jones was left intact. Blagojevich moved to expand state health care programs already in place instead of enacting his more far-reaching plan to cover uninsured Illinoisans.

Then, Blagojevich, declaring a constitutional breakdown was at hand, singled out Madigan and sued him, contending the governor has the right to set the precise day and time of a special session and that the speaker had schemed to undermine his authority by encouraging legislators to stay home. It was an odd position for Blagojevich, who spent less time in Springfield than any other governor in modern times. He found himself skewered by editorial writers around the state over stories that he often flew from Chicago to Springfield and back instead of staying in town to work out differences with lawmakers.

Blagojevich could point to accomplishments for the year. He increased education spending by more than $550 million, more than in any single previous year as governor. He signed legislation aimed at attracting a $1.4 billion cutting-edge energy plant to this state. The project could capture and bury carbon dioxide from coal. He also signed off on a negotiated agreement designed to provide electricity rate relief for consumers, legislation setting tougher restrictions on teen driving, and a new law increasing the use of interlock devices on vehicle ignitions for first-time DUI offenders.

Nevertheless, his political maneuvers in the legislative session set a bitter tone for the governor's second term.

Courtesy of Brent Hanson

President George W. Bush attended the opening of the Abraham Lincoln Presidential Library and Museum in Springfield. From left, Secretary of State Jesse White, library Director Richard Norton Smith, Lt. Gov. Pat Quinn, the president, Treasurer Judy Baar Topinka, the governor.

Courtesy of Brent Hanson

Governor Blagojevich with FEMA Director Michael Brown talking with the press after surveying the damage done by an April tornado that hit Utica in LaSalle County in 2004.

Appendix A
Roster of Governors

Name	Inauguration Dates	County of Residence
Shadrach Bond	Oct. 6, 1818	St. Clair
Edward Coles	Dec. 5, 1822	Madison
Ninian Edwards	Dec. 6, 1826	Madison
John Reynolds,[1] Dem.	Dec. 6, 1830	St. Clair
Wm. L.D. Ewing,[2] Dem.	Nov. 17, 1834	Fayette
Joseph Duncan, Dem.	Dec. 3, 1834	Morgan
Thomas Carlin, Dem.	Dec. 7, 1838	Greene
Thomas Ford, Dem.	Dec. 8, 1842	Ogle
Augustus French,[3] Dem.	Dec. 9, 1846 Jan. 8, 1849	Crawford
Joel A. Matteson, Dem.	Jan. 10, 1853	Will
Wm. H. Bissell,[4] Rep.	Jan. 12, 1857	Monroe
John Wood,[5] Rep.	Mar. 21, 1860	Adams
Richard Yates, Rep.	Jan. 14, 1861	Morgan
Richard Oglesby, Rep.	Jan. 16, 1865	Macon
John M. Palmer, Rep.	Jan. 11, 1869	Macoupin
Richard Oglesby,[6] Rep.	Jan. 13, 1873	Macon
John Beveridge,[5] Rep.	Jan. 23, 1873	Cook
Shelby Cullom,[6] Rep.	Jan. 8, 1877 Jan. 10, 1881	Sangamon
John Hamilton,[5] Rep.	Feb. 16, 1883	McLean
Richard Oglesby, Rep.	Jan. 30, 1885	Macon
Joseph W. Fifer, Rep.	Jan. 14, 1889	McLean
John P. Altgeld, Dem.	Jan. 10, 1893	Cook
John R. Tanner, Rep.	Jan. 11, 1897	Clay
Richard Yates, Rep.	Jan. 14, 1901	Morgan
Charles S. Deneen, Rep.	Jan. 9, 1905 Jan. 18, 1909	Cook
Edward F. Dunne, Dem.	Feb. 3, 1913	Cook
Frank O. Lowden, Rep.	Jan. 8, 1917	Ogle
Len Small, Rep.	Jan. 10, 1921 Jan. 12, 1925	Kankakee
Louis L. Emmerson, Rep.	Jan. 14, 1929	Jefferson
Henry Horner,[4] Dem.	Jan. 9, 1933 Jan. 4, 1937	Cook
John H. Stelle,[5] Dem.	Oct. 6, 1940	Hamilton

Name	Inauguration Dates	County of Residence
Dwight H. Green, Rep.	Jan. 13, 1941	Cook
	Jan. 8, 1945	
Adlai E. Stevenson, Dem.	Jan. 10, 1949	Lake
William Stratton, Rep.	Jan. 12, 1953	Grundy
	Jan. 14, 1957	
Otto Kerner,[7] Dem.	Jan. 9, 1961	Cook
	Jan. 11, 1965	
Samuel Shapiro,[5] Dem.	May 21, 1968	Kankakee
Richard B. Ogilvie, Rep.	Jan. 13, 1969	Cook
Daniel Walker, Dem.	Jan. 8, 1973	Lake
James R. Thompson,[8] Rep.	Jan. 10, 1977	Cook
	Jan. 8, 1979	
	Jan. 10, 1983	
	Jan. 12, 1987	
Jim Edgar, Rep.	Jan. 14, 1991	Coles
	Jan. 9, 1995	
George Ryan, Rep.	Jan. 11, 1999	Kankakee
Rod Blagojevich, Dem.	Jan. 13, 2003	Cook
	Jan. 8, 2007	

[1] Resigned to become congressman.
[2] Senate president pro tem filled vacancy.
[3] Reelected under 1848 constitution.
[4] Died in office.
[5] Lieutenant governor filled vacancy.
[6] Resigned to become U.S. Senator.
[7] Resigned to become federal judge.
[8] First term was for two years due to a provision in the Constitution of 1970.

Appendix B
The Constitutions of Illinois and the Power of the Governor

The state of Illinois has operated under four constitutions. These documents are, naturally, a product of their times. They set the boundaries for governors' powers and describe the practices of the executive branch. They also reflect the people's attitudes toward investing power in the state's chief executive. Generally speaking, the state's constitutions have provided the governors with ever greater autonomy. Today, there are few impediments — on paper anyway — to a governor's ability to execute a political agenda in Illinois.

The Constitution of 1818

The governors had less authority than the legislature during the first 30 years of Illinois statehood. The state's first Constitution set forth a "weak governor" system, giving more power to the legislative than to the executive branch. Provisions of the Constitution that particularly hampered the governors were:

- A weak veto power — The four justices of the state Supreme Court along with the governor formed the Council of Revision, which could veto the legislature's bills. Acting collectively, the council could "revise all bills about to be passed into law" and send them with objections to the originating house. The chief executive could not act alone, and by a bare majority vote the legislature could override a veto, which it usually did.
- A self-succession prohibition — Governors could not be immediately reelected. Political agendas needed to be completed in one term.
- Limited authority to make appointments — The Constitution invested the legislature — not the executive branch — with the ability to appoint the executive officers deemed "necessary."

Because of precedents set during the territorial period, the convention delegates who met at Kaskaskia to write the first Constitution had no interest in strong governors. When Illinois was part of the Northwest Territory, Governor Arthur St. Clair had been deservedly unpopular. He had visited the scattered settlements on the Wabash and Mississippi rivers only three times and had shown little interest in their problems. William Henry Harrison, who became governor of Indiana Territory in 1800, had trouble with the powerful John Edgar, Robert Morrison, and W.L.D. Morrison faction at Kaskaskia when he discouraged their questionable land speculations. After 1809, when Illinois became a separate territory, there was no legitimate complaint about Ninian Edwards, the presidentially appointed governor during the next nine years. However, the factional enemies of Edwards included Jesse B. Thomas, who was president of the convention and who had ties with the Edgar-Morrison group.

Illinois copied the Council of Revision feature from the constitution that New York adopted during the Revolutionary War. The man responsible was Elias Kent Kane, a New York-born and Yale-educated lawyer who was a Thomas ally and the chief draftsman of the Illinois Constitution. Half of the American states did not grant any veto power to their governors, which was due to the residual dislike of the unlimited authority held by the appointed colonial and territorial governors. Had it not been for Kane, Illinois might have been in the no-veto category.

The first Constitution froze the salary limit for governors at $1,000, changeable only by constitutional amendment. The governor and other state officers were elected for four-year terms, twice the term of office set forth by some states, but they were not permitted to run for immediate reelection. As population increased, the low and inflexible pay scale became one of the reasons cited by advocates of change.

The preliminary draft of the Constitution gave the chief executive the customary power to fill state and county offices by appointment. The delegates, however, knew that Shadrach Bond would be the first governor and probably would not appoint their choice for state auditor, Elijah C. Berry. As a result, they let that clause stand but added a confusing provision that gave the legislature the right to elect the auditor, attorney general, and "such other officers of the state as may be necessary." They didn't define necessity. It seemed clear that the governor could appoint the secretary of state, whose role was something like that of a confidential assistant. (But before many years, however, the relationship between the governor and the secretary of state became a major issue that involved the legislature.)

Joseph Duncan, who left the Jacksonian Democrats just before he was elected Illinois' sixth governor, was stripped of virtually all power to appoint. Thomas Ford, who became governor in 1842, was outspoken in his disapproval:

Sometimes the legislature, feeling pleased with the governor, would give him some appointing power, which their successors would take away, if they happened to quarrel with him. This constant changing and shifting of power, from one coordinate branch of government to another ... was one of the worst features of government. It led to innumerable intrigues and corruptions, and for a long time destroyed the harmony between the executive and legislative departments. And all of this was caused by the Constitution of 1818 in an attempt to get one man [Elijah C. Berry] into an office of no very considerable importance.

As a precondition for admission to statehood, the Constitution was approved by Congress but was not submitted to the voters for ratification. They were allowed to elect only the governor, lieutenant governor, members of the legislature, sheriffs, and coroners.

Because the Constitution became effective in 1818, the elections fell midway in presidential terms. The first election began the third Thursday of September and continued for two more days. After that first election, the Constitution stipulated that elections were to be held on the first Monday of August. The chief executives were not required to live at the seat of government when the legislature was not in session. The Constitution required that governors be at least 30 years old, citizens for 30 years, and residents of Illinois for two years.

Two of Illinois' strongest chief executives, Edward Coles and Thomas Ford, were in office while the "weak governor" system was in effect. Coles lost on the slavery issue when the legislature was in session but triumphed when the issue went before the voters. Ford dominated the lawmakers on the issue of state solvency. Other governors weren't as successful: Ninian Edwards battled the legislature valiantly, but Joseph Duncan was hit by a legislative steamroller.

The Constitution of 1848

The 1848 Constitution was ratified March 6, 1848, and became effective April 1. Former Governor Thomas Ford and some other officials opposed it, for a number of reasons, but it had the support of Democrats because it ended lifetime appointments and of Whigs because it outlawed alien voting.

To allow governors to be elected in presidential years, Governor Augustus French's 1846 term was cut to two years. The state and federal synchronization was completed by shifting state balloting from August to November.

Some, but not enough, of the defects in Illinois' system of government were corrected by the new document. Notably the new Constitution:

- Abolished the Council of Revision, and
- Gave the governor increased appointment powers.

Abolition of the Council of Revision removed the Supreme Court justices from the veto process and placed it exclusively in the hands of the governor. The change was largely meaningless, however, since the legislature by a majority vote could still override vetoes. During the Civil War, Governor Richard Yates blocked passage of anti-administration legislation by invoking a new proroguing provision that allowed him to prematurely terminate the 1861 legislative session.

The legislature was stripped of its much-abused power to appoint state, judicial, and county officers. Since statehood, public opinion had gradually shifted to the belief that power should be vested directly in the people, rather than in the legislative and executive branches of government. As a result, the roster of popularly elected officials was lengthened. Henceforth, the selection of subordinate state officials, such as the secretary of state, all judges, and local officers was made at polling places. Definite terms were fixed: four years for most officials, but nine years for Supreme Court justices. The long ballot meant that executive power was shared by the governor, secretary of state, and other officials. Public involvement in government also was increased by the provision that some decisions, such as banking law changes, had to be submitted to referendum. The governor retained the power to fill vacancies and make temporary appointments. The biggest gain was that the legislature no longer was politically dominant.

But a shortcoming in the 1848 Constitution encouraged petty graft. Salaries, which could be changed only by statewide referendum, were set at poverty levels — $1,500 for the governor and less for others. A clause forbidding extra compensation led to subterfuges, such as an unnecessarily large appropriation to the governor for a gardener, payments to court clerks with the understanding that they be shared with judges, and authorization for officials to collect and pocket fees for routine transactions. At session after session, the legislature demonstrated that its ingenuity was equal to the need of officials for pay supplements.

Another economy move, intended to limit the duration of sessions, fixed the pay of legislators at two dollars a day for the first 42 days and one dollar a day thereafter.

The 1848 Constitution, spawned during a series of Democratic-Whig compromises, included many verbose articles that were purely legislative in nature. A major loophole permitted wholesale passage of an increasing volume of personal and private bills for the benefit of corporations and local governments. They smelled of bribery; they overburdened Governors Richard J. Oglesby and John M. Palmer; and, they were a major reason why a third constitution was adopted in 1870.

The Constitution of 1870

After partisanship sunk an attempt to write a new constitution in 1862, the constitutional convention of 1869 produced a document that served the state for a century. The 1870 Constitution placed the executive and legislative departments in approximate equality.

The new Constitution:

- Strengthened the governor's veto powers.
- Allowed the governor to succeed himself.
- Gave the legislature the power to set salaries.
- Defined the executive branch as seven popularly elected officials.
- Established three-member House districts and instituted cumulative voting, allowing for a relatively strong minority in the legislature.
- Prohibited special legislation that affected (or favored) only selected corporate or private constituents.

The authority of the governor was strengthened — and that of the lawmakers correspondingly weakened — by a provision that only by a two-thirds vote could a veto be overridden.

To eliminate a major abuse of legislative power, the new Constitution included a triple prohibition of the special legislation that had placed the General Assembly in disrepute and had given Governor John M. Palmer the opportunity to write scholarly but ineffective veto messages. First, special laws could not be enacted if a general law could be made applicable. Next, the Constitution specifically barred special laws involving 23 topics, including those that had led to scandalous situations. Last, for emphasis, it prohibited the granting of special or exclusive privileges, immunities, or franchises to corporations or individuals.

The legislature was given the authority to set and change official salaries, which the first two constitutions had frozen at unrealistically low levels. Governor Palmer promptly was given a pay raise from $1,500 to $5,000 a year.

For the first time, governors were permitted to run for immediate reelection. Except for Palmer, Frank O. Lowden, and Louis L. Emmerson, all governors since then have wanted second terms.

While the governor was given the constitutional duty "to take care that the laws be faithfully executed," he shared administrative authority with other state officers. The U. S. Constitution had specified that executive power is vested in the president, but the new Illinois basic law said that the executive department "shall consist of the governor, lieutenant governor, secretary of state, auditor of public accounts, treasurer, superintendent of public education, and the attorney general." Each was elected independently, not necessarily from the same political party. The legislature had authority to create additional commissions and agencies. As a result, Palmer regarded the office of governor as "a mere figure-head."

Easy ratification of the 1870 Constitution soon was followed by agitation for further changes. An amendment in 1884 empowered the governor to veto line items in appropriation bills without rejecting the entire measure.

The constitutional convention, however, failed to anticipate future problems, including the growth of Chicago. An amendment in 1890 was required before the metropolis could finance the World's Columbian Exposition with a $5 million bond issue. Four years later, following an advertising campaign in downstate counties, a charter amendment for Chicago was adopted. By that time the governors' biennial messages to the legislature routinely asked that a convention be called or that revenue-raising restrictions be relaxed. In 1917 Governor Lowden also asked for a shorter ballot, which would concentrate more power in the chief executive.

The Constitution of 1970

Lowden wasn't alone in his desire for a new constitution. A convention met from 1920 to 1922, but it produced a document that was overwhelmingly rejected by voters. Absent a new constitution, a 1950 "gateway amendment" eliminated an immediate need for a new constitution by easing the amendment process. But, in 1968, the voters called for a constitutional convention by nearly a two-to-one majority. Because the Supreme Court had approved the new income tax law and an amendment reorganizing the court system had been ratified, the 1970 constitutional convention — with delegates elected on a nonpartisan basis — met without major controversy and produced a constitution that was easily ratified.

Regarding the powers of the governor, the 1970 Constitution features the following provisions:

- Statewide executive officers are elected during nonpresidential election years.
- A party's candidates for governor and lieutenant governor are elected as a team.
- The governor retains the line-item veto, and receives the power to reduce any item of appropriations in a bill presented to him. The governor is also able to send a bill back to the legislature with specific revisions.
- The Constitution abolishes the office of superintendent of public education as an elected executive office and places jurisdiction of education under a single board.

The shift to nonpresidential election years limited James R. Thompson to a two-year term upon his first election in 1976, and returned Illinois to the schedule in effect from 1818 to 1848.

The federal system of joint election of the president and vice president was adopted by requiring that the governor and lieutenant governor be elected together. In 1968 Republican Richard B. Ogilvie had been elected governor and Democrat Paul Simon lieutenant governor.

The convention delegates provoked a controversy by giving the governor amendatory authority to make changes in bills passed by the legislature, which could accept or reject the revisions. Intended to enable the correction of minor errors, the amendatory veto soon became a vehicle for major changes. Governor Dan Walker used it to adjust the state's share of financial aid to the Regional Transportation Authority.

The veto power was revised in other ways. On the theory that vetoes had been overused, the legislature was permitted to override a veto by a 60 percent vote, down from two-thirds. Also, the executive was given authority to reduce as well as to eliminate an appropriation item, but a reduction veto could be overridden by a majority vote.

The 1970 Constitution clarifies the governor's power to make appointments. It specifies that the governor has supreme executive power and allows him to reorganize agencies by executive order, subject to legislative rejection.

On paper, the power of the executive branch — particularly the governor — has been greatly enhanced by the 1970 Constitution. Coincidental to the passage of the Constitution, Governor Ogilvie engineered an astounding restructuring of Illinois government by establishing numerous departments and state agencies that ultimately report to the governor. But, in practice, this power has been offset partly as the result of the first amendment to the 1970 Constitution.

In 1980, the Cutback Amendment eliminated cumulative voting and the practice of having three representatives from each House district. This has reduced the power of the minority party and has concentrated legislative power to the party leaders in each chamber. Thus, a test for modern governors is not how they deal with the General Assembly as a whole, but how they deal with party leadership.

A 1988 call for a constitutional convention was rejected by a vote of 900,109 for to 2,727,144 against.

Appendix C
Gubernatorial Vote Totals

	Vote	%	Plurality

1818

    Shadrach Bond unopposed, returns lost.

1822

    Edward Coles . . . . .2,854 . . . . .33.2 167
    Joseph Phillips . . . . .2,687 . . . . .31.2
    Thomas C. Browne . . . . .2,443 . . . . .28.4
    James B. Moore . . . . .622 . . . . .7.2
                 Total vote 8,606 .(four candidates)

1826

    Ninian Edwards . . . . .6,280 . . . . .49.5 447
    Thomas Sloo, Jr. . . . . .5,833 . . . . .46.0
                 Total vote 12,693 (three candidates)

1830

    John Reynolds . . . . .12,837 . . . . .59.0 3,899
    William Kinney . . . . .8,938 . . . . .41.0
                 Total vote 21,776 (three candidates)

1834

    Joseph Duncan, Whig . . . . .17,330 . . . . .52.9 7,106
    William Kinney, Dem. . . . . .10,224 . . . . .31.2
    Robert K. McLaughlin, Dem. . . . . . .4,315 . . . . .13.2
                 Total vote 32,771 (four candidates)

1838

    Thomas Carlin, Dem. . . . . .30,648 . . . . .50.8 926
    Cyrus Edwards, Whig . . . . .29,722 . . . . .49.2
                 Total vote 60,370   (two candidates)

1842

    Thomas Ford, Dem. . . . . .46,507 . . . . .53.8 7,487
    Joseph Duncan, Whig . . . . .39,020 . . . . .45.1
                 Total vote 86,440 (three candidates)

1846

    Augustus C. French, Dem. . . . . .58,656 . . . . .58.2 21,623
    Thomas M. Kilpatrick, Whig . . . . . .37,033 . . . . .36.7
    Richard Eels, Liberty . . . . .5,157 . . . . .5.1
                 vote 100,846 (three candidates)

	Vote	**%**	**Plurality**

1848
Augustus C. French, Dem. . . . . .67,828 . . . . .86.8 62,169
W. L. D. Morrison, Whig . . . . .5,659 . . . . .7.2
Charles V. Dyer, Free Soil 4,692 610
Total vote 78,179 (three candidates)

1852
Joel A. Matteson, Dem. . . . . .80,789 . . . . .52.4 16,381
E. B. Webb, Whig . . . . .64,408 . . . . .41.8
D. A. Knowlton, Free Soil . . . . .9,024 . . . . .5.9
Total vote 154,221 (three candidates)

1856
Wm. H. Bissell, Rep. . . . . .111,466 . . . . .47.0 4,787
Wm. A. Richardson, Dem. . . . . . . .106,679 . . . . .45.0
Buckner S. Morris, American . . . . . .19,088 . . . . .8.0
Total vote 237,233 (three candidates)

1860
Richard Yates, Rep. . . . . .172,196 . . . . .51.5 12,943
James C. Allen, Dem. . . . . .159,253 . . . . .47.6
Total vote 334,354   .(six candidates)

1864
Richard J. Oglesby, Union . . . . . . .190,376 . . . . .54.5 31,675
James C. Robinson, Dem. . . . . .158,701 . . . . .45.5
Total vote 349,077 (two candidates)

1868
John M. Palmer, Rep. . . . . .249,912 . . . . .55.6 50,099
John R. Eden, Dem. . . . . .199,813 . . . . .44.4
Total vote 449,725 (two candidates)

1872
Richard J. Oglesby, Rep. . . . . .237,774 . . . . .54.4 40,690
Gustave Koerner, Dem. . . . . .197,084 . . . . .45.1
Total vote 437,043 (three candidates)

1876
Shelby M. Cullom, Rep. . . . . .279,263 . . . . .50.6 6,798
Lewis Steward, Dem. . . . . .272,465 . . . . .49.4
Total vote 552,093 (four candidates)

1880
Shelby M. Cullom, Rep. . . . . .314,565 . . . . .50.6 37,033
Lyman Trumbull, Dem. . . . . .277,532 . . . . .44.7
Total vote 621,117 (four candidates)

	Vote	**%**	**Plurality**

1884

Richard J. Oglesby, Rep. . . . . .334,234 . . . . .49.6 14,599
Carter H. Harrison, Dem. . . . . . . .319,635 . . . . .47.5
Total vote 673,389 (four candidates)

1888

Joseph W. Fifer, Rep. . . . . .367,860 . . . . .49.1 12,547
John M. Palmer, Dem. . . . . .355,313 . . . . .47.5
Total vote 748,447 (four candidates)

1892

John P. Altgeld, Dem. . . . . .425,558 . . . . .48.7 22,872
Joseph W. Fifer, Rep. . . . . .402,686 . . . . .46.1
Total vote 873,155 (four candidates)

1896

John R. Tanner, Rep. . . . . .587,637 . . . . .54.1 113,381
John P. Altgeld, Dem. . . . . .474,256 . . . . .43.7
Total vote 1,086,272 (six candidates)

1900

Richard Yates, Rep. . . . . .580,199 . . . . .51.5 61,233
Samuel Alschuler, Dem. . . . . .518,966 . . . . .46.1
Total vote 1,126,828 (eight candidates)

1904

Charles S. Deneen, Rep. . . . . .634,029 . . . . .59.1 299,149
Lawrence B. Stringer, Dem. . . . . . .334,880 . . . . .31.2
John Collins, Socialist . . . . 59,062 . . . . .5.5
Total vote 1,072,934 (seven candidates)

1908

Charles S. Deneen, Rep. . . . . .550,076 . . . . .47.6 23,164
Adlai E. Stevenson, Dem. . . . . .526,912 . . . . .45.6
Total vote 1,154,612 (six candidates)

1912

Edward F. Dunne, Dem. . . . . .443,120 . . . . .38.1 124,651
Charles S. Deneen, Rep. . . . . .318,469 . . . . .27.4
Frank H. Funk, Progressive . . . . . .303,401 . . . . .26.1
John C. Kennedy, Socialist . . . . . . .78,679 . . . . .6.8
Total vote 1,162,880 (six candidates)

1916

Frank O. Lowden, Rep. . . . . .696,535 . . . . .52.7 139,881
Edward F. Dunne, Dem. . . . . .556,654 . . . . .42.1
Total vote 1,322,553 (five candidates)

	Vote	**%**	**Plurality**

1920
Len Small, Rep. . . . . .1,243,148 . . . . .58.9 511,597
James Hamilton Lewis, Dem. . . . . .731,551 . . . . .34.6
Total vote 2,111,605 (ten candidates)

1924
Len Small, Rep. . . . . .1,366,436 . . . . .56.7 345,028
Norman L. Jones, Dem. . . . . .1,021,408 . . . . .42.4
Total vote 2,409,121 (seven candidates)

1928
Louis L. Emmerson, Rep. . . . . . .1,709,818 . . . . .56.8 424,921
Floyd E. Thompson, Dem. . . . . .1,284,897 . . . . .42.7
Total vote 3,012,208   (five candidates)

1932
Henry Horner, Dem. . . . . .1,930,330 . . . . .57.6 566,287
Len Small, Rep. . . . . .1,364,043 . . . . .40.7
Total vote 3,350,320   .(six candidates)

1936
Henry Horner, Dem. . . . . .2,067,861 . . . . .53.1 385,176
C. Wayland Brooks, Rep. . . . . . . .1,682,685 . . . . .43.2
Total vote 3,891,976   .(six candidates)

1940
Dwight H. Green, Rep. . . . . .2,197,778 . . . . .52.9 256,945
Harry B. Hershey, Dem. . . . . . . .1,940,833 . . . . .46.7
Total vote 4,152,622 (four candidates)

1944
Dwight H. Green, Rep. . . . . .2,013,270 . . . . .50.8 72,271
Thomas J. Courtney, Dem. . . . . .1,940,999 . . . . .48.9
Total vote 3,966,765 (four candidates)

1948
Adlai E. Stevenson, Dem. . . . . . .2,250,074 . . . . .57.1 572,067
Dwight H. Green, Rep. . . . . .1,678,007 . . . . .42.6
Total vote 3,940,257 (four candidates)

1952
William G. Stratton, Rep. . . . . . .2,317,363 . . . . .52.5 227,642
Sherwood Dixon, Dem. . . . . .2,089,721 . . . . .47.3
Total vote 4,415,864 (three candidates)

1956
William G. Stratton, Rep. . . . . . .2,171,786 . . . . .50.3 36,877
Richard B. Austin, Dem. . . . . . . .2,134,909 . . . . .49.5
Total vote 4,314,611 (three candidates)

	Vote	**%**	**Plurality**

1960
Otto Kerner, Dem. . . . . .2,594,731 . . . . .55.5 524,252
William G. Stratton, Rep. . . . . . .2,070,479 . . . . .44.3
Total vote 4,674,187 (three candidates)

1964
Otto Kerner, Dem. . . . . .2,418,394 . . . . .51.9 179,299
Charles H. Percy, Rep. . . . . .2,239,095 . . . . .48.1
Total vote 4,657,500 (two candidates)

1968
Richard B. Ogilvie, Rep. . . . . . . .2,307,295 . . . . .51.2 127,794
Samuel H. Shapiro, Dem. . . . . . .2,179,501 . . . . .48.4
Total vote 4,506,000 (three candidates)

1972
Daniel Walker, Dem. . . . . .2,371,303 . . . . .50.7 77,494
Richard B. Ogilvie, Rep. . . . . . . .2,293,809 . . . . .49.0
Total vote 4,678,804 (four candidates)

1976
James R. Thompson, Rep. . . . . . .3,000,395 . . . . .64.7 1,390,137
Michael J. Howlett, Dem. . . . . . .1,610,258 . . . . .34.7
Total vote 4,638,997 (seven candidates)

1978
James R. Thompson, Rep. . . . . . .1,859,684 . . . . .59.0 596,550
Michael J. Bakalis, Dem. . . . . . . .1,263,134 . . . . .40.1
Total vote 3,150,095 (five candidates)

1982
James R. Thompson, Rep. . . . . . .1,816,101 . . . . .49.4 5,074
Adlai E. Stevenson III, Dem. . . . .1,811,027 . . . . .49.3
Total vote 3,673,681 (four candidates)

1986
James R. Thompson, Rep. . . . . .1,655,849 . . . . .52.7 399,223
Adlai E. Stevenson III, Solidarity . . .1,256,626 . . . . .40.0
Total vote 3,143,978 (five candidates)

1990
Jim Edgar, Rep. . . . . .1,653,126 . . . . .50.7 83,909
Neil Hartigan, Dem. . . . . .1,569,217 . . . . .48.2
Total vote 3,257,410

1994
Jim Edgar, Rep. . . . . .1,984,318 . . . . .63.9 914,468
Dawn Clark Netsch, Dem. . . . . . .1,069,850 . . . . .34.4
Total vote 3,106,556

	Vote	**%**	**Plurality**

1998

George Ryan, Rep. . . . . .1,714,094 . . . . .51.0 119,903

Glenn Poshard, Dem. . . . . .1,594,191 . . . . .47.5

Total vote 3,358,705 (nine candidates)

2002

Rod Blagojevich, Dem. . . . . .1,847,040 . . . . .52.2 252,080

Jim Ryan, Rep. . . . . .1,594,960 . . . . .45.1

Total vote 3,538,891 (five candidates)

2006

Rod Blagojevich, Dem. . . . . .1,736,731 . . . . .49.8 367,416

Judy Baar Topinka, Rep. . . . . . . .1,369,315 . . . . .39.3

Rich Whitney, Green . . . . .361,336 . . . . .10.4

Total vote 3,587,676 (20 candidates)

Candidates receiving 5 percent or less of vote are omitted.

Percentages are of total vote for gubernatorial candidates, not total vote cast at election.

Sources: 1818-1820, Theodore C. Pease, *The Story of Illinois*, appendix; 1920-1952, Samuel K. Gove, ed., *Illinois Votes: A Compilation of Illinois Election Statistics*, Urbana; 1953-1988 reports of Secretary of State and State Board of Elections; 1990, Craig A. Roberts and Paul Kleppner, *Almanac of Illinois Politics — 1994*, page 386; 1994, David A. Joens and Paul Kleppner, *Almanac of Illinois Politics — 1998*, page 374; 1998, State Board of Elections web site (http://www.state.il.us/election/), December 7, 1998.

Bibliographical Essay

Author Robert Howard spent the last years of his life researching the early governors and, for the modern governors, augmenting his private "archives" — a cache of tearsheets, news releases, official documents, clippings, and memoranda that he collected in his 50 years in Illinois.

In addition to the sources cited in the following bibliography, Howard, and later the editorial staff in the publications unit of the Center for State Policy and Leadership, used the biennially published *Illinois Blue Book* as a reliable resource for fact checking. Like Howard, the editors found invaluable assistance from the administrations and the staff that oversee the collections of the Abraham Lincoln Presidential Library and Museum, the State Archives, the Illinois State Historical Society and local historical societies throughout the state.

And like Howard, we drew on *Illinois Issues* magazine as a source of background information for the Walker Administration through the first year in the second term of the Blagojevich Administration. Among the magazine's staff reporters and contributing writers we found to be most useful were Michael D. Klemens, Al Manning and Harvey Berkman for the chapters on Thompson and Edgar; Jennifer Davis and Dave McKinney for the chapter on Ryan; and Aaron Chambers, Pat Guinane and Bethany (Carson) Jaeger for the chapter on Blagojevich. *Illinois Issues* columnist Charles N. Wheeler III provided information on each of these administrations..

Boyer Long also used numerous articles from the 1981 to 1998 editions of the *Chicago Tribune* and Springfield's *State Journal-Register* to research Edgar's career as secretary of state, his campaigns, his first six months as governor, and his response to the flood of 1993. With permission from the Taxpayers' Federation of Illinois, she used her own article written for the group's newsletter on the promises Edgar made during his first campaign for governor. The governor's office provided her with files containing Governor Edgar's State of the State speeches, his budget messages, and post-session press releases. She drew information from a tape recording of a speech the governor gave on September 11, 1998, in which Edgar recapped his political career. And she learned more about the governor when she sat down with him for an exclusive interview on October 28, 1998.

She and the editorial team had an additional source that Robert Howard could not have conceived of: the Internet.

For fact checking, editors searched for a wide range of information including burial sites, civil war battles, Chicago mayors, and even the history of Mormons in Illinois.

To research and write captions for the photographs, as well as to track down elusive facts, editor Beverley Scobell used the resources of local historical societies and libraries. She sometimes spoke with local lawmakers. If they didn't know the answers, they often knew who did. Scobell also got information personally from the four living former governors.

Such resources, whether first-person, printed or online, don't discriminate for us. They can be accurate or mistaken; they can turn out to be truth or propaganda. In the bibliographical essay in the first edition of *Mostly Good and Competent Men*, Howard called the second Richard Yates' biography of his governor-father "shallow and incomplete."

Historians such as Robert Howard, Peggy Boyer Long, and Taylor Pensoneau must become the captains of the source material that they are often at the mercy of. They must make judgments on what scholarship is good and bad, whose eyewitness accounts can be trusted, and which authors are pushing what agendas. Historians become editors and framers of history.

The authors and editors of *The Illinois Governors: Mostly Good and Competent* have taken their charge as framers of Illinois history seriously. We believe that this book, though imperfect, will stand up well to scrutiny; that novice and experienced Illinois historians will value it; and that it will, in a small way, advance the cause of preserving the rich heritage of our state.

Bibliography

Affleck, James. "William Kinney, A Brief Biographical Sketch," *Illinois State Historical Society Transactions* (1908), 209-211.

Akers, Milburn P. *Chicago Sun Times* (18 July 1982).

Allswang, John M. *A House for All Peoples: Ethnic Politics in Chicago, 1890-1936*. Lexington, 1971.

Altgeld, John P. *Live Questions*. Chicago, 1890.

Altgeld, John P. *Oratory, Its Requirements and Rewards*. Chicago, 1901.

Alvord, Clarence W., ed. *Governor Edward Coles*. Springfield, 1920.

Alvord, Clarence W., ed. *The Illinois Country, 1673-1818*. Springfield, 1920.

Angle, Paul M. "Ford's History of Illinois." *Illinois State Historical Society Journal* 38, no. 1 (March, 1945): 99-104.

Angle, Paul M. "Nathaniel Pope, 1784 1850, A Memoir." *Illinois State Historical Society Transactions*, vol. 43 (1936).

Arrington, Leonard J., and Davis Bitton. *The Mormon Experience: A History of the Latter-day Saints*. New York, 1979.

Avrich, Paul. *The Haymarket Tragedy*. Princeton, 1984.

Bakalis, Michael J. *Ninian Edwards and Territorial Politics in Illinois, 1775-1818*. Ann Arbor, Michigan, 1975.

Bakalis, Michael J. *Ninian Edwards and Territorial Politics in Illinois, 1775-1818*, Northwestern University doctoral dissertation, 1966.

Ballance, Charles. *The History of Peoria, Illinois*. Peoria, 1870.

Baringer, William E. *A House Dividing: Lincoln as President Elect*. Springfield, 1945.

Barnard, Harry. *Eagle Forgotten: The Life of John Peter Altgeld.* Indianapolis, 1938.

Barnhart, Bill, and Gene Schlickman. "Intangible Rights: ...Kerner's views on civil liberties, and how his views differed from those of the man who prosecuted him." *Illinois Issues* (July/August, 1998): 32-34.

Bateman, Newton, and Paul Selby. *Historical Encyclopedia of Illinois,* Cook County edition. 2 vols. Chicago, 1901.

Benneson, Cora Agnes. "The Work of Edward Everett of Quincy in the Quarter-Master's Department in Illinois During the First Years of the Civil War." *Illinois State Historical Society Transactions* (1909).

Bennett, James O'Donnell. *Private Joe Fifer.* Bloomington, 1936. (See also his four-day interview for the *Chicago Tribune* in 1933.)

Beveridge, Albert J. *Abraham Lincoln, 1809-1858.* New York, 1928.

Beveridge, Philo J. Typescript in Illinois State Historical Library vertical file.

Bird, Fred. *Fred Bird Memoir.* Sangamon State University, Oral History Office, Springfield, 1985.

Bogart, Ernest L., and Charles Manfred Thompson. *The Industrial State, 1870-1893.* Chicago, 1922.

Bogart, Ernest L., and John Mabry Mathews. *The Modern Commonwealth, 1893-1918.* Chicago, 1922.

Bohrer, Florence Fifer. Manuscript in the Bohrer-Fifer Papers. Illinois State Historical Library.

Bonham, Jeriah. *Fifty Years' Recollections, and Portrait and Biographical Album of Coles County.* Chicago, 1887.

Bonham, Jeriah. *Fifty Years' Recollections, With Observations and Recollections on Historical Events Giving Sketches of Eminent Citizens— Their Lives and Public Services.* Peoria, 1883.

Bowen, A. L. "Personal Reminiscences of Joseph W. Fifer, an Interview with the Former Governor and a Description of his Times." *Illinois Blue Book*, 1925-26.

Boyer, Peggy. "A Prologue to Governing: The Campaign Promises of Jim Edgar." *Tax Fax: The Newsletter of the Taxpayers' Federation of Illinois* (February, 1991).

Bradley, Ralph S. *Ralph S. Bradley Memoir*. Sangamon State University, Oral History Office, Springfield 1985.

Brasler Roy P., et al., eds. *The Collected Works of Abraham Lincoln*, 9 vols. New Brunswick, NJ, 1953-1955.

Broadwater, Jeff. *Adlai Stevenson and American Politics: The Odyssey of a Cold War Liberal*. New York and Ontario, 1994.

Brown, Mark. "A man for the Millennium? Republican George Ryan...." *Illinois Issues* (February, 1998): 20-25.

Browne, Waldo R. *Altgeld of Illinois: A Record of His Life and Work*. New York, 1924.

Browning, Orville Hickman. *The Diary of Orville Hickman Browning*. eds. Theodore C. Pease and James G. Randall. 2 vols. Springfield, 1915, 1933.

Buck, Solon J. *Illinois in 1818*. Springfield, 1918.
Buley, Carlyle R. *The Old Northwest: Pioneer Period 1815-1840*. 2 vols. Indianapolis, 1950.

Burtschi, Joseph C. *Documentary History of Vandalia, Illinois: The State Capital of Illinois from 1819 to 1839*. Vandalia, 1954: 17, 32.

Byrd, Cecil K. *A Bibliography of Illinois Imprints, 1814-1858*. Chicago, 1966.

Cappon, Lester J., ed. *The Adams-Jefferson Letters: The Complete Correspondence Between Thomas Jefferson and Abigail and John Adams*, 2 vols. Chapel Hill, 1959.

Carlson, Theodore L. *The Illinois Military Tract: A Study in Land Occupation, Utilization and Tenure.* Urbana, 1951.

Carr, Clark E. *The Illini: A Story of the Prairies.* Chicago, 1906.

Carter, Clarence E. *The Territory of Illinois.* Washington, D.C., 1950.

Carter, Clarence E. *The Territory of Indiana, 1800-1810.* Washington, D. C., 1939.

Casey, Robert, and W. A. S. Douglas. *The Midwesterner: The Story of Dwight H. Green.* Chicago, 1948.

Christman, Henry M., ed. *The Mind and Spirit of John Peter Altgeld.* Urbana, 1965.

Church, Charles A. *A History of the Republican Party in Illinois, 1854-1912.* Rockford, 1912.

Clendenin, Henry W. *The Autobiography of Henry W. Clendenin.* Springfield, 1926.

Cole, Arthur C. *The Era of the Civil War, 1848-1870.* Chicago, 1922.

Coles, Edward *History of the Ordinance of 1787.* Philadelphia, 1856.

Coles, William B. *The Coles Family of Virginia: Its Numerous Connections from its Immigration to America to the Year 1915.* New York, 1931.

Collins, William H. and Cicero F. Perry, *Past and Present of the City of Quincy and Adams County.* Chicago, 1905.

Converse, Henry W. "The Life and Services of Shelby M. Cullom." *Illinois State Historical Society Transactions.* (1914): 55-79.

Corneau, Octavia. *History of the Executive Mansion.* Typescript and research notes in the Octavia Roberts Corneau Papers, Illinois State Historical Library.

Cornelius, Janet. *A History of Constitution-Making in Illinois.* Urbana, 1969.

Court of Appeals Opinion 493, *Federal Reporter*, 2nd Series, 1124.

Cullom, Shelby M. *Fifty Years of Public Service: Personal Recollections of Shelby M. Cullom*. Chicago, 1911.

Davidson, Alexander, and Bernard Stuve. *A Complete History of Illinois from 1673 to 1873, Embracing the Physical Features of the Country; Its Early Explorations; Aboriginal Inhabitants; Conquest by Virginia; Territorial Condition and the Subsequent Civil, Military and Political Events of the State*. Springfield, 1874.

Davis, George Cullom. *Governor Shelby M. Cullom, 1877-1883* . University of Illinois master's thesis, 1961.

Davis, J. McCan. *The Breaking of the Deadlock, Being an Accurate and Authentic Account of the Contest of 1903-4 for the Republican Nomination for Governor*....Springfield, 1904.

Davis, Jennifer. "The Men Who Would Be Governor." *Illinois Issues* (September, 1998): 15 - 25.

Davis, Kenneth S. *A Prophet in His Own Country: The Triumphs and Defeats of Adlai E. Stevenson*. New York, 1950.

Davis, Kenneth S. *The Politics of Honor, a Biography*. New York, 1967.

Davis, Rodney O. "Illinois Legislators and Jacksonian Democracy, 1834-1841." University of Iowa doctoral dissertation, 1966.

Davis, Rodney O. "Judge Ford and the Regulators, 1841-1842," in *1981 Selected Papers in Illinois History*. Springfield, 1982: 25-36.

de Grazia, Victor. *Victor de Grazia Memoir*. Sangamon State University, Oral History Office, Springfield, 1984.

Dilliard, Irving. "Len Small Back to Prosperity." *The Nation* . (19 Oct. 1932): 352-353.

Downey, William. *William "Smokey" Downey Memoir*. Sangamon State University Oral History Office, Springfield, 1985.

Dowrie, George W. *The Development of Banking in Illinois, 1817-1863*. Urbana, 1913.

Dunne, Edward F. *Dunne: Judge, Mayor, Governor*. ed. William L. Sullivan. Chicago, 1916.

Dunne, Edward F. *Illinois, the Heart of the Nation*. 5 vols. Chicago, 1933.

Edward Coles Papers in the Princeton University Library.

Edwards, Ninian W. *History of Illinois from 1778 to 1833; and the Life and Times of Ninian Edwards*. Springfield, 1870.

Eversole, Mildred, ed. "Richard J. Oglesby: Forty-Niner. His Own Narrative." *Papers in Illinois History, 1938*. Springfield, 1939: 158-71.

Ewing, Presley Kittredge and Mary Ellen Williams Ewing. *Ewing Genealogy with Cognate Branches, A Survey of the Ewings and Their Kin in America*. Houston, 1919.

Flanders, Robert B. *Nauvoo: Kingdom on the Mississippi*. Urbana, 1965.

Ford, Thomas. *A History of Illinois, From Its Commencement in 1818 to 1847....* Chicago, 1854 and 1945-1946.

The French-Wicker Family Papers. Manuscripts Collection of the Illinois State Historical Library, Springfield.

Gillespie, Joseph. Introduction and appendix to *Reminiscences of the Early Bench and Bar*. Usher F. Linder, ed. Chicago, 1879.

Gosnell, Harold F. *Machine Politics: Chicago Model*. Chicago, 1937 and New York, 1969.

Gove, Samuel K., ed. *Illinois Votes, 1900-1958: A Compilation of Illinois Election Statistics*. Urbana, 1959.

"Governor Coles' Autobiography," *Illinois State Historical Society Journal* no. 3 (October, 1910).

Graham, James R. History of the Sangamon County Bar. Typescript in Illinois State Historical Library, January, 1931.

Gray, Wood. *The Hidden Civil War.* New York, 1942.

Green, Dwight H. Vertical file in the Illinois State Historical Library.

Green, Paul M., and Melvin G. Holli. *The Mayors.* Carbondale, 1987.

Greene, Evarts B., and Charles M. Thompson. *The Governors' Letter-Books, 1840-1853.* Springfield, 1911.

Greene, Evarts B., and Clarence W. Alvord, eds. *The Governors' Letter-Books, 1818-1834.* Springfield, 1909.

Harper, Josephine L. *John Reynolds, The Old Ranger of Illinois.* University of Illinois doctoral dissertation, 1949.

Hartley, Robert E. *Big Jim Thompson of Illinois.* Chicago, 1979.

Hesseltine, William B. *Lincoln and the War Governors.* New York, 1955.

Hicken, Victor. *Illinois in the Civil War.* Urbana, 1966.

Hicken, Victor. "The Virden and Pana Mine Wars of 1898." *Illinois State Historical Society Journal* 52 (Summer, 1959).

Hickey, James T. "An Illinois First Family: The Reminiscences of Clara Matteson Doolittle." *Illinois State Historical Society Journal* 69, no. 1 (February, 1976).

Hickey, James T. "Oglesby's Fence Rail Dealings and the 1860 Decatur Convention." *Illinois State Historical Society Journal* 54, no. 1 (Spring, 1961): 5-14.

Hiller, Mary Jane. *William H. Bissell and the Campaign and Election of 1856.* Southern Illinois University — Carbondale, master's thesis, 1964.

History of Greene County, Illinois. Chicago, 1879.

Holden, Robert J. "Governor Ninian Edwards and the War of 1812: The Military Role of a Territorial Governor," in *1980 Selected Papers in Illinois History.* Springfield, 1982.

Howard, Robert P. "A Thompson Scorecard: Compromise and Fiscal Prudence." *Illinois Issues* (January, 1980): 8-12.

Howard, Robert P. "Abraham Lincoln, William H. Bissell and Perjury." *Lincoln Herald* (Summer, 1985).

Howard, Robert P. *Illinois: A History of the Prairie State.* Grand Rapids, 1972 and 1986.

Howard, Robert P. *James R. Howard and the Farm Bureau.* Ames, 1983.

Howard, Robert P. "Mr. Sam of Illinois." *Chicago Tribune Magazine* (12 May 1968).

Howard, Robert P. "Old Dick Richardson: The Other Senator from Quincy." *Western Illinois Regional Studies* 7, no. 1 (Spring, 1984).

Howard, Robert P. "The Great Canal Scrip Fraud: The Downfall of Governor Joel A. Matteson," in *1980 Selected Papers in Illinois History.* Springfield, 1982.

Howard, Robert P. "Thompson vs. Stevenson: A Long View." *Illinois Issues* (October, 1982): 6-11.

Howard, Robert P. "Walker, a Lone Wolf Governor." *Illinois Issues* (January, 1977): 6-7.

Hutchinson, William T. *Lowden of Illinois: The Life of Governor Frank O. Lowden.* 2 vols. Chicago, 1957.

Ickes, Harold L. *Autobiography of a Curmudgeon.* New York, 1943.

Illinois Progress, 1921-1928, Len Small, Governor. 1928.

Illinois Reports, 1846. Springfield, 1847.

Illinois State of the State: 1977 - 1991 The Thompson Administration. James R. Thompson: Springfield, 1991.

Immel, Joseph, Johnson Kanady and Frederic B. Selcke. *Joseph Immel Memoir—Johnson Kanady Memoir—Frederic B. Selcke Memoir.* Sangamon State University Oral History Office, Springfield, 1985.

Johannsen, Robert ed. *Letters of Stephen A. Douglas.* Urbana, 1961.

Johannsen, Robert *Stephen A. Douglas.* New York, 1973.

Johnson, Allen. ed., *Dictionary of American Biography.* 22 vols. New York, 1973.

Johnson, Walter. *How We Drafted Adlai Stevenson.* New York, 1955.

Jones, Robert Huhn. "Three Days of Violence: The Regulators of the Rock River Valley." *Illinois State Historical Society Journal* 59, no 2 (Summer 1966): 132-3.

Keiser, John H. "Black Strikebreakers and Racism in Illinois, 1865-1900." *Illinois State Historical Society Journal* 63, no. 3 (Autumn, 1972): 310.

Keiser, John H. *Building for the Centuries: Illinois 1865-1898.* Urbana, 1977.

Kenney, David. *A Political Passage: The Career of Stratton of Illinois.* Carbondale, 1990.

Kenney, David. *Basic Illinois Government: A Systematic Explanation.* Carbondale, 1970.

Ketcham, Ralph L. "The Dictates of Conscience, Edward Coles and Slavery." *Virginia Quarterly Review* 36, no. 1 (Winter, 1960).

Kirby, Julia Smith. *Biographical Sketch of Joseph Duncan.* Chicago, 1888.

Klement, Frank L. *The Copperheads in the Middle West.* Chicago, 1960.

Kobler, John. *Capone: The Life and World of Al Capone.* New York, 1971.

Koerner, Gustave. *Memoirs of Gustave Koerner, 1809-1896: Life Sketches Written at the Suggestion of His Children*. ed. Thomas McCormack. Cedar Rapids, 1909.

Krenkel, John H. *Illinois Internal Improvements, 1818-1848*. Cedar Rapids, 1958.

Krenkel, John H. ed. *Richard Yates, Civil War Governor*. Danville, 1966.

Krenkel, John H. ed. *Serving the Republic: Richard Yates, Illinois Governor and Congressman, Son of Richard Yates, Civil War Governor: an Autobiography*. Danville, 1968.

Langhorne, Elizabeth. "Edward Coles, Thomas Jefferson and the Rights of Man." *Virginia Cavalcade* 23, no. 1 (Summer, 1973), 30-36.

Lawrence, Mike. "Ogilvie Revisited." *Illinois Issues* (December, 1982): 25-28.

Lawrence, Mike. "The Rematch, Thompson vs. Stevenson." *Illinois Issues* (October, 1986): 10-17.

Leckie, William H. and Shirley A. Leckie. *Unlikely Warriors, General Benjamin Grierson and His Family.* Norman, OK, 1984.

Leichtle, Kurt E. *Edward Coles, an Agrarian on the Frontier.* Ph.D. dissertation, University of Illinois-Chicago Circle, 1982.

Leithold, Esther M. *Genealogy of the Evans' Family, the "Virginia Biddles" and Other Related Families.* Woodland, California, 1940.

Lewis, Donald F. Collection of Deneen papers in the Illinois State Historical Library.

Lewis, Donald Fremont. The Philadelphia Years of Gov. Edward Coles of Illinois. Typescript in Illinois State Historical Library.

Littlewood, Thomas B. *Horner of Illinois*. Evanston, 1969.

Lutes, Terry, and Joseph P. Pisciotte. *Terry Lutes Memoir—Joseph P. Pisciotte Memoir.* Sangamon State University, Oral History Office, Springfield, 1985.

McCarter, John W. *John W. McCarter, Jr. Memoir*. Sangamon State University, Oral History Office, Springfield, 1985.

McDonald, Forrest. *Insull*. Chicago, 1962.

Manning, Al. "Dan Walker Meets the Public: The Accountability Sessions." *Illinois Issues*. (January, 1975): 12-14.

Mansfield, Frank C. "The Governor and the Anarchists." *Illinois Bar Journal* 65, no. 4 (May, 1977): 600-611;

Martin, John Bartlow. *Adlai Stevenson of Illinois*. New York, 1976.

Mauldin, William Henry. *Back Home*. New York, 1947.

"Memoirs of Speaker David Shanahan." *Illinois Blue Book*. Springfield, 1925.

Merriam, Charles E. *Chicago: A More Intimate View of Urban Politics*. New York, 1929.

Messick, Hank. *The Politics of Prosecution: Jim Thompson, Richard Nixon, Marge Everett and the Trial of Otto Kerner*. Ottawa, 1978.

Michaelson, Ron. *Ron Michaelson Memoir*. Sangamon State University, Oral History Office, Springfield, 1984.

Morgenstern, George *Chicago Tribune* (11 January 1948).

Morton, Richard A. *Justice and Humanity: Edward F. Dunne, Illinois Progressive* Carbondale, 1997.

Moses, John. *Illinois Historical and Statistical*. 2 vols. Chicago, 1889.

The National Cyclopedia of American Biography. Clifton, NJ, 1926.

Neely, Mark E., Jr. *The Abraham Lincoln Encyclopedia*. New York, 1982.

Neilson, James W. *Shelby M. Cullom: Prairie State Republican*. Urbana, 1962.

Nevins, Allan. *Ordeal of the Union*, 2 vols. New York, 1947.

Norton, W. T. *Edward Coles, Second Governor of Illinois*. Philadelphia, 1911.

Nortrup, Jack Junior. "A Western Whig in Washington." *Illinois State Historical Society Journal* 64, no. 4 (Winter, 1971): 419-441.

Nortrup, Jack Junior. "Governor Yates and President Lincoln." *Lincoln Herald* (Winter, 1968): 193-206.

Nortrup, Jack Junior. "Richard Yates: A Personal Glimpse of the Illinois Soldiers' Friend." *Illinois State Historical Society Journal* 56, no. 2 (Summer, 1963): 121-58.

Nortrup, Jack Junior. *Richard Yates, Civil War Governor of Illinois*. University of Illinois doctoral dissertation, 960.

Nortrup, Jack Junior. "Yates, the Prorogued Legislature, and the Constitutional Convention." *Illinois State Historical Society Journal* 62, no. 1 (Spring, 1969): 5-31.

Oral History Office, Sangamon State University. "Stories of the Governorship." *Illinois Issues* (December, 1982): 13-23.

Palmer, George Thomas. *A Conscientious Turncoat: The Story of John M. Palmer, 1817-1900*. New Haven, 1941.

Palmer, John M. *Personal Recollections: The Story of an Earnest Life*. Cincinnati, 1901.

Palmer, John M. *The Bench and Bar of Illinois, Historical and Reminiscent*. 2 vols. Chicago, 1899.

Park, Siyoung. "Land Speculation in Western Illinois: Pike County, 1821-35," *Illinois State Historical Society Journal* 77, no. 2 (Summer, 1984): 115-28.

Pease, Theodore Calvin. *Illinois Election Returns, 1818-1848*. Springfield, 1923.

Pease, Theodore Calvin. *The Frontier State, 1818-1848*. Chicago, 1918.

Pease, Theodore Calvin. *The Story of Illinois*. Rev. ed. by Marguerite Jenison Pease. Chicago, 1965.

Pensoneau, Taylor. *Governor Richard Ogilvie: In the Interest of the State*. Carbondale, 1997.

Pensoneau, Taylor. *Powerhouse: Arrington from Illinois*. Baltimore, 2006.

Pensoneau, Taylor. "Walker, Ogilvie and Kerner Used Different Techniques in Dealing With Legislature." *Illinois Issues* (February, 1975): 51-53.

Pensoneau, Taylor and Bob Ellis. *Dan Walker: The Glory and the Tragedy*. Evansville, Indiana, 1993.

Philbrick, Francis S. *Laws of Indiana Territory, 1801-1809*. Springfield, 1930.

Phillips, Clarence. *Daily News*. Lawrenceville, Illinois, 5 February 1962

Plummer, Mark A. "Governor Richard J. Oglesby and the Haymarket Anarchists." *1981 Selected Papers in Illinois History*. Springfield, 1982: 50-59.

Portrait and Biographical Album of Coles County, Illinois. Chicago, 1887.

Pree, Edward. *Edward Pree Memoir*. Sangamon State Oral History Office, Springfield, 1984.

Putnam, Elizabeth Duncan. "The Life and Services of Joseph Duncan." *Illinois State Historical Society Transactions* (1919).

Raines, Edgar F., Jr. "The Ku Klux Klan in Illinois, 1867-1875." *Illinois Historical Journal* 78 (Spring, 1985): 17-44.

Rakove, Milton. "Gov. Thompson: What Kind of a Politician is He?" *Illinois Issues* (October, 1977): 7-9.

Raum, Green B. *History of Illinois Republicanism*. Chicago, 1900.

Reynolds, John. *My Own Times, Embracing Also the History of My Life.* Belleville, 1855 and Chicago, 1879.

Reynolds, John. *The Pioneer History of Illinois.* Belleville, 1852 and Chicago, 1887.

Richardson, Eudora Ramsey. "The Virginian Who Made Illinois a Free State." *Journal of the Illinois State Historical Society* 45, no. 1 (Spring, 1952): 5-23.

Roberts, B. H. *The Rise and Fall of Nauvoo.* Salt Lake City, 1965.

Roberts, Sidney I. "The Municipal Voters' League and Chicago's Boodlers." *Illinois State Historical Society Journal* 53, no. 2 (Summer, 1960): 117-48.

Ross, Diane. "A Few Words from the Governor." *Illinois Issues* (January, 1985): 6-19.

Schlup, Leonard. "Adlai E. Stevenson and the Gubernatorial Campaign of 1908." *International Review of History and Political Science.* 13, no. 4 (November 1976).

Schlup, Leonard C. "Adlai E. Stevenson and the Presidential Election of 1896." *Social Science Journal* 14, no. 2 (April, 1977): 118-128.

Searles, William S. "Governor Cullom and the Pekin Whisky Ring Scandal." *Illinois State Historical Society Journal* 51, no. 1 (Spring, 1958): 28-41.

Shankman, Arnold. "Partisan Conflicts, 1839-1841, and the Illinois Constitution," *Illinois State Historical Society Journal* 63, no. 4 (Winter, 1970).

Small, Len. *Illinois Progress, 1921-1928.* Springfield, 1928.

Smith, George W. *History of Illinois and Her People.* 3 vols. Chicago, New York, 1927.

Snyder, John Francis. *Adam W. Snyder and His Period in Illinois History, 1817-1842.* Springfield, 1903.

Snyder, John Francis. "Governor Ford and His Family." *Illinois State Historical Society Journal* 3, no. 2 (July, 1910): 45-51.

Snyder, John Francis. "The Army Led by Col. George Rogers Clark in His Conquest of Illinois, 1778-9." *Transactions of the Illinois State Historical Society, Collections of the Illinois State Historical Library*, vol. 21 (1903).

Spenser, Donald S. "Edward Coles: Virginia Gentleman in Frontier Politics." *Illinois State Historical Society Journal* 61, no. 2 (Summer, 1968).

Stevenson, Adlai E. *Something of Men I Have Known*. Chicago, 1909.

Stover, John F. *History of the Illinois Central Railroad*. New York, 1975.

Stuart, William H. *The Twenty Incredible Years*. Chicago, 1935.

Suppiger, Joseph Edward. *Jesse Burgess Thomas, Illinois' Pro-Slavery Advocate*. University of Tennessee doctoral dissertation, 1970.

Tarr, Joel A. *A Study in Boss Politics*. Urbana, 1971.

Thiem, George. *The Hodge Scandal: A Pattern of American Political Corruption*. New York, 1963.

Thornburn, Neil. "John P. Altgeld: Promoter of Higher Education in Illinois." *Essays in Illinois History*. Carbondale, 1968.

Tinder, Usher F. *Reminiscences of the Early Bench and Bar*. Chicago, 1879: 77.

Tingley, Donald F. *The Structuring of a State: The History of Illinois, 1899-1928*. Urbana, 1980.

Tompkins, C. David. "John Peter Altgeld as a Candidate for Mayor of Chicago in 1899." *Illinois State Historical Society Journal* 56, no. 4 (Winter 1963): 654-76.

Townsend, Walter A., ed. *Illinois Democracy: A History of the Party and Its Representative Members, Past and Present*. Springfield, 1935.

Trutter, John Thomas and Edith English Trutter. *The Governor Takes a Bride*. Carbondale, 1977.

Villard, Henry. *Memoirs of Henry Villard*. Cambridge, 1904.

Walker, Dan. *The Maverick and the Machine: Governor Dan Walker Tells His Story*. Carbondale, 2007.

Walker, Dan. *Dan Walker Memoir. Sangamon State University*, Oral History Office, Springfield, n.d.

Walton, Clyde C., ed. *An Illinois Reader.* DeKalb, 1970.

Washburne, Elihu B. *Sketch of Edward Coles, Second Governor of Illinois, and of the Slavery Struggle of 1823-4*. Chicago, 1882.

Washburne, Elihu B., ed. *The Edwards Papers*. Chicago, 1884.

Watters, Mary. *Illinois in the Second World War*. 2 vols. Springfield, 1951, 1952.

West, Roy O. "Charles S. Deneen, 1863-1940." *Illinois State Historical Society Journal* 34, no. 1 (March, 1941): 7-23.

Wheeler, Charles N. III. "Gov. James R. Thompson, 1977 - 1991: The Complete Campaigner, the Pragmatic Centrist." *Illinois Issues* (December, 1990): 12-16.

Whitney, Ellen. *The Black Hawk War, 1831-1832*. Springfield, 1970.

Williams, Deloris. *The Administration of Thomas Carlin* University of Illinois master's thesis, 1936.

Wish, Harvey. "Governor Altgeld Pardons the Anarchists." *Illinois State Historical Society Journal* 31, no. 4 (December, 1938): 424-448.

Wish, Harvey. "John Peter Altgeld and Progressive Tradition." *American History Review* (July, 1941): 813-31.

Wish, Harvey. "The Pullman Strike: A Study in Industrial Warfare." *Illinois State Historical Society Journal* 32 (September, 1939): 288-312.

Wooddy, Carroll H. *The Case of Frank L. Smith: A Study in Representative Government.* Chicago, 1931.

Wrone, David R. "Illinois Pulls Out of the Mud." *Illinois State Historical Society Journal* 58 (Spring, 1965): 69 72.

Yates Speeches. 15 major speeches, bound, and in the collection of the Illinois State Historical Library.

Index

2nd Illinois Regiment, 84
8th Illinois Cavalry, 124
8th Illinois Volunteer Regiment, 106
9/11 Commission, 284
9/11 terrorist attacks, 306, 310
14th Illinois Infantry, 116
17th Illinois Cavalry, 124
21st Illinois Regiment, 100
137th Illinois Volunteer Regiment, 91
141st Illinois Volunteers, 140

A

A.B. Plot, 25
Abraham Lincoln Presidential Library Foundation, 302
Abraham Lincoln Presidential Library & Museum, 302, 325
Accardo, Tony "Big Tuna," 260
Adamoski, Benjamin S., 217, 277
Adams County, 90
Adams, John, 10
Adams, John Quincy, 6, 26, 27, 35, 43, 45
Addams, Jane, 153, 180, 209
AFL-CIO, 242
African Americans, 16, 98, 105, 106, 107, 115, 116, 119, 126, 161, 190, 248, 281, 295, 296
Agricultural Adjustment Agency, 230
Akers, Milburn P., 217
Albion, 70, 201, 202

Alexander, Czar of Russia, 11
Allen, James C., 96, 104, 373
All Kids, 320
Allswang, John M., 208
Alschuler, Samuel, 167, 181
Altgeld, John Peter, *ix*, 114, 120, 135, 145, 148-157, 160, 161, 171, 179, 180
Alton, 6, 23, 27, 48, 55, 124
Alton College, 114
Alton Courier, 85
Alton penitentiary, 7
Altorfer, John Henry, 261
American Bottom, 4, 21, 35
American Colonization Society, 16
American Legion, 216, 218, 233
American Railway Union, 155
anarchists, 162, 165
Anna, 291
Anti-Nebraska Democrats, 78, 113, 115
Anti-Saloon League, 174, 203
Army Enlisted Reserve Corps, 260
Army of the Potomac, 97, 124
Arrington, W. Russell, 254, 255, 291, 292, 296, 355
Arthur, Chester A., 126
Art-in-Architecture Program, 280
Arvey, Jacob M., 246, 263
Associated Bank of Chicago, 243
Association of Commerce, 204
Atlanta Federal Penitentiary, 223

Atomic Energy Commission, 248
Auguste Choteau, 24
Aurora, 167, 175, 181
Aurora-Elgin highway, 182
Austin, Richard B., 241, 375
Australian ballot, 145
Aux Sable aqueduct, 78

B

Baby Richard case, 301
Bad Axe, 40
Bakalis, Michael J., 280, 376
Baker, Edward D., 65, 94
Ballance, Charles, 60
Bank of Edwardsville, 26, 27
Bank of Illinois, 27, 39, 40, 55, 62
Bank of the United States, 13, 39, 43, 46, 47, 56
Barnard, Harry, 154
Barrett, Edward J., 216, 217, 234, 239, 278
Barrett, George F., 226
Bateman, Newton, 73
Bates, Edward, 96
battle of
    Buena Vista, 84
    Cerro Gordo, 105
    Chickamauga, 116
    Corinth, 104, 106
    Gettsyburg, 124
    Island No. 10, 116
    Shiloh, 98
    Stone's River, 116
    Vera Cruz, 105
    Vicksburg, 98, 143
Bauer, Dean, 311

Beaird, Joseph A., 33
Beckman, Louis E., 242
Beckwith-Flower Colony, 201
bedsheet ballot, 249
Belleville, 27, 28, 35, 36, 46, 84, 85, 208
Bennett, James O'Donnell, 146
Bensen, Arnold, 239
Berry, Caroline, 40
Berry, Elijah, 40, 329, 330
Bethea, Sol R., 135
Beveridge, Helen May Judson, 124, 127
Beveridge, John Lourie, 109, 122-127, 132, 152, 160
Biddle, Nicholas, 13
Bilandic, Michael, 284
bimetallism, 114, 120, 156
Bird, John J., 126
Birkbeck, Morris, 12, 13
birth control, 283
Bissell, Elizabeth Kintzing Kane, 87
Bissell, Emily Susan Jones, 84
Bissell, William Henry, *ix*, 82-87, 89, 94
blacks (*see* African Americans)
black code/laws, 6, 12, 13, 99, 107, 116
Black Hawk War, 28, 35, 45, 48, 54, 90
Black Horse Troop, 246
Black, John C., 143
black Republicans, 36
Blagojevich, Patricia Mell, 316
Blagojevich, Rod, 302, 306, 312, 314-325

Blaine, James G., 134, 135

Blair, W. Robert, 292, 294

Blair, William McCormick, 233

Bland, Richard P., 156

Bloomberg, Michael, 318

Bloomington, 83, 90, 95, 106,
    120, 140, 141, 143, 144, 146,
    175, 203

Bloomington Pantagraph, 230

Board of Higher Education, 248

Bohrer, Florence Fifer, 146

Bond, Achsah, 4

Bond, Shadrach, 2-7, 22, 23, 27,
    46, 47, 329

Bonfield, John, 155

Bonham, Jeriah, 104

Bowen, Archie L., 254

Boyle, John, 21

Bradley, Omar N., 218

Brand, Rudolph, 141

Breckenridge, John C., 36

Brennan, George E., 208

Bridgeport, 47

Brookport, 269

Brooks, Charles Wayland, 211,
    221, 224, 238, 239

Brown County, 61

Browne, Thomas C., 12, 372

Browning, Orville H., 79, 91, 96,
    97

Brownsville, 45

Brundage, Edward J., 196

Bryan, William Jennings, *xi*, 114,
    120, 156, 166, 179, 194, 226,
    230

Buchanan, James, 37, 90

Buckner, Simon Bolivar, 120

Build Illinois, 280, 295

Buley, R. Carlyle, 53

Bull Moose Party, 175, 181, 187,
    203, 209, 217

Bundesen, Herman N., 211, 216,
    271

Bureau of the Budget, 263, 271,
    307

Burris, Roland, *ix*, 317

Bush, George H.W., 276, 322

Bush, George W., 284, 325

Businessmen for Kennedy, 269

Busse, Fred A., 174, 180

Butterfield, Justin, 63

Byrne, Jane, 284

Byrnes, James F., 231

C

Cahokia Downs, 216

Cairo, 72, 97, 106, 126, 131

Caldwell, B.F., 181

Calhoun, John C., 11, 26

Campbell, Bruce A., 208

Canal Scrip Fraud, 75, 78, 79,
    80

Cannon, Joseph G., 136

Canteen Corporation, 242

Canton, 115

capital punishment, *see* death
    penalty

Capitol, 79, 86, 89, 101, 107,
    108, 110, 126, 160, 238, 255,
    268, 270, 276, 294, 316, 318,
    324

Capone, Al, 195, 198, 221, 223,
    260

Carbondale, 159

Carlin, Rebecca Huitt, 54
Carlin, Thomas, 27, 35, 48, 49,
    52-57, 62, 63, 70, 71
Carlinville, 115, 116
Carlyle, 27
Carlstrom, Oscar E., 197, 198,
    202, 204
Carmi, 77
Carrollton, 54
Carter, Jimmy, 271
Carthage, 64, 65
Casey, Zodok, 40
Cassidy, John E., 216
Cellini, William F., Jr., 263
Centennial Building, 189
Centralia, 317
Centralia mine disaster, 225, 226
Century magazine, 166
Cermak, Anton J., 208, 209, 246
Chaddock College, 98
Charleston, 37, 72, 153, 240, 241,
    291, 292, 293
Chase, Salmon P., 87
Chester, 7
Chicago, 7, 35, 48, 49, 50, 55, 62,
    72, 76, 78, 95, 110, 114, 123,
    124, 126, 130, 133, 134, 136,
    141, 149, 152, 157, 167, 171,
    176, 179, 180, 183, 186, 187,
    190, 193, 194, 196, 197, 207,
    210, 211, 216, 218, 222, 225,
    227, 231, 233, 236, 237, 239,
    241, 242, 250, 260, 268, 270,
    272, 276, 278, 281, 282, 283,
    284, 294, 296, 297, 299, 305,
    306, 307, 308, 312, 314, 315,
    317, 318, 321, 323, 324, 333

Chicago, Alton and St. Louis
    Railroad, 81, 95
Chicago Bar Association, 249
Chicago Board of Education,
    268
Chicago, Burlington & Quincy
    Railroad, 186, 216
Chicago Circle, 273
Chicago City Council, 161, 173,
    189, 203
Chicago City Hall, 210, 211,
    222, 231, 233, 246, 247, 263,
    269, 271
Chicago Community Fund, 233
Chicago Council of Foreign
    Relations, 231
Chicago Crime Commission,
    233, 260, 269
Chicago Daily News, 231
Chicago Downs, 233
Chicago Election Commission,
    246
Chicago Evening Mail, 151
Chicago Fellowship Club, 111
Chicago fire, 114, 118
Chicago and Illinois Restaurant
    Association, 243
Chicago Journal, 140
Chicago-Kent College of Law,
    240, 260
Chicago Loop, 240, 249, 272,
    284
Chicago, Milwaukee, St. Paul, &
    Pacific Railroad, 264, 265
Chicago, Missouri, & Western
    Railway, 265
Chicago Municipal Court, 61

Chicago park districts, 211
Chicago parks, 243
Chicago police, 189, 290
Chicago sanitary district, 145
Chicago schools, 283, 293, 300, 316, 317
Chicago stockyards, 121
Chicago traction, 108, 154, 161, 180, 197, 203, 222
Chicago Transit Authority, 222, 263, 271, 307, 316
Chicago Tribune, 100, 126, 132, 135, 155, 165, 222, 223, 322
Children and Family Services, Department of, 297
cholera epidemic, 28, 115
Cicero, 261
Civic Center Bank, 249
Civic Federation, 186
Civil Administrative Code, 185, 188
civil rights, 238, 248, 261
civil service, 21, 45, 156, 167, 173, 195, 201, 260, 261, 295, 360
Civil Service Commission, 173, 243
Civil War, *ix, x*, 13, 16, 17, 36, 44, 59, 66, 69, 81, 84, 89, 90, 93, 98, 101, 103, 104, 114, 116, 123, 124, 129, 131, 133, 136, 139, 141, 143, 145, 147, 150, 155, 156, 160, 165, 172, 179, 190 195, 205, 215, 216, 331
Clark, George Rogers, 4

Clark, William, 24
Clark, William G., 257, 269
Class X, 279, 293
Clay County, 135, 159
Clay, Henry, 21, 43, 45, 94
Cleveland, Grover, 104, 114, 120, 126, 135, 143, 155, 156, 160, 166, 167, 230
Cloven, Will, 197
Coles County, 291, 292
Coles, Edward, *ix*, 8-17, 27, 28, 33, 44, 45, 47, 59, 90, 133, 143, 330
Coles, Sally Logan Roberts, 15
Collins, John, 374
Columbian Exposition, World's, 145, 155, 333
Comiskey Park, 280
Commission on Unemployment and Relief, 204
Committee of 800, 276
Committee on Commerce, 135
Committee on Illinois Government, 269
Committee on Territories, 131
Commonwealth Edison, 223
Compromise of 1850, 77
compulsory education, 105, 145, 152, 154
Confederates, 99, 107, 124
Congress, 3, 5, 12, 13, 14, 15, 22, 24, 27, 28, 35, 40, 43, 45, 46, 56, 60, 84, 95, 97, 107, 115, 119, 131, 151, 168, 187, 188, 238, 330
Conservation, Department of, 195, 228

Constitution of 1818, *x*, 69, 86, 328, 329, 330

Constitution of 1848, *x*, 63, 69, 71, 78, 86, 89, 96, 117, 330, 331, 332

Constitution of 1870, *x*, 118, 134, 146, 156, 212, 247, 249, 261, 263, 332, 333

Constitution of 1970, *x*, 183, 262, 263, 283, 293, 333, 334, 335

Constitution, U.S., 20, 117, 307, 369, 333

constitutional conventions, 9, 11, 12, 24, 99, 107, 108, 118, 156, 163, 188, 216, 218, 264, 297, 332, 333, 334, 335

Cook County, 61, 90, 123, 136, 168, 171, 172, 175, 182, 183, 190, 195, 198, 201, 202, 203, 204, 208, 211, 221, 225, 244, 260, 264, 277, 281, 297, 298, 299, 316

Cook County Board, 239, 240, 241, 246, 259, 261, 263

Cook County Circuit Court, 312, 322

Cook County Hospital, 261

Cook County Probate Court, 208

Cook, Daniel Pope, 5, 6, 28, 29, 45, 61

Cook Envelope Company, 249

Coolidge, Calvin, 173, 176, 191

Copperhead, 36, 220

Corrections, Department of, 263, 297

corruption, 4, 32, 34, 78, 108, 118, 132, 136, 154, 175, 194, 196, 197, 201, 233, 241, 242, 249, 250, 254, 272, 278, 294, 301, 308, 310, 311, 322, 331, 332

Council of Revision, 3, 47, 328, 329, 331

Council of Social Agencies, 204

Courtney, Thomas J., 225, 375

Crafts, Clayton E., 153

Craig, Thomas, 23, 24

Crawford County, 70, 96

Crawford, William H., 6, 11, 14, 26

Cross, Hugh W., 225

"Cross of Gold" speech, 258

Cuba, 136, 310

Cullom, Hannah Fisher, 131

Cullom, Julia Fisher, 131, 137

Cullom, Shelby Moore, *ix*, 104, 117, 118, 119, 126, 139, 146, 149, 156, 159-162, 168, 171, 174, 187, 188, 189, 190, 193, 194, 195, 196, 200, 202

Custer, Omer N., 204

Cutback Amendment, 283, 293, 335

D

Daley, Richard J., *xi*, 233, 241, 247, 248, 256, 261, 268, 269, 270, 273, 276, 278, 279, 281, 292

Daley, Richard M., 276, 297, 300, 301, 306, 310, 319

Daniels, Lee A., 302, 358, 359
Danvers, 144
Danville, 136
Darrow, Clarence, 151, 152, 157, 183
Davidson, Alexander, 94
Davis, David, 129, 130, 145, 150
Davis, Jefferson, 83, 84, 85, 86
Davis, John T., 66
Dawes, Charles G., 136
Day, J. Edward, 265
death penalty, 6, 195, 211, 228, 239, 299, 306, 311, 312, 319
Death Row, 279, 306
Debs, Eugene V., 155
Decatur, 85, 95, 105, 106, 108, 110, 218
Declaration of Independence, 10
Deerfield, 268
de Grazia, Victor, 270
DeKalb, 164, 240
DeKalb County, 123, 124, 153, 276
Democratic Federation of Illinois, 269
Democratic Party, 14, 41, 44, 46, 48, 56, 59, 62, 70, 84, 85, 90, 103, 104, 108, 113, 114, 115, 119, 133, 140, 150, 152, 155, 179, 215, 223, 229, 230, 239, 241, 256, 268, 283 (*see also*, Jacksonian, National, Peace, and War Democrats)
Democratic Republicans, 44
Deneen, Bina Day Maloney, 172, 176

Deneen, Charles Samuel, *ix, xi,* 136, 168, 170-177, 179, 181, 187, 188, 189, 193, 194, 195, 196, 202, 207, 208, 223, 230, 242, 282
Dewey, Thomas, 239
Dexter, Writ, 216
Diamond-Star Motors, 316, 338
Dietrich, William H., 212
direct primary law, 136, 137, 165
Dirksen, Everett M., 224, 242, 256, 257
Dixmoor, 261
Dixon, 135
Dixon, Alan, 293
Dixon, Sherwood, 234, 239, 375
Douglas, Emily Taft, 271
Douglas, Paul H., 231, 239, 242
Douglas, Stephen A., *xi,* 15, 36, 44, 47, 53, 56, 66, 70, 72, 77, 78, 81, 85, 93, 97, 109, 114, 115, 120, 141, 230
Downing, T. Mac, 2225
Dubois, Jesse K., 107, 117
Dubuque, Julien, 35
Duncan, Elizabeth Smith, 45
Duncan, Joseph, 13, 14, 15, 39, 60, 42-51, 55, 56, 62, 329, 330
Duncan, Polly Ann, 49
Dunne, Edward F., *ix,* 154, 168, 172, 173, 175, 178-183, 187, 188, 189, 193, 222
Dunne, Elizabeth Kelly, 180, 181
DuPage County, 248, 283, 311
Dwight, 187, 197

E

Earnfare, 297

East Moline, 153

East St. Louis, 110, 133, 190

Eastern Illinois University, 291

Eden, John R., 117, 373

Edgar, Brenda Smith, 291, 302

Edgar, Jim, 281, 282, 288-303, 308, 309, 312

Edgar, John, 4, 22, 329

Edwards, Benjamin, 20, 131

Edwards County, 201

Edwards, Cyrus, 48, 54

Edwards, Elvira Lane, 21

Edwards, Ninian, *ix*, 4, 5, 11, 12, 14, 19-29, 33, 34, 40, 44, 45, 54, 276, 329, 330

Edwards, Ninian Wirt, 20, 77

Edwards, Richard, 145

Edwardsville, 7, 11, 15, 23, 27, 28, 32, 61, 86, 172, 240

Edwardsville Spectator, 12, 25

Eels, Richard, 372

Efficiency and Economy Committee, 182

Eighteenth Amendment, 210

Eisendrath, Edwin, 322

Eisenhower, Dwight, 218, 234, 239, 241, 260, 268, 291

Elgin, 140

Elkhart Hill, 110

Elvirade, 21, 28

Emancipation Proclamation, 99

Emergency Relief Administration, 209

Emergency Relief Commission, 224

Emmerson, Anna Mathews, 202

Emmerson, Louis L., *x*, 190, 198, 200-205, 209, 238, 333

Environmental Protection Act, 264

Environmental Protection Agency, 264

Equal Rights Amendment, 307

Erickson, William N., 271

Escobedo v. Illinois, 277

Essington, Thurlow G., 194

Eustis, William, 23

Evanston, 123, 124, 126, 239, 246, 260, 292

Evanston Pier Company, 124

Everett, Marjorie Lindheimer, 285

Ewing, Caroline Berry, 40

Ewing, William L.D., 14, 38-41

Executive Mansion, 77, 83, 86, 89, 91, 107, 118, 156, 160, 166, 168, 172, 173, 181, 188, 194, 195, 203, 212, 216, 222, 279, 283, 289, 293, 301, 302, 324

F

Fair Employment Practices Commission, 233, 241, 248

Fairlie, John A., 182

Farmers Mutual Benefit Association, 120

Farnsworth, John F., 123, 125

Farrington, Frank, 189

Farwell, Charles B., 134, 141

Fawell, Scott, 311

Federal Bureau of Investigation, 306, 322
Federal Correctional Institution at Lexington, Kentucky, 250
Federal Home Loan Bank Board, 272
Federal Prison Camp in Duluth, Minnesota, 272
Fell, Jesse W., 230
Ficklin, O. B., 70
Fielden, Samuel, 121
Fifer, Gertrude Lewis, 144
Fifer, Joseph Wilson, *xi*, 104, 120, 142-147, 154, 160, 163, 188
Filan, John, 318
Finance, Department of, 197
Financial Institutions, Depatment of, 249
First American Savings and Loan Association, 272
Fisher, Walter L. 180
Fitzgerald, Patrick J., 310, 311, 321, 322
Flood of 1993, 298
Flower, George, 12
Flying Squadron, 188
Ford, Emma, 151
Ford, Frances Hambaugh, 61
Ford, Gerald, 265, 276
Ford, Thomas, *ix*, 9, 11, 26, 27, 28, 29, 31, 35, 44, 48, 53, 55, 56, 58-67, 69, 70, 71, 72, 76, 77, 84, 95, 125, 134, 144, 185, 215, 329, 330
Foreign Relations Committee, 130, 136
Forquer, George, 60, 61

Forrest, Nathan Bedford, 91
Forsyth, Thomas, 23, 24
Fort Clark, 23, 33
Fort Dearborn, 23
Fort Donelson, 98, 106
Fort Edwards, 24
Fort Russell, 23
Fort Sheridan, 248
Fort Stephenson, 45
Fort Sumter, 96, 97
Fourteenth Amendment, 107
Franklin County, 125
Freeman, Jonathan, 13
Freeport, 225
Free Soil Party, 77
French, Augustus C., 53, 68-73, 75, 82, 330
French, Clarissa Kitchell, 70
French, Lucy Southworth, 70
Fry, Jacob, 79
Fugitive Slave Act, 77
Fuller, Allen C., 107
Fulton County, 90
Funk, Frank H., 175

G

Gaines, Edmund P., 35
Galena, 54, 61, 72, 126
Galena lead mines, 46
Galesburg, 84, 204
gambling, 195, 210, 226, 297, 309
Gary, Joseph E., 155
gateway amendment, 232, 257, 264, 333
gay rights, 320

General Assembly, 5, 12, 13, 14, 22, 24, 26, 27, 34, 44, 46, 47, 48, 56, 62, 63, 70, 71, 73, 80, 84, 86, 96, 98, 99, 107, 108, 118, 132, 134, 137, 156, 161, 167, 179, 188, 196, 201, 207, 224, 232, 237, 247, 248, 255, 263, 264, 270, 282, 283, 290, 297, 300, 309, 318, 320, 328, 330, 331, 333, 335

General Assembly, special sessions, 46, 55, 72, 96, 97, 108, 118, 161, 173, 209, 210, 224, 247, 271, 310, 324

General Assistance, 297

Germano, Joseph, 241

ghost payrolling, 271

GI Bill of Rights, 218, 260

Gillespie, Joseph, 54, 86

Gillett, John D., 110

Gold Democrats, *see* National Democratic Party

gold rush, 96, 116

Gomo, 23

Goodell, R. E., 81

Goodspeed, Barney, 223

Governors State University, 283

Grand Army of the Republic, 108, 109, 116, 131, 144, 146, 216

Grand Detour, 210

Granger movement, 125, 129, 132, 134, 150, 156, 186

Grant Park Bank, 196

Grant, Ulysses S., 98, 100, 101, 106, 108, 109, 114, 118, 119, 126, 131, 132, 134, 140, 166

Granville, 124

Grayville, 202

Great Depression, x, 201, 203, 207, 208, 209, 212, 222, 224, 231, 238, 254, 261, 276

Greathouse, John S., 115

Greeley, Horace, 99, 108, 109, 119

Green, Dwight Herbert, 217, 220-227, 238, 239, 242

Green, Hugh, 225

Green, Mabel Kingston, 223

Green Party, 322

Greenback Party, 119, 140, 186, 230

Greenberg, Frank, 249

Greene County, 54, 56

Gregg, David L., 77

Gresham, Walter Q., 135

Gurnee, 238

H

Haines, Elijah M., 110, 132

Hambaugh, Frances, 61

Hamilton, Helen Williams, 140

Hamilton, John Marshall, 138-141, 144, 160

Hamilton County, 216

Hamilton, William H., 13

Hancock County, 64, 65, 90, 248

hard roads, 202, 210, 216, 219, 226, 227, 264

Hardin, John J., 64, 65

Harding, Warren G., 190, 195

Harper "high license" bill, 151

Harrison, Benjamin, 120, 135

Harrison, Carter H., 109, 120, 152, 157, 180, 181, 183
Harrison, William Henry, 4, 23, 95, 329
Harrisonville, 88
Hartigan, Neil, 270, 296
Hay, Milton, 117, 131, 146
Hayes, Rutherford B., 119, 133
Haymarket Square, 110, 120, 121, 151, 154, 160, 161
health care, 298, 315, 317, 319, 320, 321, 323, 324
Hearst newspapers, 180, 222, 230
Hearst, William R., 222, 230
Heiple, James, 301
Henry, 139
Henry Clay Whigs, 34, 102
Henry, Patrick, 9
Hershey, Harry B., 212, 217, 219, 224
Hickman, Robert, 301
Highway Commission, Illinois, 202
Highway Trust Authority, 298
Hinsdale, 239
Hispanics, 295, 296
Hiss, Alger, 233
Hodge, Orville, 241
Hoehler, Fred K., 233
Hoffman, Francis A., 90
Hooper, Warren, 12
Hoover, Herbert, 191, 201, 203, 223, 252
Hopkins, Albert J., 175
Hopkins, Harry L., 209, 210
Hopkins, John P., 155

Horner, Henry H., *ix, xi*, 146, 204, 206-213, 215, 216, 217, 223, 246, 254, 271
horse racing, 228, 248, 265, 279, 285, 309
"House Divided" speech, 124
House of Representatives, Illinois 12, 31, 40, 41, 109, 129, 134, 153, 182, 225, 240, 249, 282, 283, 293, 306, 307, 309, 316, 317, 323, 324, 332
House of Representatives, U.S., 26, 85, 95, 107, 238, 316, 317
Howard, Benjamin, 23
Howlett, Michael J., 239, 248, 256, 257, 271, 278
Hubbard, Adolphus Frederick, 14, 27
Hughes, Edward J., 211, 224
Hull, Morton D., 175, 187
Human Rights Act, 320
Human Services, Department of, 300
Humphrey, Hubert, 256
Humphrey, J. Otis, 135
Hutchingson, William H., 185

I

Ickes, Harold, L., 165, 210
Igoe, Michael L., 208, 212
Ikenberry Commission, 300
Ikenberry, Stanley, 299
Illinois Campaign Finance Task Force, 243

Illinois Central Railroad, 55, 72, 76, 118, 134, 174
Illinois College, 48, 94, 160
Illinois Commerce Commission, 197
Illinois Education Association, 349
Illinois Emergency Relief Commission, 204
Illinois Epilepsy Association, 268
Illinois FIRST, 309
Illinois Highway Improvement Association, 189
Illinois Institution for the Education of Deaf Mutes, 48
Illinois Intelligencer, 5, 12
Illinois and Michigan Canal, 6, 7, 15, 35, 46, 47, 55, 56, 59, 62, 63, 76, 118, 133
Illinois Public Aid Commission, 269
Illinois State Fair, 295, 312, 335
Illinois State Journal, 91
Illinois State Toll Highway Authority, 301
Illinois Territory, 4, 5, 11, 12, 21
Illinois Waterway, 182, 189, 196
Illinois Wesleyan, 140, 144
Illiopolis, 48
Inbau, Fred E., 277
indenture system, 12, 16, 25
Indiana Territory, 3, 4, 21
Indians, 22, 23, 24, 34, 35, 53
Ingersoll, Robert, 94, 108, 117
Inglesh, A.E., 197
Ingleside, 270
Institute of Government and

Public Affairs, 290
Insull, Martin, 223
Insull, Samuel, 197, 223
internal improvements, 6, 47, 54, 55, 56, 59, 63, 76, 125
Internal Revenue Service, 242, 20
Interstate Commerce Commission, 129, 135, 146
Iroquois County, 40
Isaacs, Theodore J., 245, 249, 250

J

jackpotism, 209
Jackson, Andrew, 14, 26, 27, 43, 44, 46, 47, 48, 53, 114, 153
Jackson County, 45, 48, 125
Jackson, Jesse, 317
Jacksonian Democrats, 14, 26, 27, 34, 43, 44, 71, 329
Jacksonville, 48, 49, 50, 73, 94, 95, 100, 101, 166, 225, 239
Jacksonville *Daily Journal*, 166, 194
James R. Thompson Center, 283, 321
Jarecki, Edmund K., 211
Jefferson, Thomas, 10, 21, 44
Jirka, Frank J., 209
Johnson, Andrew, 100, 101, 107, 114
Johnson, George E.Q., 223
Johnson, Hiram, 190
Johnson, Lyndon Baines, 248, 249, 255

Joliet, 71, 76, 77, 80, 81, 108, 110, 157
Joliet & Northern Indiana Railroad, 76
Jones, Emil Jr., 322, 323, 324
Jones, Norman L., 375
Jones, Michael, 25
Judd, Norman B., 86, 95, 96
Judson, Philo, 124
Junior College Board, 248

K

Kane, Elias Kent, 6, 40, 87, 329
Kankakee, 193, 194, 195, 196, 242, 253, 254, 256, 272, 307, 312
Kankakee County, 194, 307
Kankakee County Board of Supervisors, 350
Kankakee State Hospital, 194, 254
Kansas-Nebraska Act, 78, 85, 95
Kaskaskia, 3, 4, 5, 7, 11, 21, 22, 23, 27, 28, 32, 45, 328, 329
Keane, Thomas E., 278
Keehn, Roy D., 222
Kelley, Florence, 153
Kelly, Edward J., 207, 209, 210, 211, 215, 216, 221, 222, 223, 224, 226, 231
Kendall County, 76
Kennedy, John C., 374
Kennedy, John F., 234, 255, 291, 328
Kennelly, Martin H., 231, 233
Kenney, David, 238

Kent College of Law, 240
Kentucky Court of Appeals, 21
Kerner, Helen Cermak, 246
Kerner, Otto, *ix, xi, xii*, 211, 240, 242, 244-251, 253, 255, 256, 261, 269, 278
KidCare, 301
Kilpatrick, Thomas M., 71, 372
Kinney, William, 34, 35, 44, 46, 372
Knight, Joseph E., 249
Knowlton, D.A., 373
Know-Nothing Party, 85, 131
Knox, Frank, 231
Koerner, Gustave, 77, 95, 96, 108, 119, 373
Korean War, 268, 307

L

labor
    child, 145, 153, 167
    strike, 110, 114, 119, 126, 133, 153, 161, 190
    union, 108, 119, 151, 210, 225, 283, 319
Lake County, 223, 238, 239
Lake Forest, 309
Lake Peoria, 23, 33
Landon, Alf, 230
Lane, Elvira, 21
LaRouche, Lyndon H., Jr., 281
LaSalle County, 194, 325
Latham, James, 110
Laughlin, Edward E., 225
League of Nations, 230
League of Women Voters, 211

Lebanon, 73, 172
Legislative Reference Bureau, 182
legislature, *see* General Assembly
Lemen, Henry W., 141
Lemont, 110, 155
Levine, Stuart, 322
Lewis, James Hamilton, 180, 195, 211, 212
Lewis Institute, 276
Lewis, John L., 210
Liberal Republicans, 104, 109, 113, 119, 123, 125
Lieberman, Ernest, 241
Lincoln, Abraham, *ix, xi,* 13, 32, 36, 41, 49, 70, 71, 78, 83, 84, 85, 86, 87, 89, 90, 93, 95, 96, 97, 98, 99, 100, 101, 104, 106, 107, 108, 114, 115, 116, 123, 125, 130, 131, 137, 149, 201, 208, 230
Lincoln, city of, 173
Lincoln-Douglas debates, 87, 241
Lincoln Memorial, 137
Lincoln Monument Association, 106
Lincoln, Robert Todd, 264
Lincoln Wide-Awakes, 139
Lind, Jenny, 49
Linn, William, 49
Litchfield, W. R., 76
literacy, 333, 351
"Little Hoover" commission, 265, 268
Littlewood, Thomas B., 211
Livingston, Park, 239
Lockport, 189

Logan County, 110
Logan, John A., 86, 100, 104, 109, 116, 117, 140, 141
Lohman, Joseph D., 246
Lorenz, Francis, 257
Lorimer, William E., 136, 137, 162, 166, 167, 172, 175, 187, 194, 197
lottery, 6, 271
Lottery, Department of, 323
Louisiana Purchase, 60
Lovejoy, Elijah, 48
Lovejoy, Owen, 94
Lowden, Frank Orren, *ix, x, xi,* 129, 146, 168, 172, 175, 179, 182, 183, 184-191, 193, 195, 196, 202, 203, 224, 232, 333
Lucas, Scott W., 212, 216, 248
Lundin, Fred, 187, 195, 197, 224
Lyons, Richard J., 223

M

Macomb, 225, 240
Madigan, Lisa, 312, 321, 323
Madigan, Michael J., 281, 282, 298, 309, 312, 322
Madison County, 13, 14, 15, 33
Madison, Dolley, 9
Madison, James, 10, 11, 15, 21, 23, 24
Malone, William H., 220
Management Services of Illinois Inc., 301
Mandeville, Robert, 263
Manteno State Hospital, 254
Marcor, Inc., 269, 272

Maremont, Arnold H., 248
Marion, 80
Marshall, 48
Marshall County, 139
Martin, C. Virgule, 248
Masonic Lodge, 6, 201, 204
Massac County, 66, 72
Matteson, Joel Aldrich, *xii*, 71, 73, 74-81
Matteson, Mary Fish, 76
McCarter, John, 198, 263
McClernand, John A., 96
McCormick, Medill, 175, 176
McCormick Place, 264
McCormick, Robert R., 222
McCormick, Ruth Hanna, 176
McGovern, George, 270
McGowen, Carl, 233
McKendree College, 73, 172
McKinley, William, 114, 120, 136, 166, 167, 187
McKinley, William B., 197
McLaughlin, Robert K., 45, 46, 372
McLean County, 144
McLean, John, 5, 6
Mcleansboro, 215, 216, 217, 218
McNulta, John, 144
Medicaid, 297, 298, 301
Medicare, 320
Medill, Joseph, 135
Meek, Joseph T., 242
Mell, Richard, 316, 321
Menard penitentiary, 108, 145
Menard, Pierre, 5
mental health, 73, 240, 246, 254, 255

Mental Health Association of Greater Chicago, 243
Mental Health, Commission on, 289
Merchants and Drovers Bank, 80
Merriam, Charles E., 175
Mexican War, 64, 65, 71, 72, 83, 84, 89, 96, 105, 116
Michigan City, 49
Military Tract, 15, 40, 61, 114
militia, 21, 23, 33, 40, 45, 48, 54, 63, 64, 65, 105, 133, 139, 140, 161, 217 (*see also*, National Guard)
Miller, J. Bert, 254
Missouri Compromise, 25, 85, 115, 125
Mitchell, Stephen A., 246
Moline, 272
Monk, Lon, 318, 321
Monroe County, 60, 84
Monroe, James, 6, 11, 23, 24, 25, 26
Montgomery Ward and Company, 188, 269
Moore, James B., 12, 372
Mooseheart, 182
Morgan County, 166
Mormons, 48, 49, 55, 59, 61, 64, 65
Morris, 238, 242
Morris, Buckner S., 373
Morrison, Robert, 4, 22, 329
Morrison, W.L.D., 329`
Morrison, William R., 109
Morton, Oliver P., 99
Moses, John, 27, 89, 123

Mothers Against Drunk Driving, 351
mother's aid law, 202
Moulton, S.W., 117
Mount Carroll, 172
Mount Morris, 124, 131
Mount Pleasant, 20
Mount Vernon, 161, 202, 204, 205, 272
Mount Vernon Register-News, 234
Mulroy, James W., 233
Municipal Tuberculosis Sanitarium, 277
Municipal Voters League, 173

N

Naperville, 309
Nasby, Petroleum V., 106
Nash, Patrick A., 209, 210, 211, 212, 215, 221, 224, 226
National Commission Against Drunk Driving, 351
National Advisory Commission on Civil Disorders, 248
National Commission on the Causes and Prevention of Violence, 269
National Conference of State Legislatures, 292
National Democratic Party, 113, 114, 120
National Guard, 133, 155, 174, 186, 190, 246, 255 (*see also*, militia)
National Recovery Administration, 210

National Road, 45
National Teachers Academy, 317
Nauvoo, 48, 55, 64, 65
Nelson, Oscar, 204
Netsch, Dawn Clark, ix, 299
New Deal, 210, 230
New Design, 4, 60
New York, 47, 63, 71
Nineteenth Amendment, 189
Nixon, Richard M., 250, 256, 277
Nobel Peace Prize, 311
no-bid contracts, 284
Normal, 280
Northcott, W.A., 135
Northern Cross Railroad, 71, 76
Northern Illinois Public Service Company, 238
Northfield, 260
Northwest Ordinance of 1787, 13, 16, 22
Northwest Territory, 13, 328
Northwestern University, 124, 232, 246
    Law School, 268, 277
Nudelman, Samuel, 217

O

Oak Brook, 272
Oak Park, 260, 277, 279
Oak Ridge Cemetery, 28, 106, 137, 162
Ogilvie, Dorothy Shriver, 260
Ogilvie, Richard Buell, ix, xi, 222, 242, 256, 257, 258-265, 267, 268, 270, 271, 302, 334

Ogle County, 61, 182, 187

Oglehurst, 110, 111

Oglesby, Anna White, 107

Oglesby, Emma Keays, 110

Oglesby, John G., 110, 190, 195

Oglesby, Richard James, *ix*, 94, 100, 102-111, 115, 118, 123, 125, 134, 140, 141, 146, 160, 332

O'Hare International Airport, 310, 319

Omnibus Crime Bill, 277

Operation Safe Road, 308, 311, 312

Oquawka, 48

Oregon, 61, 187

organ donor program, 294, 333, 351

Ottawa, 161

P

Palestine, 70

Palmer, Elihu, 114, 115

Palmer, Hannah L. Kimball, 120

Palmer, John McAuley, *ix*, *xi*, 99, 100, 107, 108, 109, 112-121, 125, 133, 144, 149, 152, 156, 332, 333

Palmer, Malinda Ann Neely, 115

Pana, 161, 189

Panama Canal, 220

Panic of 1837, 47, 78

Panic of 1873, 91, 125

Paris, 70

Paris peace conference, 212

Park Forest, 292

Partridge, Jack, 23

Paschen, Herbert C., 241

Patients' Bill of Rights, 352

patronage, 21, 25, 44, 130, 132, 136, 160, 167, 168, 174, 186, 188, 194, 195, 197, 203, 209, 224, 226, 238, 260, 261, 308

Peace Democrats, 93, 96

Pearl Harbor, 256

Pease, Theodore C., 53

Peck, John Mason, 36

Pekin, 143

Pekin whiskey ring, 143

Peoples Gas Company, 223

Peoria, 5, 14, 23, 24, 33, 54, 60, 66, 80, 132, 153, 180, 216, 226, 261

pensions, 321, 323

Percy, Charles H., 247, 249, 260, 277

Philip, James, 300, 302

Philippine Islands, 136

Phillips, Joseph, 11, 12

Pierce, Frankin, 85

Pike County, 89

Pisgah, 48

Pollution Control Board, 264

Pontiac, 108

Pope County, 66, 72

Pope, John, 21

Pope, Nathaniel, 21, 22, 25

Poshard, Glenn, 309

Powell, Paul, 232, 240, 254, 257

Prairie du Rocher, 21

Price, Sterling, 124

private (special) legislation, 108, 117, 118, 119, 128, 332
prisons, 6, 7, 80, 108, 118, 167, 279, 298, 316, 332, 340
Progressive movement, 145, 156, 165, 171, 179, 182, 185, 187, 194
Progressive Party, 171, 173, 175, 183
Prohibition, 168, 186, 203, 204, 210, 223
Project Success, 298
Public Aid Commission, 224, 248
Public Aid, Department of, 248, 301
Public Service Company of Northern Illinois, 223
Public Utilities Commission, 196, 197, 210, 229
Public Welfare, Department of, 254
Pullman, Florence, 186
Pullman, George M., 155, 186, 187
Purchases and Construction, Department of, 197

Q

Quincy, 54, 65, 80, 85, 89, 90, 91, 110, 274
Quinn, Pat, 325

R

racial discrimination, 189, 241, 248

Radical Republicans, 93, 99, 116
railroads, 44, 46, 54, 55, 62, 71, 72, 118, 129, 132, 134
Railroad and Warehouse Commission, 125, 146, 160
Rainey, Henry T., 182
Ramsey, Rufus N., 164
Raum, Green B., 132
Ray, Lyman B., 238
Reagan, Ronald, 265, 322
reapportionment, 238, 240, 249, 256, 283
Red Cross, 221
Regional Transportation Authority, 270, 292, 334
Republican Party, 71, 83, 86, 90, 95, 99, 103, 106, 108, 109, 113, 114, 117, 125, 131, 133, 134, 136, 141, 143, 159, 160, 172, 183, 186, 187, 210, 223, 224, 239, 242, 264, 283, 291, 293, 306, 312, 324 (*see also,* black, Liberal, Radical)
Research Foundation for the Mentally Ill, 254
Revolutionary War, 4, 9, 40, 89, 95, 159, 187, 329
Reynolds, Catherine Manegle, 35
Reynolds, John, 12, 13, 14, 27, 30-37, 39, 40, 44, 46, 55, 72
Reynolds, Sarah Wilson, 35
Rezko, Antoin "Tony," 322
Richardson, William A., 85, 90, 373
Ridgely-Farmers State Bank, 236
Ridgely, Nicholas H., 76
Ridgeway, Thomas S., 132

Rights in Conflict, 269
Rinaker, John I., 132
road construction, 188, 196, 197, 204, 209, 224, 239, 240, 282, 309, 321
Robbins, Silas, 105
Robinson, James C., 107
Roche, John, 152
Rock Island, 46, 79, 203
Rock Island & Chicago Railroad, 76
Rock, Philip, 282, 283
Rock River Seminary, 124, 131
Ronan, James A., 282
Roosevelt, Franklin D., 168, 183, 198, 208, 210, 211, 222, 223, 224, 231, 238, 254
Roosevelt, Theodore, 146, 167, 171, 173, 175, 187
Rotary Club of Chicago, 243
Rowe, Richard Yates, 239
Rowell, J. H., 140
Rusk, Dean, 234
Russell, John, 36
Rutan v. Illinois, 284
Ryan, Dan, 240
Ryan, George, *ix*, 243, 281, 284, 304-313, 318, 320
Ryan, Jim, 318
Ryan, Lura Lynn Lowe, 307

S

Sac Indians, 35
St. Charles, 124
St. Clair, Arthur, 328
St. Clair County, 4, 73, 126
St. Louis Post-Dispatch, 217

Salem, 72
Sangamon County, 80, 196
Sangamon County Circuit Court, 80, 249
Sangamon State University, 248
Scates, Walter B., 65
Schaefer, Walter V., 232
Schircker, Henry F., 234
Schofield, John M. 116
schools, 13, 14, 45, 72, 73, 77, 80, 88, 115, 141, 145, 154, 154, 155, 164, 174, 195, 228, 243, 263, 282, 283, 290, 295, 296, 298, 299, 300, 302, 309, 319, 323, 324
Schwab, Michael, 110
Scott, William J., 260, 277
Scott, Winfield, 28, 35
Sears, Roebuck and Company, 280, 296
Second Ward Republican Club, 217
Seddon, James A., 84
Senate Foreign Relations Committee, 140, 146
Senate, Illinois, 13, 39, 40, 71, 76, 140, 144, 153, 166, 225, 232, 240, 241, 282, 283, 309, 318
Senate, U.S., 5, 14, 24, 25, 26, 40, 41, 72, 94, 99, 100, 104, 109, 110, 113, 119, 129, 130, 134, 135, 136, 140, 143, 156, 159, 174, 197, 231, 281, 293, 302
Senate Interstate Commerce Committee, 130, 136

Servicemen's Readjustment Act of 1944 (GI Bill), 218
Shapiro, Gertrude Adelman, 254, 256
Shapiro, Samuel Harvey, *ix*, 249, 252-257, 261, 262, 307
Shawneetown, 5, 14, 23, 40, 56, 62, 80, 89, 247
Shelton gang, 215
Sheridan, Philip H., 118
Sherman, Lawrence Y., 137, 183
Sherman, William T., 116, 159
Shields, James A., 66, 73
Shuman, Andrew, 140
Shurtleff College, 114
Shurtleff, Edward D., 175
Simon, Paul, 243, 256, 257, 261, 264, 267, 271, 334
Simpson, James, 239
Sinnissippi Farm, 191
Slattery, James M., 212
slavery, 3, 5, 7, 9, 10, 11, 12, 13, 14, 15, 36, 40, 48, 77, 78, 86, 89, 95, 96, 99, 100, 105, 107, 108, 109, 114, 115, 123, 139, 172, 241, 330
Sloo, Thomas, Jr., 27, 372
Small, Ida Moore, 194
Small, Lennington, *ix*, *xii*, 175, 188, 190, 192-199, 201, 202, 208, 232, 238, 239, 240, 242, 254, 307, 312
Small, Leslie, 197
Smith, Al, 203
Smith, Frank L., 187, 197
Smith, Garrett, 109
Smith, Hyrum, 64, 65

Smith, John C., 141
Smith, Joseph, 48, 54, 55, 59, 61, 64, 65
Smith, Ralph, 355
Smith, Richard Norton, 325
Smith, Theophilus T., 27
Smith, Theophilus W., 61
smokestack chasing, 296, 297
Snyder, Adam W., 35, 48, 61, 62
Snyder, John F., 20, 53, 84, 87
Solidarity Party, 281
Somonauk, 124
South Beloit, 269
Spanish-American War, 161, 186
Springdale, 66
Springfield, 27, 28, 29, 41, 72, 76, 78, 79, 89, 91, 94, 96, 97, 98, 99, 100, 104, 105, 106, 117, 119, 120, 137, 152, 153, 160, 161, 162, 168, 175, 181, 193, 204, 209, 216, 217, 225, 231, 236, 237, 239, 259, 268, 269, 272, 291, 298, 302, 307, 315, 316, 323, 324
Springfield & Meredosia Railroad, 76
Stanton, Edwin F., 99
state bank, 3, 6, 14, 33, 34, 39, 44, 45, 47, 48, 56, 62, 74, 78, 80, 134, 195
State Bank of Illinois, Shawneetown, 56, 79, 80, 81
State Board of Agriculture, 194
State Board of Canal Commissioners, 15, 78
State Board of Canvassers, 141
State Board of Education, 320

State Board of Elections, 281
State Board of Equalization, 108, 189
State Board of Health, 140
State Board of Public Charities, 156
State Council of Defense, 256
State Historical Library, 240
State Library, 280, 295
State National Bank, 131
State Police, 217, 232
Statehouse, *see* Capitol
States' Rights Doctrine, 27
Stead, William H., 174
Stelle, John H., 209, 212, 214-219
Stelle, Wilma Wisehart, 215
Stephenson, James W., 54
Stettinius, Edward R. Jr., 231
Stevenson, Adlai Ewing, 104, 153, 156, 174, 181, 203, 209, 218, 226, 230
Stevenson, Adlai Ewing II, *ix, xi,* 129, 228-235, 239, 240, 246, 268
Stevenson, Adlai Ewing, III, 230, 272, 281
Stevenson, Ellen Borden, 230, 233
Stevenson, Lewis G., 202, 230
Steward, Lewis, 119, 133
Stratton, Marion Hook, 238
Stratton, Shirley Breckenridge, 239
Stratton, William G., *ix,* 222, 236-243, 247, 261, 264, 269, 312
Stratton, William J., 238

Streator, 194
Streeter, Alson J., 134
streetcar, *see* Chicago traction
Stringer, Lawrence B., 173, 374
Stuart, John T., 131
Sturges, Jonathan, 76
Stuve, Bernard, 94
Sullivan, city of, 105
Sullivan, Roger C., 176, 181, 240
Sunburst Colonels, 189, 195, 201
Sunday, Billy, 173
Supreme Court, Illinois, 12, 14, 27, 31, 33, 47, 60, 86, 96, 118, 132, 140, 161, 197, 201, 203, 209, 232, 240, 241, 245, 249, 254, 261, 262, 269, 270, 281, 301, 319, 328, 331, 333
Supreme Court, U.S., 110, 134, 277, 284
Swett, Leonard, 95, 96
Sycamore, 124

T

Taft, William Howard, 174, 175, 187, 194
Tanner, Cora Edith English, 160
Tanner, Lauretta Ingraham, 160
Tanner, John Riley, 111, 135, 136, 141, 144, 146, 158-163, 167, 173, 194
tariff, 131, 167, 217
taxes
    auto license, 174, 189, 219, 292
    beer, 262
    cigarette, 248, 262, 300
    corporation, 248, 261, 262

gasoline, 196, 203, 228, 232, 235, 239, 240, 248, 255, 263, 264, 272, 282, 292
gross receipts, 174, 323
highway user, 232, 282
hotel/motel, 247, 262
inheritance, 308
income, *xi*, 156, 175, 188, 201, 204, 207, 210, 232, 240, 242, 247, 250, 256, 259, 260, 261, 262, 264, 269, 271, 278, 282, 290, 292, 296, 297, 299, 302, 321, 323, 333
liquor, 256, 319
property, 15, 26, 27, 56, 59, 63, 64, 77, 80, 153, 161, 189, 203, 207, 209, 279, 290, 295, 296, 297, 299, 300
riverboats, 300
sales, *xi*, 207, 209, 211, 224, 225, 238, 240, 247, 248, 256, 261, 262, 282, 297321, 323
school, 13
telephones, 300
used cars, 295
utility, 209, 248
Taylor, Zachary, 84, 105
Taylorville, 212, 224
Tazewell County, 141
teacher certification law, 155
temperance, 48, 126, 141
Third National Bank, 234, 236
Thirteenth Amendment, 107
Thomas, Jesse B., 4, 5, 11, 14, 21, 22, 24, 25, 26, 33, 34, 329
Thompson, Floyd E., 203

Thompson, James Robert, *ix*, 104, 114, 222, 243, 250, 263, 272, 274-287, 289, 293, 294, 295, 297, 302, 308, 312, 334
Thompson, Jayne Carr, 279
Thompson Proposition, 279
Thompson, William Hale, 175, 183, 187, 188, 190, 193, 195, 196, 197, 198, 201, 203, 223, 224
Thorne, Charles H., 188
Tilden, Samuel J., 119
Tingley, Donald, 196
Toll Highway Commission, 240
toll highway system, 238
Tonica & Petersburg Railroad, 95
Topinka, Judy Baar, 322, 325
traction, *see* Chicago traction
Transportation, Department of, 263
Treaty of Fort Armstrong, 35
Truman, Harry S, 226, 229, 231, 233, 239, 246
Trumbull, Lyman, 66, 70, 78, 96, 97, 99, 109, 115, 119, 120, 125, 134, 141
Tuley, Murray F., 180
Tusk, Bradley, 318
Twenty-first Amendment, 168

U

unemployment, 236, 240, 242
unemployment insurance, 243, 320, 351
Union College of Law, 180, 186
Union Progressive Party, 198

United Labor Party, 162
United Mine Workers, 210
United Nations, *xi*, 231, 234
United Steelworkers, 241
Unity Block, 151, 154
University of Chicago, 185, 222, 231, 247
University of Illinois, 108, 126, 153, 174, 182, 239, 254, 272, 277, 290, 291, 299, 311, 313
 at Springfield, 248
Urbana, 108
U.S. attorney for the Northern District, 246, 250, 276, 277, 311, 321
U.S. Court of Appeals, 7th Circuit, *xi*, 245, 249, 253, 260, 312
U.S. Court of Military Appeals, 268
U.S. Route 66, 239
U.S. Tax Court, 242
Utica, 189, 196, 325
utilities, 163, 167, 179, 189, 255

V

Vallas, Paul, 317
Van Buren, Martin, 47, 70
Van Cleve, James, 141
Vandalia, 6, 39, 40, 41, 46, 48, 49, 61, 72
Vandruff's Island, 35
Vaux, Roberts, 13
Vermilion County, 182
Versailles, 61
Veterans Administration, 218
Vietnam War, 255

Vincennes, 72
Vinson, Fred M., 268
Virden, 161
Volz, Leslie P. "Ike," 224
Von Osdell, John Murray, 91

W

Wabash College, 254
Wabash River, 13, 43, 70
Wait, Sheridan, 106
Walker, Daniel, *xi*, *xii*, 256, 263, 266-273, 276, 278, 312, 315, 316, 334
Walker, Lily Stewart, 268, 272
Walker, Roberta Dowse, 268
Walker, Roberta Nelson, 268
Walker, John H., 189
Walsh, Frank, 183
War Democrats, 106
War of 1812, 4, 5, 10, 22, 31, 45, 54, 72
Ward, Daniel P., 277
Warner, Larry, 311, 312
Warren, Earl, 226
Warren, Hooper, 12
Warsaw, 48
Washburne, Elihu B., 99, 126, 132
Washington, D.C., 5, 22, 23, 39, 43, 44, 77, 85, 86, 87, 90, 98, 107, 117, 130, 136, 187, 189, 223, 231, 233, 237, 268
Washington, Harold, 281, 283, 284
Washington Republican, 26
Washington University, 247, 313
Waterloo, 61, 84

Watson, Frank, 324
Waukegan, 196, 309
weak governor system, 328, 330
Webb, E. B., 77
welfare, 202, 203, 210, 235, 256,
    262, 264, 265, 273, 281, 297,
    298, 300, 301
West Point, 98, 116, 166
West, Roy O., 172, 175
West York, 70
Weston, 248
Whig Party, 34, 41, 43, 44, 46,
    47, 48, 49, 54, 55, 62, 64,
    65, 71, 77, 94, 95, 97, 105,
    106, 131, 330, 332
White House, *xi*, 10, 13, 43, 53,
    96, 106, 119, 124, 141, 146,
    201, 211, 229
White, J. B., 80
White, Jesse, 325
White Sox, 280
Whiteside, William B., 5
Whitney, Frank A., 208
Whitney, Henry Clay, 208
Whitney, Rich, 322
Williams, Ann, 272
Williamson County, 125
Willis, Duane "Scott," 308
Wilmington, 153
Wilmot Proviso, 73
Wilson, Woodrow, 131, 179, 185
Wines, Fredrick H., 156
Winston & Strawn, 276, 278, 284
Wirt, William, 20, 21
women's suffrage, 95, 100, 145,
    182, 185, 189
Wood, Anne M. Streeter, 90

Wood, Corinne G., 309
Wood, John, 88-91, 98
Wood, Mary A. Holmes, 90
Wood River, 114
Workmen's compensation, 174,
    189, 220
World Court, 176
World War I, 185, 189, 221, 254
World War II, 216, 218, 221,
    225, 254, 260, 291, 316
World's Fair, 321
Wray, Charles W., 233
Wright and Company, 55
Wright, Warren E., 226, 242
Wyman, Austin, 243

X

XVI Corps, 107

Y

Yates, Catherine Geers, 94
Yates, Ellen Wadsworth, 166,
    168
Yates, Richard (I), *ix*, 92-101,
    104, 105, 106, 109, 115, 116,
    120, 125, 126, 187, 331
Yates, Richard (II), *ix*, 94, 136,
    164-169, 172, 174, 181, 187,
    194
Yerkes, Charles T., 154
Young Democrats of Illinois, 254
Young Republicans, 149, 260

About the
Center for State Policy
and Leadership

The Center for State Policy and Leadership, located in the Illinois state capital, emphasizes policy and state governance. The Center identifies and addresses public policy issues at all levels of government, promotes governmental effectiveness, fosters leadership development, engages in citizen education, and contributes to the dialogue on matters of significant public concern. Working in partnership with government, local communities, citizens, and the nonprofit sector, the Center contributes to the mission of the University of Illinois at Springfield by mobilizing the expertise of its faculty, staff, students, and media units to carry out public affairs programs, research and dissemination, professional development and training, civic engagement, technical assistance, and public service activities.

About Center Publications
and *Illinois Issues*

Center Publications publishes scholarly resources and journalistic information on state government, politics, and policy for use by opinion leaders, citizens, and educators. Since 1975, *Illinois Issues* has provided independent analysis of state government and politics. The magazine reports on political trends, legislative issues, and the state's quality of life in a balanced, fair, and journalistic style. Among other print and electronic resources, Center Publications publishes the *Roster of State Government Officials*, an annual supplement to *Illinois Issues*, and *Governing Illinois*, a civics text on state and local governments for high school and middle school students.

About the Authors

The late **Robert P. Howard** was a reporter and historian. He served a long tenure as the Springfield correspondent for the *Chicago Tribune* and covered gubernatorial campaigns for *Illinois Issues* magazine. He was president of the Illinois State Historical Society, a board member of the Abraham Lincoln Association, and the author of *Illinois: A History of the Prairie State*.

Peggy Boyer Long is executive editor of *Illinois Issues* magazine. An Illinois native, she has covered Illinois government for print and public radio. As a reporter based in the Statehouse, she covered three governors: Dan Walker, James Thompson, and Jim Edgar. She is a member of the Board of Directors of the Illinois Center for the Book and a founding member of Capitolbeat, the national association of capitol reporters and editors.

Taylor Pensoneau was a political reporter for the *St. Louis Post-Dispatch* who covered five Illinois governors, including Richard Ogilvie and Dan Walker. Pensoneau is a co-author of *Dan Walker: The Glory and the Tragedy* and author of *Governor Richard Ogilvie: In the Interest of the State*. The *Chicago Sun-Times* called the Ogilvie book one of the 10 most notable political books of 1997. He is a member of the *Illinois Issues* Advisory Board.